A Good Bake

A Good Bake

The Art and Science of Making Perfect Pastries, Cakes, Cookies, Pies, and Breads at Home

Melissa Weller
with Carolynn Carreño

Photographs by Johnny Miller

ALFRED A. KNOPF
NEW YORK
2020

THIS IS A BORZOI BOOK PUBLISHED BY ALFRED A. KNOPF

www.aaknopf.com

LIBRARY OF CONGRESS CATALOGING-IN-PUBLICATION DATA
Names: Weller, Melissa, author. | Carreño, Carolynn, author.
Title: A good bake : the art and science of making perfect pastries, cakes, cookies, pies, and breads at home / Melissa Weller, Carolynn Carreño.
Description: New York : Alfred A. Knopf, 2020. | Includes index.
Identifiers: LCCN 2019048763 (print) | LCCN 2019048764 (ebook) | ISBN 9781524733438 (hardback) | ISBN 9781524733445 (ebook)
Subjects: LCSH: Pastry. | Bread. | LCGFT: Cookbooks.
Classification: LCC TX773 .W447 2020 (print) | LCC TX773 (ebook) | DDC 641.86/5—dc23
LC record available at https://lccn.loc.gov/2019048763
LC ebook record available at https://lccn.loc.gov/2019048764

Cover photograph by Johnny Miller
Cover design by Kelly Blair

Manufactured in China

First Edition

For my mother, Barbara.

Thank you for your creativity

and inspiration in the kitchen

when I was a child.

Contents

Introduction

When I first started working as a baker, I had a dreamy idea that I would be shaping and baking long elegant loaves of bread. But I was actually tasked with recording the pH of all the bread dough in the bakery. I would walk around the bakery, pH stick in hand, and diligently measure each tub of dough. This wasn't what I had in mind when I first thought of being a baker.

I am a career changer; before I became an expert on bread, sticky buns, and croissants, I was a chemical engineer. That experience is what sets me apart as a baker, and what sets this book apart from others. As a chemical engineer, I was trained to apply the principles that I learned in science to things that occur in real life, like baking, even if that's not where I ever imagined I'd end up taking that degree.

My early training is so deeply ingrained that using the scientific method has become as natural and involuntary as breathing. I use it on a daily basis. It probably sounds very complicated, as if I have test tubes and Bunsen burners in my kitchen. It's not. It's really just a way of thinking about process and organizing your ideas. What it comes down to is this: you have a theory about how something works, and you then test out your theory, like you might a formula for brownies. In chemical engineering, we call that theory a hypothesis; in cooking, we call it a recipe.

Without scaring anyone off and telling you that baking is a science (ah, but it is), let me give you an example: When I was working on my pie dough recipe, I would bake the dough and it would shrink in the oven, and the lattice would be crooked and uneven. Sure, it would taste good, but I wanted the pie to look perfect. So, I would ask myself: Why is the dough shrinking? What is happening to make it shrink? Does it have to do with the formation of gluten in the dough? Is it shrinking because of the water in the dough? I would think about the possibilities, change different things, and then observe the results. Among my experiments, I tried reducing the amount of water in the dough and noticed that my crust didn't shrink so much in the oven. My hypothesis was that reducing water in the dough and letting it rest before baking reduces the shrinkage in your crust. I tested it out and observed. What I proved is that my recipe had the desired effect, which is to say, I confirmed my theory that excess water in pie dough causes shrinkage.

Asking questions—lots of them—is integral to being an engineer: a chemical engineer or an engineer of dough. You are always asking, Why is this happening? What are the causes? How do time, temperature, heat, and mechanical movement (such as mixing a batter) affect the outcome of a baked good? I was taught to ask those questions, then develop hypotheses and test them. Curiosity allows you to ask more questions and develop better hypotheses. Passion makes you more persistent. It's all of these things—my science degree, my curiosity, and my love of baking—that have marked my culinary career and helped me become proficient in so many different areas of pastry and bread work. They've also prepared me to write this cookbook—to develop and outline recipes more thoroughly and clearly, so I can teach people at home to do what I taught myself. I learned to take the principles from cookbooks and in culinary school and apply them to baking in order to better the result, whether it's a straightforward muffin or a complex babka.

I have been baking professionally for the last fifteen years, but long before I ever stepped foot in a professional kitchen (or in a science lab), I wanted to write a cookbook. I started baking as a child, making cookies and muffins at home in central Pennsylvania with my mother, who baked from *The Fanny Farmer Cookbook* and *Hershey's Chocolate Cookbook* and recipes she had clipped from *Good Housekeeping* and collected in a recipe box, and I have baked ever since. But this was the 1980s. There was no such thing as searching the Internet for finding a recipe or clicking on Amazon.com to have a cookbook delivered to your door within days. Recipes were hard to come by, and for me, they seemed like something precious, secret codes to producing the beautiful, delicious things I wanted to create.

Cookbooks were also a gateway for me to the outside world. When I was in elementary school, someone gave my mom a cookbook as a gift: a collection of recipes from famous French restaurants across the United States. The recipes in the book were for classic fancy French dishes that I had never heard of: coquilles Saint-Jacques, duck à l'orange, île flottante, and I was enthralled. I liked reading the recipes and imagining this exotic food, but I also loved the stories behind the recipes and the accompanying pictures, the dreamy part of imagining what it would be like to be in the South of France enjoying a cherry almond tart over lunch on a warm summer afternoon. In the back of the book was a French-English dictionary, and I would use it to learn French words and pretend that I was speaking that language. My parents couldn't have afforded to take their kids on European vacations; instead we went on camping trips to the seashore. But in college, I found a way to get to France through a study-abroad program in Tours, in the Loire region. France changed me. I learned to speak the language fluently. And I fell in love with the beautiful bakeries and the pastries I bought from them, and I wanted to know how those croissants, brioche, and cookies were made. This is when my true passion for baking began.

But I didn't take that passion seriously at the time. Pragmatic by nature, I studied chemical engineering in college; I am good at science and this seemed like the wise thing to do. After college, I got an engineering job in Allentown, Pennsylvania. I didn't like it. I was discontent and bored and soon I was daydreaming of cakes I wanted to bake and elaborate dinners I wanted to host. There was a group of young engineers living in Allentown and we would get together often for dinner parties; I used these gatherings as an excuse to take on ambitious cooking and baking projects. I loved those evenings—to be able to express myself through food, and to share that with others. My friends raved about my creations, which made me like the experience even more. Once, a work colleague complimented me on a bûche de Noël that I brought to a holiday party, saying that it looked like a professional had made it, and my heart leaped.

I got my first part-time pastry position, at a French restaurant located in an industrial park, the Winesellar and Brasserie, in San Diego while still working as a chemical engineer. The chef didn't have a pastry chef, so he was grateful for the help, and he was willing to teach me. I worked there on weekends and evenings in addition to my full-time job. It brought me joy because I was learning to make things in a professional kitchen, something I had longed to do for some time. Claudia Fleming's epic dessert book *The Last Course* had just come out, and her plating style and the simple, elegant, and unfussy way she composed desserts really resonated with me. I started making things from that book for the restaurant—peach tarte tatin in the summer and chocolate caramel tarts with fleur de sel—but I was blatantly falling short. I knew I needed to go someplace where I could really learn, and in early 2003, I left San Diego for New York City and enrolled in the pastry program at the French Culinary Institute, where I learned the fundamentals of baking, pastry, chocolate work, and dessert making. I believed that if I could study and work in a city as big as New York, then regardless of my own success, that was success enough.

After I graduated, I got a job at Babbo in the West Village, and it was a dream. I worked with the revered pastry chef Gina DePalma for two years. She became my mentor and a huge influence on my life as a baker. You will see her name frequently throughout these pages, because I learned so much from Gina, and so many of my recipes originated, in different versions, with her. She had a larger-than-life personality and opinions about everything. I soaked in everything I could from her, and to this day, I still do many things the way Gina taught me to do them, like whisking dry ingredients together in a bowl rather than sifting or stirring them.

After working with Gina, I went on to work for the bread baker Jim Lahey, who is best known for his "no knead" bread dough. I learned about fermentation from Jim, and I got to make his beautiful, rustic Italian loaves of bread. After I worked for Jim, I was the head baker at Thomas Keller's

Per Se. There, I continued to learn from the formulas that I inherited from the bakers who had come before me. The recipes at Per Se were mostly all French, and very precise and exacting. I learned the art of perfection at Per Se, and I learned about seasoning and balancing pastries with salt and acid. Finally, by the time I went to work at Roberta's, the legendary pizzeria in Brooklyn, I was able to take all of that knowledge and experience I had acquired over a lifetime of baking and use it to make my own creations. I baked baguettes, sourdough bread, and bagels all in an outdoor pizza oven, and I started selling salted caramel sticky buns that were a knock-out success. The bagels that I was baking at Roberta's segued into my own bagel stand at the outdoor Williamsburg Smorgasburg market, which in turn led to a larger project, Sadelle's. When I opened Sadelle's, a contemporary remake of a traditional New York City deli, in SoHo, I took those creations a step further and really started to take my pastries to an elevated place. Pastries that I would find at local delis and old-time bakery shops became inspiration for newly imagined, tastier, more creative versions. After Sadelle's, I focused on Viennoiserie, like kouign amann and croissants. Using science, seasoning, and taste, I like to take ordinary pastries to a higher level, like pistachio sour cherry croissants and buckwheat kouign amann.

It's easy enough, now, to sum this up on the page of a résumé, but it didn't happen overnight. Along the way, I turned to cookbooks for inspiration at every turn. I baked every single bread in Nancy Silverton's *Breads from the La Brea Bakery*. I baked a lot from Claudia Fleming's *The Last Course*, which had just come out when I started getting serious about baking and pastry making. I read about flavor pairings in a book called *Culinary Artistry* by Karen Page and Andrew Dornenburg. Those were the books that I devoured as I tried to develop my palate and to teach myself how to create classic baked goods with the most flavor.

As my interest in baking increased, so did my reliance on cookbooks. I was never content if the cakes, pies, or desserts I made for friends tasted great but looked homemade. I wanted them to look as if I had bought them at a professional bakery.

After I started working in professional kitchens, I had an aha! moment. As I was learning from the more experienced bakers around me, it was clear to me: if those recipes had just given a little hint about this or that, a little more detail here or there, my baked goods would have turned out looking like those in the pictures that inspired me to want to make them to begin with. I knew then that I wanted to write a cookbook. I also knew that I was just beginning on my path and that I had a lot to learn. I continued to bake at home, and as I did, I opened an Excel document for each recipe I made—those I developed, and those I liked from cookbooks that I was baking from. I tweaked the recipes and wrote detailed notes of my findings in the margins. It was this big dream that someday, I would compile those into a cookbook that had all the information that I was looking for when I was teaching myself to bake. After fifteen years of training, perfecting, and note-taking, this is that book.

In these pages, you will find recipes for the kinds of beautiful, seductive pastries you see in your favorite bakeshop: all-American classics such as cookies and pies, layer cakes, and muffins; New York favorites, including rugelach, babka, and challah; and laminated pastries, from croissants to kouign amann, inspired by my love of France. It is equal parts educational and aspirational, with recipes written in such detail that even a novice (but focused) home baker will be able to create professional-looking baked goods at home. It is the book I wanted when I was teaching myself to bake.

If you follow these recipes, which are very detailed, and read the instructions in the Master Classes and 101s, your cookies will have the same crackle top that make your favorite bakery cookies look so appealing; your pies will turn out pretty, with a deep golden crust, sparkling with sugar and defined, crimped edges and lattice that aren't shrunken or misshapen; and your croissants will look indistinguishable from those you buy from a French patisserie. This is the cookbook I wish I'd had when first started out. It would have taught me everything I needed to achieve a "good bake" every time. Because a "good bake" is the best bake.

Setting Yourself Up for Success

Baking is all about precision, and about chemistry. You put something into a hot oven where it undergoes a transformation and emerges as something else. Each step along the way influences the final product. Because of this, I am very particular about how I execute even the most minute tasks. Below are some of the steps and considerations that I take throughout these recipes, and why.

Read the recipe
Read the recipe before you do anything else. I'm sure you've heard this piece of advice before, but I can't stress how essential it is, and how much easier it will make your life in the end.

Write a baking schedule
After reading the recipe from beginning to end, go back through the recipe with a piece of paper and pen in hand, and write out a baking schedule. I write my schedule factoring in the parameters of my own day. My baking schedule for croissants might read:

Friday morning, before work:
Feed sourdough starter.

Friday, after work:
Feed sourdough starter.
Saturday morning:
Mix croissant dough using sourdough starter.
Refrigerate dough. Make butter packet.
Laminate croissant dough and refrigerate overnight.
Sunday morning:
Pull croissant dough from refrigerator. Roll out and shape croissants.
Proof.
Bake.

Mise en place

This is a French culinary term meaning "everything in its place," and it refers to having all your ingredients in front of you and prepared. Get out all your ingredients, as well as the equipment and tools you are going to need for a recipe. Prep and measure your ingredients, and once you are done with them, put away the containers that those ingredients came in.

Work cleanly

Before you begin, clear your work area of anything you don't need. And as you proceed with a recipe, clean your work area as you go. Having a neat and clean work area is something that really separates the amateurs from the pros and it is something I really stress when I am teaching. Working clean makes you proud of what you are doing. It also results in neater looking pastries.

Preheat the oven

I am very specific about how I preheat my oven. First, I give ample time to preheat—usually about 20 to 30 minutes. Keep an oven thermometer in your oven and confirm that it has reached the desired temperature before adding your creations to the oven. Before I got a new, better oven in my apartment, I used to keep a pizza stone on the floor of the oven at all times. With a home oven—especially a weak apartment oven—the heat rushes out every time you open the oven door. But the heat penetrates the stone, so by keeping the stone in the oven, the oven better maintains its temperature when you open and close the oven door or introduce cold dough.

Weighing versus measuring

Professional bakers weigh, they do not measure, ingredients. This idea may feel foreign to you at first because you've been using measuring cups all your life. But once you get used to weighing, you'll see that it is actually easier and much less messy than measuring. The way it works is first you put a bowl on a food scale; next, tare the scale (zero it out) so you're not weighing the bowl. Then add the first ingredient you are going to weigh to the bowl. Once you've added it, tare (zero out) the scale again so it's back at zero and add the next ingredient. Continue until you've added all of the ingredients that are going into that bowl. Weighing ingredients is also much more accurate than measuring. Because there will always be variations in the density of ingredients, there will always be variations in volumetric measurements; weighed measurements, on the other hand, are always precise. I'm trained to be precise, and so I always weigh my ingredients.

Metric versus imperial weight

Metric is the system of measuring used everywhere throughout the world except in the United States. Metric weight is measured in grams and kilograms, while imperial weight refers to ounces and pounds. Where all bakers weigh rather than measure ingredients, bread bakers use almost exclusively metric measurements, rather than imperial. The reason for this is that the metric system works in increments of ten, and bakers use baker's percentage to create their recipes. Baker's percentage means the weights of the ingredients in a recipe are based on their ratio to the weight of the flour. First, you start a recipe with an amount of flour, usually 1 kilogram (or 1,000 grams). If you want water at a 70 percent ratio to the weight of the flour, then you know to add 700 grams of water. Salt is usually 2.2 percent, so you know to add 22 grams. So the math is easy. And once you have your recipe, you can easily scale it up or down because metric units are all based on multiples of ten. Even though this is not a bread baking book, I am a bread baker by nature and these recipes include metric measurements. The recipes do give the volumetric measures first, though, as a helping hand.

Temperature of ingredients

Temperature is an important factor when you're baking, especially when you're working with yeast and sourdough starter. The rate at which yeast grows and ferments is dictated by the temperature of both the ingredients and the environment. When I bake, I always consider the temperature, and throughout these recipes, you'll see me referring to temperatures often. So just be mindful of temperatures when you're baking. What's your room temperature? What's the temperature of the liquid in your recipe? What's the temperature of your butter?

Chilling dough

I learned more about the importance of working with chilled dough when I was baking at home than I did in school and in all the professional kitchens I worked at combined. At home, even as a child baking with my mother, cookie dough would stick to the surface after I'd cut it with cookie cutters.

Tart shells would rip when I was lining a pan. I didn't know what I was doing wrong, and I would get so frustrated. I wish someone had taught me then what I know now, which is that the secret trick is to work with dough that is chilled. Chilled dough does not stick to the counter or the rolling pin, and it also holds its shape in the oven, giving your baked goods a more professional look. Working with chilled dough includes more factors than simply chilling the dough before you work with it. It takes the amateur longer to roll out and work with dough, and the dough warms up in the process. Also, some bakers have cold hands; others have hot hands. If you're rolling bread dough or shaping pretzels, it makes a big difference how long you've been working with the dough (and therefore how warm the dough became in the process) and how warm your hands are. The temperature of the room is also a factor. You'll know when the dough has become warmer than you want it to be because it will be sticky and floppy and difficult to work with. The remedy is to put the dough in the refrigerator for 20 to 30 minutes until it is chilled, then start again.

Ingredients

I try to use the best ingredients I can find in whatever I am baking. At work, that's easy: I have access to every kind of specialty flour or imported chocolate or vanilla I can imagine. At home, having the right ingredients requires a bit more organization. I am by nature a planner, and an organizer, so I keep my favorite things on hand. But very often, I get the spontaneous urge to make something and I don't have everything I need. In those instances, I go to the small grocery store in my neighborhood and buy whatever brands they offer. As important as it is to use good ingredients—and I do believe it is—fresh, homemade baked goods are special in and of themselves.

Arrowroot
A few years ago, in an effort to cut down on corn-based ingredients, I started replacing the cornstarch in my recipes with arrowroot, a starch thickener made from a tropical tuber. Not only do I like that it is healthier than cornstarch, I like using arrowroot in pies because it is clear when it sets up, whereas cornstarch can make the filling cloudy. While I still use cornstarch in some of my recipes, I have converted many of them to use arrowroot.

Baking powder and baking soda
As a child, I learned to make muffins in home economics class. But when I tried to replicate them at home, they didn't rise. My mom and I put two and two together and figured out that it was the baking soda: it was old, so it had lost its leavening power, and hence my flat muffins. Nowadays, I use my baking soda so quickly that it doesn't have time to go bad, but assuming you

do not bake at home every day, or even every week, you will want to buy fresh cans of baking powder and baking soda to replace the old once a year.

Butter

I use unsalted butter exclusively (although I do love *beurre de baratte,* which is a cultured, salted butter from France, for spreading on toast or biscuits). This is common practice in professional kitchens; if you start with unsalted butter, you can control how much salt you use. These recipes have all been tested using Land O'Lakes butter, which is a very consistent product and also widely available. If you want to splurge and use European-style, use it in laminated pastries, where the butter is the focal point. For laminating, my preferred brands of European-style butter are Plugra and Beurremont. On the rare occasion when I use salted butter and you find yourself with none on hand, you can add ½ teaspoon of salt to the recipe.

Chocolate

Valrhona sells chocolate in thin oval disks called *feves.* This is my preferred chocolate, because I can use it as chocolate chunks for cookies (I cut each *feve* in half), and if I'm melting chocolate, there is no chopping involved, and no residual dust (waste) as a result. Manjari is my bittersweet chocolate of choice, and Jivara is my favorite milk chocolate.

Cocoa powder

My preferred brand is Valrhona; I just think the taste is superior to all others. I use Valrhona cocoa powder in my professional kitchen exclusively, but if I can't find it for home use, I use Ghirardelli or Hershey's cocoa powder, and that works just fine.

Eggs

I use large eggs, preferably organic, because I can count on each one weighing about 50 grams. When I'm making something that highlights a cooked egg, such as the Khachapuri with Cheese, Baked Egg, and Nigella Seeds (page 14), which has a baked, runny egg on top, I look for the best eggs I can find, ideally from a local farm.

Flour

All-purpose flour

All-purpose flour is the basic refined white flour and the base of the vast majority of these recipes. I use King Arthur Unbleached All-Purpose Flour exclusively, in both my professional and home kitchens. The main difference when it comes to refined white flours, including all-purpose flour, bread flour, cake flour, and pastry flour, is how much protein each contains. The more protein in a flour, the more gluten is developed during the process of working it. And the more gluten is formed, the stronger and more elastic your dough will be, and the chewier your baked goods will be as a result. Dough with less gluten will yield tender pastry, such as piecrust. I use all-purpose flour in place of bread flour in many of my breads, such as the Summer Focaccia with Sungolds, Corn, and Basil Pesto (page 29) and the Hot Dog Buns (page 24), because it makes for a more tender bread, with a better mouth feel, where bread flour tends to make things chewier than necessary.

Bread flour A refined white flour, bread flour has more protein than all-purpose flour, which aids in gluten development. I use it when I need to develop more gluten, and therefore more strength in my dough, such as for Cherry and Pistachio Panettone (page 82) and yeasted sandwich breads. It is also my preferred flour to use when feeding my Sourdough Starter (page xxxiii).

Buckwheat flour Don't let the name fool you: buckwheat, and hence buckwheat flour, is gluten free. Buckwheat has a distinct, brownish-gray color (I think it's pretty) and an even more distinct, earthy flavor. It is grown in Brittany, and there you find all kinds of pastry using buckwheat. I was inspired to make Buckwheat Kouign Amann (page 177) on a trip to Brittany. Look for stone-ground flour, locally milled if possible.

Cake flour Cake flour has less protein in it than all-purpose flour. King Arthur is my preferred brand. Ideally, I seek out unbleached cake flour, but often I use whatever I find at the grocery store.

Rye flour Very often, I like to switch out all-purpose flour for a more flavorful flour like rye flour, such as in the Rye Pâte Sucrée (page 291) that I use as a base for my Lemon Rosemary Curd Tart (page 288). It has almost a gray tone to it, and an unusual flavor that pairs nicely with the lemon.

Spelt flour Spelt is a strain of wheat native to Europe. It is not gluten free, but it contains less gluten than whole wheat. I use spelt flour because I like the layer of nutty flavor it adds to baked goods, such as Spelt Bull's-Eye Scones (page 348).

Whole-wheat pastry flour Because it has a lower protein content than whole-wheat flour, when you bake with whole-wheat pastry flour, you get the nice wheat flavor without the heaviness often associated with whole-grain baked goods. I "sneak" it into a lot of doughs where you'd never know it was there, from my Master Recipe for Pâte Brisée (page 232) to several muffins, scones, casual cakes, cookies, breads, and even laminated pastries, such as my Classic Croissants (page 139). I add the whole-wheat pastry flour to the dough not to make these things healthier, but because I like the layer of flavor it adds.

Nonstick cooking spray

Professional bakeries use nonstick cooking spray, not butter, to grease baking pans, muffin tins, and baking sheets. It is easy to use and efficient—it is easy to get a thin, even, and thorough coat that gets into the crevices of any shape of pan. When baking at home, I sometimes use butter instead of nonstick cooking spray, such as to butter cake pans.

Salt

Fine sea salt

I use fine sea salt exclusively in my baking. This is because I'm a bread baker first, and in bread baking, we always use fine sea salt. Sea salt can be used interchangeably with other types of salt, such as kosher salt, if you weigh it; the volumes of different types of salt vary considerably. So, invest in a tall container of La Baleine fine sea salt and use that as you bake from this book. It's the brand I use at home.

Flaky sea salt

When I want to add a pinch of salt on top of a pastry as a finishing touch, I use a large flaky, mineral-tasting sea salt. The easiest such salt to find is Maldon, which is from England. I also use a similar Nordic salt. Both have large, thin, shard-like flakes that add a wonderful crunchy element to foods.

Spices

I look for nice spices, but I don't throw them away after a certain period of time, like some cookbooks suggest you do. I cook and bake a lot, so I suppose my spices are on a pretty good rotation naturally. The one spice I do have something to say about is *nutmeg*. I buy whole nutmeg, which has such better flavor and aroma than ground. And it's so easy to grate: Just take the little nut, which is about the size of the end of your thumb, and grate it on a fine Microplane. I call for specific amounts of nutmeg in my recipes, but the truth is that I usually eyeball it. I grate the nutmeg so that it falls straight into whatever I'm making, until I think I've added enough.

Sugar

Granulated sugar

I stick with Domino or, if I'm in California, C&H, because my priority when choosing a sugar to bake with is consistent texture. Both are pure cane sugars.

Confectioners' sugar

Aka powdered sugar, confectioners' sugar is known in professional kitchens as 10X sugar, because it is ground ten times as fine as granulated sugar. It contains cornstarch, which also affects its texture. It's used often in making frostings and glazes and other applications where the goal is a smooth texture. It is the not-so-secret ingredient in my Chocolate Chunk Cookies (page 380).

Brown sugar   Brown sugar is made by combining granulated sugar with molasses. Light brown sugar has less molasses and dark brown sugar has more. I suggest you stick with Domino or C&H for the sake of consistency.

Demerara sugar   Also called turbinado sugar (sold as Sugar in the Raw), demerara sugar is a coarse, natural sugar with a pretty, light caramel color. I use it as my sanding sugar, meaning I sprinkle it on baked goods to add an organic sparkle effect. I also use it to sweeten my Blueberry Blackberry Slab Pie (page 248).

Vanilla

Vanilla beans   Vanilla beans have such a wonderful, pure flavor and aroma. When shopping for vanilla beans, look for ones that are plump and moist. Sometimes in the grocery store you don't have that option; you just get whatever bean you can find. Store them in a sealable plastic bag in your refrigerator. Use "spent" vanilla beans to make Vanilla Sugar (page 219).

Vanilla extract   Buy only pure vanilla extract; the imitation stuff is not even close. I always buy the best brand that I can find, which varies depending on where I am shopping. What I don't ever use is artificial vanilla extract.

Yeast

Instant yeast   I love fresh yeast, and in my professional kitchens, I use fresh yeast more often than not. When I bake at home, I use only instant yeast because it is so easy to get. You can buy instant yeast in little packets in the baking section of grocery stores, although I suggest you seek out one-pound bags from a baking supply store or Internet source. Store it in the freezer and dip into it as needed; you could bake every recipe in this book and never have to buy another packet of yeast. If you do buy the small packets, the most common brand you will see is Fleischmann's, which is labeled "RapidRise Instant Yeast." It is the same thing as instant dry yeast sold in one-pound bags. The yeast I buy both for home baking and in my professional kitchens is SAF-Instant Yeast, which comes in a one-pound red bag. You can find it easily from online sources and some specialty food stores. Note that instant yeast is *not* the same thing as active dry yeast. They can be used interchangeably, however, active dry yeast must be "bloomed" first. I do not use active dry yeast in any of these recipes, so don't buy that if you're shopping for this book.

Osmotolerant yeast   This is a type of instant yeast that I use for doughs that contain sugar, and in all of my Viennoiserie production. When you are working with a dough that contains sugar, the sugar and yeast both compete for the water in the dough. Osmotolerant yeast is a strain of yeast that does not compete with the sugar for the water; so, if a dough contains 5 percent or more sugar based on the weight of the flour, it is best to use osmotolerant yeast to make it. The brand I buy is SAF-Instant gold yeast. Nowhere on the package does it say "osmotolerant." I have no idea how the consumer is supposed to know the difference, but trust me when I say that the SAF gold is osmotolerant and the SAF red is regular instant yeast. Although the labeling is confusing, and although I prefer osmotolerant yeast for dough that has a high sugar content, the good news is that the two can be used interchangeably.

Sourdough starter Sourdough starter is a natural leavening, a mix of flour and water and natural yeast, that is used to ferment dough. It is what gives sourdough bread its characteristic sour or tangy flavor. See Sourdough Starter (page xxxiii) to make your own. In a pinch, you can also buy it from your local bakery, or order it online from King Arthur Flour.

Equipment and Tools

I don't want to tell anyone that they have to go out and spend a bunch of money just to make my recipes, but baking does require specific vessels— different sizes and shapes of pans are just tools of the trade. Those that I use in this book are listed here, and so is the equipment that I use in my day-to-day life baking at home or in professional kitchens to make baking easy and enjoyable. I don't always buy everything I need; I get by with what I have. I have one cooling rack when I should have two. I don't own a blender, so I use a food processor instead. And I keep things forever. I still have and use the whisk that my friend Gina DePalma gave me as a gift more than a dozen years ago. And I still use a lot of cooking gear, including a Pyrex glass pie plate, that I inherited from my grandmother, who passed away right after I graduated from college.

I have a tool kit that I take with me when I'm traveling and I think cooking will be involved. This includes a pair of tongs, a Magiwhisk, a Victorinox serrated paring knife, and my digital scale. No matter how poorly stocked the kitchen may be, if I have all of those things, I know I'll survive.

Aluminum baking sheets

I use 12-gauge commercial baking sheets that have a lip or rim around them. They conduct heat evenly and they don't buckle in the oven the way some baking sheets do. My home kitchen is stocked with half sheet pan–size baking sheets (18 x 13 inches), which is what I refer to in this book as a "baking sheet." Since this is a standardized product, it stacks well, which means you can store a lot of them in your kitchen with no problem. It's a good idea to have at least four, but two will do the trick, sometimes with some juggling involved. I also use a quarter sheet pan (13 x 9 inches) for baking Pull-Apart Parker House Rolls (page 50) and Hot Cross Buns (page 112).

Bench knife

A bench knife is a simple rectangular tool that bakers use to scrape the counter clean, and to cut dough. If you buy a good one, it will have a sharp enough edge that it functions like a knife. In a professional bread bakery, it is an everyday tool, and it functions as a knife. This is what we use to cut hundreds of pieces of dough, which we then throw on the scale for even scaling. The important thing for me in choosing a bench knife is that it is tall enough that I can cut through a block of dough without the dough hitting the handle.

Box grater

This old-school tool is still the best for grating vegetables and cheese.

Candy thermometer

I use my clip-on candy thermometer to gauge the temperature of oil when I am deep-frying, or when I'm cooking sugar syrup and jam on the stove top. It's not something that I use often, but when I do need to use one, it is essential. I still use the candy thermometer that I bought for my pastry class at the French Culinary Institute in 2004.

Cake pans

When you bake a lot, you end up with a lot of different cake pans. Mine are all anodized aluminum, which is another way to say "nonstick." I also have many stainless-steel cake pans that I acquired from my grandmother. Among the shapes of cake pans called for in this book, and that I think are part of a well-stocked kitchen, are:

8- x 2-inch round cake pans (3)
8-inch square baking pan
10-inch Bundt pan
9-inch springform pan
2-quart steamed pudding mold

Cooling racks

I use cooling racks to place baking sheets on when they first come out of the oven. And then I transfer the baked goods directly onto the cooling racks to cool completely. Placing baked goods on a cooling rack allows the air to circulate so they don't continue to cook from the residual heat of the pan. You can live without a cooling rack, but in the pursuit of perfect baked goods, one or two is worth the small investment.

Digital probe thermometer

Throughout these recipes, I often call for water and milk at specific temperatures, and the way to measure the temperature is with this inexpensive gadget. I also use it to make lemon curd and to take the internal temperature of some baked goods.

Digital scale

A food scale is an essential in any baker's kitchen. Buy a sturdy, good-quality one; you'll have it forever.

Food processor

A mini food processor comes in handy for grinding small amounts of ingredients, and they're so inexpensive that it's nice to have one around. But there is no replacement for a full-size food processor, which I call for in several recipes. I don't have a blender; this is my sole pureeing tool.

Industrial plastic wrap

I love to buy professional-grade plastic wrap, which comes in an 18-inch roll and is so much more effective than what is sold in grocery stores. It actually sticks and seals, whereas the other stuff just falls off. You can buy it online at WebstaurantStore.com, Amazon.com, or from restaurant supply stores. Buy one roll and it will last you almost forever.

Jelly-roll pan

A jelly-roll pan is an aluminum pan with a 1-inch lip. It looks just like a baking sheet, but smaller. I use a jelly-roll pan for making slab pies. The pans vary slightly in size. Mine is 10 inches by 15 inches.

Kitchen shears

Once you get used to using kitchen shears in the cooking and baking process, you won't know how you ever lived without them. I reach for them for everything from cutting parchment paper and opening packages to cutting focaccia. The key difference between kitchen shears and any other scissors is that the two sides come apart, so you can wash them thoroughly, which is important because they come into contact with food.

Loaf pans

You will need a standard 9- x 4-inch loaf pan for some recipes, and Pullman loaf pans in two sizes: 9 x 4 inches for babka and 13 x 4 inches for sandwich breads. I love the straight sides of the Pullman loaf pan and use it to make loaves such as Ricotta Chocolate Chip Pound Cake (page 341) that might otherwise be baked in a standard loaf pan. I use the larger Pullman for baking bread loaves for slicing. The Pullman pan has a lid that slides on it, which I use when I make some breads, such as the Whole-Wheat Pain au Lait Pullman (page 40); it gives the loaf square edges, which is nice for sandwiches. I leave the lid off for other loaves, such as the Sourdough Brioche Loaf (page 45), where I want a beautiful rounded, golden brown top. The lid doesn't just affect the shape of the loaf. By forgoing the lid, you get a lighter, airier loaf because you are not constricting the dough.

Microplane

I use a fine-holed Microplane to grate whole nutmeg and for zesting citrus. I like to hold the Microplane still and move the nut or fruit across the plane, not the other way around, but do what feels comfortable to you.

Muffin tins

I suggest you keep two types: one large tin that has 12 standard muffin cups and four smaller tins, each with 6 jumbo cups. I use them for muffins, of course, and I also use the jumbo tins to make the Salted Caramel Sticky Buns (page 131).

Offset spatula

An offset spatula is a long metal spatula with a handle that is offset and juts out at an angle, which gives you more control. I use both large and small offset spatulas, and I use them often for evening out batter in a cake pan, for spreading fillings over sheets of dough, and for frosting cakes, among other things.

Oven thermometer

To make sure I'm baking at the correct temperature, I keep an oven thermometer in the oven at all times. I've tried different brands and they all seem to break—or the glass gets so fogged up you can't read them. So, yes, you have to replace them from time to time. But the good news is, they aren't expensive.

Parchment paper

Once you've baked in a professional kitchen, you wouldn't think of baking on a baking sheet that wasn't lined with parchment paper. Using parchment makes easy work of cleanup: you just lift off the sheet and throw it away; no scrubbing involved. (If you want to conserve paper, you can do what is required in many professional kitchens, which is to turn the parchment over and bake on the other side before throwing it out.) Sheets of parchment paper that fit perfectly in a half sheet pan–size baking sheet are available at baking supply stores and online. They are very convenient to use because you don't have to measure and cut, and they also don't curl up the way parchment cut from a roll does. At conventional grocery stores, you can also buy folded sheets of parchment that are equally convenient.

Paring knife

My go-to small knife is a small serrated paring knife made by Victorinox. Because it is serrated, I don't have to worry about sharpening it. It has a plastic handle. It's really basic. And equally inexpensive. But it works perfectly. I use it for all small tasks, from splitting and scraping vanilla beans to hulling strawberries or slicing garlic.

Pastry bags

I use 18-inch disposable pastry bags, which I buy by the roll from a baking supply store or Amazon.com. Many home bakers are not familiar with these bags, but they're smart: they're inexpensive, easy to obtain, and there is no washing involved.

Pastry brushes

I keep two pastry brushes in my kitchen: a Swissmar washable silicone brush for brushing wet ingredients, such as water, egg, or melted butter. And a natural bristle brush, which looks like a paintbrush, which I never get wet, and which I use for brushing flour off of pastry dough.

Pastry tips

I use pastry tips for piping dough and also for decorating with royal icing. I use only a few basic tips: for example, a small round tip (Ateco #6) for icing and an open-star pastry tip (Ateco #825) for piping churros.

Pastry wheel

This rolling cutter is part of every serious baker's tool kit. I use mine constantly, for nicking dough when I am measuring, for making more precise cuts, and for cutting the dough.

Plastic bowl scraper

This simple, inexpensive handheld tool is an essential in bread baking. Bread dough tends to be very sticky. A bowl scraper is stiff, but it is flexible, and it's curved on one side to reflect the curve of a bowl so you can really scrape your bowl clean with it. It doesn't have a handle, so you hold it in your palm, and it feels like an extension of your hand. It costs about a dollar. Get one.

Roul'Pat

You may be familiar with a Silpat, which is a silicone mat used in place of parchment paper to line baking sheets. I don't use those; I use parchment instead because it's just so easy to come by. But I do use the lesser-known relative of Silpat, the Roul'Pat. Essentially a larger version of a Silpat, the mat lies on your counter and you roll dough on it. I like that it requires you to use much less flour to keep the dough from sticking, which is a good thing because too much flour can change the texture and the flavor of what you're baking. I still use the Roul'Pat that Gina DePalma gave me more than a decade ago. She was cleaning out the kitchen at Babbo and said, "Here, Melissa. Take this." I remember thinking: I don't want it. I'll never use it. But I did anything Gina told me to do, so I took it home and started using it. Now, I use a Roul'Pat any time I roll out dough at home.

Rolling pin

I use an 18-inch straight rolling pin, which bakers refer to as a "French rolling pin," exclusively. I've always called it a French rolling pin, but it's actually called a "straight rolling pin." This is a rolling pin without handles, which allows me to feel how much pressure I am putting on the dough. French rolling pins come with tapered edges or straight all the way across; I like the straight ones. I don't use a rolling pin with handles, ever. But I understand that using a rolling pin with handles can be easier for the novice, and it is also more ergonomically correct, so if you want to use a rolling pin with handles, look for a ball-bearing one.

Rubber spatulas

Silicone rubber spatulas are essential for cleaning mixing bowls. I have a few shapes and sizes, all heat proof, that I reach for at different moments.

Pie plate

I use a Pyrex glass 9-inch pie plate because it makes for the most evenly browned piecrust. You don't get the same golden brown crust from fancy ceramic pie plates. And crusts tend to burn or brown unevenly in aluminum pie tins. The glass pie plates are inexpensive, easy to find, and the best for the job.

Pie weights or dried beans

I own a set of pie weights that I bought at a fancy cookware store, but the set doesn't contain enough weights to fill the pie shell as deeply as I like to. I almost always bypass my pie weights and use two pounds of dried beans instead. Either works equally well.

Dried beans are cheap, easy to find, and, like "official" pie weights, you can reuse them. Put them in a container and label it "pie weights" so you don't accidentally cook them.

Santoku knife

A Santoku is a Japanese knife, similar in size to a classic European chef's knife, but with a straighter blade that is not meant for chopping using a rocking motion the way a chef's knife is. My 8-inch Wüsthof Santoku is the knife I use for all my chopping, whether it's for rhubarb, apples, onions, or herbs. A Santoku also has a dimpled edge, which keeps whatever you are chopping from sticking to the blade.

Serrated bread knife

I have two serrated knives, one offset and one regular. I use the offset serrated knife for slicing bread. By using an offset serrated knife, when you are slicing downward through the loaf, your hand doesn't hit the cutting board when it gets to the bottom, as the knife blade gets there first. I use a standard serrated knife to cut through cake layers. Having both is ideal, but one or the other is fine. If you were going out to buy only one, I would suggest the offset knife, which is more versatile.

Spice grinder

I use a spice grinder, which looks exactly like a coffee grinder (and a coffee grinder can be used in its place) for grinding spices and seeds, such as sesame seeds for the Black Sesame Kouign Amann (page 176).

Stand mixer

A stand mixer is an essential in a baker's kitchen. There are some things, like creaming butter and sugar together, where handheld beaters could be substituted. But for making bread dough, which requires some strength, only a stand mixer will do. You can also walk away from a stand mixer while it's working, which means you can multitask: get ingredients ready or clean up while the mixer is doing its work. I use a 6-quart KitchenAid mixer, but the 8-quart mixer is amazing, and if I were buying one again, that is the one I would buy.

Stainless-steel bowls

Stainless-steel bowls are really important in baking. They're more efficient than ceramic bowls because they're lightweight and they don't break. You need stainless-steel bowls when you're setting up a double boiler, and when you're weighing ingredients into a bowl, a lightweight bowl is important, so the scale doesn't top out. Stainless-steel bowls are also practical from a storage point of view because they nest. And, they are inexpensive; I suggest you buy a set of nesting bowls for everyday use. Save the beautiful ceramic bowls for serving purposes.

Straightedge

A straightedge, or ruler, is essential for measuring dough when you're rolling it, and to use as a guide for a pastry wheel when cutting dough for more precise pastries, such as croissants.

Strainers

It's nice to have fine-mesh strainers in a few different sizes for rinsing grains, draining anything you've soaked (such as dried fruit), or straining citrus juice.

Tart pans

I call for French removable-bottom tart pans in two recipes: I use a 9-inch pan for the Lemon Rosemary Curd Tart with Rye Crust (page 288) and a 10½-inch pan for the Chestnut Honey Walnut Tart (page 281). The removable bottom means that the tart stands on its own, out of the pan, which is such a pretty look. You can use either fluted or not fluted interchangeably, whichever you find, or like the look of better.

Tongs

Something that surprises me when I'm cooking in other people's homes or in a rented Airbnb is how many people don't have metal tongs. Tongs are your best friend in the kitchen, especially when you're cooking at the stove. They're like an extension of your hand. When you're sautéing, you can turn things much more easily using tongs than with a spatula. They're also great for turning vegetables that are roasting in the oven. And nothing else will do when you're deep- or shallow-frying. I wish more people would think about using tongs.

Whisk

Hands down the best whisk is a Magiwhisk. It's small, compact, lightweight, and it does the job better than any other type. I use it for small jobs, such as whisking eggs for egg wash or making salad dressing. I have a 14-inch piano whisk for everything else.

Yeast Tutorial

If you have never worked with yeast, I know it can be intimidating. Even the language can seem mysterious when you are not familiar with it. This is not a book about bread baking, so I am going to skip over some of the intricacies, but I do use yeast throughout these recipes—in the Savory Breads, Sweet Yeasted Breads, and Laminated Pastries chapters—so I want to give you a basic understanding of yeast and how it works.

The basic principle behind yeast is that it is a leavener: like baking soda or baking powder, it causes baked goods to rise. The difference is that baking soda and powder are chemical leaveners, where yeast is a natural, organic leavener. (A third type of leavener is "mechanical." An example of that is whipped egg whites.) Whether you are working with dry yeast, fresh yeast (compressed or cake), or natural yeast (sourdough starter), yeast eats the sugars and damaged starches in your dough and produces carbon dioxide and alcohol. The carbon dioxide leavens the dough. Different types of yeast are used to leaven different baked goods. Some recipes are leavened with commercial yeast (such as the instant dry yeast I use in many of these recipes), some with sourdough starter, and some with a combination of the two. I often use a combination: the commercial yeast for reliability and consistency and the sourdough starter for the flavor it adds to baked goods. (For more detail, see Sourdough Starter, page xxxiii.)

The two principal factors in activating yeast are temperature and time: the temperature of the dough and the amount of time you let it ferment and proof.

The following is a short glossary of terms related to yeast.

Autolyse   Autolyse is a technique that was developed in France by a baker named Raymond Calvel, who discovered that—because both salt and yeast inhibit gluten formation—if you let flour and water sit together before adding salt and yeast, gluten forms better. I use autolyse in doughs for which crumb structure and stretch of gluten are important, such as for baguette dough. In this book, I use it with my focaccia dough because focaccia dough is stretched, and the dough stretches better with stronger gluten formation. Most professional bakers autolyse their dough for about 30 minutes and that is what I call for. Some bakers hold back the salt and yeast completely. I introduce them in two distinct piles on top of the dough, so they begin to dissolve into the dough but don't inhibit the gluten. I don't like them to touch because the salt will take the water away from the yeast and the yeast will start to die.

Biga   An Italian stiff sourdough starter, biga is a type of preferment (see page xxxii). Its hydration is much lower than the liquid sourdough starter I normally use. I convert my liquid starter to a stiff starter to make my Cherry and Pistachio Panettone (page 82).

Crumb   The crumb refers to the texture inside a baked good. It is defined by the gelatinized starch and the holes that are produced during leavening. A croissant should have a nice, big, open-holed honeycomb structure. Brioche should have a tighter crumb, with a lot of small, wide, uniform holes and no big ones.

Fermentation   Professional bakers refer to the first rise as the "fermentation," and that is how I refer to it in this book. The first rise, or fermentation period, comes at the point in the process when you have just finished mixing the dough and the yeast has begun to feed on it. Your dough will be what we call "in bulk," which means it will be in the mixing bowl, covered, in a warm place, which allows the yeast to grow. Fermentation can also take place in the refrigerator, where, because of the colder temperature, the yeast growth slows down; this slow growth contributes a lot of flavor. Oftentimes, I like to start my fermentation in a warm room and then move the dough to the refrigerator to give it a long and slow rise; extending the time improves the baked good's flavor.

Poolish   A poolish is a type of preferment (see below). A poolish is equal parts water and flour and a small amount of commercial yeast. It is mixed between 12 and 24 hours before mixing the dough into which it will be added. I use a poolish in making focaccia because it adds extensibility to the dough, which enables me to stretch the dough into the pan in which the focaccia is baked.

Preferment   A preferment is dough that is fermented before it is added to the main dough, which will also be fermented. The types of preferments used in this book are sourdough starter, poolish, sponge, and biga. All preferments add flavor to dough, and also boost fermentation.

Proofing   Proofing refers to the second rise of the dough. This takes place after the fermentation stage. You remove the dough from the bowl and shape it according to the requirements of the finished product: a loaf of bread, a roll, or a croissant, etc. After being shaped, the dough needs to rise again, or proof. A professional baker often relies on time and the size of a product to judge when something is proofed properly, but this can be tricky to judge for the novice baker. When you are starting out, the best way to tell if something is proofed is by poking it with your fingertip. Bread and pastry products proof from the outside toward the center, so you want to poke the dough in two places: the tip or end of the pastry, and also in the center. When dough is done proofing, the tip should really hold the indentation, while the center should hold the indentation but spring back a little.

The same dough, shaped into a small roll, will take less time to proof than that dough shaped into a large loaf. The longer you proof an enriched dough (any dough that has fat such as oil or butter or eggs in it), the lighter and fluffier and bigger it will become. At a certain point in proofing any dough, you will reach the point of no return where the dough will proof no more and will start to collapse either before it goes into the oven or during the bake.

Retard   Retarding dough means to slow down the fermentation process. This is done by cooling the dough, which you do by putting it in the refrigerator. Yeast growth slows down in cooler temperatures, so by cooling the dough, you slow down the fermentation process. Besides fermentation, the other thing that is happening when you are retarding dough is that the enzymes that occur in flour and yeast break down the damaged starches (complex sugar) in the flour into simple sugars. Simple sugars contribute to the flavor of the dough and also cause it to brown in the oven. By retarding the dough, you give the enzymes the opportunity to break down the starches into sugars, which enhances the flavor of the dough. Also, increased sugar in the dough means increased browning. So, by waiting, you get that deep, burnished exterior on breads and pastries. Due to the Maillard reaction—a chemical reaction between naturally occurring amino acids in food and sugars that reduce as a product of heat—browned foods not only look better, they also taste better.

Sponge　　A sponge is a type of preferment. I use it to boost the fermentation of Rum and Raisin Stollen (page 115) because that dough is laden with butter, rum, dried fruits, and nuts, all of which impede fermentation.

Turn/Fold　　Turning and folding are the same thing and I use the words interchangeably. You turn/fold dough during the fermentation process. The dough at this point will be in a bowl, covered with plastic wrap or a towel. To turn the dough (which I generally do every hour, so in the middle of a two-hour fermentation, or at the end of a one-hour fermentation), first, uncover the bowl. Wet your hands, which prevents the dough from sticking to them, and pick up one edge of the dough and bring it toward the center. Do the same with the opposite edge of the dough, then with the top and bottom edges. This is a more orderly method of what is also called punching down the dough. This little bit of movement helps to redistribute the yeast and strengthen the dough. (Folding can also refer to the process during lamination of folding the dough and butter layers into a book or letter shape.)

Sourdough Starter

My formula for sourdough starter is for what is known as a liquid starter, as opposed to a biga, or stiff starter. If you were someone who enjoyed chemistry class, as I did, I think you'll enjoy making sourdough starter. It is a natural leavening made from a culture of flour, water, and natural yeast found in the air; bacteria work in harmony with the yeast to create flavor in the culture, so each sourdough starter has a unique character. You can buy sourdough starter from an established bakery or online, or you can make yours from scratch.

To make sourdough starter from scratch, you start with flour, water, and a small amount of honey. Choosing the flour that you build your starter from is important. Many organic stone-ground flours contain a fair amount of natural yeast, because yeast spores attach themselves to grains, and in the case of organic stone-ground flours, that yeast remains attached to the grain during the process of milling it into flour. Rye flour in particular is known to have a very high natural yeast content, which is why I start with rye flour when building a starter from scratch. (You may have heard about people beginning a starter with grapes; that is because natural yeast is found on the skins of grapes. I believe there is more yeast found in stone-ground rye flour than grapes, so that's the strategy I use.) Yeast feed off of sugar, which is why I add honey to my starter; it acts like a vitamin boost, kick-starting the growth of the yeast. As the days progress and I am building my starter, I scale back the amount of rye flour and replace it with bread flour and whole-wheat flour.

Yeast is like a pet. It needs food (flour),
water, and a warm environment to thrive.

It takes six days for sourdough starter to ripen fully to a point where you can use it. When you are building your starter, you "feed" it twice a day. Yeast feeds off of flour, so "feeding" your starter means mixing a small amount of the "mother" starter (that is the starter that you are working with, which has already fermented) with flour and water. The point of doing this is to build up the concentration of yeast in the culture. (Sourdough starter should really be called sourdough *culture* because it is the yeast culture that starts your sourdough loaf.)

The most important factor in the success of ripening a starter from scratch, or maintaining a starter, besides feeding it every day, is temperature. The ideal water and air temperature for ripening starter is approximately 75°F. If the water or air is too cold, the yeast won't thrive, and you won't notice much activity. Likewise, if you forget to feed your starter, it will start to look gray and liquidy and sad.

A healthy, ripened sourdough starter that is ready to use to make bread will have grown in volume, and there will be bubbles, lots of bubbles. If you use a clear container, you will be able to see the bubbles on the sides and you will also notice bubbles on the top of the starter when you remove the lid from the container.

Sourdough starter is constantly growing and changing. The yeast will start feeding on the damaged starches and sugars immediately. When you first feed it, the starter will look like a thick paste with no bubbles. As the yeast grows and the starter ripens, bubbles form and become more voluminous and the gluten proteins break down, taking the starter from a stiff paste to a light, airy, bubbly slurry.

There is a window of time in which starter will ferment and proof bread at an optimal rate. How long the starter takes to get to this point depends on how much mother is used to make the sourdough culture. If you use a lot of mother, your sourdough starter could be ready in as little as two hours. Using the proportion of mother to flour and water in my sourdough starter recipe, the starter should be ripe and ready to properly raise bread after fermenting and growing for eight hours, and can be used until up to fourteen hours after it was last fed.

I can't tell you how many people tell me, "I killed my starter!" But, in fact, once you've got it going, a starter is nearly impossible to kill. To revive a seemingly dead starter, first, drain any liquid that has formed on top. Then feed the starter according to the maintenance feed (see page xxxviii). If the starter is not active, wait a full day before feeding it again. At this point, you may want to double or triple the amount of ripened starter (the mother) you add to the feed. Wait another full day before feeding it again, and within a day or two, you will start to see some activity. Once you can see that the starter is beginning to bubble and grow, resume feeding it twice a day.

You can make sourdough starter in a glass or plastic container; the important thing is that it have a tight-fitting lid and that it hold at least 1½ quarts. (If you use a 1-quart container, when the starter expands, the pressure of it will cause it to explode out of the container.) Because in feeding the starter you move it from one container to another, it's ideal to have two such containers.

Note Making starter from scratch requires a lot of flour. It will be more than you anticipate. I like to keep a 5-pound bag of bread or all-purpose flour on hand when I know that I will be growing a starter from scratch.

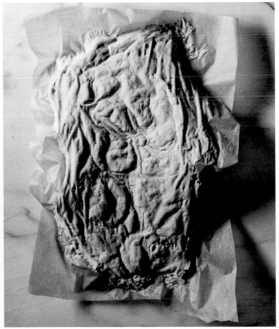

Day One: Morning

Organic rye grains have natural yeast on them, so starting with stone-ground flour from this grain is key to developing yeast in the starter. The honey acts as a vitamin booster for the yeast. You will give the starter a full day to begin to ferment before feeding it again. Still, this is the beginning stage and there won't be a high enough concentration of yeast in the mixture for you to notice a visible difference after the first day.

Water (70°F to 75°F)	1½ cups	352 grams
Organic stone-ground rye flour	1½ cups	300 grams
Mild-flavored honey (such as wildflower or clover)	1 teaspoon	7 grams

Put the water in a 1½-quart or larger container with a tight-fitting lid. Add the flour and honey and stir with a spoon to combine. Cover the container and set it in a warm place, such as near or on your stove (approximately 75°F), for 24 hours.

Day Two: Morning feed

Your starter will still look like flour mixed with water. To continue to encourage the yeasts to grow, take a portion of the yeast culture—this is "ripened starter" or "mother"—and mix it with flour and water. This is "feeding" your starter.

When feeding your starter, you begin with a small amount (about 1 tablespoon) of the mother starter. If you were baking with the starter, after using what you need for your recipe, the amount left would be just about what you need. But if you're not baking it, you discard the rest. Although it might feel wasteful to discard it, unless you're baking with it, or sharing it with friends, there is no alternative. If you were to feed the entire starter instead of just this small amount, the amount of flour you would add would not be enough food for the yeast and the yeast would eventually starve; your bread volume would shrink, and your starter would stop rising as a result. Starting with a small amount of ripened starter helps the yeast to grow at a good rate without starving it. Because your starter on day two will not be very active, you will use a larger amount of mother than what you use with an active starter (1 cup versus 1 tablespoon).

Water (70°F to 75°F)	1 cup	235 grams
Mother (the mixture from Day One)	1 cup	200 grams
Organic stone-ground rye flour	1 cup	110 grams
Bread flour (or all-purpose flour)	¾ cup	90 grams

Put the water in a 1½-quart (or larger) container with a tight-fitting lid. Scoop out 200 grams (1 cup) of the original starter and add it to the container; discard the remaining starter. Add the rye flour and bread flour and stir with a metal spoon to combine. Cover the container and set the starter in a warm place (approximately 75°F) for approximately 12 hours.

Day Two: Evening feed

Depending on how warm it is in your home and other factors, such as humidity, by this time, your starter may already be very active. If it is active, you will see bubbles on the top of the starter (and from the side if you are using a glass container); yeast produces carbon dioxide and alcohol and those bubbles indicate that there is yeast activity. The starter may also be rising considerably in the container. That is the carbon dioxide and gluten at work. Some gluten has formed in the starter, and the carbon dioxide is getting trapped inside the gluten network. (Be warned: when I recently made starter in a too-small container, I came home on the evening of Day Two to find my starter exploding out of the container.)

Evening feed

Water (70°F to 75°F)	½ cup	118 grams
Ripened starter	½ cup	100 grams
Organic rye flour	½ cup	55 grams
Bread flour (or all-purpose flour)	½ cup	60 grams

Put the water in a 1½-quart (or larger) container with a tight-fitting lid. Scoop out 100 grams (½ cup) of the ripened starter and add it to the container; discard the remaining ripened starter. Add the rye flour and bread flour and stir with a metal spoon to combine. Cover the container and set the starter in a warm place (approximately 75°F) for approximately 12 hours.

Days Three, Four, and Five

At this point, you switch from rye flour to whole-wheat flour because the yeast from the rye flour has already begun growing. I use a combination of whole-wheat flour instead of all bread flour because the whole-wheat flour contains natural yeast. So as the days go on and the yeast in my starter becomes more concentrated, I am gradually moving from yeast-containing grains to more refined bread flour (or all-purpose flour), which does not contain the natural yeast.

Morning feed

Water (70°F to 75°F)	½ cup	118 grams
Ripened starter	½ cup	100 grams

| Organic whole-wheat flour | ½ cup | 60 grams |
| Bread flour (or all-purpose flour) | ½ cup | 60 grams |

Put the water in a 1½-quart (or larger) container with a tight-fitting lid. Measure out 100 grams (½ cup) of the ripened starter and add it to the container; discard the remaining ripened starter. Add the whole-wheat flour and bread flour and stir with a metal spoon to combine. Cover the container and set the starter in a warm place (approximately 75°F) for approximately 12 hours.

Evening feed

Water (70°F to 75°F)	½ cup	118 grams
Ripened starter	½ cup	100 grams
Organic whole-wheat flour	½ cup	60 grams
Bread flour (or all-purpose flour)	½ cup	60 grams

Put the water in a 1½-quart (or larger) container with a tight-fitting lid. Measure out 100 grams (½ cup) of the ripened starter and add it to the container; discard the remaining ripened starter. Add the whole-wheat flour and bread flour and stir with a metal spoon to combine. Cover the container and set the starter aside at room temperature for approximately 12 hours.

Day Six

Your starter is now ready to use. From here out, refer to the feed schedule in Maintaining a Starter (below).

Float test

To test whether your starter is ready to use, fill a small bowl with water. Wet the fingers of one hand and use them to carefully pinch off a piece of the starter, taking care not to deflate the starter in the process. Place the starter in the water. If it floats, the starter is good to use. The reason it is floating is that the yeast has produced a sufficient amount of carbon dioxide. If the concentration of yeast has produced enough carbon dioxide to cause the starter to float, it is also high enough to leaven dough. If the starter sinks, feed it for a few more days, testing it every day, until it floats. This is the "float test." I ask the bakers who work with me to make sure the starter passes the float test each time before adding it to dough.

Maintaining a starter

Now that you have built a starter, you have to maintain it, which means feeding it on a regular basis. If you are maintaining your starter just to have on hand to use someday, it is enough to feed it once a day. If you are actively baking with it or are getting ready to bake with it in the very near future, feed it twice a day. This ensures less bacteria and more active yeast in the starter, which results in a higher rise in your baked goods.

Morning maintenance feed

Water (70°F to 75°F)	⅔ cup	157 grams
Ripened starter	1 tablespoon	25 grams
Bread flour (or all-purpose flour)	1⅓ cups	160 grams

Put the water in a 1½-quart (or larger) container with a tight-fitting lid. Measure out 25 grams (1 tablespoon) of the ripened starter and add it to the container; discard the remaining ripened starter. Add the flour and stir with a metal spoon to combine. Cover the container and set the starter aside in a warm place (approximately 75°F) for approximately 12 hours.

Evening maintenance feed

Water (70°F to 75°F)	⅔ cup	157 grams
Ripened starter	1 tablespoon	25 grams
Bread flour (or all-purpose flour)	1⅓ cups	160 grams

Put the water in a 1½-quart (or larger) container with a tight-fitting lid. Measure out 25 grams (1 tablespoon) of the ripened starter and add it to the container; discard the remaining ripened starter. Add the flour and stir with a metal spoon to combine. Cover the container and set the starter aside in a warm place (approximately 75°F) for approximately 12 hours.

Saving your starter

If you are unable to feed your starter because you are leaving town, put the ripened starter in the refrigerator until you return. Do not put just-fed starter in the refrigerator. Starter that was just fed has a low (or no) concentration of yeast; the yeast hasn't had time to feed and grow. If you put just-fed starter in the refrigerator, when you remove the starter from the refrigerator, it may not come back to life. To prevent this from happening, put your starter in the refrigerator at its ripest point, when it is very active and bubbly.

When you are ready to resume a maintenance feeding schedule, remove the starter from the refrigerator and drain off any liquid that has formed on top. Resume feeding the starter twice a day using the feed routine for Maintaining a Starter (page xxxviii) until the yeast has concentrated enough that the starter passes the float test.

Wrapping Dough

After I have made any dough that I will be rolling out, I roll it between plastic wrap into a square. I'm pretty meticulous about this; the square is usually about 8 inches, and the corners of my dough block have distinct 90-degree angles. Starting with a squared-off block of dough sets you up to succeed in rolling out a sheet of dough with squared edges. When laminating, it is particularly important to start with an even, squared-off block of dough so that it wraps around the butter evenly.

To wrap dough this way, start by laying a long sheet of plastic wrap on your work surface. Use a plastic bowl scraper to scoop the dough out of the bowl onto the plastic in the center. Loosely fold the plastic over the dough, leaving a couple of inches of slack on both sides. Gently run a rolling pin over the dough into the slack to begin to flatten it out slightly. Take a second, long sheet of plastic wrap and lay it over the dough in the other direction, leaving a couple of inches of slack. Gently run the rolling pin in the direction of the slack created by the second sheet of plastic. Using kitchen shears, snip the plastic wrap near the corners to let the air escape. Run a rolling pin over the dough to create a roughly 8-inch, ½-inch-thick square, making sure to get the dough into the corners so that you have squared edges. If you are rolling the dough out round, such as for a classic round pie, roll the dough into a ½-inch-thick disk instead.

A Good Bake

Savory Breads

Even though I am both a chemical engineer and bread baker, this book is not a deep dive into the science of sourdough. It is a collection of recipes that I love and make often at home, and the savory breads I include in this chapter reflect that. The difference between these breads and those in a hard-core bread-baking primer is that none of these rely solely on sourdough starter to rise. Instead, they use a combination of starter and commercial yeast, which makes them easier to achieve, and more forgiving. These are also enriched breads; they have something *in* them or *on* them, such as sugar, eggs, nuts, seeds, or cheese. These are my go-to breads that I want to share with you.

Potato Onion Buns

Makes 13 burger-size buns

These buns make for perfect bacon, egg, and cheese sandwiches. The secret to how special they are lies in the balance of ingredients. First, the dough contains onions that are dehydrated in a low oven, which intensifies their flavor and also improves their texture. Removing water from the onion creates tougher cell walls, which means the onion doesn't break down during the mixing process, so the buns have bits of sweet onion in them. The buns also contain baked potato, which is pure starch; the potato in the dough causes the dough to ferment quickly, giving the buns an ethereal texture. The acidity of the buttermilk softens the dough, and the dough also contains a small amount of sugar. All of these components work together to create an umami effect, and the perfect balance of sweet, salty, and savory. It is really the perfect bun.

Plan ahead to make these. I suggest you dehydrate the onion and bake the potato the day before you plan to make the dough.

For the dough		
Yellow onions	2 large	1,000 grams
Yukon gold potato	1 medium to large	200 grams
Olive oil	2 tablespoons plus more for coating the potatoes	30 grams
Fresh chives	3 large bunches	50 grams
All-purpose flour	5 cups plus more for dusting	600 grams
Instant yeast	2 teaspoons	6 grams
Granulated sugar	1 tablespoon plus 1 teaspoon	17 grams
Fine sea salt	3½ teaspoons	21 grams
Buttermilk, well shaken	¾ cup	188 grams
Whole milk	⅔ cup	160 grams
Large egg	1	50 grams
Large egg yolk	1	17 grams

For baking the buns		
Nonstick cooking spray		
Extra-virgin olive oil	2 tablespoons	30 grams

Dehydrate the onions

- Arrange the oven racks so one is in the top third of the oven and the other is in the bottom third. Preheat the oven to 200°F.
- Line two baking sheets with parchment paper.
- Cut the onions into a ½-inch dice and spread them out over the surface of the two prepared baking sheets.
- Place one baking sheet on each oven rack and cook the onions for about 4 hours, until the onions have shriveled and are almost completely dried out, stirring them every hour so the onions around the edges of the pans don't

burn. Remove the onions from the oven and set them aside to cool to room temperature. If you are making the onions in advance of making the dough, consolidate them on one baking sheet and set them aside, for as long as several hours, until you're ready to use them. Or transfer them to a sealable plastic bag and refrigerate for up to 2 days.

Cook the potato
- Arrange the oven racks so one is in the center position. Preheat the oven to 400°F.
- Rinse and dry the potato. Place it on a piece of aluminum foil large enough to wrap it in, drizzle it with enough olive oil to cover (about 1 teaspoon), and rub the oil into the potato. Wrap the potato in the foil and place it on the center oven rack to bake until it is very soft when pierced with the tip of a paring knife, 1 hour to 1 hour 20 minutes. Remove the potato from the oven and set it aside to cool to room temperature. (If you are cooking the potato in advance of making the dough, leave it wrapped in foil and refrigerate it until you're ready to use it.)

Prepare to mix the dough
- Finely chop the chives and set them aside.
- Unwrap the potato and cut it into ⅜- to ½-inch pieces, leaving the skin on. Set aside.
- Place the dehydrated onions in a small bowl, cover with hot tap water, and set aside to soak for 10 minutes. Drain the onions in a fine-mesh strainer and then gently squeeze the pieces in your fist to remove the excess water.

Mix the dough
- Put the flour, yeast, sugar, and salt in a medium bowl and stir with a whisk to combine.
- Combine the buttermilk, milk, egg, egg yolk, chives, potato, and onions in the bowl of a stand mixer. Add the dry ingredients. Fit the mixer with the dough hook and mix on low speed for 3 minutes. Increase the speed to medium and mix for 5 minutes. Turn off the mixer and remove the bowl from the stand. Remove the dough hook and wipe it clean with a wet hand. Cover the bowl with plastic wrap. Set the dough in a warm place in your kitchen and let it ferment for 1 hour. Uncover the bowl and turn the dough. To turn the dough, use a wet hand to fold the top edge down two-thirds and fold the bottom edge to meet the top edge, so the dough is folded like a letter. Fold the sides inward in the same way to form a sort of ball, then re-cover the bowl. Place the bowl in the refrigerator overnight to retard the dough.

Retarding dough improves its flavor. This is true of straight or enriched dough (dough that is enriched with eggs, butter, sugar, or cream).

Form and proof the buns
- Line two baking sheets with parchment paper and spray the paper on both trays with nonstick cooking spray.
- Remove the dough from the refrigerator and uncover it. Lightly dust your work surface with flour. Using a plastic bowl scraper, scoop the dough out of the bowl onto the floured surface. Dust the top of the dough with flour and use a bench knife to divide the dough into 13 (approximately 110-gram) pieces. Put one piece of dough on the work surface. Dust your hands lightly with flour. Gently rest your palm on the dough and roll the dough into a tight round ball. Put the ball on a prepared baking sheet and continue, rolling the rest of the pieces of dough into balls and adding them to the baking sheets, leaving about 2 inches between each round.
- Once you have shaped all of the buns, dust your palms with flour and gently pat each bun into a flat patty 3 to 4 inches in diameter. Cover each baking sheet with a damp, lightweight kitchen towel and set the sheets aside in a warm place for 1½ to 2 hours, to proof the buns until they have doubled in size and do not spring back when poked in the center.

This is a very sticky dough; it will be easiest to shape when it is cold and your hands are amply floured.

Bake the buns
- Arrange the oven racks so one is in the top third of the oven and the other is in the bottom third. Preheat the oven to 350°F.
- Pour the olive oil into a small bowl. Remove the kitchen towels and lightly brush the buns with the oil, using about half of it.
- Place one baking sheet on each oven rack and bake the buns for 30 minutes, until they are lightly browned and emit a hollow sound when you tap on the bottom of a bun with your finger, rotating the baking sheets from front to back and from one rack to the other halfway through the baking time. (Watch out that the bottoms do not brown too quickly. If they are getting too brown before they are done, slip a second baking sheet directly under each baking sheet to create a doubled baking sheet, shielding the dough from the direct heat.) Remove the buns from the oven and brush again very lightly with the remaining olive oil. Transfer the buns to a rack to cool completely.

Soft Pretzels

Makes 9 to 10 pretzels

Traditionally, New York pretzels are dipped in a lye solution before being baked. Lye is an alkaline chemical that speeds up the browning process. It is what gives the pretzel its characteristic burnished exterior and also contributes to its distinct flavor. But lye is caustic, and if you get any of it on you, undiluted, it will burn you. When making pretzels at home, I was afraid that no matter how careful I was, my dog might find a drop on the floor and lick it up. So instead of lye, in this recipe I recommend a baking soda solution. Where lye is sodium hydroxide ($NaOH$), baking soda is sodium bicarbonate ($NaHCO_3$). It is the hydrogen molecule (represented by the *H* in the chemical formulas) in each of these chemicals that is key. The hydrogen bonds with the starch molecules on the surface of the pretzel to gelatinize, and this gelatinization results in the brown, shiny crust when the pretzel is baked. Because the quantity of baking soda needed to gelatinize the surface is so large, the water needs to be boiling in order for the baking soda to dissolve.

For the pretzels		
Bread flour	4¾ cups plus more for dusting	570 grams
Granulated sugar	2 tablespoons	26 grams
Fine sea salt	2 teaspoons	12 grams
Water (70°F to 75°F)	1¼ cups	294 grams
Instant yeast	1½ teaspoons	4.5 grams
Large egg	1	50 grams
Unsalted butter, cubed and softened	8 tablespoons (1 stick)	113 grams
Nonstick cooking spray		
For boiling and finishing the pretzels		
Water	8 cups	1,880 grams
Baking soda	6 tablespoons	90 grams
Flaky sea salt	2 to 3 tablespoons	

Mix and ferment the dough

- Place the flour, sugar, and fine sea salt in a large bowl and stir with a whisk to combine.
- Place the water in the bottom of the bowl of a stand mixer. Add the yeast and whisk briefly to help it dissolve. Add the egg and whisk to combine. Add the dry ingredients and the butter. Fit the mixer with the dough hook and mix on low speed for 2 minutes. Increase the speed to medium and mix the dough for 5 minutes to develop the gluten. Turn off the mixer and remove the bowl from the stand. Remove the dough hook and wipe it clean with a wet hand. Cover the bowl with a clean kitchen towel or plastic wrap. Place the bowl in a warm

place to ferment the dough for 1 hour. Uncover the bowl and turn the dough. To turn the dough, use a wet hand to fold the top edge down two-thirds and fold the bottom edge to meet the top edge, so the dough is folded like a letter. Fold the sides inward in the same way to form a sort of ball, then re-cover the bowl.

Get prepared

- Line a baking sheet with parchment paper and spray the paper with nonstick cooking spray.
- Dust a large work surface very lightly with flour. Use a plastic bowl scraper to scrape the dough out of the bowl and onto the work surface. Lightly dust the top of the dough with flour and use a bench knife to cut the dough into 10 (105-gram) pieces.

Shape the pretzels

- Put one piece of dough on the work surface. Dust your hands lightly with flour. Gently rest your palm on the dough and roll the dough into a tight round ball. Put the ball on the prepared baking sheet and continue, rolling the rest of the pieces of dough into balls and adding them to the baking sheet.
- Place the baking sheet in the refrigerator to chill the dough for 2 hours or as long as overnight. (If you are refrigerating the balls overnight, after 1 hour, remove the baking sheet from the refrigerator and cover it with plastic wrap to prevent the balls from developing a "skin." Return it to the refrigerator.)
- Line a second baking sheet with parchment paper and spray the paper with nonstick cooking spray.
- Lightly dust a work surface that is at least 3 feet from side to side with flour. (My counter isn't big enough, so I use my kitchen table.)
- Remove one ball from the refrigerator and place it on the flour-dusted surface. Gently press on it with the palm of your hand to flatten it into a thick pancake. Using both hands, pick up the top edge of the round and fold it down by one-fourth, pinching the top edge into the round of dough. Repeat, rolling the top edge toward the center and pinching it into the dough, forming the pancake shape into a log in the process. Do this two or three more times, until you reach the bottom of the log, which will now be tight and not floppy. Doing this creates tension in the dough, which helps it to hold its shape because you are stretching and tightening the gluten on the surface of the pretzel.

Don't add so much flour on your work surface that the log slides around on it; you need tension to get the dough to roll into a long rope.

- Lightly dust your hands with flour and place the fingertips of both hands on the center of the log. Gently roll the log into a 30-inch rope, dusting your work surface and hands very lightly with flour as needed. When you begin to feel tension preventing you from rolling the dough any longer, set the rope aside for 5 to 10 minutes to let the gluten relax, then resume rolling. While the rope is relaxing, remove another ball from the refrigerator and roll it to the same point, then let it rest.

- As each rope reaches 30 inches long, lay it in front of you, parallel to the edge of the counter. Pick up each end of the rope and bring the ends together away from you as if you were forming a circle. Cross the two ends so you have about 10 inches of rope from the point at which they cross. Twist the two ropes once and then lay them down so you have one pointing toward four o'clock and the other to eight o'clock, creating a classic pretzel shape. Pinch the dough in place at the point where it meets the rounded triangle at the bottom.
- Place the shaped pretzel on the prepared baking sheet, adjusting it to return it to a pretty pretzel shape if needed. Continue shaping all of the pretzels in this way, working in rotation, rolling the logs into ropes and shaping the pretzels, and when the ropes are ready, placing 5 pretzels on each baking sheet.
- Cover each baking sheet with a damp, lightweight kitchen towel and set the sheets aside in a warm place to proof the pretzels for 45 minutes, until they have puffed up slightly. Place the baking sheets in the refrigerator for about 30 minutes, and up to overnight, to chill the pretzels so they firm up. (You can prepare the pretzels to this point up to 1 day in advance.)

Dip and bake the pretzels

- Arrange the oven racks so one is in the top third of the oven and the other is in the bottom third. Preheat the oven to 375°F.
- Bring the water to a boil in a large stockpot over high heat. Add half of the baking soda and whisk to combine, taking care, as the water will boil furiously when you add the baking soda. Add the remaining baking soda and whisk it in.
- Remove one baking sheet of pretzels from the refrigerator and uncover it. Pick up one pretzel and gently drop it into the boiling water. Boil for 15 seconds, gently turn it with tongs, and boil for 15 seconds on the other side. Use the tongs to remove the pretzel from the water and return it to the baking sheet. Continue boiling the pretzels and placing them on the baking sheets until you have boiled all of the pretzels from both baking sheets.
- Sprinkle the pretzels generously with flaky salt.
- Place one baking sheet on each oven rack and bake the pretzels for 20 to 25 minutes, rotating them from front to back and from one rack to the other halfway through the baking time. Remove the pretzels from the oven and set aside to cool slightly. Serve warm or at room temperature.

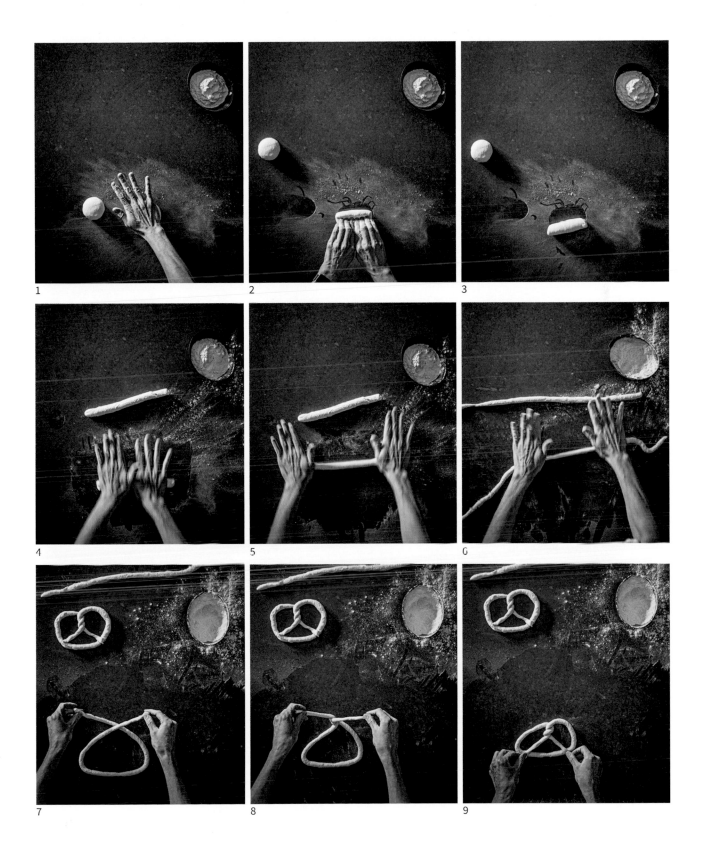

Khachapuri with Cheese, Baked Egg, and Nigella Seeds

Makes 4 khachapuri; serves 4

Khachapuri is a traditional yeasted flatbread from the Eurasian country of Georgia. The sides are rolled inward to create a boat-like shape, which is topped with cheese and a baked egg. (Khachapuri can include any number of toppings, including ground meat or beans.) I try to replicate the cheese commonly used to make khachapuri by combining cheddar, Gruyère, and feta. I sprinkle nigella seeds over the top edge of the dough; these small black seeds, used in Indian and Middle Eastern cuisines, have a mild onion flavor and also look pretty.

You can either bake all four khachapuri at one time, or bake fewer and refrigerate the remaining dough and topping until you're ready to assemble and bake them, or for up to four days. I usually bake two on one day and two a couple of days later.

For the dough		
All-purpose flour	3 cups plus more for dusting	360 grams
Granulated sugar	2 tablespoons	26 grams
Instant yeast	2 teaspoons	6 grams
Fine sea salt	1½ teaspoons	9 grams
Water	1 cup	235 grams
Unsalted butter	2 tablespoons	28 grams
Nonstick cooking spray		
For the filling		
Aged cheddar cheese	8 ounces	226 grams
Gruyère cheese	8 ounces	226 grams
Feta (preferably sheep's milk)	8 ounces	226 grams
For finishing the flatbread		
Nigella seeds	1 tablespoon	9 grams
Flaky sea salt		
Large eggs	4	200 grams

Mix and ferment the dough

- Put the flour, sugar, yeast, and fine sea salt in a large mixing bowl and whisk to combine the ingredients.
- Place the water in the bowl of a stand mixer. Add the dry ingredients and the butter. Fit the mixer with a dough hook and mix on low speed for 2 minutes. Increase the speed to medium and mix for 5 minutes. Turn off the mixer and remove the bowl from the stand. Remove the dough hook and wipe it clean with a wet hand. Cover the bowl with a clean kitchen towel or plastic wrap and set aside in a warm place to let the dough ferment for 2 hours, turning it once halfway through that time. To turn the dough, uncover the bowl and use a wet hand to fold the top edge down two-thirds and fold the bottom edge to

meet the top edge, so the dough is folded like a letter. Fold the sides inward in the same way to form a sort of ball, then re-cover the bowl.

Divide and round the dough

· Line a baking sheet with parchment paper and spray the paper with nonstick cooking spray.

· Lightly flour a large flat work surface and use a plastic bowl scraper to scrape the dough out of the bowl onto the floured surface. Lightly dust the top of the dough with flour and use a bench knife to divide the dough into 4 equal (160-gram) pieces.

· Put one piece of dough on the work surface. Dust your hands lightly with flour. Gently rest your palm on the dough and roll the dough into a tight round ball. Put the ball on the prepared baking sheet and continue, rolling the rest of the pieces of dough into balls and adding them to the baking sheet.

· Place the baking sheet in the refrigerator until the balls are chilled and firm, about 1 hour, and up to overnight. (If you are resting the rounds overnight, remove them from the refrigerator after one hour, spray a sheet of plastic wrap with nonstick cooking spray, and place the plastic, sprayed side down, over the baking sheet.)

Roll out the dough

· Line a baking sheet with parchment paper.

· Lightly dust a large flat work surface with flour.

· Remove one ball of dough from the refrigerator and place it on the floured surface. Lightly dust the dough and rolling pin with flour and roll the dough to a 10-inch circle. (For more detailed instructions, see Rolling Dough 101, page 250.) If the dough begins to spring back, set it aside to rest to give the gluten a chance to relax while you roll another ball of dough. Place the finished round of dough on the prepared baking sheet. Dust the top of the round lightly with flour. Lay a sheet of parchment paper on the dough and dust it with flour. Continue rolling (and resting the dough as needed) until you have rolled all of the balls of dough into 10-inch rounds, stacking them on top of one another with sheets of flour-dusted parchment between them. Place the baking sheet in the refrigerator to chill the rounds while you make the filling. (You will use the baking sheet that the dough was resting on in the refrigerator for the final shaping and baking of the khachapuri.)

Make the filling

· Grate the cheddar and Gruyère on the small to medium holes of a box grater. Combine the grated cheeses in a large bowl and crumble in the feta. Mix the cheeses together using your hands or a rubber spatula.

Prepare to bake the khachapuri

· Arrange the oven racks so one is in the top third of the oven and the other is in the bottom third. Preheat the oven to 400°F.

Shape the khachapuri

- Remove one dough round from the refrigerator and place it on a flat work surface. Spread 2 cups (170 grams; or one-fourth) of the cheese mixture evenly across the surface of the dough, leaving about ¼ inch free of cheese around the edges. Repeat with a second dough round.
- Roll the top edge (the one farthest from you) of one round down a third of the way toward the center, pinching the dough so that it stays in place. Repeat, rolling the bottom edge one-third of the way upward, toward the center; there will be 2 to 3 inches of exposed cheese between the top and bottom edges of the dough. Continue to roll the top and bottom edges of the dough together at the sides until they meet. Pinch the sides of the dough together and gently twist to seal them closed. Place the shaped khachapuri on the prepared baking sheet. Repeat, shaping a second khachapuri with a second round of dough in the same way. Place the second boat on the same baking sheet and place them in the refrigerator. If you are baking only 2, cover the baking sheet with the remaining 2 dough rounds with plastic wrap and return it to the refrigerator; refrigerate the toppings for up to 3 days. When you are ready to bake them, remove the remaining rounds from the refrigerator, unwrap them, and proceed with the recipe. Otherwise, remove the remaining 2 rounds of dough from the refrigerator. Top and shape them in the same way and place them on the parchment-lined baking sheet that the dough was resting on.

Finish and bake the khachapuri

- Brush the edges of the boat lightly with water and sprinkle with the nigella seeds and flaky salt.
- Place one baking sheet on each oven rack and bake the khachapuri for 20 minutes, rotating them from front to back and from one rack to the other halfway through the baking time.
- After 20 minutes, open the oven door and slide an oven rack out so you can work quickly with the khachapuri. Crack an egg into the center of each khachapuri. (If the cheese has puffed up so much that there is no room for the egg, push the cheese down in the center with the tines of a fork to make room.)
- Sprinkle the eggs with flaky salt and close the oven door.
- Increase the oven temperature to 450°F.
- Bake the khachapuri for an additional 10 minutes, until the egg whites are opaque. Remove the khachapuri from the oven and set aside to cool slightly. Serve warm.

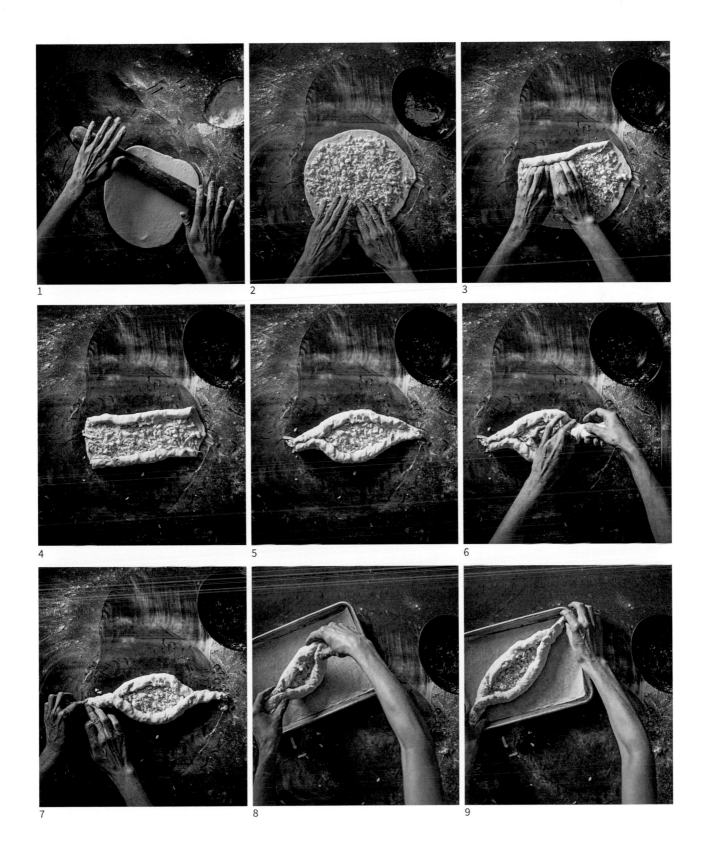

1

2

3

4

5

6

7

8

9

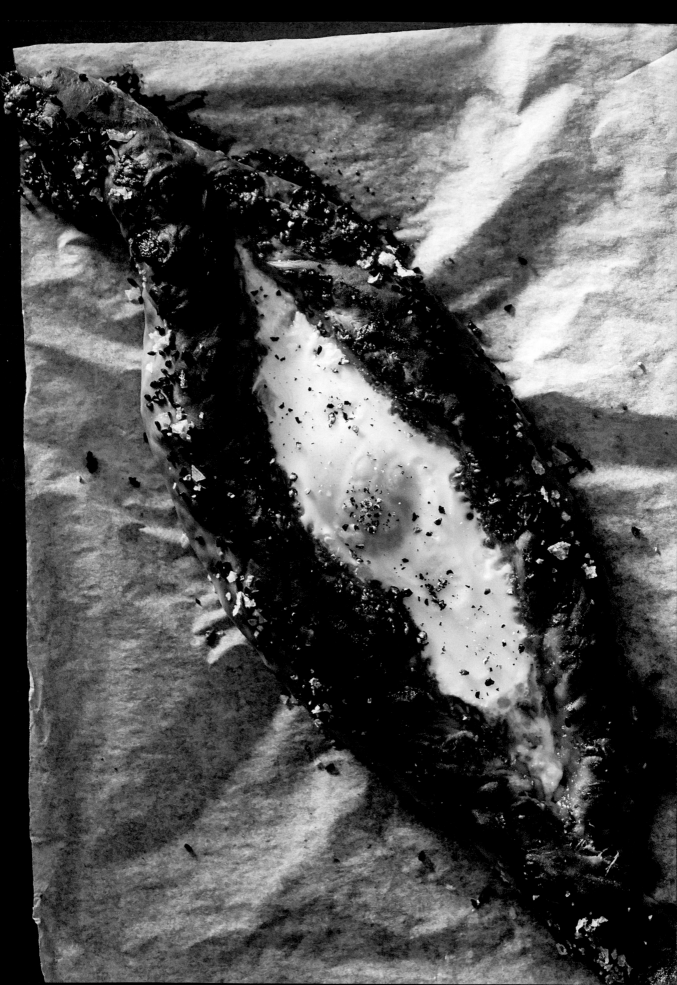

Kale and Cheese Khachapuri with Zhoug

This is another take on khachapuri, inspired by a visit I made to Oda House, a Georgian restaurant in Manhattan. This khachapuri is topped with a second sheet of dough, like a double-crusted pizza, or a thin, savory two-crust pie. The filling is drizzled with zhoug, which is a mix of herbs, spices, and olive oil—the Middle Eastern version of Italian salsa verde. The recipe for zhoug makes more than you'll need for this, but it's nice to have in the refrigerator to spoon on anything from eggs in the morning to grilled meat, fish, or vegetables.

Makes 2 khachapuri; serves 2 to 4

For the dough

All-purpose flour	3 cups plus more for dusting	360 grams
Granulated sugar	2 tablespoons	26 grams
Instant yeast	2 teaspoons	6 grams
Fine sea salt	1½ teaspoons	9 grams
Water	1 cup	235 grams
Unsalted butter	2 tablespoons	28 grams
Nonstick cooking spray		

For the filling

Curly kale	1 bunch	
Yellow onion	1 large	
Unsalted butter	2 tablespoons	28 grams
Extra-virgin olive oil	1 tablespoon	15 grams
Fine sea salt	1 teaspoon	6 grams
Gruyère cheese	4 ounces	113 grams
Aged cheddar cheese	4 ounces	113 grams
Feta (preferably sheep's milk)	4 ounces	113 grams
Zhoug (recipe follows)	2 tablespoons	

For finishing the flatbread

Nigella seeds	1 teaspoon
Flaky sea salt	1 teaspoon
Extra-virgin olive oil	for brushing

Mix and ferment the dough

· Put the flour, sugar, yeast, and fine sea salt in a large mixing bowl and whisk to combine the ingredients.

· Place the water in the bowl of a stand mixer. Add the dry ingredients and the butter. Fit the mixer with a dough hook and mix on low speed for 2 minutes. Increase the speed to medium and mix for 5 minutes. Turn off the mixer and remove the bowl from the stand. Remove the dough hook and wipe it clean with a wet hand. Cover the bowl with a clean kitchen towel or plastic wrap and set aside in a warm place to let the dough ferment for 2 hours, turning it once halfway through that time. To turn the dough, uncover the bowl and use a wet hand to fold the top edge down two-thirds and fold the bottom edge to meet the top edge, so the dough is folded like a letter. Fold the sides inward in the same way to form a sort of ball, then re-cover the bowl.

Divide and round the dough

- Line a baking sheet with parchment paper and spray the paper with nonstick cooking spray.
- Lightly flour a large flat work surface and use a plastic bowl scraper to scrape the dough out of the bowl onto the floured surface. Lightly dust the top of the dough with flour and use a bench knife to divide the dough into 4 equal (160-gram) pieces.
- Put one piece of dough on the work surface. Dust your hands lightly with flour. Gently rest your palm on the dough and roll the dough into a tight round ball. Put the ball on the prepared baking sheet and continue, rolling the rest of the pieces of dough into balls and adding them to the baking sheet.
- Place the baking sheet in the refrigerator until the balls are chilled and firm, about 1 hour, and up to overnight. (If you are resting the rounds overnight, remove them from the refrigerator, spray a sheet of plastic wrap with nonstick cooking spray, and place the plastic, sprayed side down, over the baking sheet.)

Make the filling

- Rip the leaves of kale off the stems and discard the stems. Wash the leaves, dry them in a colander, and roughly chop them.
- Bring a large pot of salted water to a boil. Fill a large bowl with ice water to make an ice bath. Place a colander in the sink.
- Place the kale leaves in the boiling water, using tongs to submerge them, and boil for 3 minutes, until the leaves are bright green and tender. Lift the kale out of the water and plunge it in the ice bath to cool completely. Drain the kale in the colander. Pick up the kale and squeeze it in your fists to extract as much water as possible. Transfer the drained kale to a large bowl.
- Cut the tops off the onion, peel it, and cut it in half, root to tip. Lay the onion halves flat on a cutting board and slice the onion ⅛ inch thick.
- Heat the butter and olive oil in a large sauté pan over medium-high heat until the butter melts. Add the onion slices, reduce the heat to medium, and sauté, stirring frequently, for about 7 minutes, until the onion has softened and is just beginning to take on a faint color. Add the onion to the bowl with the kale. Add the salt to the bowl and fold together with a rubber spatula to combine.
- Grate the Gruyère and cheddar on the small to medium holes of a box grater. Combine the grated cheeses in a large bowl and crumble in the feta. Mix the cheeses together using your hands or a rubber spatula.

Roll out the dough

- Line a baking sheet with parchment paper. Lightly dust a large flat work surface with flour.

- Remove one ball of dough from the refrigerator and place it on the floured surface. Lightly dust the dough and rolling pin with flour and roll the dough to an 11-inch circle. (For more detailed instruction, see Rolling Dough 101, page 250.) If the dough begins to spring back, set it aside to rest to give the gluten a chance to relax while you roll another ball of dough.
- Place the circle on the prepared sheet. Arrange half of the kale-onion mixture evenly on the round, leaving about 1 inch clear of filling along the edge. Brush the edges of the dough with water. Drizzle 2 tablespoons of the zhoug over the kale mixture and arrange half of the cheese over the top. Set aside.
- Lightly dust the work surface with more flour as needed. Remove a second round from the refrigerator, place it on the floured surface, and roll it out into an 11-inch circle. Fold the circle in half, pick it up, and gently place it over the khachapuri and its filling, centering it. Unfold the round so it completely covers the filling. Roll the edges of the bottom and top sheets of dough together toward the center of the khachapuri. Pinch the dough together so the edges do not unroll.
- Lightly brush the top of the khachapuri with water. Sprinkle with ½ teaspoon nigella seeds and ½ teaspoon flaky salt. Place the sheet in the refrigerator to chill for 30 minutes, or up to 1 hour.
- Repeat, making a second khachapuri with the remaining dough and filling and placing it on the baking sheet that the dough was resting on in the refrigerator. Place the baking sheet in the refrigerator to chill for 30 minutes, or up to 2 hours.

Prepare to bake the khachapuri

- Arrange the oven racks so one is in the top third of the oven and the other is in the bottom third. Preheat the oven to 400°F.
- Remove the khachapuri from the refrigerator. Cut 2 (2-inch) slits to form an X in the top of each khachapuri; this allows the steam to escape so the pastry does not get soggy while it is cooling after baking.

Bake the khachapuri

- Place one baking sheet on each oven rack to bake the khachapuri for 35 to 40 minutes, until the top and bottom crusts are golden brown, rotating the baking sheets from front to back and from one rack to the other halfway through the baking time. Remove the baking sheets from the oven. Use a large spatula to move the khachapuri to a cooling rack to cool slightly. Transfer the khachapuri to a cutting board and use a pizza cutter or large knife to cut each pastry into 6 slices. Serve warm or at room temperature.

Zhoug

**Makes about
1 cup**

Fresh cilantro (leaves and stems)	1 cup	40 grams
Fresh flat-leaf parsley (leaves and stems)	½ cup	15 grams
Serrano pepper	1, halved, ribs and seeds removed and chopped	
Garlic, thinly sliced	3 cloves	
Ground cumin	1 teaspoon	
Ground cloves	⅛ teaspoon	
Ground cardamom	⅛ teaspoon	
Fine sea salt	½ teaspoon	3 grams
Olive oil	3 tablespoons	45 grams
Apple cider vinegar	¼ cup	59 grams

Place the cilantro and parsley leaves and stems, serrano pepper, garlic, cumin, cloves, cardamom, and salt in the bowl of a food processor (or a blender). Process until the ingredients have broken down. Add the olive oil and cider vinegar and process until smooth. Transfer to a covered container and refrigerate until ready to use, or for up to 2 weeks.

Hot Dog Buns

Makes 16 buns

One year I was asked to make hot dog buns for a client for the Fourth of July. When the buns came out of the oven, I looked at them and thought: Something isn't right. I checked the dimensions, and they were fine. Then I looked at the buns again, and I realized that the problem was that I hadn't baked them close enough together, so they weren't pull-apart buns. Hot dog buns have to grow together when they're proofed and baked. That's what gives them their signature look, but it also helps keep them soft and tender, with a minimal amount of crust.

These hot dog buns are my take on Martin's Potato Rolls. I add buttermilk to the dough, the acidity of which tenderizes the dough and makes the buns soft and squishy, like commercial hot dog buns, but, of course, better.

Yukon gold potatoes	8 ounces (about 2 medium)	250 grams
Extra-virgin olive oil	for brushing	
All-purpose flour	6½ cups plus more for dusting	780 grams
Granulated sugar	1½ tablespoons	20 grams
Fine sea salt	1 tablespoon plus ¼ teaspoon	19.5 grams
Instant yeast	2½ teaspoons	8 grams
Whole milk	1 cup	240 grams
Buttermilk, well shaken	1 cup	245 grams
Large egg	1	50 grams
Large egg yolks	2	34 grams
Nonstick cooking spray		

Bake the potatoes

▪ Arrange the oven racks so one is in the center position. Preheat the oven to 400°F.

▪ Rinse and dry the potatoes and coat them with about 1 teaspoon of olive oil. Wrap the potatoes in aluminum foil and bake in the oven until they are very soft when pierced with the tip of a paring knife, 1 hour to 1 hour 20 minutes. Remove from the oven and let cool to room temperature in the foil. The potatoes can be baked the day before making the dough. Refrigerate them in the foil and unwrap them when you're ready to use them.

Mix and proof the dough

▪ Put the flour, sugar, salt, and yeast in a large bowl and stir to combine.

▪ Unwrap the potato and cut it into roughly ⅜-inch pieces, leaving the skin on, and put in the bowl of a stand mixer. (If the potato has been refrigerated, it's fine to add it to the mix cold.) Add the milk, buttermilk, egg, and egg yolks to the bowl. Add the dry ingredients. Fit the mixer with the dough hook and mix on low speed for 3 minutes. Increase the speed to medium and mix for 5 minutes to develop the gluten. Turn off the mixer and remove the bowl from

the stand. Remove the dough hook and wipe it clean with a wet hand. Cover the bowl with a clean kitchen towel or plastic wrap and set the dough in a warm place to ferment for 1 hour. Uncover the bowl and turn the dough. To turn the dough, use a wet hand to fold the top edge down two-thirds and fold the bottom edge to meet the top edge, so the dough is folded like a letter. Fold the sides inward in the same way to form a sort of ball, then re-cover the bowl.
▪ Place the dough in the refrigerator overnight to retard the dough.

Shape and proof the hot dog buns

▪ Remove the dough from the refrigerator. Lightly dust a large flat work surface with flour and use a plastic bowl scraper to scrape the dough out of the bowl and onto the floured surface. Dust the top of the dough with flour and use a bench knife to divide it into 16 (approximately 100-gram) pieces.
▪ Dust your hands lightly with flour. Take one piece of dough and gently rest your palm on the dough and roll the dough into a tight round ball. Place the ball off to the side of the work surface and continue, rolling the rest of the pieces of dough into balls and moving them off to the side. Let the rounds rest for about 15 minutes.
▪ Lightly dust your hands with flour and pick up one ball of dough. Put the ball on your work surface in front of you and gently press on it with the palm of your hand to flatten the dough into a thick pancake. Fold the top down two-thirds of the way toward you and press it into the dough. Then bring the bottom two-thirds up and press it into the dough like you are forming a letter. Using both hands, pick up the top edge of the letter and fold it down to the center, pinching the edge into the dough. Repeat, moving the top edge toward the bottom of the dough, pinching it into the dough to form a log. Push down on the dough with the palm of one hand to flatten the log until it is 5 inches long. If the dough sticks to your work surface, use a bench knife to scrape under it and release it. Set the flattened log to the side and repeat, shaping the remaining balls of dough in the same way.

This classic bread baker's shaping technique creates tension in the dough, which helps the dough proof more uniformly.

Finish shaping the hot dog buns

▪ Spray the perimeters of a baking sheet with nonstick cooking spray. Line with parchment paper and spray the parchment with nonstick cooking spray.
▪ Place the flattened dough logs on the prepared pan so that there are two rows of 8 logs, each with their long sides parallel to the short length of the pan, leaving ⅛ to ¼ inch between each bun.
▪ Pour ⅓ cup olive oil into a small dish and lightly brush the buns with half of the olive oil. (Reserve the remaining oil; you will use it later.) Cover the baking sheet with a damp, lightweight kitchen towel and set it aside in a warm place to proof the buns for 1½ to 2 hours, until they have doubled in size; they will

have grown into each other and the dough will not spring back when poked in the center.

Bake the hot dog buns

▪ Arrange the oven racks so one is in the center position. Preheat the oven to 350°F.

▪ Lightly brush the rolls with about half of the remaining olive oil. Place the baking sheet on the center rack of the oven to bake the hot dog buns for 40 minutes, until the buns are golden brown, rotating the baking sheet from front to back halfway through the baking time.

▪ Remove the buns from the oven and brush the remaining olive oil on top. Holding the baking sheet with both hands, gently hit the bottom of the sheet pan on a cooling rack to release the buns so they slide in one piece onto the rack. (If they are resisting sliding off the baking sheet, gently slide a spatula under them to nudge them off.)

It is important that pull-apart rolls, such as hot dog buns, cool in one piece so that the parts of the rolls that are touching one another do not dry out from being exposed to air.

Summer Focaccia with Sungolds, Corn, and Basil Pesto

Makes 1 large focaccia; serves 12 to 16

The summer that I was working on this book, I was also consulting for a Philadelphia bakery-restaurant called Walnut Street Café. I was making focaccia and needed toppings. Sweet corn, which was in season, came to my mind, and I thought it would taste even better balanced by the acidity of summer tomatoes. But the real magic of this focaccia is the cream, which is whipped and then spread onto the dough. It acts as a bed for the corn and tomatoes, and then caramelizes when baked. It's divine.

The focaccia starts with a "poolish," which is a type of preferment. Poolish is a dough that is fermented before the fermentation of the main dough. The poolish adds stretchiness to the dough, which in this case is needed to stretch the focaccia dough into the baking sheet.

Note You will need one baking sheet pan (18 x 13 inches, or a pan of similar dimensions) to make this.

For the poolish		
Water (70°F to 75°F)	½ cup	118 grams
Instant yeast	1⁄16 teaspoon	0.15 gram
Bread flour	1 cup	120 grams
For the dough		
Water (70°F to 75°F)	1⅓ cups	313 grams
All-purpose flour	3¾ cups	450 grams
Instant yeast	1 teaspoon	3 grams
Fine sea salt	2 teaspoons	12 grams
Extra-virgin olive oil	5 to 6 tablespoons	75 grams
For the topping		
Heavy cream	¾ cup	179 grams
Sungold tomatoes (or another small, sweet variety), halved	1 pint	315 grams
Corn, 1 ear shucked, kernels removed	about ¾ cup	120 grams
Fresh chives, chopped	1 tablespoon	5 grams
Red pepper flakes	¼ teaspoon	
Flaky sea salt	1½ teaspoons	6 grams
Pecorino Romano, finely grated	⅓ cup (not packed)	20 grams
For finishing the focaccia		
Basil Pesto (recipe follows)	3 tablespoons	
Pecorino Romano, finely grated	⅓ cup (not packed)	20 grams

Make the poolish

· The evening before you plan to make the focaccia (12 hours before you plan to mix the dough), pour the water into a quart-size container (ideally one with a lid). Sprinkle the yeast on top of the water and sprinkle the bread flour on top of that. Mix with a spoon until no flour is visible, cover with the lid (or plastic wrap), and set the poolish aside at room temperature to ferment for

12 to 18 hours. (To check that the poolish has fermented sufficiently, fill a small bowl with water. Wet the fingers of one hand and gently use your fingers to lift a small portion of the poolish out of the container and drop it in the water. If the poolish floats, it is ready. If not, let it ferment until it is ready, as long as 6 additional hours. If you find that it is taking too long, set it in a warmer place, such as near the stove.) If your poolish is ready before you are ready to use it, place it in the refrigerator. If your poolish is cold when you use it, bring your water to 80°F instead of 70°F when mixing your focaccia dough.

Mix and ferment the dough

· Place the water in the bowl of a stand mixer and add the poolish and all-purpose flour. Fit the mixer with the dough hook and mix on low speed for 2 to 3 minutes, until no flour is visible and very few lumps remain. Turn off the mixer and remove the bowl from the mixer stand; you can leave the dough hook in the bowl.

· Place the yeast and fine sea salt in separate piles on the top of the dough. Set the dough aside in a warm place to rest, uncovered, for 30 minutes. (For more information on why we are resting the dough before mixing the yeast and salt into the dough, see "Autolyse" in the Yeast Tutorial, page xxxi.)

· Return the bowl to the stand and mix with the dough hook for about 2 minutes on low speed. Increase the speed to medium and mix for 3 minutes to develop the gluten. Turn off the mixer and remove the bowl from the stand. Remove the dough hook and wipe it clean with a wet hand. Cover the bowl with plastic wrap and set the dough in a warm place to ferment for 2 hours, turning the dough once halfway through that time. To turn the dough, uncover the bowl and use a wet hand to fold the top edge down two-thirds and fold the bottom edge to meet the top edge, so the dough is folded like a letter. Fold the sides inward in the same way to form a sort of ball, then re-cover the bowl.

Shape the focaccia

· Uncover the bowl. Pour the olive oil onto a baking sheet and spread it around with your fingers to completely coat the bottom and sides. Use a plastic bowl scraper to scrape the dough in a big lump onto the baking sheet. Dip your fingers in the olive oil on the baking sheet and use the oil to coat the top of the dough. Let the dough rest for about 20 minutes without disturbing it. (It does not need to be covered because the oil provides a protective barrier to prevent the surface of the dough from drying out.) Dip your fingers in the oil on the baking sheet. Slide your fingers under the lump of dough and gently stretch it out toward the sides of the baking sheet. Press your fingertips into the surface of the dough to dimple it and stretch it evenly toward the sides of the baking sheet. When the dough starts to spring back, stop dimpling and stretching and let it rest for 20 minutes, then resume, dimpling and stretching the dough until it reaches the edges of the baking sheet. Set the dough aside in a warm place to proof for 45 minutes.

Top and bake the focaccia

· Arrange the oven racks so one is in the center position. Preheat the oven to 425°F.

· Put the cream in the bowl of a stand mixer. Fit the mixer with the whisk attachment and whip on medium-high speed until stiff peaks form. Turn off the mixer. Spoon the whipped cream onto the dough and use a small offset spatula to spread it to cover the surface. Place the tomatoes, cut side up, on the whipped cream layer, pushing down gently so they adhere to the cream. Sprinkle on the corn, followed by the chives, red pepper flakes, flaky salt, and pecorino.

· Place the focaccia on the center rack of the oven to bake for 30 to 35 minutes, until the surface and underside of the focaccia are golden brown (use an offset spatula to lift up and peek at the underside), rotating the baking sheet from front to back halfway through the baking time. Remove the focaccia from the oven. Using a large offset spatula, carefully slide the focaccia out of the baking sheet and onto a cooling rack.

Finish the focaccia

· While the focaccia is still warm, use a spoon to dot the surface of the focaccia with the pesto in small spoonfuls.

· When the focaccia has cooled, sprinkle the pecorino over the top. Use scissors to cut the focaccia into pieces.

Basil Pesto

**Makes about
1 cup**

This makes more than you will need for the focaccia. Use the leftover for pasta or spoon it on sandwiches or grilled vegetables and meats.

Garlic	2 cloves	
Fine sea salt	1 teaspoon	6 grams
Basil leaves, julienned	2 cups (lightly packed)	60 grams
Extra-virgin olive oil	½ cup	115 grams
Pecorino Romano, finely grated	½ cup	60 grams

· Put the garlic, fine sea salt, and basil in the bowl of a food processor fitted with a metal blade and pulse until the leaves are finely chopped but not pulverized. With the machine running, add the olive oil through the feed tube in a slow drizzle. Add the pecorino and process until the pesto is almost smooth, with flecks of basil remaining.

· Refrigerate the pesto in a covered container until you're ready to use it, and for up to 1 week.

Variation
Onion Board

**Makes 1 large
onion board;
serves 12 to 16**

Onion board, also called pletzel, is a Jewish flatbread similar to focaccia that is covered with caramelized onions and sprinkled with poppy seeds. Onion boards used to be a Jewish deli staple, but you don't see them much anymore, which is too bad, because they're delicious. To make an onion board, make, shape, and proof the dough for Summer Focaccia with Sungolds, Corn, and Basil Pesto (page 29). Cook the onions and use them, along with the poppy seeds, to top the dough as described here.

Note You will need one baking sheet pan (18 x 13 inches, or a pan of similar dimensions) to make this.

For the onions		
Yellow onions	3½ pounds (4 to 5 large)	1,670 grams
Unsalted butter	4 tablespoons (½ stick)	56 grams
Fine sea salt	2½ teaspoons	15 grams
For the topping		
Poppy seeds	2 teaspoons	6 grams
Flaky sea salt	½ teaspoon	3 grams
Bread crumbs	3 tablespoons	30 grams

Cook the onions

- Arrange the oven racks so one is in the lowest position. Preheat the oven to 300°F.
- Cut the tops off the onions, peel the onions, and cut them in half, root to tip. Lay the onion halves flat on a cutting board and slice the onions ⅛ inch thick.
- Melt the butter in a large Dutch oven (or another oven-safe pot with a lid) over medium heat. Add the onion slices and fine sea salt and cook without browning them for 15 minutes, stirring frequently. (If the onions begin to brown, reduce the heat slightly.) Turn off the heat, cover the pot, and place it in the oven to cook the onions for 30 minutes. Remove from the oven and let them rest, covered, for another 30 minutes. Remove the lid from the pot and put the onions in a large fine-mesh strainer to strain out the liquid. Set the onions aside for 30 minutes to cool to room temperature. (You can prepare the onions to this point up to a day in advance. Refrigerate in an airtight container until you're ready to use them.)

**Assemble and bake the
onion board**

- Arrange the oven racks so one is in the center position. Preheat the oven to 425°F.
- Transfer the onions to the prepared focaccia dough and use your fingers to spread them evenly over the surface of the dough. Sprinkle the poppy seeds over the onions, followed by the flaky salt and bread crumbs.
- Place the onion board on the center rack of the oven to bake for 30 to 35 minutes, until the surface and underside of the onion board are golden brown, rotating the pan halfway through the baking time. (Use an offset spatula to lift up and peek at the underside of the onion board to make sure that it has browned and is crispy before removing it from the oven.) Remove from the oven. Using a large offset spatula, carefully slide the onion board out of the pan and onto a cooling rack. Use scissors to cut it into pieces.

Carrot Currant Pecan Loaf

Makes 1 loaf

After I left Babbo, I wanted to learn to make bread, so I went to work for the great baker Jim Lahey, of Sullivan Street Bakery, in New York City. Jim is simply one of the most knowledgeable (and passionate) bread bakers in this country. This recipe uses his famous "no-knead" bread dough, which went viral after being published in *The New York Times*. Even though the words *carrot* and *pecan* in the title might lead you to believe this is a carrot bread along the lines of a quick bread or carrot cake, it is not that at all. It is a delicious, nutty, savory bread, perfect for serving with a cheese plate or for pre-meal snacking. I was enamored with it from the first time I made and tasted it. The year after my year with Jim, I made this loaf for Thanksgiving. Ten years later, it is still an annual tradition.

The bread is baked in a Lodge 3.2 Quart Cast Iron Combo Cooker, which is comprised of a cast-iron Dutch oven with a skillet lid. The pair is inverted so the skillet is on the bottom and the Dutch oven rests on top like a "cloche." Baking the bread in this heavy, closed vessel results in a beautiful, brown crusty exterior like that produced by a good bread bakery. The combo is not expensive, and after you taste this bread, you will be glad you bought one. This dough takes 18 hours to ferment and then proofs for 2 hours, so if you want to enjoy it with dinner, start mixing your dough about six o'clock the evening before.

Note You will need a Lodge 3.2 Quart Cast Iron Combo Cooker (Dutch oven with skillet lid) to make this.

Whole pecans	1 cup	115 grams
Dried currants	1 cup	130 grams
Bread flour	3⅓ cups plus more for dusting	400 grams
Fine sea salt	2 teaspoons	12 grams
Instant yeast	¼ teaspoon	1 gram
Carrot juice (70°F to 75°F)	1½ cups	360 grams
Rye flour	½ cup for dusting	60 grams

Get prepared

- Arrange the oven racks so one is in the center position. Preheat the oven to 300°F.
- Spread the pecans on a baking sheet and toast them in the oven for 18 to 20 minutes, shaking the pan once during that time for even toasting, until the nuts are golden brown and fragrant. Remove the baking sheet from the oven and set aside to cool the nuts to room temperature. Roughly chop the pecans and set aside.
- Place the currants in a small bowl and cover with hot water. Set aside to soak for 5 minutes. Drain the currants in a fine mesh strainer and let them sit in the strainer so they continue to drain until you're ready to use them.

Mix and ferment the dough

· Combine the bread flour, salt, and yeast in a medium bowl and stir to distribute the ingredients.

· Place the carrot juice in a deep mixing bowl (such as the bowl of a stand mixer, although you won't be using the mixer). Add the dry ingredients, pecans, and currants. Stir the dough with a large rubber spatula or wooden spoon until the currants and pecans are evenly incorporated and no pockets of dry ingredients remain. Cover the bowl tightly with plastic wrap (or a tight-fitting lid) and put the bowl in a warm place for about 18 hours, until the dough looks swollen.

Controlling the temperature is an important part of making this bread. Insulating the dough by mixing and fermenting it in a deep container helps it to stay at a good fermentation temperature (ideally between 75°F and 80°F).

Form and proof the loaf

· Line a baking sheet with a large, clean, lightweight kitchen towel and dust heavily with the rye flour. Dust a large flat work surface heavily with bread flour. Use a plastic bowl scraper or rubber spatula to scoop the dough out of the bowl and gently place the dough on the floured surface.

It's important when working with no-knead bread dough that you handle it gently. Because we usually develop the gluten by kneading, or mixing, this dough relies solely on the gluten that is formed during fermentation. We don't want to deflate that by manhandling the dough.

· Handling the dough gently, fold the top edge gently two-thirds of the way toward the bottom edge. Fold the bottom edge to meet the top edge, as if you were folding a letter, pressing on the dough just enough to get it to stay in place, but not patting the dough. Do the same with the two sides, folding the right edge two-thirds of the way toward the left edge, and folding the left edge to meet the right edge. Flip the dough upside down onto the prepared kitchen towel. Use the ends of the towel to cover the loaf so it doesn't dry out while proofing. Set the dough aside in a warm place to proof for 2 hours, until it does not bounce back when you indent it with your finger.

Bake the bread

- About 30 minutes before the dough is done proofing, arrange the oven racks so one is in the center position and no oven racks are above it. Place the Dutch oven, skillet side down, in the oven and preheat the oven and the Dutch oven to 450°F.

- Open the oven and carefully slide the oven rack out partway. Remove the Dutch oven from the skillet lid. Uncover the dough and use the towel to rock the ball of dough into the palm of your free hand. Place the dough, right side up, on the skillet lid. Return the Dutch oven to cover the dough and slide the oven rack back into the oven. Bake the bread for 25 minutes. Remove the top of the Dutch oven from the skillet lid and bake the bread for 20 to 25 minutes more, until it has a deeply burnished crust. Remove the skillet with the bread from the oven. Slide a large metal spatula under the bread with one hand on the spatula and the other, protected by a clean kitchen towel, holding the bread, remove the bread from the skillet lid. Place the bread on a cooling rack to cool completely.

Whole-Wheat Pain au Lait Pullman

**Makes 1
(13-inch) loaf**

This is my favorite bread for making toast. I eat it with salted butter and jam, and I also like to use it to make sandwiches. What I particularly like about this loaf is that, where most whole-wheat breads are made with 10 or 20 percent wheat flour and 80 or 90 percent white flour, this one is made with one-third whole-wheat flour, so it has an intense, wheat-y, nutty flavor. The other thing that sets it apart from other whole-wheat loaves is that the dough contains butter. The butter imparts great flavor, of course, and it also gives the bread a delicately crispy exterior. I often give it as a gift: a loaf of bread with a jar of homemade jam—so simple, and people really go crazy for it.

In this recipe, I call for you to pinch off a hunk of the dough before putting the rest in the loaf pan. By giving more space to the dough in the pan, the resulting bread is lighter and airier, with a more delicate crumb. The recipe will leave you with some excess dough to make into dinner rolls. If you're wondering why I don't just make the recipe a little bit smaller, it has to do with bread baking, which is done in metric measurements, which means it is scaled larger or smaller in multiples of ten.

Note You will need a 13- x 4-inch Pullman loaf pan to make this.

All-purpose flour	3¾ cups	450 grams
Whole-wheat flour	1¾ cups	210 grams
Instant yeast	2 teaspoons	6 grams
Fine sea salt	1 tablespoon plus 1 teaspoon	24 grams
Whole milk	1½ cups	360 grams
Sourdough Starter (page xxxiii)	¾ cup	128 grams
Large eggs	2	100 grams
Mild-flavored honey (such as wildflower or clover)	2 tablespoon plus 1 teaspoon	45 grams
Unsalted butter, cubed and softened	16 tablespoons (2 sticks)	226 grams
Nonstick cooking spray		

Mix and ferment the dough

· Combine the all-purpose flour, whole-wheat flour, yeast, and salt and stir to distribute the ingredients.

· Put the milk in a medium saucepan and heat over medium heat, stirring with a wooden spoon, until it is just warm to the touch but not hot (about 90°F). Turn off the heat and transfer the milk to the bowl of a stand mixer. Add the starter, eggs, honey, and dry ingredients.

· Fit the mixer with the dough hook and mix on low speed for 2 minutes. Increase the speed to medium and mix for 5 minutes to develop the gluten. Reduce the speed to low, add the butter, and mix for 7 to 10 minutes, until the butter is mixed in. Turn off the mixer and remove the bowl from the stand. Remove the dough hook and wipe it clean with a wet hand. Cover the bowl with a clean kitchen towel or plastic wrap and set the bowl aside in a warm place to ferment the dough for 2 hours, turning the dough once during that time. To turn the dough, uncover the bowl and use a wet hand to fold the top edge down two-thirds and fold the bottom edge to meet the top edge, so the dough is folded like a letter. Fold the sides inward in the same way to form a sort of ball, then re-cover the bowl.

Turning the dough halfway through the fermentation helps to develop the gluten and distribute the yeast.

Form and proof the loaf

- Lightly spray the insides and the underside of the lid of a 13- x 4-inch Pullman loaf pan with nonstick cooking spray.
- Pinch off a 250-gram piece of the dough (about the size of an orange) and set it aside.
- Using a plastic bowl scraper, scrape the remaining dough out of the bowl into the prepared pan. Wet your hands and use them to pat the dough into the corners of the pan and to even out the surface of the dough. Slide the lid closed on the pan, leaving it cracked open by 1 inch.
- Place the loaf in a warm place for 1½ to 2 hours to proof the dough, until it begins to peek out of the opening in the lid. Close the lid completely and discard any dough that has been pinched off by closing the lid.

Bake the bread

- While the dough is proofing, arrange the oven racks so one is in the center position. Preheat the oven to 375°F.
- Place the loaf on the center rack of the oven to bake for 45 to 50 minutes, until the top is dark golden brown, rotating the pan from front to back halfway through. (To check for doneness, using oven mitts or kitchen towels, slide the Pullman loaf lid open enough to see the color, being careful of any steam that will arise when you open the pan.) Remove the loaf from the oven.
- Using oven mitts or kitchen towels to protect your hands from the heat, immediately slide the lid off the loaf pan. Invert the pan so the bread falls onto a cooling rack. Let the loaf cool completely and slice as desired.

When making bread, start preheating your oven before the dough is finished proofing; if you wait until the dough is ready, it will over proof. Over-proofed bread will grow too large and bake out of the pan. And it will have an unappealing "fluffy" texture, and might also cave in.

Multigrain Loaf

**Makes 1
(13-inch) loaf**

I call this bread multigrain even though, in reality, it contains more seeds than grains, but whatever you call it, it's a really beautiful loaf of healthy bread. At Sadelle's, we used it to make our healthy egg sandwich, which consisted of an egg-white omelet, arugula, and salsa verde. At Walnut Street Café, we used the bread for avocado toast. At home, I like it toasted with French butter, and my son likes it with butter and jam. In other words: it is very versatile.

It is not difficult to make, and the ingredients are not hard to find, but you have to plan ahead, as the grains need to be soaked overnight before you mix the dough; the soaked mixture is referred to as a "soaker." Starting with a soaker is a traditional bread baker's technique when baking with whole grains. Dry grains will absorb any water available to them. If you don't soak them before adding them to bread dough, they will take the water they find in the dough, resulting in bread that is dry, with chewy, undercooked grains in it.

Note You will need a 13- x 4-inch Pullman loaf pan to make this.

For the soaker		
Steel-cut oats	½ cup	80 grams
Polenta	⅓ cup	52 grams
Brown flaxseeds	⅓ cup	50 grams
Black sesame seeds	⅓ cup	42 grams
Water (95°F to 100°F)	1 cup	235 grams
For the dough		
Bread flour	3 cups	360 grams
Spelt flour	2⅓ cups	245 grams
Fine sea salt	1 tablespoon	18 grams
Instant yeast	2 teaspoons	6 grams
Water (about 80°F)	1¾ cups	411 grams
Sourdough Starter (page xxxiii)	½ cup	85 grams
Nonstick cooking spray		

Make the soaker

· The evening before you want to bake the bread, combine the oats, polenta, flaxseeds, and sesame seeds in a 2-cup (or similar size) container or bowl and stir to combine. Add the water and stir again to distribute the water among the grains and seeds. Cover the container with a lid or plastic wrap and set it aside at room temperature overnight, or for at least 12 hours.

Mix and ferment the dough

· Put the bread flour, spelt flour, salt, and yeast in a medium bowl and stir to combine. Scoop the seed soaker into the bowl of a stand mixer. Add the water and starter, as well as the dry ingredients. Fit the mixer with the dough hook and mix on low speed for 3 minutes. Increase the speed to medium and mix for 2 minutes. Turn off the mixer and remove the bowl from the stand. Remove the dough hook and wipe it clean with a wet hand. Cover the bowl with a clean kitchen towel or plastic wrap and set the dough aside in a warm place for 2 hours to ferment, turning the dough once halfway through that time. To turn the dough, uncover the bowl and use a wet hand to fold the top edge down two-thirds and fold the bottom edge to meet the top edge, so the dough is folded like a letter. Fold the sides inward in the same way to form a sort of ball, then re-cover the bowl.

Form and proof the loaf
- Lightly spray the insides and the underside of the lid of a 13- x 4-inch Pullman loaf pan with nonstick cooking spray.
- Using a plastic bowl scraper, scrape the dough out of the bowl into the prepared pan. Wet your hands and use them to pat the dough into the corners of the pan and to even out the surface of the dough. Slide the lid on the pan, leaving it cracked open by 1 inch.
- Place the loaf in a warm place for about 1 hour, until the dough starts to rise through the lid opening. Close the lid completely and discard any dough that has been pinched off by closing the lid.

Bake the bread
- While the dough is proofing, arrange the oven racks so one is in the center position. Preheat the oven to 400°F.
- Place the loaf on the center rack of the oven to bake for about 50 minutes, until the top is dark golden brown, rotating the pan from front to back halfway through. (To check for doneness, using oven mitts or kitchen towels, slide the Pullman loaf lid open enough to see the color, being careful of any steam that will arise when you open the pan.) Remove the loaf from the oven.
- Using oven mitts or kitchen towels to protect your hands from the heat, immediately slide the lid off the loaf pan. Invert the pan directly onto a cooling rack. Let the loaf cool completely and slice as desired.

Sourdough Brioche Loaf

Makes 1 (13-inch) loaf

This rich, tender bread is great toasted, with butter and jam. It also makes delicious Deep-Fried French Toast (page 226).

Note You will need a 13- x 4-inch Pullman loaf pan to make this.

All-purpose flour	4 cups plus more for dusting	480 grams
Granulated sugar	¼ cup plus 2 tablespoons	76 grams
Instant yeast	2 teaspoons	6 grams
Fine sea salt	2 teaspoons	12 grams
Large eggs	5	250 grams
Whole milk	⅓ cup	80 grams
Sourdough Starter (page xxxiii)	1 cup	170 grams
Unsalted butter, cubed and softened	20 tablespoons (2½ sticks)	283 grams
For baking the loaf		
Egg	1	
Fine sea salt	pinch	

Mix and ferment the dough

- Put the flour, sugar, yeast, and salt in a medium bowl and stir to combine the ingredients.
- Put the eggs, milk, and starter in the bowl of a stand mixer and place the dry ingredients on top. Fit the mixer with the dough hook and mix on low speed for 2 to 3 minutes to combine the wet and dry ingredients. Increase the mixer speed to medium and mix for 5 minutes to develop the gluten. Turn off the mixer and wipe the dough hook clean with a wet hand; the dough tends to climb up the hook during the mixing of this dough. Add the butter and mix on low speed until it is incorporated into the dough, 5 to 10 minutes (depending on the softness of the butter), stopping to clean the dough hook with a wet hand once or twice during this time. Turn off the mixer and remove the bowl from the stand. Remove the dough hook and wipe it clean with a wet hand. Cover the bowl with a clean kitchen towel or plastic wrap and set the dough aside in a warm place for 2 hours to ferment, turning the dough once halfway through that time. To turn the dough, uncover the bowl and use a wet hand to fold the top edge down two-thirds and fold the bottom edge to meet the top edge, so the dough is folded like a letter. Fold the sides inward in the same way to form a sort of ball, then re-cover the bowl. After 2 hours, turn the dough again. Cover the bowl and place it in the refrigerator overnight to retard the dough.

Form and proof the loaf

· Lightly dust a large flat work surface with flour. Remove the dough from the refrigerator and uncover it. Use a plastic bowl scraper to scoop the dough out onto the floured work surface. Gently pat the dough into a rectangle about the length of the pan you will be baking it in, with the long edge parallel to you. Use your hands to get underneath the top edge of the dough and fold it down about two-thirds of the way from the top like a letter. Scoop your hands under the bottom edge of the dough (the edge closest to you) and fold it up over the top so the bottom edge is even with the top edge. Lift the dough and flip it over into the pan so the seam is on the bottom. Use your hands to pat the dough into the corners of the pan and even out the surface of the dough.

· Cover the dough with a damp, lightweight kitchen towel and set aside in a warm place for about 3 hours, until the dough has risen and is about ¼ inch from the top rim of the pan.

Bake the bread

· Arrange the oven racks so one is in the center position. Preheat the oven to 350°F.

· Whisk the egg with a pinch of salt to make an egg wash. Brush the top of the loaf with the egg wash; discard the remaining egg wash.

· Put the loaf on the center rack to bake for about 35 minutes, until the top is a beautiful mahogany brown, rotating the pan from front to back halfway through. Remove the loaf from the oven.

· Invert the pan so the loaf falls onto a cooling rack. Turn the loaf right side up and let it cool completely. Slice as desired.

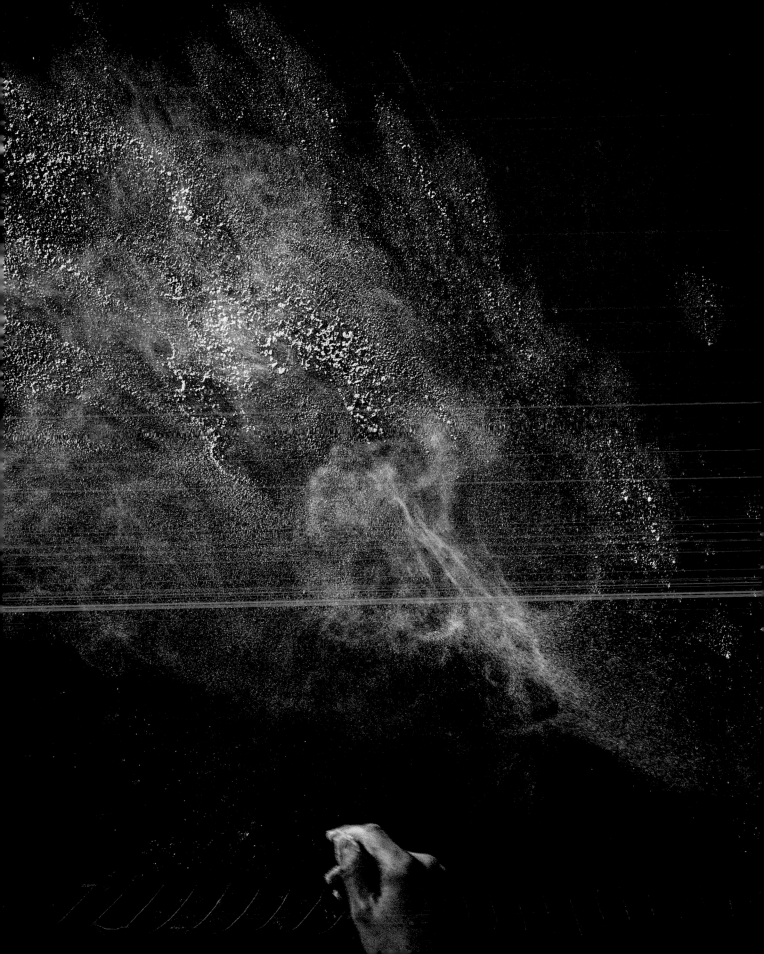

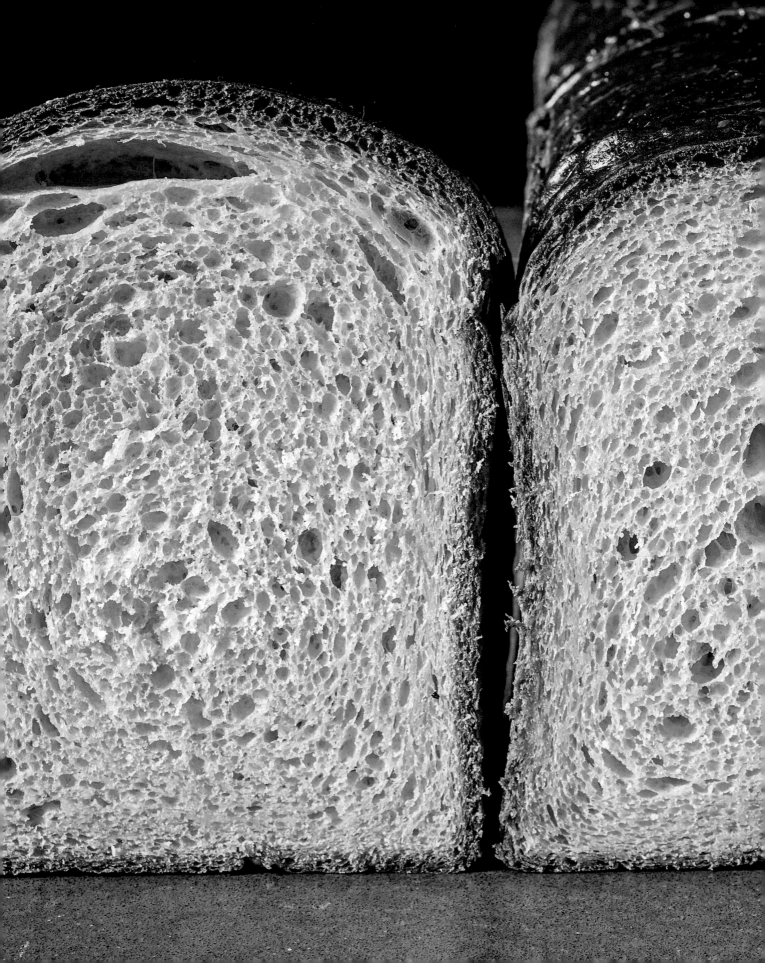

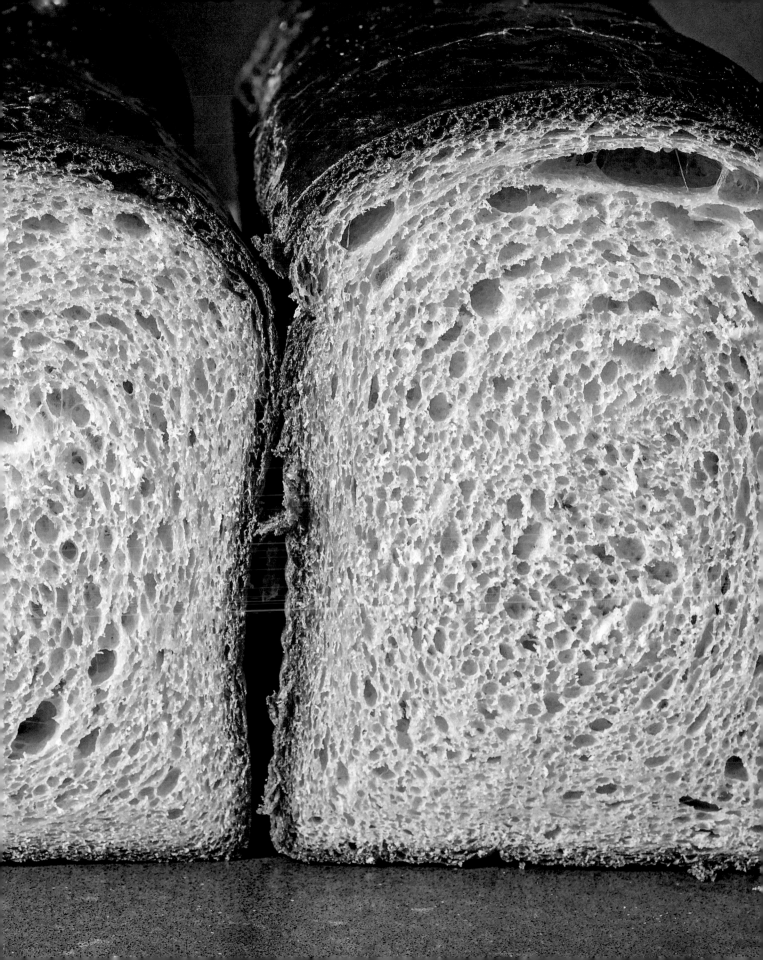

Pull-Apart Parker House Rolls

Makes 15 rolls

When I was at Per Se, Jonathan Benno, the chef de cuisine, tasked me with creating a warm roll for bread service. He told me about the rolls at the restaurant Craftsteak, which he considered the *ne plus ultra* of Parker House rolls. I studied those rolls and started experimenting with different dough variations. These rolls are still on the menu, ten years later. They're that good. At home, I prefer a pull-apart shape to a Parker House roll shape, which is mostly a matter of putting the rolls closer together on the baking sheet before baking them. Baking them close together like this keeps them really tender, because the sides stay soft and squishy, and really old-school.

Note You will need a quarter sheet pan (13- x 9½-inches) or a pan of similar dimensions) to make this.

All-purpose flour	3½ cups plus more for dusting	420 grams
Granulated sugar	2 tablespoons	26 grams
Fine sea salt	2 teaspoons	12 grams
Instant yeast	1½ teaspoons	4.5 grams
Whole milk	1 cup	240 grams
Sourdough Starter (page xxxiii)	⅓ cup	57 grams
Large egg	1	50 grams
Unsalted butter, cubed and softened	12 tablespoons (1½ sticks)	170 grams
Nonstick cooking spray		
For baking the rolls		
Unsalted butter, melted and cooled slightly	3 tablespoons	42 grams
Flaky sea salt	Pinch	

Mix and ferment the dough

▪ Place the flour, sugar, salt, and yeast in a medium bowl and stir with a whisk to combine the ingredients.

▪ Place the milk, starter, and egg in the bowl of a stand mixer. Add the dry ingredients. Fit the mixer with the dough hook and mix on low speed for 2 minutes. Increase the mixer speed to medium and mix the dough for about 5 minutes, until it is smooth and no longer sticky. Add the cubed butter and mix on low speed until there are no chunks of butter remaining, 5 to 10 minutes, stopping to scrape down the sides of the bowl if the butter is sticking.

▪ Turn off the mixer and remove the bowl from the stand. Remove the dough hook and wipe it clean with a wet hand. Cover the bowl with a clean kitchen towel or plastic wrap and set the bowl in a warm place to allow the dough to ferment for 2 hours, turning the dough once halfway through that time.

To turn the dough, uncover the bowl and use a wet hand to fold the top edge down two-thirds and fold the bottom edge to meet the top edge, so the dough is folded like a letter. Fold the sides inward in the same way to form a sort of ball, then re-cover the bowl.

- While the dough is fermenting, line a baking sheet with parchment paper and spray the paper with nonstick cooking spray.
- Transfer the dough to the baking sheet and spread it out. Put it in the refrigerator for 1 hour, until it's chilled and no longer sticky, and up to overnight. (If you are refrigerating the dough overnight, remove the baking sheet from the refrigerator after 1 hour, cover it with plastic wrap, and return it to the refrigerator.)

Shape and proof the rolls

- Spray the bottom and sides of a quarter sheet pan with nonstick cooking spray. Line the pan with parchment paper and spray the parchment with nonstick cooking spray.
- Remove the dough from the refrigerator. Lightly dust a large flat work surface with flour and use a plastic bowl scraper to scrape the dough out of the bowl and onto the floured surface. Lightly dust the top of the dough with flour and use a bench knife to divide the dough into 15 (65-gram) pieces.
- Put one piece of dough in front of you on the work surface. Dust your hands lightly with flour. Gently rest your palm on the dough and roll the dough into a tight round ball. Put the ball on the prepared baking sheet and continue, rolling the rest of the pieces of dough into balls and adding them to the baking sheet, spacing the rounds out evenly with 3 rounds lined up across the short side and 5 lined up on the long side. Cover the balls with a damp, lightweight kitchen towel. Set aside in a warm place to proof the rolls for 2½ to 3 hours, until the rolls are swollen looking and touching each other.

Bake the rolls

- While the rolls are proofing, arrange the oven racks so one is in the center position. Preheat the oven to 350°F.
- Brush the tops of the rolls with half of the melted butter. Reserve the remaining butter.
- Put the baking sheet on the center rack of the oven to bake the rolls for 25 to 30 minutes, until they are light golden brown, rotating the rolls from front to back halfway through. Remove the rolls from the oven and brush with the remaining melted butter. Holding the pan with both hands, tap the pan on a cooling rack to slide the rolls out onto the rack in a single piece. Sprinkle a generous pinch of flaky salt on top of each roll. Serve warm.

Master Recipe
for Challah Dough

**Makes 1,000 grams dough,
enough for 1 Sectional Challah
(page 59) plus 3 Challah Rolls,
9 Challah Rolls (page 62), or
1 Six-Strand Challah Loaf (page 65)**

Challah is the ultimate Jewish bread. It's the bread that's traditionally broken for the Friday Sabbath. There are many different shapes, and I give you instructions here for shaping several different kinds of them; but whatever shape you choose, the important thing is that the bread is torn, not cut with a knife.

I learned to make challah when I was at Per Se, where I inherited an excellent recipe from the baker who came before me. It had egg yolks, whole eggs, water, oil, honey and sugar for sweeteners, flour, salt, and yeast. We would mix the dough, ferment it for two hours, and then shape it into a six-strand braided loaf, and proof and bake it. Because we sold the braided loaf at our Bouchon Bakery, I started retarding the shaped and proofed loaves overnight in the walk-in refrigerator so the overnight baker needed only to pull them out of the refrigerator and bake them. I did this to accommodate our production schedule, but I very quickly noticed that the challah loaves that had been retarded had better flavor, and the very best challahs were made from dough that was retarded *before* being shaped. I took this knowledge with me to my next job, at Roberta's. There, in addition to retarding the dough, I increased the proofing time from 2 hours to as long as 4, until the dough was so light it practically deflated when you poked it with your finger. The long proofing time is what makes my challah as light and feathery as it is, where too often challah is tight (a baker's term for bread that doesn't have the characteristic open holes that indicate it has been properly proofed) and dry. Even after I'd created a challah that was very flavorful, from retarding the dough, and light and airy, from the long proofing time, I thought it could still be a bit more moist. So, I began adding sourdough starter to the dough, which, consisting of half flour and half water, adds moisture to the bread, and also prolongs the shelf life. In the end, I created a challah that is light and feathery, flavorful, and moist. It is, in my opinion, the best challah I have ever baked.

Golden raisins (optional)	1¼ cups	188 grams
All-purpose flour	4 cups	480 grams
Granulated sugar	2 tablespoons	26 grams
Fine sea salt	2 teaspoons	12 grams
Instant yeast	2 teaspoons	6 grams
Mild-flavored honey (such as wildflower or clover)	2 tablespoons	40 grams
Large egg	1	50 grams
Large egg yolks	2	34 grams
Canola or vegetable oil	¼ cup plus 2 tablespoons	83 grams
Water (70°F to 75°F)	⅔ cup	157 grams
Sourdough Starter (page xxxiii)	⅔ cup	113 grams

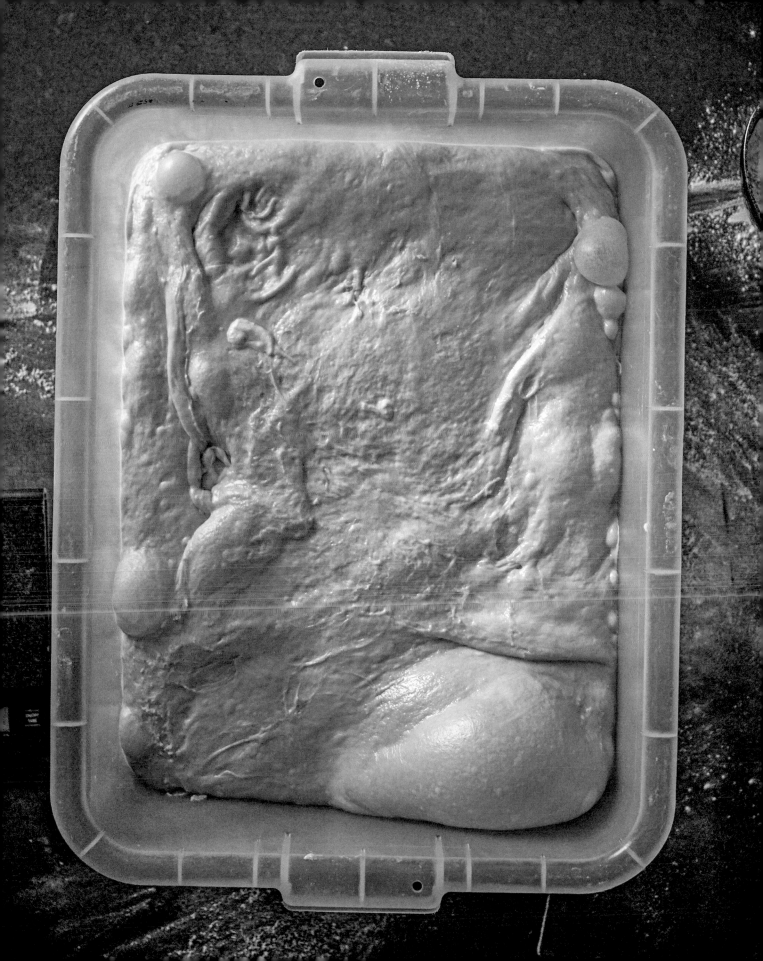

**Soak the raisins
(if you are using them)**

- Place the raisins in a small bowl, cover with hot tap water, and set aside to soak for 10 minutes. Drain the raisins in a strainer and let them sit in the strainer to continue to drain while you mix the dough.

Mix and ferment the dough

- Place the flour, sugar, salt, and yeast in a medium bowl and stir with a whisk to combine. Place the honey, egg, egg yolks, canola oil, water, and starter in the bottom of the bowl of a stand mixer. Then place all of the dry ingredients on top. Fit the mixer with the dough hook attachment and mix on low for 2 minutes. Hold on to the mixing bowl to steady it and increase the speed to medium. Mix on medium for 5 minutes to develop the gluten, holding on to the mixer the entire time; the dough is stiff and can cause the mixer to jump around. Add the raisins, if you are using them, and mix on low speed until they are incorporated.
- Turn off the mixer and remove the bowl from the stand. Remove the dough hook and wipe it clean with a wet hand. Cover the bowl with a clean kitchen towel or plastic wrap and set the bowl in a warm place to allow the dough to ferment for 2 hours, turning the dough halfway through that time and again after 2 hours. To turn the dough, uncover the bowl and use a wet hand to fold the top edge down two-thirds and fold the bottom edge to meet the top edge, so the dough is folded like a letter. Fold the sides inward in the same way to form a sort of ball, then re-cover the bowl. Place the dough in the refrigerator overnight or for at least 8 hours to retard the dough.

Sectional Challah

Make 1 (9-inch) loaf

Challah is customarily ripped rather than sliced, so it is traditionally formed into pull-apart shapes. A six-stranded challah is the most ubiquitous and also considered the most symbolic. But challah doesn't need to be limited to that shape. The way a pull-apart loaf works is that when you put balls or logs of dough together in a pan, they proof and grow into each other, so they form a cohesive loaf, but the individual pieces of dough maintain their structure, so they can be easily pulled apart. I had seen brioche shaped like this; called "Brioche Nanterre," it is comprised of separate balls. When I saw something similar at Walls' Bake Shop, a classic Jewish bakery on Long Island, it was a eureka moment. The Walls' challah was comprised of logs rather than balls, creating rip-apart slices, which seemed like a fun way to enjoy French toast. I also knew it would save the bakery a lot of time, because it is a lot quicker to shape logs than it is to braid a six-strand loaf. For the same reason, this is a convenient way of shaping challah for the home cook.

Note You will need a 9- x 4-inch Pullman loaf pan (or a 9- x 4-inch standard loaf pan) to make this.

Nonstick cooking spray		
Master Recipe for Challah Dough (page 54)	1 recipe	1,000 grams
All-purpose flour	for dusting	
For baking the challah		
Large egg	1	
Fine sea salt	pinch	

Get prepared
- Spray the bottom and insides of a 9- x 4-inch Pullman loaf pan (or a 9- x 4-inch standard loaf pan) with nonstick cooking spray.
- Remove the dough from the refrigerator, uncover it, and use a plastic bowl scraper to scrape it onto a flour-dusted flat work surface. Lightly dust the top of the dough with flour and use a bench knife to cut the dough into 9 (110-gram) pieces.

Shape the challah
- Put one piece of dough on the work surface. Dust your hands lightly with flour. Gently rest your palm on the dough and roll the dough into a tight round ball. Place the ball on a lightly flour-dusted corner of your work surface, away from where you are rolling, and continue rolling the remaining pieces of dough into balls and moving them aside to rest. (If you don't have enough

space on your counter, place the balls on a flour-dusted baking sheet instead.) Let the balls rest for 10 to 15 minutes to allow the gluten to relax.

• Lightly dust your hands with flour and pick up one ball of dough. Put the ball on your work surface and gently press on it with the palm of your hand to flatten it into a thick pancake. Using both hands, pick up the top edge of the round and fold it down by one-fourth, pinching the top edge into the log with the tips of your fingers. Repeat, moving the top edge toward the center and pinching it into the dough. Do this two or three more times, until you reach the bottom of the log. (This is a classic bread baker's shaping technique to create tension in the dough, which helps the dough proof more uniformly.)

• Roll out the log until it is 4 inches long (the width of your pan), dusting your hands very lightly with flour if the dough is sticking to the work surface. Lay the log widthwise in the prepared loaf pan. Repeat, rolling the remaining balls into tight logs and adding them to the pan one at a time and stopping once you have filled the pan with 6 logs. (Roll the remaining balls into logs and shape them to make Challah Rolls, page 62.)

Proof and bake the challah

• Spray a sheet of plastic wrap with nonstick cooking spray and lay it, sprayed side down, on the pan. Set the loaf aside in a warm place to proof for about 3 hours, until the dough has risen to just below the rim of the pan.

• While the challah is proofing, arrange the oven racks so one is in the center position. Preheat the oven to 350°F.

• Whisk the egg with the salt to make an egg wash. Uncover the loaf pan and brush the wash generously over the challah; discard the remaining egg wash.

• Put the challah on the center rack of the oven to bake for 35 to 40 minutes, until the top is a deep caramel color and the loaf emits a hollow sound when you tap on the bottom with your finger, rotating the loaf pan from front to back halfway through the baking time. Remove the loaf from the oven and let it cool slightly in the loaf pan. Invert the pan so the loaf falls onto a cooling rack. Turn the loaf right side up and cool completely.

Challah Rolls

Makes 9 rolls

This is a traditional challah roll shape. The rolls are made to resemble a knot and are very pretty.

All-purpose flour	for dusting	
Master Recipe for Challah Dough (page 54)	1 recipe	1,000 grams
For baking the rolls		
Large egg	1	
Fine sea salt	pinch	

Get prepared

· Line two baking sheets with parchment paper and set aside.

· Remove the dough from the refrigerator, uncover it, and use a plastic bowl scraper to scrape it onto a flour-dusted flat work surface. Lightly dust the top of the dough with flour and use a bench knife to cut into 9 (110-gram) pieces.

Shape the challah

This classic bread baker's shaping technique creates tension in the dough, which helps it proof more uniformly. The tension also works the gluten, helping your bread expand to its fullest potential.

· Put one piece of dough on the work surface. Dust your hands lightly with flour. Gently rest your palm on the dough and roll the dough into a tight round ball. Place the ball in a flour-dusted corner of your work surface, away from where you are rolling, and continue, rolling the remaining pieces of dough into balls and moving them aside to rest. (If you don't have enough space on your counter, place the balls on a flour-dusted baking sheet instead.) Let the balls rest for 10 to 15 minutes to allow the gluten to relax.

· Lightly dust your hands with flour and pick up one ball of dough. Put it on your work surface and gently press with the palm of your hand to flatten it into a thick pancake. Using both hands, pick up the top edge of the round and fold it down by one-fourth, pinching the top edge into the log with your fingertips. Repeat, moving the top edge toward the center and pinching it into the dough. Do this two or three more times, until you reach the bottom of the log.

· Lightly dust a flat work surface and your hands with flour. (You want to have enough flour on your hands so that the dough is not sticking to your hands or the counter, but not so much that the dough slides on the work surface; you need tension between the dough and the work surface to shape the dough.) Place one log on the work surface and roll it under the palms of both hands into a 12-inch-long strand. Dust a space to the side of where you are working and place the strand there to rest. (If you do not have room on your counter for the strands, put them on a flour-dusted baking sheet.) Roll all the remaining logs into strands and move them to the side with the first one.

· Pick up one strand and lay it parallel to you. Cross the ends of the strand over each other into a loose circle, adjusting the "tail" of the top end so it is longer than the other. Bring the "tail" over, down, and back up through the hole in the center of the circle like you are starting to tie a knot. Loop this end again over, around the outside, and up through the middle of the circle, popping up like a little knob out of the center. Pull the other end of dough down through the center hole, so the knob of this end pokes through the bottom. Lay the roll on a prepared baking sheet. Repeat, forming the remaining strands into rolls and placing them on the baking sheets, leaving about 3 inches between each.

Proof and bake the rolls

- Cover the rolls with a damp, lightweight kitchen towel and proof for 2 hours, until a roll holds the indentation of a fingertip poked into its side.
- While the rolls are proofing, arrange the oven racks so one is in the top third of the oven and the other is in the bottom third. Preheat the oven to 350°F.
- Whisk the egg with the salt to make an egg wash. Uncover the rolls and brush the wash generously over them; discard the remaining egg wash.
- Put one baking sheet of challah rolls on each oven rack and bake for 25 to 30 minutes, until the tops are a deep caramel color and the rolls emit a hollow sound when you tap on the bottom of one with your finger, rotating the baking sheets from front to back and from one rack to the other halfway through the baking time. Remove the baking sheets from the oven and place them on cooling racks; let the challah rolls cool on the baking sheets.

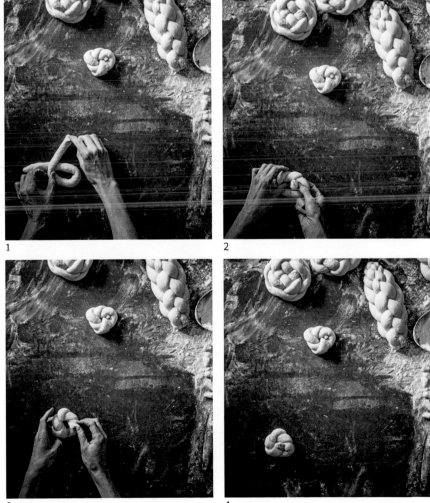

1

2

3

4

Six-Strand Challah Loaf

Makes 2 loaves

A six-strand braided loaf is the classic, iconic challah shape. At Roberta's, we offered it only on Fridays, and it was so popular, we sold out every week. Enjoy it as a dinner bread. I love a fried egg and cheese sandwich on toasted challah.

This loaf takes 3 to 4 hours to proof. Dough proofs from the outside in, so a large loaf like this takes longer to proof than, say, a roll. What's more, because this challah is formed into long strands that are fairly tightly braided, the gluten in the dough has been worked significantly, which adds to the proofing time. The long proofing time results in light, feathery challah, so be patient. Slow bread equals good bread.

This recipe calls for you to top the dough with natural sesame seeds, which leave the hull still intact. These are used often in bread baking, but they can be hard to find for the home cook. You can find them on Nuts.com, or the best option in grocery stores are Japanese toasted sesame seeds, which come in a shaker canister. These have the hull intact and they're really flavorful. (The seeds come in black and white; use white for this.) The difference is that the Japanese seeds are lightly toasted, but this won't affect your baked goods. What you don't want are the pearly white hulled sesame seeds, which don't have the same delicious flavor.

For the challah braid		
Master Recipe for Challah Dough (page 54)	1 recipe	1,000 grams
All-purpose flour	for dusting	
For baking the challah		
Natural white sesame seeds	½ cup	70 grams
Large egg	1	
Fine sea salt	pinch	

Get prepared

• Remove the dough from the refrigerator, uncover it, and use a plastic bowl scraper to scrape it onto a flour-dusted flat work surface. Lightly dust the top of the dough with flour and use a bench knife to cut the dough into 12 (80-gram) pieces.

Shape the dough into strands

• Put one piece of dough on the work surface. Dust your hands lightly with flour. Gently rest your palm on the dough and roll the dough into a tight round ball. Place the ball in a flour-dusted corner of your work surface, away from where you are rolling, and continue rolling the remaining pieces of dough into balls and moving them aside to rest. (If you don't have enough space on your counter, place the balls on a flour-dusted baking sheet instead.) Let the balls rest for 10 to 15 minutes to allow the gluten to relax.

- Lightly dust your hands with flour and pick up one ball of dough. Put the ball on your work surface and gently press on it with the palm of your hand to flatten it into a thick pancake. Using both hands, pick up the top edge of the round and fold it down by one-fourth, pinching it into the dough log with the tips of your fingers. Repeat, moving the top edge toward the center and pinching it into the dough, two or three more times until you reach the bottom of the log.
- Lightly dust a flat work surface and your hands with flour. (You want to have enough flour on your hands so that the dough is not sticking to your hands or the counter, but not so much that the dough slides back and forth on the work surface; you need tension between the dough and the work surface to shape the dough.) Place one log on the work surface and roll it under the palms of both hands into a 12-inch-long strand. Dust a space to the side of where you are working and place the strand there to rest. (If you do not have room on your counter for the strands, put them on a flour-dusted baking sheet.) Roll all the remaining logs into strands and move them to the side with the first one.

Braid the strands

- Lay 6 of the strands side by side perpendicular to you on your work surface. Pinch the strands together at the top, and then move the 3 strands on the left to the left and the 3 on the right to the right to create two sections of strands.
- Move the bottom of the outer right strand diagonally up to the left so it begins to form an X. Move the outer left strand diagonally to the upper right quadrant to form an X, with 4 strands on the bottom and 2 on the top. Next, pick up the strand in the upper left quadrant, and bring it diagonally down to the center, placing it inside the 2 strands that are on the bottom right. Take the outermost right strand on the bottom of the X and move it up and across diagonally so that it is in the upper left quadrant.
- Pick up the strand in the upper right quadrant of the X and move it diagonally downward, to the center, placing it inside the 2 strands that are on the bottom left. Take the outermost left strand on the bottom and move it up and across diagonally so that it is in the upper right quadrant.
- Continue braiding in this way, moving the upper left strand down to the center and the bottom outer right strand up and then moving the upper right strand down to the center and the bottom outer left strand up until the challah is braided. Once you've braided as far as you can go, pinch the ends together. Use the edge of your hand to press down on the end of the challah and make a sawing motion to pinch off the end. This makes a tight, clean end to the braid. Do the same on the other side of the challah.
- Slide your hands under the challah and gently push the two ends of the challah closer together so that the challah is not too long and skinny. Set aside while you braid the second challah in the same way.

Do not tug on the strands as you braid. They become shorter as you go, and they will feel awkward and you will want to pull on them to make it easier to braid, but don't. Doing it will cause the challah to look less like a braid and more like a lobster.

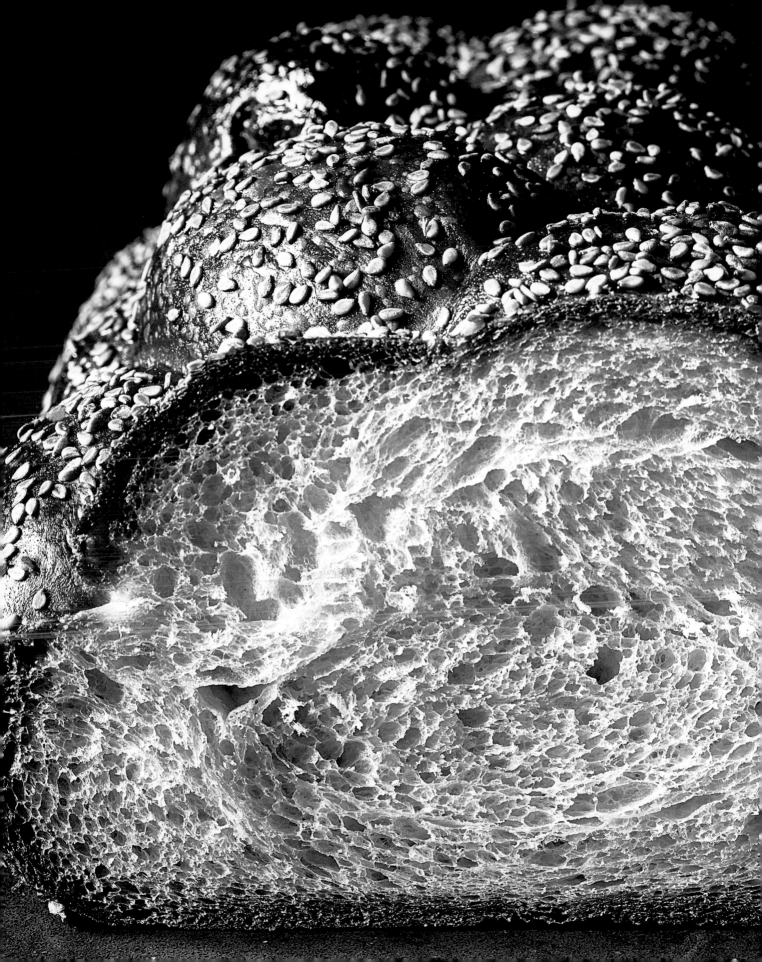

Finish the challah loaves

- Line two baking sheets with parchment paper.
- Place the sesame seeds in a large shallow bowl. Whisk the egg and salt together in a small bowl to make an egg wash.
- Brush both challah loaves with egg wash. Cover the bowl and refrigerate the remaining egg wash. You will use it again later, after the challah proofs. Pick up one loaf and place the top in the bowl of seeds. Move the challah around to coat the top all over with the seeds. Picking it up by the bottom so you don't disturb the seed coating, place the challah loaf diagonally on one of the prepared baking sheets. Dip the second challah in the sesame seeds and place it on the second baking sheet.

Proof and bake the loaves

- Cover the loaves with damp, lightweight kitchen towels and proof for 3 to 4 hours, until the dough holds the indentation of a fingertip poked into the side.

When challah is properly proofed, it will feel almost as if it wants to deflate when you poke it with your finger.

- While the challah loaves are proofing, arrange the oven racks so one is in the top third and the other is in the bottom third. Preheat the oven to 350°F.
- Uncover the loaves and brush the wash generously over them; discard the remaining egg wash.
- Place one baking sheet on each oven rack and bake the loaves for 30 to 35 minutes, until the tops are a deep caramel color and the loaves emit a hollow sound when you tap on the bottom with your finger, rotating the baking sheets from front to back and from one rack to the other halfway through the baking time. Remove the baking sheets from the oven and place them on cooling racks to cool.

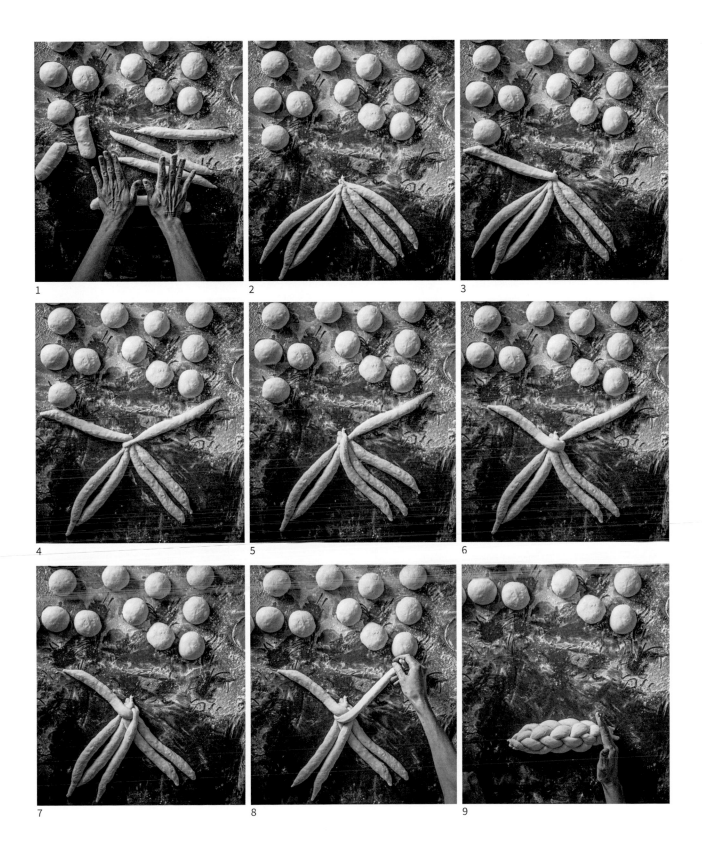

1 2 3

4 5 6

7 8 9

Challah Crowns

Makes 2 crowns

This is a really classic shape for challah, which my friend Joe Bowie taught me how to make. It is traditionally served for Rosh Hashanah, the Jewish New Year, to represent how things come full circle.

Master Recipe for Challah Dough (page 54)	1 recipe	1,000 grams
All-purpose flour	for dusting	
For baking the challah		
Large egg	1	
Fine sea salt	pinch	

Get prepared

· Remove the dough from the refrigerator, uncover it, and use a plastic bowl scraper to scrape it onto a flour-dusted flat work surface. Lightly dust the top of the dough with flour and use a bench knife to cut the dough into 8 (125-gram) pieces.

Shape the dough into strands

· Put one piece of dough on the work surface. Dust your hands lightly with flour. Gently rest your palm on the dough and roll the dough to create a tight round ball. Place the ball in a flour-dusted corner of your work surface, away from where you are rolling, and continue rolling the remaining pieces of dough into balls and moving them aside to rest. (If you don't have enough space on your counter, place the balls on a flour-dusted baking sheet instead.) Let the balls rest for 10 to 15 minutes to allow the gluten to relax.

· Lightly dust your hands with flour and pick up one ball of dough. Put the ball on your work surface and gently press on it with the palm of your hand to flatten it into a thick pancake. Using both hands, pick up the top edge of the round and fold it down by one-fourth, pinching it into the dough log with the tips of your fingers. Repeat, moving the top edge toward the center and pinching it into the dough, two or three more times until you reach the bottom of the log.

· Lightly dust a flat work surface and your hands with flour. (You want to have enough flour on your hands so that the dough is not sticking to your hands or the counter, but not so much that the dough slides on the work surface; you need tension between the dough and the work surface to shape the dough.) Place one log on the work surface and roll it under the palms of both hands into a 15-inch-long strand. Dust a space to the side of where you are working and place the strand there to rest. (If you do not have room on your counter for the strands, put them on a flour-dusted baking sheet.) Roll all the remaining logs into strands and move them to the side with the first one.

Weave the crown

- Line two baking sheets with parchment paper. Lay 2 of the strands 1 inch apart, parallel to you on your work surface. Lay the remaining 2 strands 1 inch apart, across the first 2 strands in a tic-tac-toe formation.
- To start the weave pattern, lift up the parallel rope that is farthest from you and slide the perpendicular rope on the right side underneath it so the 2 are woven together. Do the opposite on the other side, slipping the perpendicular rope on the left side underneath the parallel rope that is closest to you.
- As you weave the crown, you will first move 360 degrees clockwise and then 360 degrees counterclockwise. Take the top left perpendicular rope and move it over the top right perpendicular rope, bending it at a 90-degree angle so it is parallel to you. Take the top right parallel rope and move it over the bottom right parallel rope, bending it 90 degrees so it is perpendicular to you. Take the bottom right perpendicular rope and cross it over the bottom left perpendicular rope, bending it 90 degrees to the left so that it is parallel to you. Finally, take the bottom left parallel rope, cross it over the top left parallel rope, and move it up 90 degrees. This is one rotation.
- Repeat this rotation in a counterclockwise direction, starting first with the top right perpendicular rope, crossing it over the top left perpendicular rope, and moving it to the left 90 degrees so that it is parallel to you. Repeat this pattern to complete the rotation.
- After you have completed one clockwise rotation and one counterclockwise rotation, you should be able to complete one more clockwise rotation and then you will run out of room to weave. When you have no more room to weave, pull the ends of the strands underneath the crown and pinch them together. Place the crown on a prepared baking sheet. Repeat, weaving the second crown with the remaining dough strands and placing the crown on the second prepared baking sheet.

Proof and bake the crowns

- Cover the crowns with damp, lightweight kitchen towels and proof for 3 hours, until the dough holds the indentation of a fingertip poked into their sides.
- While the crowns are proofing, arrange the oven racks so one is in the top third of the oven and the other is in the bottom third. Preheat the oven to 350°F.
- Whisk the egg with the salt to make an egg wash. Uncover the crowns and brush the wash generously over them; discard the remaining egg wash.
- Place one baking sheet on each oven rack to bake the challah crowns for 30 to 35 minutes, until the tops are a deep caramel color and the crowns sound hollow when you tap their undersides with your finger, rotating the baking sheets from front to back and from one rack to the other halfway through the baking time. Remove the baking sheets from the oven and place them on cooling racks; let the crowns cool on the baking sheets.

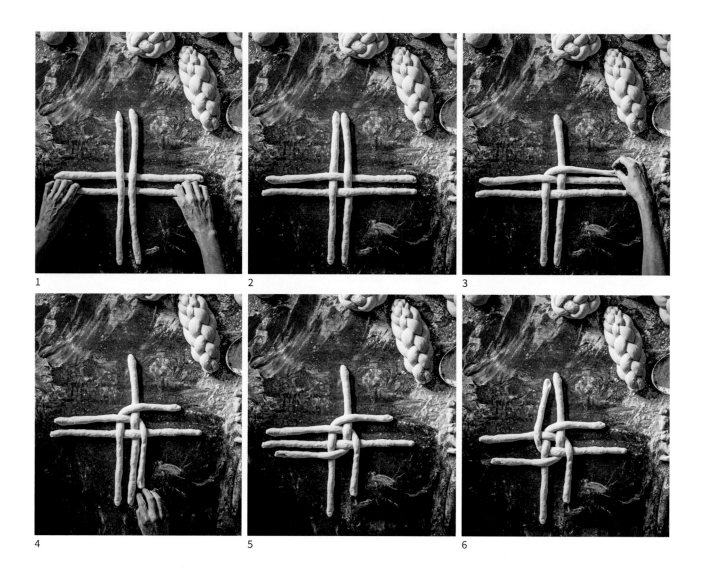

1   2   3

4   5   6

Cherry and Pistachio Panettone

Makes 2 large panettone

Traditional panettone is an Italian Christmas cake filled with dried fruits and nuts and baked in a large cylindrical paper mold. Perfect panettone has a big, domed top, a fine, tender crumb, and a lot of holes in it. It is incredibly involved and tricky to make, but it's a special cake, which is why people love it and want to be able to make it at home. With this recipe, I stayed as close as possible to the traditional way of doing things—it contains the usual mix of dried fruits and nuts, and I add chopped orange and vanilla bean seeds to the dough to make it really flavorful. And I made some adjustments to my professional formula to make it attainable for anybody who wants to take on the challenge.

The principal difference between this panettone and one I would make in a professional kitchen has to do with the yeast. A traditional panettone is leavened only with sourdough starter, where here I use a combination of sourdough starter and commercial yeast. Panettone made exclusively with sourdough starter can take as long as 8 hours to proof, so I add the commercial yeast, which cuts the proofing time in half. Even with the reduced proofing time, this recipe is still a three-day process. Panettone takes time, which is one of the things that makes it special.

Traditional panettone is made with a *biga,* which is an Italian word for stiff sourdough starter. Stiff sourdough starter contains twice as much flour as liquid sourdough starter, so, where a liquid sourdough starter, such as my Sourdough Starter (page xxxiii), is light and airy, stiff sourdough starter is stiff and solid, like clay. In old black-and-white photographs, you see panettone bakers in Italy holding their stiff sourdough starters, like bricks of stiff dough, wrapped in burlap tied closed with a string. Stiff sourdough starter is often more acidic because it contains more acetic acid, which is what gives sourdough bread its sour taste. Liquid sourdough starter, by contrast, has more lactic acid, which is not as vinegary in flavor. In my desire to replicate a traditional panettone, in the first step of this recipe, I convert my liquid sourdough starter to a stiff sourdough starter.

One of the main pitfalls for the home baker is that panettone can completely sink the minute you take it out of the oven. The delicate crumb and hole structure that result from the long proofing time can't hold up the weight of butter in the dough, so it collapses in on itself. To prevent this, you flip it upside down the second you pull it out of the oven. By flipping the panettone upside down, gravity is on your side; then the butter cools and solidifies, at which point the panettone is no longer at risk of collapsing. Italian bakeries use a ladder-like spike contraption called a *spillone* to hold the panettone upside down until they are cooled. I have created a similar system using wooden dowels and skewers.

Refresh (or "feed") your starter the evening before you intend to start this recipe. If you don't already have a starter going, postpone your panettone project for a couple of weeks while you build one. And if you do have a starter, you still need to plan ahead for this: I like to begin this recipe on a Friday, bake on Sunday, and have panettone to enjoy on Sunday evening.

Note You will need two (5¼-inch) paper panettone liners, two (3-foot) wooden dowels and four (12-inch) wooden skewers to make this.

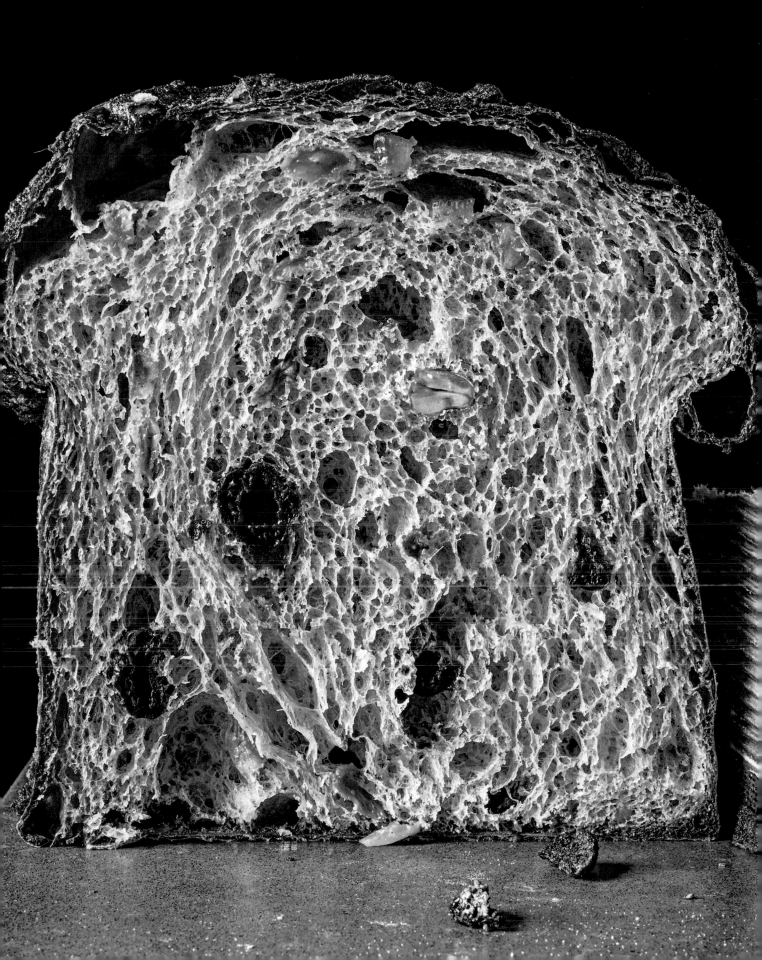

For the stiff starter

Sourdough Starter (page xxxiii)	¾ cup	128 grams
Water (about 95°F)	¼ cup	59 grams
Bread flour	1 cup plus more for dusting	120 grams

For the first dough

Bread flour	3 cups minus 2 tablespoons	342 grams
Water (about 70°F)	¾ cup	176 grams
Large egg yolks	4	68 grams
Mild-flavored honey (such as wildflower or clover)	1 teaspoon	7 grams
Unsalted butter, cubed and softened	6 tablespoons	84 grams
Granulated sugar	¼ cup plus 2 tablespoons	76 grams

For the second dough

Dried cherries	⅔ cup	100 grams
Golden raisins	⅓ cup	50 grams
Vanilla bean	1	
Orange	1	100 grams
Pistachios (preferably Sicilian)	½ cup	65 grams
Candied orange peel, chopped finely	½ cup	80 grams
Mild-flavored honey (such as wildflower or clover)	1 tablespoon	20 grams
Ground cardamom	1 teaspoon	2 grams
Freshly grated nutmeg	1 teaspoon	1 gram
Ground cloves	½ teaspoon	1 gram
Bread flour	½ cup plus 1 tablespoon plus additional for dusting	69 grams
Instant yeast	1 teaspoon	3 grams
Granulated sugar	¼ cup	50 grams
Large egg yolk	1	17 grams
Fine sea salt	1½ teaspoons	9 grams
Unsalted butter, cubed and softened	6 tablespoons	84 grams
Nonstick cooking spray		

For the glaze

Pistachios (preferably Sicilian)	¼ cup	33 grams
Granulated sugar	1½ teaspoons	6.5 grams
Confectioners' sugar	⅓ cup	40 grams
All-purpose flour	1½ teaspoons	5 grams
Fine sea salt	pinch	
Large egg white	2 tablespoons	25 grams
Canola or vegetable oil	1 teaspoon	5 grams
Fresh lemon juice	½ teaspoon	2.5 grams

Panettone Schedule for a Weekend Baking Project

Making panettone takes time, but most of the time is just waiting while the yeast does its work. This schedule will help you to plan it out.

Day One: Friday
This day is about getting ready. Refresh your starter as you normally would in the morning and evening.

8:00 a.m. Feed the starter.
8:00 p.m. Feed the starter.

Day Two: Saturday
Today you will convert your liquid starter (the one you've been maintaining) to a stiff starter. Then you will mix the first dough in the evening. To make the panettone schedule doable, I mix the stiff starter at midday. It's completely okay that the starter you refreshed the evening before is left to sit out until noonish. It will just be hungrier and should activate faster.

Noon Mix the stiff starter.
6:00 p.m. Mix the first dough; let the first dough ferment overnight.

Day Three: Sunday
Today you will make the second dough, ferment it, then shape, proof, and bake the panettone.

7:00 a.m. Mix the second dough.
7:15 a.m.–9:15 a.m. Ferment the dough; while the dough ferments, get everything else ready: the paper liners, skewers, dowels, and glaze.
9:15 a.m.–9:30 a.m. Shape the panettone.
9:30 a.m.–12:30 p.m. to 2:30 p.m. Proof the dough.
2:30 p.m.–3:00 p.m. Bake the panettone.
3:00 p.m. Cool upside down for at least several hours.

mixed in and no butter chunks remain, 5 to 10 minutes, stopping to wipe the dough hook clean once or twice with a wet hand. (The time will depend on the softness of the butter.) Turn off the mixer.

Ferment the dough

- Remove the bowl from the mixer and wipe the dough hook clean with a wet hand. Cover the bowl with a clean kitchen towel or plastic wrap and set it in a warm place to allow the dough to ferment for 2 hours, turning the dough after 1 hour. To turn the dough, uncover the bowl and use a wet hand to fold the top edge down two-thirds and fold the bottom edge to meet the top edge, so the dough is folded like a letter. Fold the sides inward in the same way to form a sort of ball, then re-cover the bowl.
- Line a baking sheet with parchment paper and generously spray with nonstick cooking spray.
- Lightly dust a large flat work surface with flour. Uncover the bowl and transfer the dough to the floured work surface. If you are making babka with the dough, use your hands or a bench knife to divide it in half. (Each half will be approximately 500 grams.) If you are making New York Cheese Danishes or the blueberry blackberry cheese Danish braid, leave the dough in one piece.

Even when it seems like I don't have room in my refrigerator to place a baking sheet, I move things around and often balance the baking sheet on top of things to make room in whatever way I can.

- Place the dough on the prepared baking sheet and use your hands to gently coax and pat the mound or mounds of dough into even squares. Put the baking sheet in the refrigerator to chill the dough for at least 2 hours, until it feels firm. (If you are making the dough in advance, remove the baking sheet from the refrigerator after 2 hours, wrap the baking sheet in plastic wrap so the dough doesn't dry out and develop a skin, and return it to the refrigerator for up to 2 days.)

Wrapping dough in plastic after it is chilled prevents it from sticking to the plastic wrap.

Cinnamon Babka with Brown Butter Cinnamon Glaze

Makes 2 babkas

Whenever I think of cinnamon babka, I remember the *Seinfeld* episode where Elaine and Jerry stop at a bakery to buy babka for a party. The customer in front of them takes the last chocolate babka. Elaine and Jerry go on about how cinnamon is the "lesser babka" of the two, and they are embarrassed at the thought of showing up at the party with the cinnamon babka. That might be the popular opinion, but, in fact, I actually prefer cinnamon babka to chocolate. I add almond paste to the brown sugar–cinnamon filling, which makes it really moist. After it comes out of the oven, I glaze my cinnamon babka with a cinnamon glaze, which adds another layer of cinnamon flavor to the babka, and also makes it seem more moist.

Note You will need two 9- x 4-inch Pullman loaf pans (or two 9- x 4-inch standard loaf pans) to make this.

For the dough

All-purpose flour	for dusting	
Master Recipe for Babka Dough (page 92)		

For the filling

Almond paste	⅓ cup	80 grams
Light brown sugar	1 cup (lightly packed)	200 grams
Ground cinnamon	¼ cup	30 grams
Fine sea salt	1 teaspoon	6 grams
Unsalted butter, cubed and softened	14 tablespoons (1 stick plus 6 tablespoons)	197 grams
Mild-flavored honey (such as wildflower or clover)	1 tablespoon plus 2 teaspoons	33 grams
Nonstick cooking spray		

For baking the babka

Large egg	1	50 grams
Fine sea salt	big pinch	

Brown Butter Cinnamon Glaze (recipe follows)

Roll out the babka dough

- Line a baking sheet with parchment paper. Dust the parchment lightly with flour and set the baking sheet aside.
- Dust a large flat work surface lightly with flour. Unwrap and remove one square of dough from the refrigerator and place it on the floured surface, working as quickly as possible so the dough does not warm up and become sticky. Dust the top of the dough and a rolling pin with flour. Working from

the center outward, roll the dough into a 16-inch square, rotating the dough and dusting the work surface, dough, and rolling pin with flour as needed to prevent the dough from sticking. If the dough does become too sticky while being rolled out, return it to the refrigerator to chill before continuing to roll it out.

- Place the sheet of dough on the prepared baking sheet, folding the edges that are hanging off the baking sheet over the sheet of dough, as if you were folding a shirt. Place the baking sheet in the refrigerator while you roll the second square of dough.

- Dust the work surface with flour and remove the second square of dough from the refrigerator. Place it on the floured surface, and roll it into a 16-inch square as you rolled the first one. Remove the baking sheet with the dough from the refrigerator. Place a sheet of parchment paper on top of the refrigerated dough, dust the paper lightly with flour, and place the second sheet of dough on the paper, folding in the edges that are hanging off the baking sheet. Return the baking sheet to the refrigerator for about 30 minutes, until the dough firms up slightly.

Make the filling
- Combine the almond paste, brown sugar, cinnamon, and salt in the bowl of a stand mixer. Fit the mixer with the paddle attachment and mix on medium speed to break up the almond paste. Add the butter and mix on low speed until the butter is mixed with the paste. Turn off the mixer, scrape down the sides of the bowl with a rubber spatula, and add the honey. Mix on low speed until the honey is just combined.

- If you are making the babka the same day, transfer the filling to a small bowl and set it aside at room temperature until you're ready to use it. If you are making the filling to assemble the babka another day, refrigerate it, covered, for up to 2 days. If you refrigerated the filling, you will need to warm it up to 75°F to 80°F in a small saucepan over low heat, or in a microwave. Divide the filling in half and use half for each babka.

Prepare to fill and shape the babkas
- Spray two 9- x 4-inch Pullman loaf pans or two standard loaf pans with nonstick cooking spray.
- Make sure the filling is an easily spreadable consistency.

Fill and shape the babkas
- Remove the dough from the refrigerator. Lift up the parchment paper holding the top square of dough and lay it on a flat work surface. Return the baking sheet with the remaining sheet of dough to the refrigerator.
- Use an offset spatula to spread two-thirds of one portion of the filling evenly over the surface of the dough, taking care to spread the filling to the edges. Gently roll the dough away from you to form a fat roll. Pick the babka roll up with two hands and give it a gentle pull on both ends to elongate it slightly. Set

the roll down and cut it in half through the middle so you have 2 rolls, each approximately 10 inches long.

- Spread the remaining portion of filling across the top of one of the 2 halves and place the second half on top of the filling to form an X with the 2 rolls of dough. Twist the ends of the bottom roll up and over the top roll to cover the filling. Pick up the babka with two hands and place it into a prepared loaf pan.
- Repeat, removing the second sheet of dough from the refrigerator and assembling the second babka using the remaining filling.

Adding a layer of filling between the rolled babka dough helps keep the layers separate when the babka bakes, resulting in a more layered babka.

Proof and bake the babkas

- Cover each babka with a clean kitchen towel or plastic wrap and set it in a warm place to proof for 2 to 3 hours, until the loaves have doubled in size.
- Arrange the oven racks so one is in the center position. Preheat the oven to 350°F.
- Whisk the egg with the salt in a small bowl to make an egg wash. Uncover the babka loaves and brush the wash generously over their surfaces; discard the remaining egg wash.
- Place the babka loaves on the center rack of the oven to bake for 45 to 50 minutes, until they are deep golden brown, rotating the pans from front to back halfway through the baking time. Remove the babkas from the oven and set aside to cool for 5 to 10 minutes, until they are cool enough to touch. Place a clean kitchen towel on the counter and flip the babkas upside down to release them from the pans. Place them, right side up, on a cooling rack to cool slightly.

Make the glaze and glaze the babkas

- While the babkas are baking, make the Brown Butter Cinnamon Glaze (see next page).
- Spoon the warm glaze over the top of the warm babka loaves. Wait for the glaze to set before slicing the babka, about 20 minutes.

Babka filling needs to be very soft so it spreads easily on the dough. My kitchen tends to be on the cool side, so I usually microwave the filling for a few seconds and then stir and microwave again if needed.

Brown Butter Cinnamon Glaze

Topping babka with a glaze rather than the more traditional crumb topping makes it more moist, and also allows me to bring in another layer of flavor—in this case, the nutty flavor of brown butter and an extra hit of cinnamon.

Unsalted butter	4 tablespoons (½ stick)	56 grams
Confectioners' sugar	1 cup	120 grams
Fine sea salt	pinch	1 gram
Whole milk	2 tablespoons	30 grams

• Heat the butter without stirring in a medium saucepan over medium-high heat for 3 to 5 minutes, until the bubbles subside and the butter is dark brown with a toasty smell, swirling the pan occasionally so the butter browns evenly. Turn off the heat and set the butter aside to cool to room temperature.

• While the butter is cooling, whisk the confectioners' sugar and salt in a medium bowl. Whisk the milk into the bowl with the dry ingredients, making sure to whisk out any lumps. Add the butter and whisk until the glaze is smooth.

Variation
Golden Raisin Walnut Babka

Makes 2 babkas

When I set out to perfect babka for Sadelle's, I wanted to stick with classic fillings, raisin and walnut being one of them. I already had a raisin puree in my repertoire as a pastry chef, and after a few tries at raisin walnut babka, I got the idea to use the puree for the filling rather than scattering raisins over the dough, which is the way the babka is typically prepared. The puree, which contains brown sugar and cinnamon, was a delicious addition, and it turned out to have the added benefit of making the babka more moist.

When you're spreading the filling over the babka dough, it may seem scant and as if it is not enough, but trust me: the amount is correct. The filling is heavy, so if you put more filling than this on the dough, you will weigh down the babka, and it won't rise as it should, and the resulting babka will be dense and leaden.

Note You will need two 9- x 4-inch Pullman loaf pans (or two 9- x 4-inch standard loaf pans) to make this.

For the dough		
Master Recipe for Babka Dough (page 92)		
For the filling		
Walnuts	1½ cups	158 grams
Golden raisins	2 cups	300 grams
Light brown sugar	½ cup (lightly packed)	100 grams
Ground cinnamon	2 teaspoons	4 grams
Fine sea salt	1 teaspoon	6 grams
Unsalted butter, softened	4 tablespoons (½ stick)	56 grams
For baking the babka		
Large egg	1	50 grams
Fine sea salt	big pinch	
For the glaze		
Brown Butter Cinnamon Glaze (page 97)	1 recipe	

Make the filling

- Arrange the oven racks so one is in the center position. Preheat the oven to 300°F.
- Spread the walnuts on a baking sheet and toast them for about 20 minutes, until they are golden brown and fragrant. Remove them from the oven and set aside to cool to room temperature. Finely chop the walnuts to about the size of peas.
- Place the raisins in a small bowl, cover with hot tap water, and set aside to soak for 10 minutes. Drain the raisins in a fine-mesh strainer and let them sit in the strainer to continue to drain until you're ready to use them.

· Put the raisins, brown sugar, cinnamon, salt, and butter in the bowl of a food processor fitted with a metal blade and process to form a smooth puree, about 1 minute. If you will be assembling the babka another day, refrigerate the filling, covered, for up to 2 days. Warm the filling in a microwave or a saucepan over medium-low heat, stirring often, before using it. Divide the filling in half to use half for each babka.

Fill, shape, proof, and bake the babkas

· Refer to the instructions for filling and shaping the babka loaves in Cinnamon Babka with Brown Butter Cinnamon Glaze (page 97). Sprinkle half of the chopped walnuts over the filling for each babka, and proof and bake the loaves as directed.

Make the glaze and glaze the babkas

· While the babkas are baking, make the brown butter cinnamon glaze. Remove the babka loaves from the oven and set aside to cool for 5 to 10 minutes, until they are cool enough to touch. Place a clean kitchen towel on the counter and flip the babkas upside down to release them from the pans. Place them right side up on a cooling rack to cool slightly. Spoon the warm glaze over the tops of the babkas while they are still warm. Wait for the glaze to set before slicing, about 20 minutes.

Variation
Chocolate Babka

Makes 2 babkas

As pleased as I was when a slice of this babka ended up on the cover of *Food & Wine* magazine, for me, the real testament to my babka came when I brought a loaf with me when I went to eat at Zahav, an Israeli restaurant in Philadelphia. I brought the babka as a gift for the chef/owner, Michael Solomonov. I was a little nervous because Michael is an expert on Jewish food, but he loved it, and his staff loved it. And he confirmed that it was a traditional Ashkenazi babka. I top mine with a glaze rather than the traditional crumb topping, but otherwise, this is a classic.

Note You will need two 9- x 4-inch Pullman loaf pans (or two 9- x 4-inch standard loaf pans) to make this.

For the dough		
Master Recipe for Babka Dough (page 92)		
For the filling		
Chocolate Shortbread (page 404; or store-bought chocolate cookies)	7 to 8	140 grams
Milk chocolate	6 ounces (1 cup chips)	170 grams
Bittersweet chocolate	2.5 ounces (½ scant cup chips)	71 grams
Unsalted butter, cubed	9 tablespoons (1 stick plus 1 tablespoon)	127 grams
Mild-flavored honey (such as wildflower or clover)	⅓ cup	105 grams
For baking the babka		
Large egg	1	50 grams
Fine sea salt	big pinch	
For the glaze		
Milk chocolate	4 ounces (⅔ cup chips)	113 grams
Bittersweet chocolate	4 ounces (⅔ cup chips)	113 grams
Unsalted butter, cubed	8 tablespoons (1 stick)	113 grams
Mild-flavored honey (such as wildflower or clover)	1 tablespoon	20 grams

Make the filling

• Put the cookies in a food processor fitted with a metal blade and process them to crumbs.

• Pour 1 to 2 inches of water into the bottom of a small saucepan and choose a bowl that fits over the saucepan to make a double boiler. Make sure the water is not touching the bottom of the bowl; if it is, pour some water out. Bring the water to a boil over high heat, then reduce the heat to medium-low to maintain a gentle simmer.

- If the chocolate for the filling or the glaze is in a chunk or bar, roughly chop it.
- Add the milk chocolate, bittersweet chocolate, and butter to the bowl of the double boiler and heat them until they melt, stirring occasionally with a heat-proof rubber spatula and scraping down any chocolate that collects on the sides of the bowl to make sure it melts evenly and doesn't burn. Turn off the heat.
- Remove the bowl from the double boiler and wipe the bottom of the bowl to make sure no water drips. Add the cookie crumbs and honey, and stir to combine. Set the filling aside to cool slightly; you want it to be warm enough to be still spreadable. If you are making the filling in advance of the babka, allow it to cool to room temperature. If you are making the filling to assemble the babka another day, refrigerate it, covered, for up to 2 days. Warm it up in a microwave or a saucepan over medium-low heat, stirring often, before using. Divide the filling in half to use half for each babka.

Fill, shape, proof, and bake the babkas

- Refer to the instructions for filling, shaping, proofing, and baking the babkas in Cinnamon Babka with Brown Butter Cinnamon Glaze (page 97).

Make the glaze and glaze the babkas

- While the babkas are baking, pour 1 to 2 inches of water in the bottom of a small saucepan and choose a bowl that fits over the saucepan to make a double boiler. Make sure the water is not touching the bottom of the bowl; if it is, pour some water out. Bring the water to a boil over high heat, then reduce the heat to medium-low to maintain a gentle simmer.
- If the chocolate is in a chunk or bar, roughly chop it. Place the milk chocolate and bittersweet chocolate in the bowl of the double boiler. Add the butter and honey and warm them until they melt, using a heat-proof rubber spatula to stir and scrape down the sides of the bowl so the chocolate doesn't burn. Remove the bowl from the double boiler and set it aside to cool the glaze slightly
- Remove the babka loaves from the oven and set them aside to cool for 5 to 10 minutes, until they are cool enough to touch, Place a clean kitchen towel on the counter and flip the babkas upside down to release them from the pans. Place them right side up on a cooling rack to cool slightly. Spoon the warm glaze over the top of the babkas while they are still warm. Wait for the glaze to set before slicing the babka, about 20 minutes.

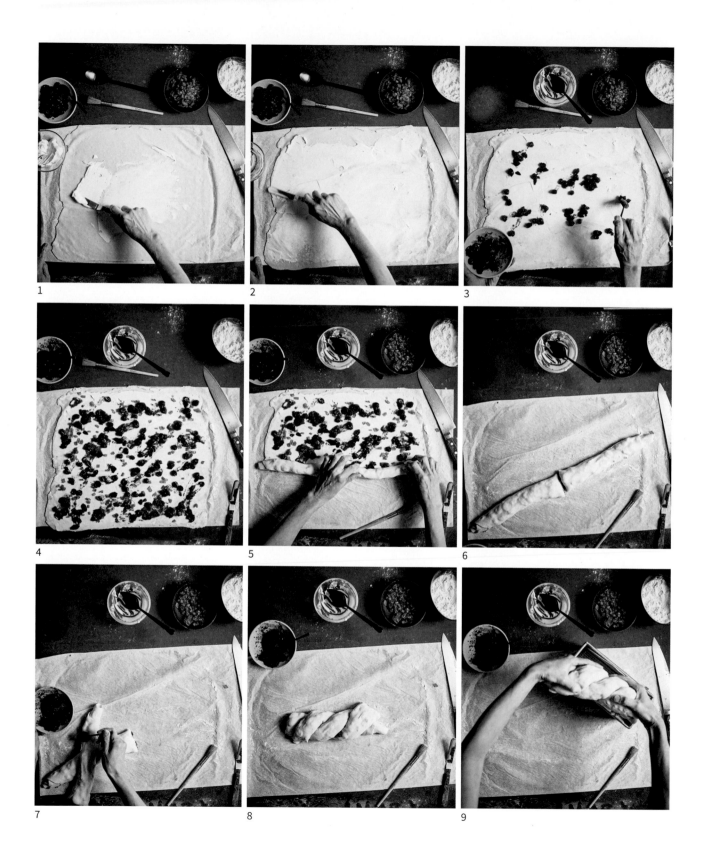

1

2

3

4

5

6

7

8

9

Variation
Cranberry Cream Cheese Babka

Makes 2 babkas

This is my version of a holiday babka. At Per Se, I made babka with cranberry-orange filling starting around Thanksgiving time and extending through Hanukkah and Christmas. At some point during my intense babka research period, I merged that filling with a traditional cheese babka, which has always reminded me of a cheese Danish, which I love. I especially like the way the acidity of the fruit in this babka contrasts with the sweet cheese filling. The cheese melts into the dough, so the babka is really rich and decadent. It's a sort of ne plus ultra holiday babka.

Note You will need two 9- x 4-inch Pullman loaf pans (or two 9- x 4-inch standard loaf pans) to make this.

For the dough		
Master Recipe for Babka Dough (page 92)		
For the cranberry compote		
Cranberries, fresh or frozen	16 ounces	454 grams
Light brown sugar	1½ cups (lightly packed)	300 grams
Fresh orange juice	½ cup	123 grams
Cinnamon sticks	2	
Black peppercorns	8	
Whole allspice berries	6	
Whole cloves	3	
Red pepper flakes	¼ teaspoon	
Candied orange peel, chopped	¼ cup plus 2 tablespoons	80 grams
For the cheese filling		
Whole milk ricotta	½ cup	110 grams
Cream cheese, cubed and softened	4 ounces	113 grams
Granulated sugar	2 tablespoons	26 grams
Arrowroot	2 tablespoons	16 grams
Fine sea salt	pinch	
For the baking the babka		
Large egg	1	50 grams
Fine sea salt	big pinch	
For the glaze		
Brown Butter Cinnamon Glaze (page 97)		

Make the cranberry compote

- Combine the cranberries, brown sugar, and orange juice in a medium saucepan. Place the cinnamon sticks, peppercorns, allspice berries, cloves, and red pepper flakes in a small piece of cheesecloth and tie closed with butcher's twine to make a spice bundle. Place the bundle in the saucepan and bring the mixture to a boil over medium-high heat. Reduce the heat to medium-low to maintain a steady simmer and simmer for 20 to 25 minutes, until the sauce has thickened, stirring frequently to prevent the ingredients from sticking to the pan. (You need to be especially careful about stirring near the end of the cooking time when much of the liquid has evaporated.) Remove the compote from the heat and set it aside to cool to room temperature. Transfer to a container with a lid, cover, and refrigerate for at least 1 hour, and preferably overnight. Just before using, stir in the candied orange peel and divide in half for each babka.

Make the cheese filling

▪ Place the ricotta, cream cheese, granulated sugar, arrowroot, and salt in the bowl of a food processor fitted with a metal blade and process until smooth, scraping down the sides of the bowl as needed. Transfer the filling to a container with a lid, cover, and chill for at least 1 hour, and up to overnight. Divide the filling in half to use half for each babka.

Make the cranberry cheese babka

▪ Refer to the recipe for Cinnamon Babka with Brown Butter Cinnamon Glaze (page 97). Instead of cinnamon filling, spread the babka with the cheese filling, then spoon the cranberry compote over the cheese filling. Where the recipe calls for you to spread the remaining filling across the top of one of the 2 halves, use the compote. Glaze the babka with the brown butter cinnamon glaze.

Cardamom Cinnamon Rolls with Buttermilk Glaze

These are a classic cinnamon roll made with a buttery, brioche dough that can be completed from start to finish in one day. They're old-school, pull-apart style, baked together in a cake pan and topped with a white glaze. The dough contains whole-wheat flour, but don't be fooled; these are not "healthy" cinnamon buns. I simply like the layer of flavor that the whole wheat adds to the cinnamon rolls.

Note You will need a 9-inch springform pan to make these.

Makes 8 cinnamon rolls

For the dough

All-purpose flour	2 cups plus more for dusting	240 grams
Whole-wheat pastry flour	1½ cups	158 grams
Granulated sugar	½ cup plus 1 tablespoon	63 grams
Instant yeast	2 teaspoons	6 grams
Ground cardamom	1½ teaspoons	4 grams
Fine sea salt	2 teaspoons	12 grams
Large eggs	4	200 grams
Whole milk	⅓ cup	80 grams
Unsalted butter, cubed and very soft	16 tablespoons (2 sticks)	227 grams
Nonstick cooking spray		

For the filling

Dark brown sugar	1 cup (lightly packed)	200 grams
Unsalted butter, cubed and very soft	8 tablespoons (1 stick)	113 grams
Ground cinnamon	2 teaspoons	4 grams
Fine sea salt	pinch	

For the glaze

Confectioners' sugar	3⅓ cups	400 grams
Buttermilk, well shaken	½ cup	125 grams
Fine sea salt	⅛ teaspoon	

Make the dough

- Place the all-purpose flour, whole-wheat pastry flour, granulated sugar, yeast, cardamom, and salt in a large bowl and stir to combine.
- Place the eggs and milk in the bowl of a stand mixer and add the dry ingredients. Fit the mixer with the dough hook and mix on low speed for about 3 minutes to combine. Increase the speed to medium and mix for 5 minutes to develop the gluten. Reduce the speed to low, add the butter, and mix until the butter is incorporated into the dough (this will take 5 to 10 minutes, depending on how soft the butter is), stopping to scrape down the dough hook with a wet hand and the sides of the bowl once or twice with a rubber spatula during that time. Remove the bowl from the mixer and use

a wet hand to scrape the dough off the hook. Place a clean kitchen towel over the bowl and set the bowl aside to ferment for 2 hours, turning the dough halfway through the fermentation. To turn the dough, uncover the bowl and use a wet hand to fold the top edge down two-thirds and fold the bottom edge to meet the top edge, so the dough is folded like a letter. Fold the sides inward in the same way to form a sort of ball, then re-cover the bowl.

▪ Line a baking sheet with parchment paper and spray the parchment with nonstick cooking spray.

▪ Use a plastic bowl scraper to scoop the dough out of the bowl onto the prepared baking sheet. Gently pat and form the dough into a roughly 8-inch square. Refrigerate the dough for at least 2 hours, and as long as overnight. (If you are leaving the dough overnight, after 2 hours, wrap the baking sheet in plastic wrap to prevent a skin from forming on the dough and return the baking sheet to the refrigerator.)

Prepare the filling

▪ Just before rolling out the dough, combine the brown sugar, butter, cinnamon, and salt in the bowl of a stand mixer. Fit the mixer with the paddle attachment and mix on low speed to combine the ingredients. Set the filling aside at room temperature while you roll out the dough so it stays soft and spreadable.

Roll out the dough and form the rolls

▪ Spray the bottom and sides of a 9-inch springform pan with nonstick cooking spray.

▪ Lightly flour a large flat work surface. Remove the dough from the refrigerator, unwrap it if it is wrapped, and peel it from the parchment paper using a plastic scraper. Place the dough on the floured surface. Lightly dust your rolling pin and the dough with flour and, starting in the center of the dough and working outward, roll the dough out to a 12- x 16-inch rectangle with the long edge parallel to you. (For more detailed instruction, see Rolling Dough 101, page 250.) Lift the dough and dust underneath lightly with flour. Use a small offset spatula to spread the filling evenly over the surface of the dough, leaving a ½-inch border with no filling at the top edge of the dough. Gently roll the dough away from you to form a log.

▪ With the seam facedown on the countertop, trim the sides of the log with a serrated knife and cut the log into 8 equal-size spiral rounds; each will be about 2 inches wide. Put one segment, cut side up, in the center of the prepared pan and arrange the remaining segments in a circle around the center segment.

▪ If you are baking the cinnamon rolls the same day, cover the rolls with plastic wrap or a damp, lightweight kitchen towel and set them aside to proof for 2 hours, until the dough looks swollen. (If you plan to bake the rolls the following morning, spray a sheet of plastic wrap with nonstick cooking spray and place it, sprayed side down, to cover the pan. Set the rolls aside to proof for 1½ hours. Refrigerate the cinnamon rolls overnight.)

Bake the cinnamon rolls

· Arrange the oven racks so one is in the center position. Preheat the oven to 350°F.

· If the rolls are in the refrigerator, remove the rolls from the refrigerator. In either case, uncover them.

· Place the pan of cinnamon rolls on the center rack of the oven to bake for 45 to 50 minutes for freshly proofed rolls (50 to 55 minutes if the rolls were refrigerated), until the tops of the cinnamon rolls are deep golden brown, rotating the pan from front to back halfway through baking. Remove the pan from the oven and place it on a cooling rack. Carefully remove the side of the springform pan. Allow the buns to cool slightly while you prepare the glaze.

Prepare the glaze

· Whisk the confectioners' sugar, buttermilk, and salt together in a medium bowl. Spoon the glaze over the top of each bun. Serve warm or at room temperature.

Hot Cross Buns

Makes 15 buns

Hot cross buns, spiced sweet rolls filled with currants or raisins, are traditionally served to mark the end of Lent, on Good Friday, and also on Easter. They have a cross on top that is made of flour and baked into the buns. I pipe the crosses on at the end using a confectioners' sugar icing, which makes them a little sweeter and I think makes them look nicer. My spice blend, which has a nice kick from the addition of white pepper, was inspired by that used in Elizabeth David's book *English Bread and Yeast Cookery*.

Note You will need a quarter baking sheet (13 x 9½ inches) and a large disposable pastry bag to make this.

For the buns

Dried currants	2 cups	255 grams
All-purpose flour	4¼ cups plus more for dusting	510 grams
Dark brown sugar	½ cup (lightly packed)	100 grams
Instant yeast	1 tablespoon plus 2 teaspoons	15 grams
Fine sea salt	2½ teaspoons	15 grams
Ground white pepper	1 teaspoon	2 grams
Ground cinnamon	1 teaspoon	2 grams
Ground ginger	1 teaspoon	2 grams
Freshly grated nutmeg	¼ teaspoon	<1 gram
Ground cloves	¼ teaspoon	½ gram
Whole milk	¾ cup	180 grams
Large eggs	2	100 grams
Crème fraîche	¼ cup	55 grams
Orange	1	
Unsalted butter, cubed and softened	8 tablespoons (1 stick)	113 grams
Nonstick cooking spray		

For baking the buns

Large egg	1	
Fine sea salt	pinch	

For the icing

Confectioners' sugar	1⅔ cups	200 grams
Whole milk	2 tablespoons	30 grams

Soak the currants

· Put the currants in a small bowl. Cover with hot tap water and set aside to soak for about 10 minutes. Drain the currants in a fine-mesh strainer and let them sit in the strainer to drain any remaining water while you mix the dough.

Make and ferment the dough

- Put the flour, brown sugar, yeast, salt, white pepper, cinnamon, ginger, nutmeg, and cloves in a medium bowl and stir with a whisk to combine.
- Pour the milk into the bowl of a stand mixer. Add the eggs and crème fraîche. Use a fine Microplane to grate the orange zest over a bowl, grating only the outermost, bright-colored layer. Add the dry ingredients. Fit the mixer with the dough hook and mix on low speed for 2 minutes. Increase the speed to medium and mix for 3 minutes. Add the butter, reduce the speed to low, and mix until the butter is incorporated, about 5 minutes, stopping to scrape down the sides of the bowl with a rubber spatula and clean the hook once or twice with a wet hand. Add the currants and mix on low speed for about 5 minutes, until they are evenly distributed throughout the dough. Turn off the mixer and remove the bowl from the stand. Remove the dough hook and wipe it clean with a wet hand. Cover the bowl with a clean kitchen towel or plastic wrap. Place the bowl in a warm place to ferment the dough for 2 hours, turning the dough once halfway through the fermentation. To turn the dough, use a wet hand to fold the top edge down two-thirds and fold the bottom edge to meet the top edge, so the dough is folded like a letter. Fold the sides inward in the same way to form a sort of ball, then re-cover the bowl.

Divide the dough and form the buns

- While the dough is fermenting, spray the perimeters of a quarter baking sheet with nonstick cooking spray. Line the bottom of the baking sheet with parchment and spray the top of the parchment with the nonstick cooking spray.
- Lightly dust your work surface with flour. Using a plastic bowl scraper, scrape the dough out of the bowl onto the floured surface. Use a bench knife to divide the dough into 15 (85-gram) pieces.
- Working with one piece of dough at a time, place the dough on the floured surface and roll it under the palm of your hand in a circular motion, pushing against the counter gently to create a ball. (This dough is not terribly sticky, so you shouldn't need much if any flour on the counter or your hands to shape the balls. If you use too much flour on your work surface the dough will slip and slide instead of rounding. If this happens, scrape the extra flour away with a bench knife and continue.)
- Place the ball in one corner of the prepared baking sheet. Continue rolling the remaining pieces of dough in the same way, lining the balls up 3 across and 5 down on the baking sheet. Cover the baking sheet with a clean kitchen towel or lightly spray a piece of plastic wrap with nonstick cooking spray and lay it, sprayed side facing down, on the dough. Set it in a warm place to proof the dough for about 2 hours, until the balls have approximately doubled in size and are touching each other.

Bake the buns

- While the buns are proofing, arrange the oven racks so one is in the center position. Preheat the oven to 350°F.
- Whisk the egg and salt in a small bowl to make an egg wash. Brush the tops and sides of the buns with the egg wash; discard the remaining egg wash.
- Put the baking sheet on the center rack of the oven to bake the buns for 30 to 35 minutes, until the buns are nicely browned and sound hollow when tapped on the top, rotating the baking sheet from front to back halfway through the baking time. Remove the baking sheet from the oven, giving the pan a little jerk to help slide the buns off the baking sheet onto the cooling rack in one piece. (If the buns are sticking to the sides of the pan, loosen them with a paring knife before sliding them off the baking sheet.) Let the buns cool to room temperature before icing them.

Make the icing and ice the buns

- While the buns are cooling, put the confectioners' sugar and milk in a small bowl and stir with a fork or whisk until the icing is smooth. Transfer the icing to a disposable pastry bag and make a cut about 3/16 inch wide at the tip.
- Pipe the icing in a line down the center of each row of buns. Pipe another line down the center of each column of buns, perpendicular to the first lines, to create a cross on each bun.

Rum and Raisin Stollen

Makes 3 stollen

Stollen is a sweet, spiced, fruit- and nut-filled holiday bread from Dresden in Germany. It is baked in an oval shape, with a log of marzipan nestled in the center, which is supposed to represent the baby Jesus in swaddling clothes. This recipe makes three stollen, but they are fairly small. I can eat a whole loaf in one sitting. I love to serve and eat it with a cup of coffee on Christmas Day.

This recipe starts with a sponge, which is a preferment, or dough that is fermented prior to being added to the main dough. The point of any fermentation, in addition to adding flavor, is to boost fermentation. (For more on this, see the Yeast Tutorial, page xxx.) The boost is necessary with this dough because it is very heavy with butter, rum, and dried fruits and nuts, all of which impede fermentation.

For the nuts and raisins		
Whole almonds	heaping ½ cup	85 grams
Golden raisins	1½ cups	225 grams
For the sponge		
Whole milk	⅓ cup plus 1 tablespoon	95 grams
Instant yeast	3 teaspoons	9 grams
All-purpose flour	2 cups plus more for dusting	240 grams
For the dough		
Unsalted butter, cubed and softened	12 tablespoons (1½ sticks)	169 grams
Granulated sugar	2 tablespoons	26 grams
Almond paste	¾ cup plus 1 tablespoon	198 grams
Fine sea salt	1 teaspoon	6 grams
Ground cinnamon	1 teaspoon	2 grams
Freshly grated nutmeg	1 teaspoon	1 gram
Ground cloves	½ teaspoon	1 gram
Dark rum	¼ cup	59 grams
Candied lemon peel, chopped	½ cup	80 grams
For finishing the stollen		
Unsalted butter, melted and cooled slightly	4 tablespoons (½ stick)	57 grams
Granulated sugar	1 tablespoon	13 grams
Confectioners' sugar	½ cup	60 grams

Get prepared

- Arrange the oven racks so one is in the center position. Preheat the oven to 300°F.
- Spread the almonds on a baking sheet and toast until they are golden brown and fragrant, about 20 minutes, shaking the pan at least once while the nuts

are toasting. Remove the pan from the oven and set aside for the almonds to cool slightly.

· Place the raisins in a small bowl, cover with hot tap water, and set aside to soak for about 10 minutes. Drain the raisins in a fine-mesh strainer and let them sit in the strainer to drain any remaining water while you make the dough.

Make the sponge

· Place the milk in a small saucepan and heat over low heat for about 30 seconds, until it is warm to the touch. (The milk should be between room temperature and body temperature.)

· Pour the milk into the bowl of a stand mixer and sprinkle the yeast over it. Whisk to dissolve the yeast. Add ¼ cup of the flour and stir with a rubber spatula to form a wet batter. Sprinkle the remaining 1¾ cups flour over the batter and place the bowl in a warm place to let the sponge rest, uncovered, for 30 minutes, until there are visible cracks on the surface; cracks are signs that the sponge is growing or fermenting.

Make the dough

· Add the butter, granulated sugar, 2 tablespoons (36 grams) of the almond paste, salt, cinnamon, nutmeg, and cloves to the bowl with the sponge. Fit the mixer with the dough hook and mix on low speed for 2 minutes. Turn off the mixer and use a rubber spatula to scrape the dough from the sides to the center of the bowl. Mix the dough on medium speed for 3 minutes, stopping once or twice to scrape the dough in toward the center, to ensure it is being kneaded evenly. Turn off the mixer and let the dough rest on the stand for 30 minutes, leaving the dough hook in place. (Like the sponge, this rest is another way to boost the fermentation of the dough.)

· Add the rum, raisins, and almonds and mix on low speed for 1 to 2 minutes, until the additions are dispersed throughout the dough. Turn off the mixer and remove the bowl from the stand. Remove the dough hook and wipe it clean with a wet hand. Cover the bowl with plastic wrap and put the dough in a warm place to ferment for 30 minutes.

Shape the stollen

· Line a baking sheet with parchment paper and dust it lightly with flour.

· Divide the remaining almond paste into 3 equal pieces (54 grams or 3 tablespoons each). Roll each piece of almond paste into a 6-inch log and set aside.

· Lightly dust a large flat work surface with flour. Place the dough on the floured surface and use a bench knife to divide it into 3 equal pieces (about 330 grams). Pat each piece gently into a 6- x 4-inch oval that is ¾ inch thick. Lay one almond paste log down the center of each oval and push the logs gently to nestle them into the dough. Fold the top edge of dough over the log to come about 1 inch from the bottom edge of the dough. Pinch the edges of the dough to seal them together and encase the almond logs. Flip the stollen over onto the prepared baking sheet, leaving an equal amount of space between each. Cover the baking sheet with a damp, lightweight kitchen towel and put the stollen in a warm place to proof for about 1½ hours, until they are slightly swollen. (This dough is so dense that it won't grow much.)

Prepare to bake the stollen

- Place the baking sheet with the stollen in the refrigerator for 30 minutes; this helps the stollen hold their shape, and makes it easier to flip them over before baking them.
- Arrange the oven racks so one is in the center position. Preheat the oven to 350°F.
- Line a baking sheet with parchment paper.

Bake and finish the stollen

- Remove the stollen from the refrigerator. Flip them right side up and line them up in a row parallel with the short side of the baking sheet, leaving an even amount of space between each stollen.
- Place the baking sheet with the stollen on the center rack of the oven to bake for about 40 minutes, rotating the pan from front to back halfway through the baking time. Remove the baking sheet from the oven and put it on a cooling rack.
- Immediately after the stollen come out of the oven, brush them with the melted butter, sprinkle with the granulated sugar, and allow them to cool completely. (If you are making the stollen to serve later, wrap each one tightly in plastic wrap until you're ready to serve them or for up to 1 week.) Before serving, put the confectioners' sugar in a fine-mesh strainer and dust the stollen generously with the sugar.

Laminated Pastries

I fell in love with Viennoiserie, or laminated pastries, when I studied in France in college. During that year, when I lived in Tours, at least once a day and usually more than that, I stopped into a bakery to buy a *pain aux raisins, pain au chocolat,* or a simple *croissant au beurre.* I loved the bakeries themselves, how beautiful and charming they were. And I was enthralled with the look and flavor of these delicate pastries.

Laminated pastries are those made with laminated dough: a block of dough composed of many layers of dough and butter. The process of laminating dough consists of *encasing* a solid block of butter, called a *beurrage,* in a sheet of dough. The dough with the butter locked inside is then rolled out and folded, rolled out again and folded again, and again, creating a distinct layering of dough and butter. When laminated dough is baked, the heat causes the water in the butter to evaporate, resulting in light, layered, flaky, and delicately crisp pastries.

After my year abroad, when I came home and started baking more seriously, I would ask: How on earth did they make those things? It was the most daunting task I could have imagined doing in the kitchen. I'm not sure if at the time I would have truly believed I could replicate such beautiful pastries myself. The fact that I was able to learn—and to learn to teach others how to do it—is one of my greatest accomplishments. I couldn't be happier or prouder to be able to share these recipes, and all the tricks I've learned along the way, in this chapter.

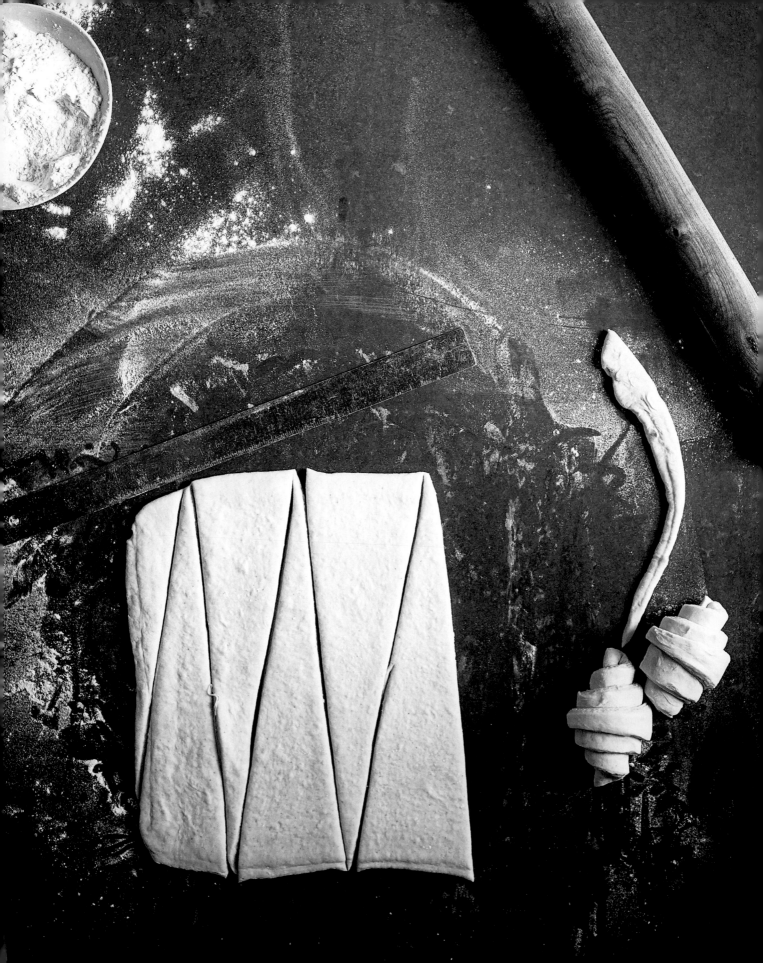

Master Class
A Step-by-Step Tutorial to Laminated Pastry Perfection

Successful lamination is all about evenness: creating and maintaining perfectly even layers of butter and dough that are consistent all the way across the dough. The steps that we take during the lamination process are all working toward this goal.

The two most familiar types of laminated dough are croissant dough and puff pastry, both of which you will find here. But, in fact, you can laminate many types of dough. In this chapter, I laminate brioche dough, for instance, to make Salted Caramel Sticky Buns (page 131); and laminated babka dough is the base for the Blueberry Blackberry Cheese Danish Braid (page 193). My rugelach (see pages 161 and 165) and Flaky Buttermilk Biscuits (page 167) are also laminated, but they differ from the others in that they are not laminated with a sheet of laminating butter (the *beurrage* or "butter block"); instead, the butter is quickly mixed into the dough and remains in large chunks. The pastries get their layers from folding in these chunks. (This is called "rough" lamination.)

Different types of dough are laminated with different ratios of dough to laminating butter. It is the baker's choice how much butter they use in lamination. My croissant dough (page 135) is laminated with 25 percent butter in proportion to the total weight of the dough. Brioche dough already contains a lot of butter, so I use less laminating butter in my sticky bun recipe. The same is true for my fantails and Danishes. My Kouign Amann (page 171) recipe contains more laminating butter than all of the others because kouign amann are all about the butter.

Make the dough and wrap it in plastic

After making the dough you are going to be laminating, you will chill it until you're ready to roll it out in the following steps.

Make the butter packet

A *butter packet* is a term I use to refer to what is technically called a *beurrage,* which is the sheet of solid butter that is placed on a sheet of dough to begin the lamination process. For my professional kitchens, I order the *beurrage,* which comes as a 1-kilogram, ½-inch-thick sheet of unsalted French Normandy butter. When the bakers go to laminate their dough, they unwrap the sheet of butter and place it on their sheet of dough. It's very convenient and efficient. I re-create this for hand laminating.

With the butter packet, I have essentially replicated this experience for home use, creating a butter packet that is the size that suits an amount of dough suitable for the home baker. Many recipes for home bakers call for you to smear the butter onto the dough, which is not a good alternative. Making a butter packet ensures that you create a really smooth, even layer. In my opinion, it is a must for anyone trying to make professional-looking Viennoiserie at home (see A Short and Sweet Chapter on Fried Dough, page 210). The packet also gives you total control over the temperature of the butter. I like to make butter packets in advance. I keep a stack in my refrigerator so they're ready to go when I want to make laminated dough.

To make a butter packet, place a 12- x 15- or 16-inch piece of parchment paper on a flat work surface with the long side parallel to you. Fold the side edges inward and the top and bottom inward to create a 10- x 6-inch rectangle.

Slice the butter ¼ inch thick lengthwise.

Open the paper packet and lay the butter slices in a single layer like tiles within the rectangle created in the center of the folded paper. Refold the packet to enclose the butter and flip the packet so the seam is facing down. Let the butter packet rest at room temperature for 30 to 45 minutes, until the butter is very soft but not greasy. Roll a rolling pin over the packet to distribute the butter in an even layer to the edges and corners of the packet with no spaces between the tiles. Put the butter packet in the refrigerator to chill until it is firm, about 20 minutes, and for up to 2 weeks. I suggest you label the packet with the name of the recipe it is for; different recipes call for different amounts of laminating butter.

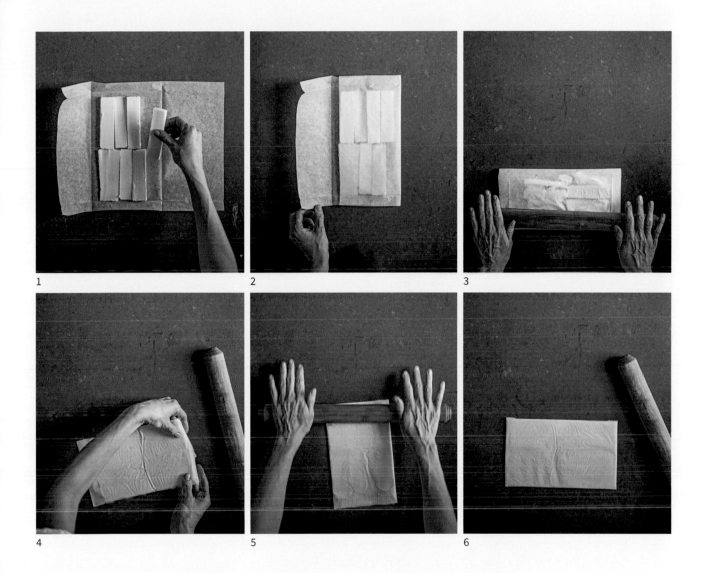

1
2
3
4
5
6

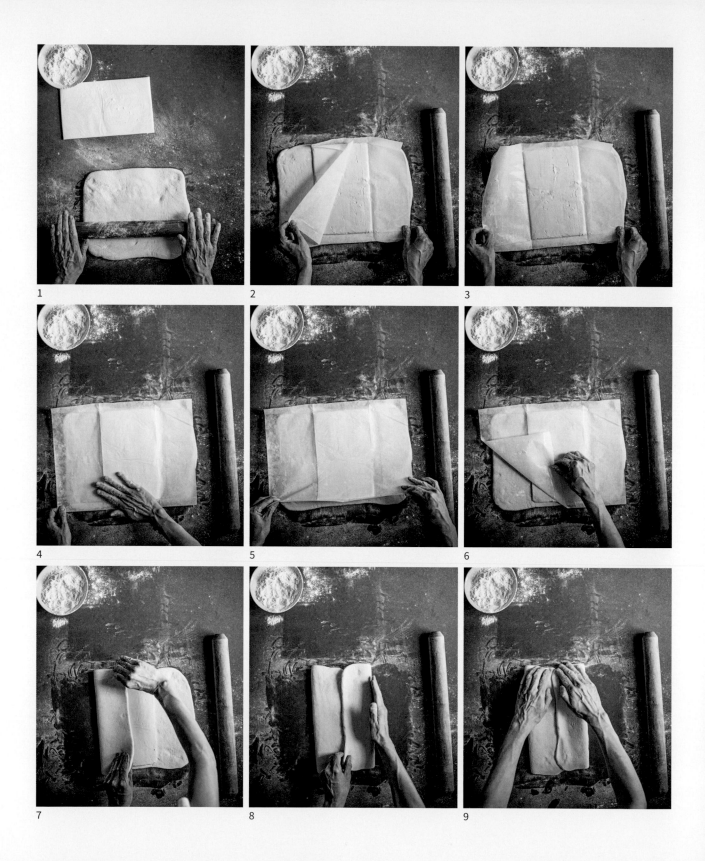

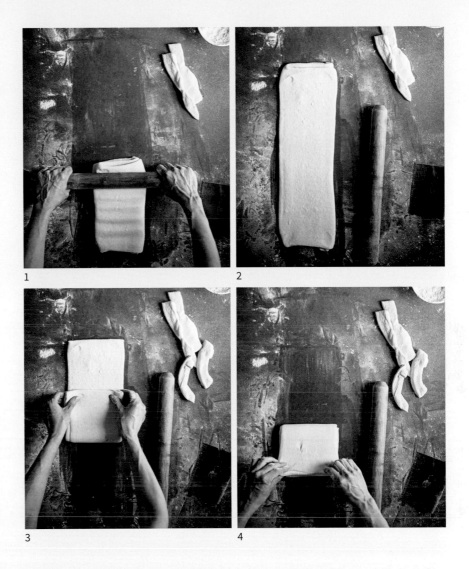

1 2 3 4

Baked Trimmings

Since lamination is all about evenness, there is a lot of measuring and trimming involved. You will be left with trimmings when making your laminated block of dough, and again when you are rolling out the laminated block to cut and shape it into individual pastries. Trimmings are made of delicious, layered and buttery bits of dough. Rather than waste them, I suggest you make a pastry out of them. Roll them in sugar, put them in muffin tins, filling each cup one-half to three-quarters full. Cover with a damp kitchen towel and proof them in a warm place until they double in size. Bake in a 350°F oven until they're golden brown. You can also freeze the scraps until you have enough to fill a larger pan, such as a loaf pan.

Salted Caramel Sticky Buns

Makes 2 dozen buns

I debuted these laminated sticky buns when I worked as head baker at Roberta's, and people went nuts for them. *The New York Times* named them the number-one dish of the year, and they are what I've become best known for. I've been asked for the recipe many times over the years, but this is the first time I've shared it.

To make them, I start with classic French brioche dough, which is enriched with butter and eggs. The brioche dough is moist and flavorful on its own, but then I laminate it, which lifts up the dough a bit and adds that little *je ne sais quoi*. I bake these individually, in muffin tins, so the entire exterior of each bun is covered in gooey caramel. Finally, I sprinkle Maldon sea salt on the buns when they come out of the oven, which balances out the sweetness. They really are the perfect sticky bun: sweet, salty, and rich, without being heavy.

You want to make your butter packet in advance, or while the dough is in the refrigerator. Place the packet in the refrigerator to chill until you're ready to laminate the dough, then remove it from the refrigerator to soften it slightly when called to do so in the recipe.

Note You will need four (6-cup) jumbo muffin tins to make these.

For the dough		
All-purpose flour	3⅔ cups plus more for dusting	440 grams
Instant yeast	1 tablespoon plus 2 teaspoons	15 grams
Granulated sugar	¼ cup	50 grams
Fine sea salt	2 teaspoons	12 grams
Whole milk	¼ cup	60 grams
Large eggs	4	200 grams
Unsalted butter, cubed and softened	16 tablespoons (2 sticks)	226 grams
Nonstick cooking spray		
Butter packet (page 122), chilled	12 tablespoons (1½ sticks)	168 grams
For the filling		
Granulated sugar	2 tablespoons	26 grams
Ground cinnamon	2 tablespoons	12 grams
For the topping		
Unsalted butter, cubed and softened	26 tablespoons (3 sticks plus 2 tablespoons)	364 grams
Light brown sugar	1¾ cups plus 1 tablespoon (lightly packed)	363 grams
Heavy cream	½ cup	119 grams
Flaky sea salt	for sprinkling	

Make the dough

· Whisk the flour, yeast, granulated sugar, and fine sea salt together in a large bowl.

· Pour the milk into the bowl of a stand mixer. Add the eggs and put the dry ingredients on top. Fit the mixer with the dough hook and mix on low speed for 3 minutes to combine the ingredients. Turn the mixer speed up a couple of notches to medium and mix for 5 minutes to develop the gluten and create a homogenous dough. Reduce the mixer speed to low and add the butter all at once. Continue to mix on low until the butter is incorporated into the dough, stopping to scrape down the hook and the bowl once or twice with a plastic bowl scraper while you are incorporating the butter; depending on how soft the butter is, this will take between 10 and 15 minutes. Once the butter is incorporated, remove the bowl from the stand and wipe the hook clean with a wet hand. Place a clean kitchen towel or plastic wrap over the bowl and set the dough aside at room temperature to ferment for 1 hour.

• Meanwhile, line a baking sheet with parchment paper and spray it with nonstick cooking spray.

• Use a plastic bowl scraper to scrape the dough out of the bowl and onto the prepared baking sheet. Using wet hands, pat and form the dough gently into an 8-inch square. Refrigerate the dough for at least 1 hour and up to 8 hours. (The dough is very sticky, so I don't wrap it in plastic wrap. However, if you are refrigerating the dough for longer than 1 hour, remove the baking sheet from the refrigerator after 1 hour, wrap it in plastic wrap, and return it to the refrigerator.)

Laminate the Dough

Lock in the butter • Remove the butter packet from the refrigerator and set it on the counter to soften until it is bendy but still cool; this could take anywhere from 5 to 20 minutes, depending on how cold it is, and depending on the texture of the dough. You want the butter to be slightly softer and more malleable than the dough but not so soft that it will ooze out of the dough.

• Lightly dust a large flat work surface with flour. Remove the baking sheet from the refrigerator. Unwrap the dough, if it has been refrigerated for more than an hour, and place it on the floured surface. Lightly dust the top of the dough and a rolling pin with flour and roll the dough out to 14 inches from side to side and 11 inches from top to bottom, dusting the work surface, rolling pin, and top of the dough lightly with flour as you roll the dough, so it doesn't stick.

I try to reuse a sheet of plastic wrap whenever possible. When I unwrap a block of dough, I set the plastic wrap to the side and use it later in the recipe if plastic wrap is needed.

• Open the parchment packet to expose the butter and flip the packet over to place the butter on the dough, centering the 10-inch edge of the butter packet on the 11-inch length of dough. Run your hand over the parchment paper so that the heat of your hand helps to peel off the paper. Then peel off and discard the parchment paper. Fold the left and right sides of the dough over the butter so they meet in the middle and pinch the edges of dough together with your fingers. Gently press the top and bottom edges of the dough together to seal the packet closed and lock in the butter.

Make two letter folds

- Dust your work surface with a bit more flour. Dust the top of the dough and the rolling pin with flour and roll the dough lengthwise to 18 inches from top to bottom, dusting with flour as needed.
- Using a pastry wheel or bench knife, trim the top and bottom edges of the dough just enough to expose the layer of butter in the center of the dough. Reserve the trimmings to make Baked Trimmings (page 129) or discard them. Fold the top edge down two-thirds and fold the bottom edge to meet the top edge, so the dough is folded into thirds, like a letter.
- Rotate the dough 90 degrees so that the folded, closed edges are facing left and right and one of the open edges (with the visible layers) is facing you, dusting lightly underneath the dough with flour. Dust the top of the dough and the rolling pin with flour and roll the dough to 18 inches from top to bottom, dusting with flour as needed. Trim the top and bottom edges to expose the butter layers and add the trimmings to your baked trimmings or discard. Fold the top edge down and the bottom edge up to make a second letter fold.
- Wrap the laminated block of dough in plastic wrap and place it in the freezer to chill for 1 hour. Move the dough from the freezer to the refrigerator for at least 8 hours and up to 12 hours to retard the dough.

Prepare to fill the buns

- When you are ready to fill and bake the buns, remove the laminated block of dough from the refrigerator and set it on the counter to rest for 20 to 30 minutes, until you can feel that the butter layers inside the dough are just becoming malleable (but not soft) when you bend the block slightly.
- Meanwhile, stir the granulated sugar and cinnamon for the filling together in a small bowl and set it aside.
- Lightly dust a large flat work surface with flour. Unwrap the dough and place it on the floured surface. Lightly dust the top of the dough and rolling pin with flour and roll the dough out into a rectangle that is 19 inches from side to side and 12 inches from top to bottom, dusting with flour as needed.

Fill and cut the buns

- Using a pastry wheel or bench knife, cut the dough across the middle so that you have two strips 19 inches from side to side and 6 inches top to bottom. Brush the surfaces of both lengths of dough with water. Sprinkle the cinnamon sugar over the surface of the dough, dividing it evenly between the two strips and leaving ½ inch at the top free of cinnamon sugar.
- Beginning with the edge closest to you, make one small, tight roll away

from you. Continue to roll the dough away from you as tightly as you can until you've rolled the sheet into a tight roll. Adjust the roll so the seam is on the bottom. Roll the second length of dough in the same way. Place the rolls diagonally on a baking sheet and place them in the refrigerator to chill for 30 minutes. (If you are planning ahead, remove the logs from the refrigerator, wrap them in plastic, and place them in the freezer for up to 1 week.)

Make the topping
- Combine the butter and brown sugar in the bowl of a stand mixer. Fit the mixer with the paddle attachment and mix on low speed until the butter and sugar are incorporated, about 1 minute, stopping once to scrape down the sides of the bowl with a rubber spatula. With the mixer running, drizzle in the cream and mix until it is combined.

Form and proof the buns
- Spray the muffin cups lightly with nonstick cooking spray.
- Scoop the caramel topping into the bottom of the tins, dividing it evenly; you will use about 2 tablespoons (30 grams) in each cup. Use your fingers to pat the topping down into an even layer in each cup.
- Remove the dough logs from the refrigerator and place them on a cutting board. Use a serrated knife to cut the rough end off of the right side of one of the logs. Continue cutting down the length of the log, cutting it into 1½-inch pieces. Cut the rough end off the left side of the log when you get there.
- Place one piece of dough, cut side facing up, in each muffin cup. Repeat with the second log. Cover each muffin tin with a damp, lightweight kitchen towel and set aside in a warm place for the buns to proof for about 2 hours, until they have started to grow and fill out the muffin cups; they will not fill them out completely.

Bake the sticky buns
- While the sticky buns are proofing, arrange the oven racks so one is in the top third of the oven and the other is in the bottom third. Preheat the oven to 350°F.
- Put two muffin tins on each oven rack to bake the sticky buns for 25 to 27 minutes, rotating the pans from front to back and from one rack to the other halfway through the baking time so the cinnamon buns brown evenly. Remove the pans from the oven and let the sticky buns rest in the pans for about 3 minutes, to let the caramel set up. Lay a sheet of parchment paper out on your work surface. Quickly invert the muffin tins over the parchment paper to release the buns onto the paper so that the bottoms of the cinnamon buns, which are coated with caramel, will be the tops. Sprinkle a big pinch of flaky salt on each sticky bun. Serve warm or at room temperature.

Master Recipe
for Croissant Dough

**Makes 1 (1,260-gram) block;
or enough for 7 Classic Croissants
(page 139), 12 Pain aux Raisins
(page 147), or 10 Pain au Chocolat
(page 153)**

This dough is used to make croissants, pain au chocolat, and pain aux raisins. It's a classic yeasted dough, laminated with butter. Some croissant dough recipes have a little butter in the dough, some do not. Mine does. I think the fat in the dough helps the fat in the lamination and makes for an easier laminating process—the fat molecules can slip and slide together. I wrote this recipe with the home baker in mind. It is a small amount of dough with minimal rolling out, which enables you to create nice, even, perfect layers. Because you're going to go to the effort of making and laminating croissant dough, I suggest you make a double batch. Double the amount of dough you mix, then divide the dough in half. Make two separate butter packets and laminate each batch of dough individually. Use one block and store the other one in the freezer for up to a week. When you are ready to use the frozen dough, transfer it to the refrigerator overnight. This dough is pretty easy to handle; it is not too soft or sticky, so it's a great recipe for those who are new to laminating.

You want to make your butter packet in advance, or while the dough is in the refrigerator. Place the packet in the refrigerator to chill until you're ready to laminate the dough, then remove it from the refrigerator to soften it slightly when called to do so in the recipe.

For the dough		
Whole milk	1¼ cups	300 grams
Bread flour	3¾ cups	450 grams
Whole-wheat pastry flour	½ cup	52.5 grams
Granulated sugar	3 tablespoons	39 grams
Unsalted butter, cubed and softened	3 tablespoons	42 grams
Instant yeast	1 tablespoon	9 grams
Fine sea salt	2½ teaspoons	15 grams
Sourdough Starter (page xxxiii)	½ cup	85 grams
All-purpose flour	for dusting	
Butter packet (page 122), chilled	19 tablespoons (2 sticks plus 3 tablespoons)	266 grams

Make the dough

- Line a baking sheet with parchment paper.
- Put the milk in a small saucepan and heat it over low heat until it reaches 70°F on a digital thermometer.
- Put the bread flour, whole-wheat pastry flour, sugar, butter, yeast, and salt in a medium bowl and stir to combine.
- Put the milk and starter in the bowl of a stand mixer. Place the dry ingredients on top. Fit the mixer with the dough hook and mix on low speed

for 2 minutes. Increase the speed to medium-high and mix for 5 minutes to develop the gluten in the dough.

▪ Place a long sheet of plastic wrap on your work surface. Use a plastic bowl scraper to scrape the dough out of the mixer onto the plastic wrap and pat the dough into a square shape. Wrap the plastic wrap around the dough and run a rolling pin over the dough to form an even 8-inch square. (For more detail, see Wrapping Dough, page xl.) Place the dough in the refrigerator for 1 hour.

Laminate the Dough

Lock in the butter
▪ Remove the butter packet from the refrigerator and set it on the counter to soften until it is bendy but still cool; this could take anywhere from 5 to 20 minutes, depending on how cold it is and on the texture of the dough. You want the butter to be slightly softer and more malleable than the dough but not so soft that it will ooze out of the dough.

▪ Lightly dust a large flat work surface with all-purpose flour. Remove the dough from the refrigerator, unwrap the dough, and place it on the floured surface. Lightly dust the top of the dough and a rolling pin with flour and roll the dough out to a rectangle that is 14 inches from side to side and 11 inches from top to bottom, dusting with flour as needed.

▪ Open the butter packet to expose the butter and flip the packet over to place the butter on the dough, centering the 10-inch edge of the butter packet on the 11-inch length of dough. Run your hand over the parchment paper so that the heat of your hand helps to peel off the paper. Then peel off and discard the parchment paper. Fold the left and right sides of the dough over the butter so they meet in the middle, and pinch the two edges of dough together with your fingers. Gently press the top and bottom edges of the dough together to seal the packet closed and lock in the butter.

Make a book fold
▪ Dust your work surface with a bit more all-purpose flour. Dust the top of the dough and the rolling pin with flour and roll the dough to 32 inches from top to bottom, dusting with flour as needed. (Standard kitchen counters are 26 inches deep, so to roll this, one end of the dough will be hanging over the counter while you roll the other end.) Using a pastry wheel or bench knife, trim the top and bottom edges of the dough just enough to expose the layer of butter in the dough. Reserve the trimmings to make Baked Trimmings (page 129) or discard them. Fold the top edge of the dough toward the bottom and the bottom edge of the dough toward the top so the two edges meet slightly off-center. Fold the bottom edge to meet the top, like a book.

Make a letter fold

- Rotate the dough 90 degrees so the closed, folded edges are facing left and right, and the open edge, where the layers are visible, is facing you. Lightly dust the work surface, rolling pin, and dough with all-purpose flour and roll out the dough to 18 inches from top to bottom, dusting with flour as needed. Using a pastry wheel or bench knife, trim the top and bottom edges of the dough just enough to expose the layers of butter in the center of the dough. Add the trimmings to your baked trimmings or discard them. Fold the top edge down two-thirds and the bottom edge to meet the top edge, so the dough is folded into thirds, like a letter.
- Wrap the laminated block of dough in plastic and place it in the freezer to chill for 1 hour. Move the dough from the freezer to the refrigerator and let it rest for at least 8 hours and up to 12 hours to retard the dough.

Classic Croissants

Makes 7 croissants

As a baker, my heart is in France, and croissants are such a big part of the French culinary tradition, I was determined to include a recipe in this book that would make perfect-looking croissants at home possible. A cross section of a perfect croissant would show a beautiful, open honeycomb crumb structure. In a professional kitchen, you get this open structure from the gluten that is developed by using a commercial dough sheeter, which you just can't get when rolling by hand. Through a lot of trial and error, I was able to create a recipe for a croissant with the same even layers and honeycomb look as that you see in a professional bakery.

Master Recipe for Croissant Dough (page 135)	1 recipe	
All-purpose flour	for dusting	
For baking the croissants		
Large egg	1	50 grams
Fine sea salt	big pinch	

Roll out the dough

- Remove the laminated block of dough from the refrigerator and set it on the counter to rest for 20 to 30 minutes, until you can feel that the butter layers inside the dough are just becoming malleable (but not soft) when you bend the block slightly.
- Line two baking sheets with parchment paper.
- Lightly dust a large flat work surface with flour. Unwrap the dough and place it on the floured surface. Lightly dust the top of the dough and a rolling pin with flour and roll the dough out to a rectangle that is 13 inches from side to side and 12 inches from top to bottom, dusting with flour as needed.

Cut the croissants

- Using a pastry wheel or bench knife, trim the top and bottom edges of the dough. Reserve the trimmings to make Baked Trimmings (page 129) or discard them.
- Starting on the right edge and moving left, use a small sharp knife to score along the bottom edge of the dough every 3 inches. Score one mark 1½ inches from the right edge on the top edge of the dough. Continuing left, from the first mark, score the dough every 3 inches.
- Using a long knife, cut from the lower right corner of the dough to the first score on the top edge of the dough. Then rotate your knife to cut from the top cut to the next mark on the bottom to create a triangle. Continue working your way across the dough, cutting from one mark to another, until you have

cut 7 triangles in a backgammon-like formation. Add the misshapen pieces on either end to your baked trimmings or discard them.

Shape and proof the croissants

· Working with one triangle at a time, make a ½-inch-long, perpendicular cut in the center of the short side of the triangle; this cut helps when forming the croissant, to give it an elongated shape. Fold the small flaps of dough created by the small cut from the center toward the outside edges of the triangle.
· Roll the triangle from the base away from you, toward the point, trying to get three full rolls in the dough, ending with the tip of the triangle underneath the croissant, facing the countertop. Place the croissant on one of the prepared baking sheets. Repeat, shaping the remaining croissants in the same way and spacing them evenly between the two baking sheets.
· Gently cover each baking sheet with a damp, lightweight kitchen towel and set the sheets aside in a warm place for 2½ to 3 hours to proof the croissants until they have swelled to one and a half times their size.

Covering dough with a damp kitchen towel prevents it from forming a skin.

Bake the croissants

· While the croissants are proofing, arrange the oven racks so one is in the top third of the oven and the other is in the bottom third. Preheat the oven to 375°F.
· Whisk the egg and salt together in a small bowl to make an egg wash. Uncover the croissants and lightly brush them with the egg wash; discard the remaining egg wash.
· Place one baking sheet on each oven rack to bake the croissants for 25 to 30 minutes, until they are deep golden brown, rotating the baking sheets from front to back and from one rack to the other halfway through the baking time so the croissants brown evenly. Remove the baking sheets from the oven and let the croissants cool on the baking sheets for a few minutes. Use a metal spatula to transfer the pastries to a cooling rack to cool completely. Serve warm or at room temperature.

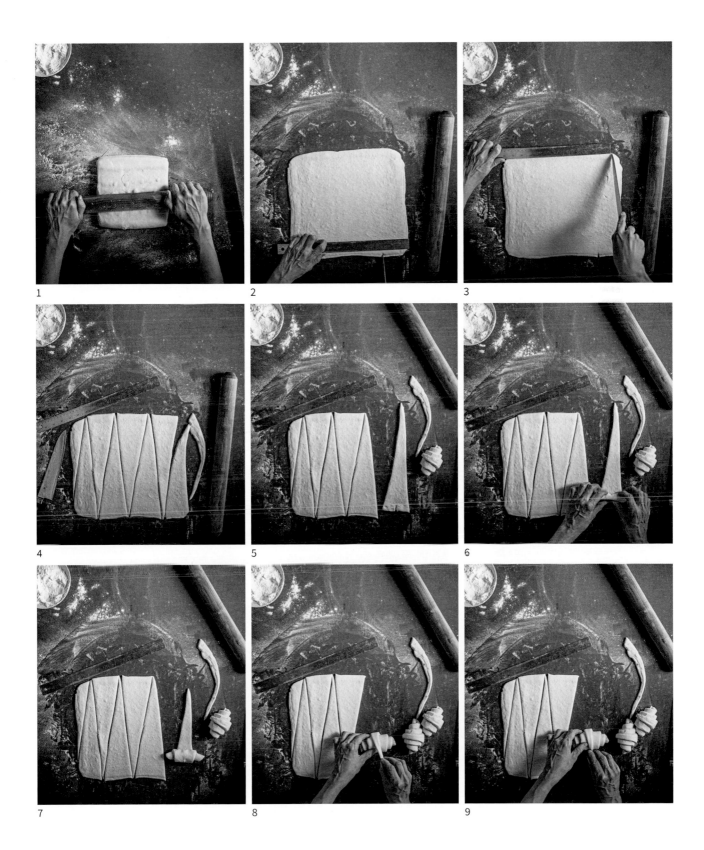

Twice-Baked Croissants with Sour Cherries and Pistachios

Makes 6 croissants

Around the time I started working on this book, I was working as a consultant, developing the menu for the Walnut Street Café in Philadelphia. I knew I wanted to include a twice-baked croissant on the menu. In the United States, a typical way to make an almond croissant is to pipe almond cream on croissant dough, then roll up the croissant, proof, and bake it. To make the French version, first you start with day-old croissants, which, when you're running a professional kitchen, is always a great thing. You take the croissant and cut it in half like a sandwich, and then you dunk it in simple syrup. Next you open the croissant like a sandwich, pipe almond cream down the center, close the sandwich, and bake it, so it has this delicate, browned, crunchy exterior and this very moist, flavorful, sweet filling. I love that. I thought of different nut creams I might like in a croissant, and my first instinct was pistachios because I just love them. I also wanted to incorporate jam into the croissant—sour cherry seemed like the perfect pairing. I like that the tart, sour cherry jam balances the sweetness and richness of the pistachio cream. When I first made the pistachio cream, I thought its flavor was too muddled; I couldn't distinguish it from almond cream. I added apricot kernel oil, which really heightened the distinct pistachio flavor.

Note   You will need one large disposable pastry bag.

For the pistachio cream		
Granulated sugar	½ cup	100 grams
Pistachio flour	1 cup	100 grams
Unsalted butter, cubed and softened	7 tablespoons	98 grams
Fine sea salt	¼ teaspoon	2 grams
Large eggs	2	100 grams
Apricot kernel oil (optional)	⅛ teaspoon	1 gram
For the simple syrup		
Granulated sugar	2 cups	400 grams
Water	2 cups	450 grams
For the croissants		
Croissants, day-old (page 139; or store-bought)	6	
Simple syrup	1 recipe	
Sour cherry jam (store-bought)	2 tablespoons	40 grams
Pistachios (preferably Sicilian), chopped	¼ cup	33 grams
Confectioners' sugar	¼ cup	30 grams

Make the pistachio cream

· Put the granulated sugar, pistachio flour, butter, and salt in the bowl of a stand mixer. Fit the mixer with the paddle attachment and mix on low speed until the ingredients are combined and no visible chunks of butter remain, about 2 minutes. Add the eggs, one at a time, mixing on low speed until the first egg is integrated with the rest of the ingredients before adding the second egg, and stopping the mixer to scrape down the sides of the bowl after each addition. Add the apricot kernel oil, if you are using it, and mix to combine.

· Spoon the pistachio cream into a large disposable pastry bag and refrigerate for at least 1 hour for it to set, and up to overnight. (The cream can also be frozen for up to several months.)

Make the simple syrup

- Combine the granulated sugar and water in a medium saucepan and stir so there are no dry patches of sugar. Bring to a boil over high heat, reduce the heat to medium, and boil for 1 minute. Turn off the heat and transfer the simple syrup to a heat-proof medium bowl; you want to choose a bowl that is large enough to hold a croissant easily and deep enough that you can immerse a croissant in it. Set aside to cool to room temperature.

Halve and dip the croissants

- Arrange the oven racks so one is in the center position. Preheat the oven to 350°F.
- Line two baking sheets with parchment paper.
- Using a large serrated knife, slice the croissants in half lengthwise and place them on the prepared baking sheet, dividing them evenly. Picking up one croissant at a time, with one half in each hand, quickly dip the two halves in the syrup, making sure to immerse them completely. Lift the croissant halves out of the simple syrup, sandwich them together in between both hands, and gently squeeze the two halves together, letting the excess syrup drip back into the bowl. Return the dipped croissant, top side up, to the baking sheet and repeat with the remaining croissants, dipping them in the same way.

Fill the croissants

- Remove the tops from the croissants and set them aside. Remove the pistachio cream from the refrigerator and cut a ¾-inch opening in the tip of the pastry bag. Pipe the cream in a 1-inch wide strip down the center of each croissant bottom.
- Using a small spoon, create a crater in the cream beginning 1 inch from the start of the strip of cream and running down the middle of each strip of cream, stopping about 1 inch before you reach the end of the cream; each crater will be about 3 inches long and ⅜ inch deep. Spoon ½ to 1 teaspoon of jam into each crater scraped out of each line of cream so that the jam is flush with the cream. Place the tops on the croissants and press down on each one gently to adhere the croissant top to the filling.
- Pipe about 1 tablespoon of the pistachio cream in a round on the center of each croissant top. Pick up a big pinch of the chopped pistachios and press them gently into the cream topping.

Bake the croissants

- Put the croissants on the center rack of the oven to bake for about 30 minutes, until the cream topping is gently browned and the edges of the croissants are slightly crisp, rotating the baking sheet from front to back halfway through. Remove the croissants from the oven and transfer them to a cooling rack to cool to room temperature.
- Put the confectioners' sugar in a fine-mesh strainer and dust it over the croissants.

Ham and Cheese Twice-Baked Croissants

Makes 7 croissants

I lived for a year in France during college. I was in Tours, in the Loire Valley, and I used to purchase these croissants often at the counter of my neighborhood bakery. I would get them heated up—*à emporter,* which essentially means "to take away"—and eat them on my way to school. It was such an American thing to do—getting lunch like that and eating it on the street! But I enjoyed it. These are made with day-old croissants, so in running a bakery, where you try not to waste anything, it's a great use for leftovers.

For the béchamel		
Unsalted butter	2 tablespoons	28 grams
Small yellow onion, cut into ¼-inch dice	⅓ cup	45 grams
Fine sea salt	½ teaspoon	3 grams
All-purpose flour	1½ tablespoons	13.5 grams
Whole milk, warm	1 cup	240 grams
Freshly grated nutmeg	½ teaspoon	< 1 gram
For the croissants		
Croissants, day-old (page 139; or store-bought)	7	
Black Forest ham, thinly sliced	14 ounces	397 grams
Gruyère cheese	8 ounces (7 ounces thinly sliced; 1 ounce grated)	226 grams
Dijon mustard	2 tablespoons plus 1 teaspoon	20 grams

Make the béchamel

- Put the butter in a small saucepan and heat it over medium heat until it has melted and begins to bubble. Add the onion and sauté over medium heat until the onion has softened but has not begun to brown, about 3 minutes. Add the salt and flour and cook, stirring constantly, for about 1 minute to cook off the flour taste. Add the warm milk in a steady stream, stirring constantly while you add it. Stir in the nutmeg. Bring the béchamel sauce to a gentle boil, stirring constantly, and cook for about 2 minutes, until it is thick enough to coat the back of a spoon. Transfer the béchamel to a small bowl and set aside to cool to room temperature.

Assemble the croissants

- Line two baking sheets with parchment paper.
- Using a large serrated knife, slice the croissants in half lengthwise. Put the croissants on your counter or a cutting board. Take off the tops and put the tops, cut side up, in back of the bottoms; you are forming a sandwich production line. Use a small offset spatula to spread about 1 tablespoon (25 grams) of the béchamel over the bottom half of each croissant. Fold

2 ounces (50 grams) of the ham like a letter and place on each croissant, folding the ham further so it doesn't hang over the edges. Place 1 ounce (28 grams) of the sliced Gruyère on top of each portion of ham and spread a small dollop (about 1 teaspoon) of mustard on the cheese with the back of a spoon. Place the tops on the croissants and press down gently to seal the sandwiches closed. Place the croissants on the prepared baking sheets, dividing them evenly between the baking sheets. Dollop a spoonful of béchamel on top of each croissant and sprinkle with the grated Gruyère cheese, dividing it evenly among the sandwiches.

- Arrange the oven racks so one is in the top third of the oven and the other is in the bottom third. Preheat the oven to 350°F.
- Place one baking sheet on each baking rack to bake the croissants for approximately 30 minutes, until the béchamel is golden brown and the grated cheese has melted, rotating the baking sheets from front to back and from one rack to the other halfway through the baking time so the croissants brown evenly. Remove the croissants from the oven and transfer them to a cooling rack to cool. Serve warm or at room temperature.

Pain aux Raisins

Makes 1 dozen pains aux raisins

In France this spiral pastry is often called an *escargot,* or "snail." Germans have a similar pastry called a *zimtschnecke,* or "cinnamon snail." Although it does look a bit like a snail, I always just call it pain aux raisins. The dough is sweet and caramelized, so it's a little bit crunchy, and between the spirals are layers of dried currants and vanilla pastry cream. I changed the traditional raisins to currants; I like currants better than raisins because of their slightly tarter flavor. I soak the currants in grappa or brandy, which gussies up the flavor and also softens them, but if you don't have these spirits or don't want to use them, soak the currants in water instead. Otherwise, I stayed true to the original and my memory of enjoying them when I was a college student in France.

Dried currants	1 cup	135 grams
Grappa or brandy (optional)	¼ cup	56 grams
Master Recipe for Croissant Dough (page 135)	1 recipe	
All-purpose flour	for dusting	
Vanilla Bean Pastry Cream (recipe follows)	1½ cups	380 grams
For baking and finishing the pain aux raisins		
Large egg	1	50 grams
Fine sea salt	big pinch	
Blood Orange Jam (page 224; or store-bought apricot jam)	¼ cup	85 grams
Water	1 tablespoon	

Soak the currants

- Put the currants in a small bowl. Add the grappa or brandy, if you are using it. Add enough hot tap water to cover the currants. Set the currants aside to soak for 10 minutes. Drain the currants in a fine-mesh strainer and let them sit in the strainer to drain any remaining water while you roll out the dough.

Roll out the dough

- Remove the laminated block of dough from the refrigerator and set it on the counter to rest for 20 to 30 minutes to soften the butter layers, until you can feel that the butter layers inside the dough are just becoming malleable (but not soft) when you bend the block slightly.
- Lightly dust a large flat work surface with flour. Unwrap the dough and place it on the floured surface. Lightly dust the top of the dough and a rolling pin with flour and roll the dough out to a 15-inch square, dusting the work surface, rolling pin, and top of the dough lightly with flour as you roll the dough, so it doesn't stick. The dough will want to spring back; when you feel resistance, let the dough rest for a minute or two and resume rolling until you reach the desired dimensions.

Roll, cut, and shape the pastries

- Line two baking sheets with parchment paper.
- Dollop the pastry cream onto the dough. Use a large offset spatula to spread the pastry cream in an even layer to cover the surface of the dough, making sure to spread it all the way to the edges. Sprinkle the currants in an even layer over the pastry cream.
- Beginning with the edge closest to you, make one small, tight roll away from you. Continue to roll the dough away from you as tightly as you can until you've rolled the sheet into a tight roll. Adjust the roll so the seam is on the bottom. Use a serrated knife to trim the ends of the roll. Reserve the trimmings to make Baked Trimmings (page 129) or discard them. Slice the roll into 1-inch-thick "snails."
- Pick up one pain aux raisins and tuck the tail end of the dough toward the center. Then place the pastry with the tucked end down on one of the prepared baking sheets. Repeat, shaping the remaining pastries in the same way and dividing them evenly between the baking sheets.

Tucking the tail of the dough under the pastry prevents it from springing open or coming unraveled when it bakes.

- Cover each baking sheet with a damp, lightweight kitchen towel and set the sheets aside in a warm place to proof the pastries for about 2 hours, until they have swelled to one and a half times their size.

Bake the pastries

- While the pastries are proofing, arrange the oven racks so one is in the top third of the oven and the other is in the bottom third. Preheat the oven to 375°F.

Stacking two baking sheets together is a useful trick when you need to keep the bottoms of a pastry from darkening too much while the tops brown.

- Place one baking sheet on each oven rack to bake the pastries for 25 to 30 minutes, until they are deep golden brown, rotating the baking sheets from front to back and top to bottom halfway through the baking time so the snails brown evenly.
- While the pains aux raisins are baking, combine the jam and water in a small saucepan over medium heat and bring to a boil, whisking to break up the jam. Turn off the heat.
- Remove the pains aux raisins from the oven and brush the tops with the jam glaze. Return the pastries to the oven for 1 to 2 minutes, until the glaze is set; it will look sticky, not glistening. Remove the baking sheets from the oven and let the pastries cool on the baking sheets for a few minutes. Use a metal spatula to transfer the pastries to a cooling rack to cool completely. Serve warm or at room temperature.

Vanilla Bean Pastry Cream

**Makes about
2½ cups**

Pastry cream is a thick, egg-based custard used often in French pastry. Where other custards, such as crème anglaise and lemon curd, are thickened with eggs, pastry cream is thickened with cornstarch. The cornstarch prevents the eggs from curdling, which is a constant worry when making other egg-based custards. When cooked, starch absorbs heat and water and swells. This swelling is what causes the pastry cream to thicken. Egg proteins also react to heat. The egg proteins, which start out wound up like little balls, begin to unwind. They cross-link to each other as they unwind, and moisture gets trapped between them; this is what causes egg-based custard to set. A little too much heat, though, and egg-based custard goes from set to curdled instantly. But if there is starch in the mix, it gets in the way of the egg proteins and prevents them from cross-linking. The starch molecules absorb liquid, swell, and link to each other, which causes the starch to thicken. This thickening happens in pockets and clumps. So, when making pastry cream, you have to whisk vigorously while cooking to smooth out the lumps of swollen starches and break them up into smaller pieces. It is the same when you make gravy or béchamel. Unlike custards made with only eggs, it is almost impossible to curdle pastry cream.

Whole milk	2 cups	480 grams
Vanilla bean	1	
Granulated sugar	½ cup	100 grams
Cornstarch	3 tablespoons	25.5 grams
Fine sea salt	⅛ teaspoon	1 gram
Large egg yolks	6	102 grams
Unsalted butter, cubed and softened	4 tablespoons (½ stick)	56 grams

▪ Put the milk in a medium saucepan. Split the vanilla bean down the middle with a small sharp knife and use the knife to scrape the seeds out of the bean. Add the bean and seeds to the saucepan with the milk.

▪ Pour half of the sugar into a medium bowl and add the remaining sugar to the saucepan with the milk. (The halves of sugar can be eyeballed; they don't need to be exact. The sugar added to the milk helps to keep the milk from scorching on the bottom of the pan.) Warm the milk and sugar over medium-high heat, stirring occasionally, until the mixture begins to bubble around the edges.

▪ Meanwhile, place a dampened kitchen towel under the bowl with the sugar; this will prevent it from sliding around when you begin whisking. Add the cornstarch and salt to the bowl and whisk to combine. Add the egg yolks and whisk for about 30 seconds to lighten them slightly. Drizzle in 1 cup of the hot milk, whisking constantly. Add the remaining milk 1 cup at a time, whisking constantly. Return the mixture to the saucepan and bring it to a boil over high heat, stirring constantly with the whisk. (You need to be able to see that it's boiling, and if you're whisking too furiously, it froths and you can't see it.) When the mixture starts to boil, reduce the heat to medium-low and cook for 2 minutes to swell the cornstarch, whisking furiously to work out any lumps that have formed in the cream. (The reason we're cooking the custard at this point is not to thicken it—it will be thick before the 2 minutes are up—but to cook the starch in the cornstarch so you don't taste it, and also to destroy the alpha amylase enzyme in the egg, which can cause the custard to break down after it's cooked.) Remove the saucepan from the heat, add the butter, and whisk until the butter has melted and combined with the cream. Remove the vanilla bean. (Use the bean to make Vanilla Sugar, page 219, or discard it.)

▪ Set a fine-mesh strainer over a bowl or storage container. Pass the pastry cream through the strainer to remove any lumps, pressing on the cream with a rubber spatula to push it through the strainer. Place a sheet of plastic wrap on top of the pastry cream and press it so it sits directly on the surface to prevent a skin from forming. Cover the container with a lid and refrigerate for at least 1 hour and up to 3 days.

Pain au Chocolat

**Makes 10
pains au chocolat**

These are often called chocolate croissants, but I prefer to use their French name, *pain au chocolat*, which translates as "chocolate bread." Originally, pains au chocolat were made by wrapping bread dough around a stick of chocolate, then at some point, bakers started using croissant dough instead. I started making these when I was working at Roberta's and my son was two years old. I would take a pastry with me to his swim class for an after-class treat. He would get so excited; he would rip it open and eat the chocolate stick inside first. It is still his favorite. To this day, it's the first thing he orders when we go to France, and the first thing he does when he gets one is open it up to eat the chocolate first. He's become somewhat of an expert on them: When he opens up the pastry, we both count to see how many sticks of chocolate the baker used. If the number is fewer than two, we give each other a disapproving look.

Note Chocolate batons are sticks of dark chocolate, formed and sold specifically for making croissants. You can find them at baking supply stores and online. If you cannot find them, use Valrhona *feves*.

Master Recipe for Croissant Dough (page 135)	1 recipe	
Semisweet chocolate batons	20 (or 40 semisweet chocolate *feves*)	
For baking the pain au chocolat		
Large egg	1	50 grams
Fine sea salt	big pinch	

Roll out the dough

If the butter in the laminating dough is too cold and hard, it will shatter when you roll it, resulting in an uneven lamination; the finished pastry won't have even layers, and it will not rise as high.

· Remove the laminated block of dough from the refrigerator and set it on the counter to rest for 20 to 30 minutes, until you can feel that the butter layers inside the dough are just becoming malleable (but not soft) when you bend the block slightly.

· Lightly dust a large flat work surface with flour. Unwrap the dough and place it on the floured surface. Lightly dust the top of the dough and a rolling pin with flour and roll the dough out into a rectangle that is 20 inches from side to side and 12 inches from top to bottom, dusting with flour as needed. The dough will want to spring back; when you feel resistance, let the dough rest for a minute or two and resume rolling until you reach the desired dimensions.

Cut the pains au chocolat

Using a straightedge and pastry wheel or large knife, trim the edges of the dough, cutting as little as needed to make straight, even edges. Reserve the trimmings to make Baked Trimmings (page 129) or discard them. Cut the dough in half lengthwise so you have 2 (6-inch-wide) strips of dough.

▪ Use a straightedge and pastry roller to cut the dough into 3½-inch-wide rectangles. Add the end pieces to your baked trimmings or discard them. Cut the second strip of dough in the same way.

Shape and proof the pains au chocolat

▪ Line two baking sheets with parchment paper.

▪ Without moving the dough rectangles, place 1 stick of chocolate (or 2 *feves*) along the bottom short edge of the dough and fold the dough over the chocolate as if you are wrapping fabric around a rectangular bolt of cardboard. Once the chocolate is no longer visible, place another chocolate stick (or 2 *feves*) along the edge of the dough and fold the dough over the chocolate again to "close" the pain au chocolat. The seam should be in the center of the bottom, otherwise the pain au chocolat will pop open when it bakes. If the seam isn't underneath, gently roll the pastry to shift it. Gently press on the pastry with the palm of your hand to give the pastry the shape of a rectangle with rounded edges. Place it on one of the prepared baking sheets and repeat, filling the remaining rectangles with the remaining chocolate and shaping them as you did the first one. Place 5 on each baking sheet.

▪ Cover each baking sheet with a damp, lightweight kitchen towel and set the sheets aside in a warm place to proof the pains au chocolat for about 2 hours, until they look swollen and are about one and a half times their original size.

When you are working with delicate dough, such as laminated dough, you want to use a very lightweight kitchen towel when proofing to prevent squishing the pastries in the process.

Bake the pastries

▪ While the pains au chocolat are proofing, arrange the oven racks so one is in the top third of the oven and the other is in the bottom third. Preheat the oven to 375°F.

▪ Whisk the egg and salt together in a small bowl to make an egg wash. Uncover the sheets and brush the pains au chocolat with the egg wash.

▪ Place one baking sheet on each oven rack to bake the pastries for 25 to 28 minutes, until the tops are golden brown, rotating the baking sheets from front to back and from one rack to the other halfway through the baking time so the pastries brown evenly. Remove the baking sheets from the oven and let the pains au chocolat cool on the baking sheets for a few minutes. Use a metal spatula to transfer the pastries to a cooling rack to cool. Serve warm or at room temperature.

Double Chocolate Croissants

Makes 10 croissants

I got the idea for these croissants after making a chocolate babka with a chocolate dough (instead of the traditional plain dough and chocolate filling) and a white chocolate filling. The babka was so delicious that I decided to try making chocolate-on-chocolate croissants, and I loved them. The dough contains cocoa powder, which has a slightly savory quality to it, so to make them sufficiently sweet, I increase the sugar in the dough, and I fill them with more chocolate than I do with traditional pains au chocolat.

The cocoa powder absorbs some of the liquid in the dough, creating a tighter dough that is more difficult to roll, both during the lamination process and when cutting. This recipe calls for you to rest the dough periodically during the rolling process, which helps to relax the gluten.

You want to make your butter packet in advance, or while the dough is in the refrigerator. Place the packet in the refrigerator to chill until you're ready to laminate the dough, then remove it from the refrigerator to soften it slightly when called to do so in the recipe.

Note Chocolate batons are sticks of dark chocolate, formed and sold specifically for making croissants. You can find them at baking supply stores and online. If you cannot find them, use Valrhona *feves*.

For the dough		
Whole milk	1⅓ cups plus 1 tablespoon	335 grams
Bread flour	4 cups plus 2 tablespoons	498 grams
Cocoa powder (preferably Valrhona)	¾ cup	64 grams
Granulated sugar	½ cup plus 1 tablespoon	63 grams
Instant yeast	1 tablespoon	9 grams
Fine sea salt	2½ teaspoons	15 grams
Sourdough Starter (page xxxiii)	⅔ cup	113 grams
Unsalted butter, cubed and softened	4 tablespoons (½ stick)	56 grams
Butter Packet (page 122)	19 tablespoons (2 sticks plus 3 tablespoons)	266 grams
For shaping the croissants		
All-purpose flour	for dusting	
Semisweet chocolate batons	20 (or 40 semisweet chocolate *feves*)	
For baking the croissants		
Large egg	1	50 grams
Fine sea salt	big pinch	

Make the dough

- Put the milk in a small saucepan and heat it over low heat until it reaches 70°F on a digital thermometer.
- Put the bread flour, cocoa powder, sugar, yeast, and salt in a medium bowl and stir to combine.
- Put the milk, starter, and 4 tablespoons butter (56 grams) in the bowl of a stand mixer. Place the dry ingredients on top. Fit the mixer with the dough hook and mix on low speed for about 3 minutes, until the dough comes together and no chunks of butter are visible.
- Place a long sheet of plastic wrap on your work surface. Use a plastic bowl scraper to scrape the dough out of the mixer onto the plastic wrap and pat the dough into a square shape. Wrap the plastic wrap around the dough and run a rolling pin over the dough to form an even 8-inch square. (For more detail, see Wrapping Dough, page xl.) Place the dough in the refrigerator for 1 hour.

Laminate the Dough

Lock in the butter

- Remove the butter packet from the refrigerator and set it on the counter to soften until it is bendy but still cool; this could take anywhere from 5 to 20 minutes, depending on how cold it is and on the texture of the dough. You want the butter to be slightly softer and more malleable than the dough but not so soft that it will ooze out of the dough.
- Lightly dust a large flat work surface with all-purpose flour. Remove the dough from the refrigerator, unwrap the dough, and place it on the floured surface. Lightly dust the top of the dough and the rolling pin with flour and roll the dough out to a rectangle that is 14 inches from side to side and 11 inches from top to bottom, dusting with flour as needed.
- Open the parchment packet to expose the butter and flip the packet over to place the butter on the dough, centering the 10-inch edge of the butter packet on the 11-inch length of dough. Run your hand over the parchment paper so that the heat of your hand helps to peel off the paper. Peel off and discard the parchment paper. Fold the left and right sides of the dough over the butter so they meet in the middle and pinch the two edges of dough together with your fingers. Gently press the top and bottom edges of the dough together to seal the packet closed and lock in the butter.

Make a book fold

- Dust your work surface with a bit more all-purpose flour. Dust the top of the dough and the rolling pin with flour and roll the dough lengthwise to 32 inches from top to bottom, dusting the work surface, rolling pin, and top of the dough lightly with flour as you roll the dough. (Standard kitchen counters are 26 inches deep, so to roll this, one end of the dough will be hanging over the counter while you roll the other end.) Using a pastry wheel or bench knife, trim the top and bottom edges of the dough just enough to expose the layer of butter in the center of the dough. Reserve the trimmings to make Baked

Trimmings (page 129) or discard them. Fold the top edge of the dough toward the bottom and the bottom edge of the dough toward the top so the two edges meet slightly off-center. Fold the bottom edge to meet the top, like a book.

Make a letter fold

· Rotate the dough 90 degrees so the closed, folded edges are facing left and right, and the open edge, in which the layers are visible, is facing you. Lightly dust the work surface, rolling pin, and dough with all-purpose flour and roll out the dough to 18 inches from top to bottom, dusting with flour as needed. Using a pastry wheel or bench knife, trim the top and bottom edges of the dough just enough to expose the layers of butter in the center of the dough. Add the trimmings to your baked trimmings or discard them. Fold the top edge down two-thirds and fold the bottom edge to meet the top edge, so the dough is folded into thirds, like a letter.

· Wrap the laminated block of dough in plastic wrap and place it in the freezer to chill for 1 hour. Move the dough from the freezer to the refrigerator and let it rest for at least 8 hours and up to 12 hours to retard the dough.

Roll out the dough

· Remove the laminated block of dough from the refrigerator and set it on the counter to rest for 20 to 30 minutes, until you can feel that the butter layers inside the dough are just becoming malleable (but not soft) when you bend the block slightly.

· Lightly dust a large flat work surface with all-purpose flour. Unwrap the dough and place it on the floured surface. Lightly dust the top of the dough and the rolling pin with flour and roll the dough out into a rectangle that is 20 inches from side to side and 12 inches from top to bottom, dusting with flour as needed. The dough will begin to spring back and resist being rolled to these dimensions. You will need to stop to let the gluten relax for a few minutes two or three times during the rolling process.

Cut the croissants

· Using a straightedge and pastry wheel or large knife, trim the edges of the dough, cutting as little as needed to make straight, even edges. Add the trimmings to your baked trimmings or discard them. Cut the dough in half lengthwise so you have 2 (6-inch-wide) strips of dough.

· Use a straightedge and pastry roller to cut the dough into 3½-inch-wide rectangles. Add the end pieces to your baked trimmings or discard them. Cut the second strip of dough in the same way.

Shape and proof the croissants

· Line two baking sheets with parchment paper.

· Place 1 stick of chocolate (or 2 *feves*) along the bottom short edge of the dough and fold the dough over the chocolate, as if you are wrapping fabric around a rectangular bolt of cardboard. Once the chocolate is no longer visible, place another chocolate stick (or 2 *feves*) along the edge of the dough and fold the dough over the chocolate again. Add 1 more baton (or 2 more *feves*) and fold the dough to "close" the croissant. The seam of the croissant should be in the center of the bottom of the croissant; if it isn't, gently roll the croissant so the seam is underneath the croissant. Gently press on the croissant with the palm of your hand to give the croissant the shape of a rectangle with rounded edges. Place the croissant on one of the prepared baking sheets. Repeat, filling the remaining croissants with the remaining chocolate and shaping them as you did the first one. Place the croissants on the prepared baking sheets as they are done, placing 5 croissants on each baking sheet.

· Cover each baking sheet with a damp, lightweight kitchen towel and set the sheets aside in a warm place to proof the croissants for 1½ to 2 hours, until they look swollen and about one and a half times their original size.

Bake the croissants   · While the croissants are proofing, arrange the oven racks so one is in the top third of the oven and the other is in the bottom third. Preheat the oven to 375°F.

· Whisk the egg and salt together in a small bowl to make an egg wash. Uncover the sheets and brush the croissants with the egg wash; discard the remaining egg wash.

· Place one baking sheet on each oven rack to bake the croissants for 25 to 28 minutes, until the tops are deep brown, rotating the baking sheets from front to back and from one rack to the other halfway through the baking time so the croissants brown evenly. Remove the baking sheets from the oven and let the croissants cool on the baking sheets for a few minutes. Use a metal spatula to transfer the pastries to a cooling rack to cool. Serve warm or at room temperature.

Strawberry Jam and Hazelnut Rugelach

Makes 2 dozen rugelach

These classic Jewish cookies are laminated with sugar, meaning the counter is dusted with sugar instead of flour for rolling the dough. Sugar is hydroscopic, which means it has the ability to absorb moisture from its surroundings. The result is that the sugar between the layers pulls water from the dough and becomes syrupy, so the cookies have a crispy, flaky exterior, and are soft and moist on the inside. Rugelach purists debate the merits of triangular versus rectangular rugelach. I like both shapes, but in terms of making them, I am pro rectangle, because the triangles tend to burn on the bottom when I bake them. These are rectangles. If I don't already have Strawberry Jam (page 228) or it isn't the season to make it, I use Bonne Maman jam for these; it is good quality and widely available.

Note You will need four baking sheets to make this: two for the cookies and two to line those baking sheets. Stacking two baking sheets allows the rugelach to brown on top without burning on the bottom.

For the filling		
Hazelnuts	¾ cup	105 grams
Strawberry Jam (page 228; or store-bought)	¾ cup	218 grams
For the dough		
Unsalted butter, cold	16 tablespoons (2 sticks)	226 grams
Cream cheese, cold	8 ounces	226 grams
All purpose flour	1½ cups plus more for dusting	180 grams
Whole-wheat pastry flour	½ cup	53 grams
Granulated sugar	1 tablespoon	13 grams
Fine sea salt	½ teaspoon	3 grams
For laminating the dough		
Granulated sugar	¼ cup plus 2 tablespoons for sprinkling	50 grams plus 25 grams

Toast the hazelnuts for the filling

· Arrange the oven racks so one is in the center position. Preheat the oven to 300°F.

· Spread the hazelnuts on a baking sheet and toast them in the oven for 20 to 25 minutes, until they are golden brown and fragrant, shaking the pan once during that time for even toasting. Remove the baking sheet from the oven and set aside for about 10 minutes to allow the nuts to cool slightly.

· Put the nuts in the center of a clean kitchen towel, close the towel, and rub the nuts in the towel between your hands to rub off as much of the skins as possible. Pick up the nuts with your hands, leaving the skins in the towel. Put the nuts in a large sealable plastic bag and seal the bag closed, letting any excess air escape as you seal it. Lay the bag on your countertop and roll your rolling pin over it to crush the hazelnuts into small pieces; you don't want to crush them so much that they are powdery.

Make the dough
- Cut the butter and cream cheese into 1-inch cubes. Spread them out on a plate and put the plate in the freezer for 10 minutes.
- Meanwhile, put the all-purpose flour, whole-wheat pastry flour, sugar, and salt in the bowl of a stand mixer. Fit the mixer with the paddle attachment and mix on low speed to combine. Turn off the mixer, add the butter and cream cheese, and mix on the lowest speed to avoid flour flying out of the bowl when you turn the mixer on, until the dough completely comes together and wraps around the paddle, about 2 minutes.
- Lightly dust a large flat work surface with all-purpose flour. Scoop the dough out of the bowl with a rubber spatula and place it on the floured surface. Pat the dough into an 8-inch square.

Make a letter fold
- Lightly dust the top of the dough and the rolling pin with all-purpose flour and roll the dough lengthwise to 20 inches from top to bottom. Fold the top edge down two-thirds and fold the bottom edge to meet the top edge, so the dough is folded into thirds, like a letter.

Make a second letter fold
- Put ¼ cup of the laminating sugar in a small bowl. Lift up the dough and dust your work surface with one-third of the sugar. Place the dough on the sugar-dusted surface, rotating it 90 degrees so the closed, folded edges are facing left and right, and one of the open edges (with visible layers) is facing you. Sprinkle the top of the dough with some of the remaining sugar and roll the dough out to 20 inches from top to bottom, dusting the dough, rolling pin, and work surface with the remaining laminating sugar as you roll. Fold the top edge down and the bottom edge up to make a second letter fold.
- Wrap the dough in plastic wrap and place it in the refrigerator to chill until the dough is firm, about 45 minutes and up to 2 days.

Fill and form the rugelach
- Lightly dust a large flat work surface with all-purpose flour. Remove the dough from the refrigerator and place it on the floured surface. Lightly dust the dough and rolling pin with flour and roll it out to a rectangle that is 21 inches from side to side and 13 inches from top to bottom, dusting with flour as needed.
- Using a pastry wheel and straightedge, trim all four sides of the dough to create straight, even edges. Reserve the trimmings to make Baked Trimmings (page 129) or discard them. Use the pastry wheel to cut the dough in half lengthwise so you have 2 (roughly 6-inch-wide) strips of dough.

- Spoon half of the jam onto the strip of dough closest to you and use a small offset spatula to spread the filling evenly over the dough, leaving ½ inch on the edge farthest from you clear of filling. Sprinkle half of the hazelnuts over the jam. Brush the bare edge of the length of dough with water.
- Begin with the edge closest to you and fold the jam-covered edge of the dough away from you by ¾ inch. Repeat, flopping the dough over itself until you have rolled the strip of dough into a long log. Move the log aside. Spread the remaining jam on the second length of dough, sprinkle the nuts over the jam, and roll it up in the same way.
- Line a baking sheet with parchment paper.
- Place the logs on the baking sheet and place the baking sheet in the refrigerator to chill the logs for at least 30 minutes, and up to overnight, to firm up the dough. (If you are preparing the rugelach in advance, remove the baking sheet from the refrigerator after the dough is firm. Wrap each log in plastic wrap and freeze for up to 1 month. When you are ready to bake them, remove the logs from the freezer and place them on your counter to defrost for about 30 minutes, until they are soft enough to slice, or place them in the refrigerator overnight to defrost, before proceeding with the recipe.)

Cut the rugelach
- Line two more baking sheets with parchment paper.
- Remove the rugelach logs from the refrigerator. Place one on a cutting board with the seam facing down. Use a large sharp knife to cut the log into 1½-inch lengths and place the pieces, seam side down, on the prepared baking sheets, leaving about 2 inches between each rugelach. Repeat, cutting the remaining log and adding the remaining pieces to the baking sheets. Place the baking sheets in the refrigerator for at least 1 hour, and up to overnight, to firm up the dough before baking.

Prepare to bake the rugelach
- Arrange the oven racks so one is in the top third of the oven and the other is in the bottom third. Preheat the oven to 350°F.
- Remove the baking sheets from the refrigerator. Brush the tops of the rugelach with water and sprinkle with the remaining 2 tablespoons sugar.
- Place a baking sheet under each baking sheet of rugelach so the baking sheets are a double thickness; this allows the cookies to brown on top without burning (the sugar they are rolled in causes the bottoms to burn easily).

Bake the rugelach
- Place one doubled baking sheet on each oven rack to bake the cookies for 25 to 30 minutes, until the rugelach are light golden, rotating the baking sheets from front to back and from one rack to the other halfway through the baking time so the rugelach brown evenly. Remove the baking sheets from the oven. Use an offset spatula or thin metal spatula to move the rugelach to a cooling rack to cool to room temperature.

Variation
Poppy Seed Rugelach

Although jam-filled hazelnut rugelach tend to be more popular, these are my personal favorite. You need a spice grinder to grind the poppy seeds for these, and a digital instant-read thermometer.

For the filling

Poppy seeds	½ cup	58 grams
Large egg	1	50 grams
Crème fraîche (or whole milk)	¼ cup	55 grams
Granulated sugar	2 tablespoons	26 grams
Mild-flavored honey (such as wildflower or clover)	2 tablespoons	40 grams
Unsalted butter	1 tablespoon	14 grams
Zest from 1 lemon		
Juice from ½ lemon	1 tablespoon	15 grams
Fine sea salt	¼ teaspoon	1.5 grams

Make the filling

- Grind one-third of the poppy seeds in a spice grinder for a few seconds, until they are broken up and powdery. Pour the ground seeds into a small bowl, and repeat, grinding the remaining seeds in two more batches and adding the ground seeds to the bowl with the first batch of ground seeds. Set aside.
- Whisk the egg in a medium bowl to break it up; set it near your stove. Place a fine-mesh strainer in a medium bowl and set aside.
- Place the crème fraîche, sugar, honey, butter, lemon zest, lemon juice, and salt in a small saucepan and heat over medium heat, stirring with a whisk until the butter melts and the sugar dissolves. Gradually add this mixture to the bowl with the egg and return the mixture to the saucepan. Cook on low heat, whisking constantly, until the mixture is a thick, custard-like consistency and registers 180°F on a digital thermometer. Remove the saucepan from the heat and pour the mixture through the strainer into the bowl. Stir in the poppy seeds. Cover the bowl with plastic wrap, pressing the plastic wrap to touch the filling to prevent a skin from forming. Refrigerate the filling until it is cool to the touch and has set up to the consistency of peanut butter, or for up to 3 days.
- Spoon and spread the poppy seed filling as if it were the jam in the recipe above, dividing it between the 2 (6-inch-wide) strips of dough, and proceed with the recipe.

Flaky Buttermilk Biscuits

I am very clear about what I like in biscuits: I like them soft and flaky, rich with butter, and with a lot of layers that you can see from the side. That's what these are. They're not a light, fluffy Southern biscuit that you would pour gravy over. In fact, these have a crunchy, burnished exterior. I like to eat them with salty butter and jam.

Makes 16 biscuits

Unsalted butter, cold	16 tablespoons (2 sticks)	226 grams
All-purpose flour	1½ cups plus more for dusting	180 grams
Whole-wheat pastry flour	1⅔ cups	175 grams
Baking powder	1½ teaspoons	8 grams
Granulated sugar	2 teaspoons	9 grams
Fine sea salt	1½ teaspoons	9 grams
Buttermilk, well shaken	1 cup plus 2 tablespoons	265 grams

Make the dough

- Cut the butter into ½-inch-thick pieces. Lay the pieces in a single layer on a plate and put the plate in the freezer for 10 minutes.
- Place the all-purpose flour, whole-wheat pastry flour, baking powder, sugar, and salt in the bowl of a stand mixer. Fit the mixer with the paddle attachment and mix on low speed for about 30 seconds to combine the ingredients. Add the butter and mix on low for 1 to 2 minutes, until there are no large chunks of butter remaining. Turn off the mixer and use your hands to check the size of the butter; if there are any pieces larger than a nickel, pinch them between your fingertips to flatten them. Add 1 cup of the buttermilk and mix on low speed just until the mixture comes together, and no dry pockets remain; it will be slightly lumpy.

Roll out the dough

- Dust a large flat work surface with all-purpose flour.
- Use a plastic bowl scraper to scoop the dough out of the bowl onto the floured surface. Pat the dough into a 6-inch square. Lightly dust the top of the dough and a rolling pin with flour and roll the dough to 14 inches from top to bottom, dusting with flour as needed. Slide a bench knife under the top edge of the dough and fold it down two-thirds. Slide the bench knife under the bottom edge and fold it up to meet the top edge to fold the dough into thirds, like a letter.
- Rotate the dough 90 degrees so the folded, closed edges are facing left and right and one of the open edges (with the visible layer) is facing you, dusting underneath and on top of the dough and the rolling pin with all-purpose flour.

Roll the dough out until it is 14 inches from top to bottom, dusting with flour as needed. Slide a bench knife under the top edge of the dough and fold it down two-thirds. Slide the bench knife under the bottom edge and fold it up to meet the top edge to fold the dough into thirds, like a letter.

- Line a baking sheet with parchment paper.
- Pat the dough into an 8-inch square and place the square of dough on the prepared baking sheet and refrigerate for 30 minutes to chill.

Prepare to bake the biscuits

- Arrange the oven racks so one is in the top third and the other is in the bottom third. Preheat the oven to 400°F.
- Line a second baking sheet with parchment paper.
- Take the baking sheet with dough out of the refrigerator.
- Lift the parchment paper with the dough off the sheet and lay it on a flat work surface. Line the baking sheet with a fresh sheet of parchment paper.
- Use a large chef's knife to cut the dough into 2-inch squares. Transfer the biscuits to the two prepared baking sheets, dividing them evenly and leaving 2 inches between each biscuit.
- Brush the tops of the biscuits with the remaining buttermilk.

Bake the biscuits

- Place one baking sheet on each oven rack to bake the biscuits for 25 to 30 minutes, until the tops are deep golden brown, rotating the baking sheets from front to back and from one rack to the other halfway through the baking time so the biscuits brown evenly. Remove the baking sheets from the oven and let the biscuits cool for about 2 minutes on the baking sheets. Serve warm or at room temperature.

Kouign Amann

**Makes 1 dozen
kouign amann**

If you've never heard of kouign amann, you're not alone: they are relatively new to the American baking scene. Pronounced "queen amann"—the name means "buttery cake" in Breton—they are a traditional pastry from Brittany, France. They have butter and sugar laminated into the dough, and the dough itself is also very buttery. I add sourdough starter to the dough, which gives it a nice flavor. Brittany is known for its butter, so when I make these, I use good, high-fat European-style butter such as Plugrá, which is now widely available.

You want to make your butter packet in advance, or while the dough is in the refrigerator. Place the packet in the refrigerator to chill until you're ready to laminate the dough, then remove it from the refrigerator to soften it when called to do so in the recipe.

Note You will need two (6-cup) jumbo muffin tins to make these.

For the dough		
Bread flour	3¾ cups	450 grams
Granulated sugar	2 teaspoons	9 grams
Fine sea salt	2 teaspoons	12 grams
Instant yeast	1½ teaspoons	4.5 grams
Water (75°F)	1 cup plus 2 tablespoons	265 grams
Sourdough Starter (page xxxiii)	½ cup	85 grams
Unsalted butter, cubed, softened	1 tablespoon	14 grams
Butter Packet (page 122), chilled	25 tablespoons (3 sticks plus 1 tablespoon)	350 grams
All-purpose flour	for dusting	
Granulated sugar	¾ cup	150 grams
For finishing the kouign amann		
Nonstick cooking spray		
Granulated sugar	12 teaspoons	52 grams

Make the dough

- Line a baking sheet with parchment paper.
- Put the bread flour, sugar, salt, and yeast in a medium bowl and stir to combine.
- Put the water and starter in the bowl of a stand mixer. Add the dry ingredients and the butter. Fit the mixer with the dough hook and mix on low speed for about 3 minutes, until the dough just comes together and no chunks of butter are visible.
- Place a long sheet of plastic wrap on your work surface. Use a plastic bowl scraper to scrape the dough out of the mixer onto the plastic wrap and pat the dough into a square shape. Wrap the plastic wrap around the dough and run a

rolling pin over the dough to form an even 8-inch square. (For more detail, see Wrapping Dough, page xl.) Place the dough in the refrigerator for 1 hour.

Laminate the Dough

Lock in the butter
· Remove the butter packet from the refrigerator and set it on the counter to soften until it is bendy but still cool; this could take anywhere from 5 to 20 minutes, depending on how cold it is and on the texture of the dough. You want the butter to be slightly softer and more malleable than the dough but not so soft that it will ooze out of the dough.

· Lightly dust a large flat work surface with all-purpose flour. Remove the dough from the refrigerator, unwrap the dough, and place it on the floured surface. Lightly dust the top of the dough and the rolling pin with flour and roll the dough out to a rectangle that is 14 inches from side to side and 11 inches from top to bottom, dusting with flour as needed.

· Open the parchment packet to expose the butter and flip the packet over to place the butter on the dough, centering the 10-inch edge of the butter packet on the 11-inch length of dough. Run your hand over the parchment paper so that the heat of your hand helps to peel off the paper. Peel off and discard the parchment paper. Fold the left and right sides of the dough over the butter so they meet in the middle and pinch the two edges of dough together with your fingers. Gently press the top and bottom edges of the dough together to seal the packet closed and lock in the butter.

Make three letter folds
· Lightly dust a large flat work surface with all-purpose flour and place the dough on the floured surface. Lightly dust the top of the dough and the rolling pin with flour and roll the dough to 18 inches from top to bottom, dusting the work surface, rolling pin, and top of the dough lightly with flour as you roll the dough, so it doesn't stick. Using a pastry wheel or a bench knife, trim the top and bottom edges of the dough just enough to expose the layer of butter in the center of the dough. Reserve the trimmings to make Baked Trimmings (page 129) or discard them. Fold the top edge down two-thirds and fold the bottom edge to meet the top edge, so the dough is folded into thirds, like a letter.

· Rotate the dough 90 degrees so the closed edges are facing left and right and one of the open edges (with the visible layers) is facing you. Lightly dust the work surface, rolling pin, and dough with flour and roll out the dough until it is roughly 18 inches from top to bottom, dusting with flour as needed. Using a pastry wheel or a bench knife, trim the top and bottom edges to expose the butter layers. Add the trimmings to your baked trimmings or discard them. Fold the top edge down and the bottom edge up to make a second letter fold.

· Wrap the dough in plastic and place it in the refrigerator to relax the gluten for 30 minutes. (Don't worry about cleaning up your counter as you will be making one more letter fold during this lamination process.)

· Lightly dust your work surface with more all-purpose flour if needed. Remove the dough from the refrigerator, unwrap the dough, and place it on the floured surface with the closed edges facing left and right. Lightly dust the top of the dough and the rolling pin with flour and roll out the dough to 18 inches from top to bottom, dusting with flour as needed. Trim the top and bottom edges to expose the butter layers and add the trimmings to your baked trimmings or discard them. Fold the top edge down and the bottom edge up to make a third letter fold.

· Wrap the laminated block of dough in plastic and place it in the freezer to chill for 1 hour. Move the dough from the freezer to the refrigerator for at least 8 hours and up to 12 hours to retard the dough.

Make the fourth letter fold with sugar

· Remove the laminated block of dough from the refrigerator and set it on the counter to rest for 20 to 30 minutes, until you can feel that the butter layers inside the dough are just becoming malleable (but not soft) when you bend the block slightly.

· Put the laminating sugar in a small bowl. Lightly dust a large flat work surface with about one-third of the sugar.

· Unwrap the dough and place it so the closed, folded edges are facing left and right, and one of the open edges (with visible layers) is facing you. Lightly dust the top of the dough and the rolling pin with more sugar and roll the dough out to a rectangle that is 18 inches from top to bottom, dusting the dough, rolling pin, and work surface with sugar as needed to keep the dough from sticking. Fold the top edge down and the bottom edge up to make a fourth letter fold. Wrap the dough in plastic wrap and let it rest on your counter for 20 minutes before proceeding.

Roll out and shape the kouign amann

· Spray 12 jumbo muffin cups with nonstick cooking spray. Sprinkle 1 teaspoon of sugar into each muffin cup. Swirl the tins to distribute the sugar over the bottom and sides of the cups.

· Dust your work surface with some of the remaining laminating sugar. Unwrap the dough and place the dough on the sugared surface. Dust the top of the dough and the rolling pin with additional sugar and roll the dough out to a rectangle that is 12 inches from top to bottom and 16 inches from side to side, dusting with the remaining laminating sugar as you roll. Using the straightedge as a guide, cut the dough into 4-inch squares.

· Working with one square of dough at a time, bring two opposite corners of the dough together and press down to seal them together in the center of the square. Fold the two remaining corners together and press to seal them together in the center. Place the dough in a muffin cup with the folds facing up. Repeat with the remaining squares of dough, folding in the same way and placing them in the remaining prepared muffin cups.

· Cover each muffin tin with a damp, lightweight kitchen towel and set them aside in a warm place for 50 to 60 minutes to proof, until the kouign amann start to puff up and expand.

Bake the kouign amann

· While the kouign amann are proofing, arrange the oven racks so that one is in the center position. Preheat the oven to 375°F.

· Place the muffin tins on the center rack to bake the kouign amann for 25 to 30 minutes, until the tops are golden brown and the undersides are caramelized and a bit of the caramelizing sugar begins to peek out around the sides of the pastries, rotating the muffin tins from front to back halfway through the baking time so the pastries brown evenly.

· While the kouign amann are baking, lay a sheet of parchment paper on your countertop. Remove the kouign amann from the oven and immediately flip the tins upside down so the pastries fall out onto the paper. If the pastries are sticking to the sides, run an offset spatula around the edges to loosen them. Turn the pastries right side up to cool. Serve warm or at room temperature.

Variation
Black Sesame
Kouign Amann

I love pastries with black sesame seeds. Supposedly they have more flavor than white ones, but I like them just as much for how they look. What really makes a difference when choosing sesame seeds is that they are toasted, as untoasted sesame seeds have very little flavor. You can toast your sesame seeds in a skillet or buy already-toasted sesame seeds; these are sold with the hulls on in the Japanese section of grocery stores, often in a shaker can. The toasted sesame seeds have a sweet, toasty flavor that makes these crisp, buttery pastries really special.

Black sesame seeds	¼ cup plus 2 tablespoons	50 grams
Granulated sugar	¾ cup	150 grams

· If you are starting with untoasted sesame seeds, put them in a medium skillet and toast over medium-high heat for 1 to 2 minutes, shaking the pan frequently so they toast evenly and don't burn, until they are fragrant and begin popping in the pan. Turn off the heat and transfer the seeds to a medium bowl to cool to room temperature.

· Working in three batches, put the sesame seeds in a spice grinder with about 1 tablespoon of the sugar. Pulse to break up the seeds without pulverizing them. (Three quick pulses.) Put the ground seeds and sugar in a medium bowl. Repeat, grinding the rest of the seeds in two additional batches with about 1 tablespoon of the sugar in each batch. Add the ground seeds to the bowl. Add the remaining sugar to the bowl and stir to combine.

· Reserve 12 teaspoons to put 1 teaspoon in each muffin cup. Use this mixture of seeds and sugar in place of the laminating sugar in the kouign amann recipe.

Buckwheat Kouign Amann

**Makes 10
kouign amann**

Buckwheat is a grain commonly grown in Brittany and used in many Breton pastries, most famously galettes, or savory crêpes. Kouign amann are also from Brittany, so after a recent trip there, I was inspired to marry the two, creating these delicious buckwheat kouign amann. The nutty and earthy flavors of the buckwheat provide the perfect contrast to the butter and sugar. I shape these into spirals instead of folding in the corners as I do with the plain kouign amann.

Make your butter packet in advance or while the dough is in the refrigerator. Place the packet in the refrigerator to chill until you're ready to laminate the dough, then remove it from the refrigerator to soften it when called to do so in the recipe.

Note You will need two (6-cup) jumbo muffin tins to make these.

For the dough		
Bread flour	2½ cups plus more for dusting	300 grams
Buckwheat flour	1¼ cups	150 grams
Granulated sugar	2 teaspoons	9 grams
Fine sea salt	2 teaspoons	12 grams
Instant yeast	1½ teaspoons	4.5 grams
Water (75°F)	1 cup plus 2 tablespoons	265 grams
Sourdough Starter (page xxxiii)	½ cup	85 grams
Unsalted butter, softened	1 tablespoon	14 grams
Butter Packet (page 122)	25 tablespoons (3 sticks plus 1 tablespoon)	350 grams
Granulated sugar	1¼ cups	250 grams
For finishing the kouign amann		
Nonstick cooking spray		
Granulated sugar	10 teaspoons	43 grams

Make the dough

- Line a baking sheet with parchment paper.
- Place the bread flour, buckwheat flour, sugar, salt, and yeast in a medium bowl and stir to combine the ingredients.
- Put the water and starter in the bowl of a stand mixer. Add the dry ingredients and the butter. Fit the mixer with the dough hook and mix on low speed for about 3 minutes, until the dough just comes together and no chunks of butter are visible.
- Place a long sheet of plastic wrap on your work surface. Use a plastic bowl scraper to scrape the dough out of the mixer onto the plastic wrap and pat the dough into a square shape. Wrap the plastic wrap around the dough and run a rolling pin over the dough to form an even 8-inch square. (For more detail, see Wrapping Dough, page xl.) Place the dough in the refrigerator for 1 hour.

Laminate the Dough

Lock in the butter

· Remove the butter packet from the refrigerator and set it on the counter to soften until it is bendy but still cool; this could take anywhere from 5 to 20 minutes, depending on how cold it is and on the texture of the dough. You want the butter to be slightly softer and more malleable than the dough but not so soft that it will ooze out of the dough.

· Lightly dust a large flat work surface with bread flour. Remove the dough from the refrigerator, unwrap the dough, and place it on the floured surface. Lightly dust the top of the dough and the rolling pin with flour and roll the dough out to a rectangle that is 14 inches from side to side and 11 inches from top to bottom, dusting with flour as needed.

· Open the parchment packet to expose the butter and flip the packet over to place the butter on the dough, centering the 10 inch edge of the butter packet on the 11-inch length of dough. Run your hand over the parchment paper so that the heat of your hand helps to peel off the paper. Peel off and discard the parchment paper. Fold the left and right sides of the dough over the butter so they meet in the middle and pinch the two edges of dough together with your fingers. Gently press the top and bottom edges of the dough together to seal the packet closed and lock in the butter.

Make three letter folds

· Lightly dust a large flat work surface with bread flour and place the dough on the floured surface. Lightly dust the top of the dough and the rolling pin with flour and roll the dough lengthwise to 18 inches from top to bottom, dusting the work surface, rolling pin, and top of the dough lightly with flour as you roll the dough so that it doesn't stick. Using a pastry wheel or a bench knife, trim the top and bottom edges of the dough just enough to expose the layer of butter in the center of the dough. Reserve the trimmings to make Baked Trimmings (page 129) or discard them. Fold the top edge down two-thirds and fold the bottom edge to meet the top edge, so the dough is folded into thirds, like a letter.

· Rotate the dough 90 degrees so the closed edges are facing left and right and one of the open edges (with the visible layers) is facing you. Lightly dust the work surface, dough, and rolling pin with flour and roll the dough to 18 inches from top to bottom, dusting with flour as needed. Using a pastry wheel or a bench knife, trim the top and bottom edges to expose the butter layers. Add the trimmings to your baked trimmings or discard them. Fold the top edge down and the bottom edge up to make a second letter fold.

· Wrap the dough in plastic and place it in the refrigerator to relax the gluten for 20 minutes. (Don't worry about cleaning up your counter as you will be making one more fold during your lamination process.)

· Lightly dust your work surface with more bread flour if needed. Remove the dough from the refrigerator, unwrap it, and place it on the floured surface with the closed edges facing left and right. Lightly dust the top of the dough and rolling pin with flour and roll out the dough to 18 inches from top to bottom, dusting with flour as needed. Trim the top and bottom edges to expose the butter layers. Add the trimmings to your baked trimmings or discard them. Fold the top edge down and the bottom edge up to make a third letter fold.

- Wrap the laminated block of dough in plastic and place it in the freezer to chill for 1 hour. Move the dough from the freezer to the refrigerator for at least 8 hours and up to 12 hours to retard the dough.

Make a fourth letter fold

- Remove the laminated block of dough from the refrigerator and set it on the counter to rest for 20 to 30 minutes, until you can feel that the butter layers inside the dough are just becoming malleable (but not soft) when you bend the block slightly.
- Put the laminating sugar in a small bowl. Lightly dust a large flat work surface with one-third of the sugar.
- Unwrap the dough and place it so the closed, folded edges are facing left and right, and one of the open edges (with visible layers) is facing you. Lightly dust the top of the dough and the rolling pin with more sugar and roll the dough out to a rectangle that is 18 inches from top to bottom, dusting the dough, rolling pin, and work surface with the sugar as needed to keep the dough from sticking. Fold the top edge down two-thirds and fold the bottom edge to meet the top edge to make a fourth letter fold. Wrap the dough in plastic wrap and let it rest on your counter for 20 minutes before proceeding.

Roll out and shape the kouign amann

- Spray 10 jumbo muffin cups with nonstick cooking spray. Sprinkle 1 teaspoon of sugar into each muffin cup. Swirl the tins to distribute the sugar over the bottom and sides of the cups.
- Dust your work surface with the remaining laminating sugar. Unwrap the dough and place the dough on the sugared surface. Dust the top of the dough and the rolling pin with additional sugar and roll the dough out to a rectangle that is 18 inches from top to bottom and 13 inches from side to side. Using a straightedge and a pastry wheel or long knife, trim the edges of the dough, cutting as little as needed to make straight, even edges. Add the trimmings to your baked trimmings or discard them. Using the straightedge as a guide, cut the dough into 10 (1¼-inch) strips.
- Pick up one strip and roll it away from you into a spiral. Lay the spiral with the concentric circles facing up in one of the prepared muffin cups. Repeat with the remaining strips, rolling and placing each in a prepared muffin cup.
- Cover each muffin tin with a damp, lightweight kitchen towel and set aside in a warm place for 50 to 60 minutes to proof, until the kouign amann start to puff up and expand.

Bake the kouign amann

- While the kouign amann are proofing, arrange the oven racks so that one is in the center position. Preheat the oven to 375°F.
- Place the muffin tins on the center rack to bake the kouign amann for 25 to 30 minutes, until the tops are golden brown and the undersides are caramelized and a bit of the caramelizing sugar begins to peek out around the sides of the pastries, rotating the muffin tins from front to back halfway through the baking time so the pastries brown evenly.
- While the kouign amann are baking, lay a sheet of parchment paper on your countertop. Remove the kouign amann from the oven and immediately flip the tins upside down so the pastries fall out onto the paper. If the pastries are sticking to the sides, run an offset spatula around the edges to loosen them. Turn the pastries right side up to cool completely.

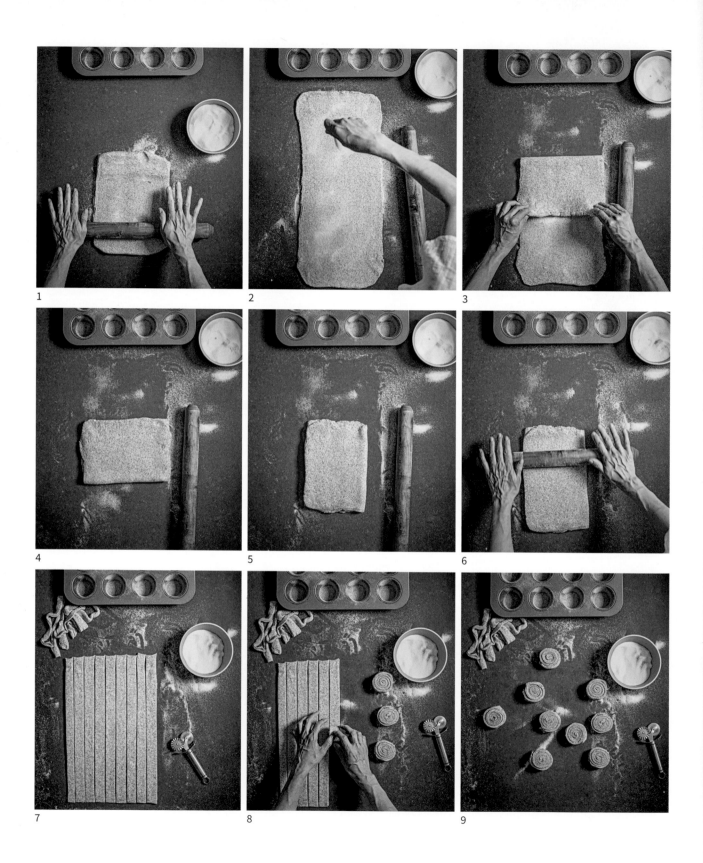

Chaussons aux Pommes

Makes 7 chaussons; makes 1 (1-kilogram) block of puff pastry dough or enough for 2 sheets. (You will need only one sheet for this recipe. Freeze the second sheet for up to 2 weeks. Place it in the refrigerator to thaw overnight before using it.)

A *chausson aux pommes* is basically the French version of an apple turnover, and a classic after-school treat for French schoolchildren. In addition to Ham and Cheese Twice-Baked Croissants (page 144) and Pain aux Raisins (page 147), this was one of my go-to snacks when I studied in France.

Chaussons are made with puff pastry, which differs from croissant dough in that it doesn't contain yeast. Instead, puff pastry gets its height and lightness solely from folding the dough. When the water in the butter evaporates during the baking process, it pushes the layers of dough upward, creating a layered, flaky dough. Traditionally puff pastry is made with six letter folds, considerably more than yeasted laminated dough. I make this puff pastry with five folds; I think the sixth letter fold makes it *too* flaky. I don't want it to shatter and fall apart when I bite into it. The other difference in my puff pastry is that it contains some whole-wheat pastry flour, which adds a subtle nutty flavor that you don't usually get in this delicate dough.

Puff pastry dough can be really irritating to work with because the gluten in the dough gets really strong from being rolled out and folded so many times. You need to relax it in the refrigerator between folds, and then pay attention to how the dough feels when you pull it back out before rolling it again. Give the dough a gentle bend. If you feel the butter is hard, like it is going to break, let it warm up slightly before rolling the dough. I don't recommend puff pastry for the laminating novice. You want to make your butter packet in advance of starting this recipe. Place it in the refrigerator to chill until you're ready to laminate the dough, then temper it when called to do so in the recipe.

Note You will need an oval turnover cutter to make these. They aren't the most common cutter you'll find (not in the United States anyway) and when you do find them, they can be expensive. I have provided a traceable pattern for you to use to make your own cutter if you don't want to buy one (see page 189). Trace the pattern onto a piece of cardstock (a discarded cereal box would work perfectly). Cut the oval out of the cardstock to create a stencil and use the stencil as a guide to cut ovals from the puff pastry dough.

For the dough

Bread flour	3⅓ cups	400 grams
Whole-wheat pastry flour	¾ cup	79 grams
Fine sea salt	2½ teaspoons	15 grams
Cold water	1 cup plus 1 tablespoon	250 grams
White vinegar	1 teaspoon	5 grams
Unsalted butter, cubed and slightly softened	5 tablespoons	70 grams
Butter Packet (page 122)	28 tablespoons (3½ sticks)	400 grams
All-purpose flour	for dusting	

For the filling

Unsalted butter	1 tablespoon	14 grams
Granny Smith apples	3 medium to large	
Light brown sugar	½ cup (lightly packed)	100 grams
All-purpose flour	2 tablespoons	18 grams
Ground ginger	½ teaspoon	1 gram
Fine sea salt	¼ teaspoon	2 grams
Apple cider vinegar	2 teaspoons	10 grams
Pure vanilla extract	1 teaspoon	5 grams

For shaping and finishing the pastries

All-purpose flour	for dusting
Large egg	1
Fine sea salt	big pinch

Make the dough

▪ Combine the bread flour, whole-wheat pastry flour, and salt in a medium bowl.

▪ Put the water and white vinegar in the bowl of a stand mixer. Add the dry ingredients and butter on top of the liquid ingredients. Fit the mixer with the dough hook and mix on low speed for about 3 minutes, until the dough just comes together and no chunks of butter are visible.

▪ Place a long sheet of plastic wrap on your work surface. Use a plastic bowl scraper to scrape the dough out of the mixer onto the plastic wrap and pat the dough into a square shape. Wrap the plastic wrap around the dough and run a rolling pin over the dough to form an even 8-inch square. (For more detail, see Wrapping Dough, page xl.) Set the dough aside to rest for 20 to 30 minutes.

Laminate the Dough

Lock in the butter

▪ Remove the butter packet from the refrigerator and set it on the counter to soften until it is bendy but still cool; this could take anywhere from 5 to 20 minutes, depending on how cold it is and on the texture of the dough. You want the butter to be slightly softer and more malleable than the dough but not so soft that it will ooze out of the dough.

- Lightly dust a large flat work surface with all-purpose flour. Remove the dough from the refrigerator, unwrap the dough, and place it on the floured surface. Lightly dust the top of the dough and the rolling pin with flour and roll the dough out to a rectangle that is 14 inches from side to side and 11 inches from top to bottom, dusting with flour as needed.
- Open the parchment packet to expose the butter and flip the packet over to place the butter on the dough, centering the 10-inch edge of the butter packet on the 11-inch length of dough. Run your hand over the parchment paper so that the heat of your hand helps to peel off the paper. Peel off and discard the parchment paper. Fold the left and right sides of the dough over the butter so they meet in the middle and pinch the two edges of dough together with your fingers. Gently press the top and bottom edges of the dough together to seal the packet closed and lock in the butter.

Make five letter folds

- Dust your work surface with a bit more all-purpose flour. Dust the top of the dough and the rolling pin with flour and roll the dough lengthwise to 18 inches from top to bottom, dusting the work surface, rolling pin, and top of the dough lightly with flour as you roll the dough, so it doesn't stick. Using a pastry wheel or bench knife, trim the top and bottom edges of the dough just enough to expose the layer of butter in the center of the dough. Reserve the trimmings to make Baked Trimmings (page 129) or discard them.
- Fold the top edge down two-thirds and fold the bottom edge to meet the top edge, so the dough is folded into thirds, like a letter.
- Rotate the dough 90 degrees so the folded, closed edges are facing left and right, and one of the open edges (with the visible layers) is facing you. Lightly dust the work surface, dough, and rolling pin with all-purpose flour and roll the dough to 18 inches from top to bottom, dusting with flour as needed. Using a pastry wheel or a bench knife, trim the top and bottom edges to expose the butter layers. Add the trimmings to your baked trimmings or discard them. Fold the top edge down and the bottom edge up to make a second letter fold.
- Wrap the dough in plastic and place it in the refrigerator to relax the gluten for 20 to 30 minutes. (Don't worry about cleaning up your counter as you will be making three more letter folds during this lamination process.)
- Lightly dust your work surface with more flour if needed. Remove the dough from the refrigerator, unwrap it, and place it on the floured surface with the closed edges facing left and right. Lightly dust the top of the dough and rolling pin with flour and roll out the dough to 18 inches from top to bottom, dusting with flour as needed. Trim the top and bottom edges to expose the butter layers. Add the trimmings to your baked trimmings or discard them. Fold the top edge down and the bottom edge up to make a third letter fold.
- Wrap the dough in plastic again and refrigerate it for 20 to 30 minutes before

making a fourth letter fold. Let the dough rest again for 20 to 30 minutes, then repeat, rolling the dough out again and making a fifth letter fold.

· Wrap the dough in plastic wrap again and place the dough in the refrigerator overnight or for at least 8 hours to let the gluten relax completely. (The dough can also be frozen for up to 3 months; place it in the refrigerator overnight to thaw it, then proceed with the recipe.)

Make the filling

· Arrange the oven racks so one is in the center position. Preheat the oven to 350°F.

· Grease the bottom of a 9-inch pie plate or another medium baking dish with the butter.

· Peel the apples and discard the peels. Working one at a time, core and cut each apple into quarters. Lay the apple quarters flat on your cutting board and slice them ⅛ inch thick. Place the slices in a large bowl and set aside.

· Put the brown sugar, all-purpose flour, ginger, and salt in a small bowl and stir to combine. Sprinkle the sugar mixture over the apples. Add the cider vinegar and vanilla and toss with your hands to coat the apples with the other ingredients.

· Transfer the apple filling to the prepared pie plate and cover with aluminum foil.

· Place the pie pan on the center rack of the oven to bake for 45 minutes, until the apples are soft and the liquid is thick and bubbly. Remove the pan from the oven and remove the aluminum foil, being careful of the escaping steam. Gently stir the apples and set aside to cool to room temperature. (You can make the filling to this point up to 1 day in advance. Cover the cooled apples and refrigerate until you're ready to use them.)

Roll out the dough

· Remove the laminated block of dough from the refrigerator and set it on the counter to rest for 20 to 30 minutes, until you can feel that the butter layers inside the dough are just becoming malleable (but not soft) when you bend the block slightly.

· Line a baking sheet with parchment paper and have a second sheet of parchment handy.

· Lightly dust a large flat work surface with all-purpose flour. Unwrap the dough and place it on the floured surface. Dust the top of the dough and the rolling pin with flour and roll the dough out to a 13- x 20-inch rectangle, dusting the work surface, rolling pin, and top of the dough lightly with flour as you roll the dough, so it doesn't stick. Use a pastry wheel or a large knife to cut the dough in half through the middle. Transfer one half to the prepared baking sheet. Lay the second sheet of parchment paper on top of the dough and lay the second sheet of dough on top of the parchment. Place the baking sheet in the refrigerator to let the dough relax for about 30 minutes.

Roll out and form the chaussons

- Lightly dust a large flat work surface with all-purpose flour. Remove the puff pastry from the refrigerator. Place one sheet of puff pastry on the work surface. Wrap the baking sheet with the remaining pastry sheet in plastic wrap and freeze. Let the first sheet rest at room temperature for 20 to 30 minutes.
- Lightly dust the top of the puff pastry and the rolling pin with flour and roll out the pastry to 20 inches from side to side and 13 inches from top to bottom, dusting with flour as needed.
- Using a small sharp knife and a turnover cutter or the stencil you made from the traceable pattern, cut 7 ovals from the pastry.

Fill the chaussons

- Place about 3 tablespoons (60 grams) of the filling on the bottom half of each oval, leaving a ¼-inch border with no filling around the edges of the pastry. Fill a small bowl with water and use a pastry brush to brush the bare edges of the ovals with water. Fold the top half of the dough over to cover the filling. Press the top and bottom edges of dough together with the tines of a fork to seal each chausson closed. Gather the scraps and add them to your baked trimmings or discard them.
- Line a baking sheet with parchment paper. Transfer the chaussons to the prepared baking sheet.
- Place the baking sheet in the refrigerator to chill the chaussons for 20 minutes. (If preparing the chaussons in advance, remove them from the refrigerator after they have chilled. Wrap each chausson individually in plastic wrap and freeze for up to 1 month. Bake as per the instructions that follow.)

Bake the chaussons

- Arrange the oven racks so that one is in the center position. Preheat the oven to 375°F.
- Remove the chaussons from the refrigerator. Working one at a time, hold the chausson in place with one hand and use a paring knife to score their tops decoratively with the other, making sure that the scores go completely—or almost all the way—through the dough, which will allow the steam to escape when the chaussons are baked.
- Whisk the egg with the salt in a small bowl to make an egg wash. Brush the tops with egg wash; discard the remaining egg wash.
- Place the baking sheet on the center rack and bake the chaussons for 25 to 30 minutes, until they are golden brown, rotating the baking sheet from front to back halfway through the baking time so the pastries brown evenly. Remove the baking sheet from the oven and allow the chaussons to cool for a few minutes on the baking sheet. Use a metal spatula to transfer the pastries to a cooling rack to cool. Serve warm or at room temperature.

Master Recipe
for Laminated Babka Dough

**Makes enough for
2 Blueberry Blackberry Cheese
Danish Braids (page 193) or
9 New York Cheese Danishes
(page 201)**

I started to make cheese Danishes in anticipation of the opening of Sadelle's. I wanted to create a New York–style Danish, which is soft and buttery, but not crispy. At the time I was also working on my babka dough, so I started with that. I give the dough a light lamination to produce some flakiness, while still maintaining that soft, bready texture.

You want to make your butter packet in advance, or while the dough is in the refrigerator. Place the packet in the refrigerator to chill until you're ready to laminate the dough, then remove it from the refrigerator to soften it slightly when called to do so in the recipe.

All-purpose flour	3¾ cups plus more for dusting	450 grams
Granulated sugar	½ cup	100 grams
Instant yeast	1 tablespoon	9 grams
Fine sea salt	2 teaspoons	12 grams
Whole milk	1 cup	240 grams
Large egg	1	50 grams
Large egg yolk	1	17 grams
Unsalted butter, cubed and softened	10 tablespoons (1 stick plus 2 tablespoons)	140 grams
Nonstick cooking spray		
Butter Packet (page 122), chilled	12 tablespoons (1½ sticks)	170 grams

Make the dough

- Combine the flour, sugar, yeast, and salt in a large bowl.
- Place the milk, egg, and egg yolk in the bowl of a stand mixer. Fit the mixer with the dough hook. Add the dry ingredients and mix on low speed for 3 minutes to create a homogenous dough. Increase the speed to medium and mix for 5 to 8 minutes, until the dough is completely wrapped around the hook and cleans the sides of the bowl. With the mixer still running on medium speed, add the butter and mix until it is completely mixed in and no butter chunks remain, 5 to 10 minutes (depending on the softness of the butter), stopping to wipe the dough hook clean once or twice with a wet hand. Turn off the mixer.

Ferment the dough

- Remove the bowl from the mixer and wipe the dough hook clean with a wet hand once more. Cover the bowl with a clean kitchen towel or plastic wrap and set aside in a warm place to allow the dough to ferment for 2 hours, turning the dough after 1 hour. To turn the dough, uncover the bowl and use a wet hand to fold the top edge down two-thirds and fold the bottom edge to meet the top edge, so the dough is folded like a misshapen letter; fold the sides inward in the same way to form a sort of ball, then re-cover the bowl.

· Line a baking sheet with parchment paper and generously spray the paper with nonstick cooking spray.

· Uncover the bowl and transfer the dough to the prepared baking sheet. Use your hands to gently coax and pat the dough into an even square. Place the dough in the refrigerator to chill for at least 2 hours, until it feels firm. (If you are making the dough in advance, remove it from the refrigerator after 2 hours, wrap the baking sheet in plastic wrap, and return it to the refrigerator for up to 2 days; this prevents the dough from developing a skin.)

Laminate the Dough

Lock in the butter
· Remove the butter packet from the refrigerator and set it on the counter to soften until it is bendy but still cool; this could take anywhere from 5 to 20 minutes, depending on how cold it is and on the texture of the dough. You want the butter to be slightly softer and more malleable than the dough but not so soft that it will ooze out of the dough.

· Lightly dust a large flat work surface with flour. Remove the dough from the refrigerator, unwrap the dough, and place it on the floured surface. Lightly dust the top of the dough and the rolling pin with flour and roll out the dough to a rectangle that is 14 inches from side to side and 11 inches from top to bottom, dusting with flour as needed.

· Open the parchment packet to expose the butter and flip the packet over to place the butter on the dough, centering the 10-inch edge of the butter packet on the 11-inch length of dough. Run your hand over the parchment paper so that the heat of your hand helps to peel off the paper. Peel off and discard the parchment paper. Fold the left and right sides of the dough over the butter so they meet in the middle and pinch the two edges of dough together with your fingers. Gently press the top and bottom edges of the dough together to seal the packet closed and lock in the butter.

Make two letter folds
· Lightly dust your work surface with a bit more flour. Dust the top of the dough and the rolling pin with flour and roll the dough to 18 inches from top to bottom, dusting the work surface, rolling pin, and top of the dough lightly with flour as you roll the dough, so it doesn't stick. Using a pastry wheel or a bench knife, trim the top and bottom edges of the dough just enough to expose the layer of butter in the center of the dough. Reserve the trimmings to make Baked Trimmings (page 129) or discard them. Fold the top edge down two-thirds and fold the bottom edge to meet the top edge, so the dough is folded into thirds, like a letter.

· Rotate the dough 90 degrees so that the folded, closed edges are facing left and right and one of the open edges (with the visible layers) is facing you.

Lightly dust the work surface, dough, and rolling pin with flour and roll the dough to 18 inches from top to bottom, dusting with flour as needed. Using a pastry wheel or a bench knife, trim the top and bottom edges to expose the butter layers and add the trimmings to your baked trimmings or discard them. Fold the top edge down and the bottom edge up to make a second letter fold.

- If you are using the dough to make a Danish braid, use a bench knife to cut the dough in half through the middle, so you are cutting perpendicular to the counter's edge. If you are using the dough to make cheese Danishes, leave it in one piece.
- Wrap the laminated block, or blocks, of dough in plastic wrap and place it in the freezer to chill for 1 hour. Move the dough from the freezer to the refrigerator for at least 8 hours and up to 12 hours to retard the dough.

Blueberry Blackberry Cheese Danish Braid

**Makes 1 Danish braid;
10 to 12 slices**

This is a beautiful Danish braid—made with babka dough that is laminated, so it is both flaky and soft—with a sweet-tart berry filling combined with a rich cream cheese filling. The berries are cooked in a pie plate in the oven, basically imitating a pie filling without the crust. The braid is not difficult to make, but you do have to take care along the way when you are rolling, measuring, and cutting, as it is a pastry where evenness counts.

Note You will need one large disposable pastry bag.

For the cream cheese filling		
Cream cheese, softened	8 ounces	226 grams
Granulated sugar	1 tablespoon	13 grams
Large egg yolk	1	17 grams
For the berry filling		
Blueberries	6 ounces (about 1 heaping cup)	170 grams
Blackberries	6 ounces (about 1 heaping cup)	170 grams
Dark brown sugar	¼ cup (lightly packed)	50 grams
Arrowroot	2 teaspoons	5 grams
Fine sea salt	pinch	1 gram
Fresh lemon juice	1 ounce (about ½ lemon)	28 grams
For the dough		
Master Recipe for Laminated Babka Dough (page 190)	½ recipe	
All-purpose flour	for dusting	
For finishing the braid		
Large egg	1	
Fine sea salt	big pinch	
Demerara (turbinado) sugar	1½ tablespoons	20 grams

Make the fillings

· Arrange the oven racks so one is in the center position. Preheat the oven to 375°F.

· To make the cream cheese filling, combine the cream cheese and granulated sugar in the bowl of a stand mixer fitted with the paddle attachment (or a food processor fitted with a metal blade) and mix on low speed just to combine; don't mix longer than necessary as you don't want to aerate the mixture. Add the egg yolk and mix until it is blended in, stopping to scrape down the sides of the bowl with a rubber spatula as needed. Transfer the filling to a large disposable pastry bag and refrigerate for about 2 hours, until the filling sets up, or for up to 2 days.

- To make the berry filling, combine the blueberries and blackberries in a pie plate. Pick out and discard any blueberry stems you find.
- Combine the brown sugar, arrowroot, and salt together in a small bowl and stir or whisk to break up any lumps and to combine the ingredients. Sprinkle the brown sugar mixture over the berries and stir with a rubber spatula to coat the berries with the sugar. Stir in the lemon juice.
- Place the pie plate on the center rack of the oven and bake the berries, uncovered, for 20 minutes, stirring them halfway through the baking time. Remove the berries from the oven and set aside to cool slightly. Turn off the oven.
- Transfer the berries to a small container and cover the container while the berries are still warm; refrigerate until they've completely cooled and for up to 3 days. (Covering the container while the berries are warm creates steam inside the container and prevents a skin from forming.)

Roll out the dough

- Remove the laminated block of dough from the refrigerator and set it on the counter to rest for 20 to 30 minutes, until you can feel that the butter layers inside the dough are just becoming malleable (but not soft) when you bend the block slightly.
- Line a baking sheet with parchment paper.
- Lightly dust a large flat work surface with flour. Remove and discard the plastic wrap and place the dough on the floured surface. Lightly dust the top of the dough and the rolling pin with flour and roll the dough out to a rectangle that is 10 inches from side to side and 16 inches from top to bottom, dusting with flour as needed. (If the dough is springing back before you can roll it to those dimensions, transfer it to a parchment-lined baking sheet and refrigerate for 20 to 30 minutes to relax the gluten. Remove the dough from the refrigerator and continue rolling it out until you reach the correct dimensions.) Place the dough on the prepared baking sheet and place it in the refrigerator for 20 minutes to rest and chill the dough before you cut and braid it.

The more you work dough, the more the gluten develops.
Cold temperature and time relax it.

- Lay parchment paper on your work surface and transfer the dough to the parchment.

Cut the dough

- Using a straightedge to measure, nick the dough 3¼ inches from the left edge and 3¼ inches from the right edge on the bottom edge of the dough. Do the same on the top edge of the dough. Use the straightedge as a guide to score the dough between the top and bottom marks on both sides to visually divide the dough into 3 segments.

- Start at the top of the left vertical line you just cut and use a bench knife to cut downward toward the left edge of the dough at a 45-degree angle. (You can eyeball the first cut; it doesn't need to be exactly 45 degrees.) Make diagonal cuts parallel to the first cut, using the bench knife. Start from the diagonal cut you just made, and cut the dough every inch moving downward on the left segment of dough. Repeat on the right side: start at the top of the right vertical line and use a bench knife to cut downward toward the right edge of the dough at a 45-degree angle. Make diagonal cuts that are parallel to the

1

2

3

4

first cut, using the bench knife. Starting from the diagonal cut you just made, cut the dough every inch moving downward on the right segment of dough. Transfer the parchment paper with the dough on it to a baking sheet.

- Remove the cheese filling from the refrigerator and cut a ¾-inch opening at the tip of the pastry bag. Pipe 4 lines of cream cheese filling down the length of the center segment of dough. Use a small offset spatula to spread the filling over to the edges of this segment.

- Remove the berry filling from the refrigerator and spoon about 1 cup (250 grams) of the berry filling on top of the cream cheese layer and use the back of the spoon to spread it to cover the cheese filling. (You will have 1 to 2 tablespoons extra filling. Stir it into plain yogurt or enjoy it however you prefer.)

Braid and proof the Danish

- Starting at the edge farthest from you, lift the top left triangular flap of dough and fold it to the right to cover the filling (the edge will be perpendicular to the top edge of the center segment of dough). Fold the top right flap of dough to the left in the same way. Fold the first strip on the left length of dough downward toward the right at a 45-degree angle. Do the same on the right. Continue alternating left and right, braiding the dough as you work your way down the length of the Danish. When you have braided all the strips, seal the top edge of the dough closed by pressing down gently on the top and bottom sheets of dough. Seal the lower edge in the same way.

- Cover the baking sheet with a damp, lightweight kitchen towel and set it aside in a warm place for about 1 hour to proof the braid until it looks puffy.

Prepare to bake the Danish braid

- Arrange the oven racks so one is in the center position. Preheat the oven to 350°F.

- Whisk the egg and salt together in a small bowl to make an egg wash. Uncover the Danish braid and brush the wash over the surface of the braid; discard the remaining egg wash. Sprinkle the demerara sugar on top of the braid.

Bake the Danish braid

Baking the braid on a doubled baking sheet prevents the bottom of the braid from burning in the time it takes the top to brown.

- Slip a baking sheet underneath the baking sheet with the braid to create a baking sheet of double thickness. Place the baking sheets on the center rack of the oven to bake the braid for 30 to 40 minutes, until it is golden brown on top, rotating the baking sheet from front to back halfway through the baking time so the Danish braid browns evenly. Remove the baking sheets from the oven and place them on a cooling rack to cool the braid for at least 10 minutes before slicing.

- Slide the braid onto a cutting board and slice it into 2-inch-wide strips. Serve warm or at room temperature.

New York Cheese Danishes

Makes 16 to 18 Danishes

These are New York Danishes, not to be confused with European-style Danishes, which are made from a dough similar to croissant dough, making them crispier and flakier. New York Danishes are softer, with a homier feel. They are about the size of a sticky bun, so there is a lot of filling relative to the amount of dough, which I like.

Note You will need one large disposable pastry bag.

For the filling		
Cream cheese, softened	8 ounces	226 grams
Granulated sugar	1 tablespoon	13 grams
Large egg yolk	1	17 grams
For the dough		
Master Recipe for Laminated Babka Dough (page 190)	1 recipe	
All-purpose flour	for dusting	
For finishing the Danishes		
Large egg	1	50 grams
Fine sea salt	big pinch	
Apricot jam	2 tablespoons	
Water	1 teaspoon	

Make the filling

- Put the cream cheese and sugar in the bowl of a stand mixer fitted with the paddle attachment (or a food processor fitted with a metal blade) and mix on low speed to combine; don't mix longer than necessary as you don't want to aerate the mixture. Add the egg yolk and mix until it is blended in, stopping to scrape down the sides of the bowl with a rubber spatula as needed. Transfer the filling to a large disposable pastry bag and refrigerate for about 2 hours, until the filling sets up, and for up to 2 days.

Roll out the dough

- Remove the laminated block of dough from the refrigerator and set it on the counter to rest for 20 to 30 minutes, until you can feel that the butter layers inside the dough are just becoming malleable (but not soft) when you bend the block slightly.
- Line two baking sheets with parchment paper.
- Lightly dust a large flat work surface with flour. Remove and discard the plastic wrap and place the dough on the floured surface with the long edge parallel to you. Lightly dust the top of the dough and the rolling pin with flour and roll the dough out to a rectangle that is 18 inches from side to side and 12 inches from top to bottom, dusting with flour as needed. (If the dough

is springing back before you can roll it to those dimensions, transfer it to a parchment-lined baking sheet and refrigerate for 20 to 30 minutes to relax the gluten. Remove the dough from the refrigerator and continue rolling it out until you reach the correct dimensions.) Using a pastry wheel, trim the top, bottom, and sides so you have clean, straight edges. Use the trimmings to make Baked Trimmings (page 129) or discard them.

· Using the pastry wheel, score the dough at every inch mark on the top and bottom edges. Using the straightedge as a guide, cut the dough into 16 to 18 (1-inch-wide) strips.

An unfloured surface gives you the surface tension you need to twist the dough. If the dough is sticking to the surface, which it will if the dough is warm, flour your hands.

· Pick up one strip and lay it horizontally on a section of your work surface that has no flour on it. Twist both ends in opposite directions several times until the length of the strip is completely twisted. Place both hands gently on the twisted strip and move one hand toward you and the other hand away from you to get one more twist into the strip. Pick up the strip and coil it into a tight spiral. Bring the outside end of the coil underneath the Danish and pinch it together with the end that is at the center of the Danish. Place the Danish with the pinched coil underneath on one of the prepared baking sheets. Continue shaping the remaining Danishes in the same way, putting them on the baking sheets, with 2 to 3 inches between them, as you work.

· Cover the baking sheets with damp, lightweight kitchen towels and set the pastries aside in a warm place to proof for 1½ to 2 hours, until they look puffy.

Finish and bake the Danishes

· Arrange the oven racks so one is in the top third of the oven and the other is in the bottom third. Preheat the oven to 350°F.

· Whisk the egg with the salt in a small bowl to make an egg wash. Brush the wash over the surface of each Danish; discard the remaining egg wash. Press both of your thumbs into the center of each Danish to create a flat-bottomed crater about 1½ inches wide.

· Remove the pastry bag from the refrigerator and cut a ¾-inch opening at the tip. Pipe a heaping tablespoon of the filling to fill the center well of each Danish.

· When you have filled all of the Danishes, use wet fingertips to dab down any peaks of cheese that were created during piping, as these will burn in the oven.

· Place one baking sheet on each oven rack and bake the Danishes for 18 to 22 minutes, until they are golden brown and the cheese has puffed up (but not so long that the filling cracks), rotating the baking sheets from front to back and from one oven rack to the other halfway through the baking time so the

Danishes brown evenly. Remove the baking sheets from the oven and place them on cooling racks to cool while you prepare the apricot glaze.

▪ While the Danishes are cooling, combine the apricot jam and water in a small saucepan. Heat over medium heat, whisking, to melt the jam and make a smooth glaze. (Or place the jam in a bowl and heat it in a microwave for about 30 seconds, until the jam liquefies.)

▪ Use a pastry brush to brush the glaze onto the tops of the warm Danishes. Serve warm or at room temperature.

I tend to be conservative about how much glaze I put on any pastry. Supposedly it seals the pastry, keeping it from drying out, but mostly it makes the pastry shine and sparkle and look beautiful. Don't overdo it. For me, the most important thing in a pastry is the way it tastes, not the way it looks.

Black Pepper Fantails with Salted Honey Butter

Makes 1 dozen fantails

Fantails are a laminated pastry; the name refers to their shape. They are made by cutting laminated dough into squares, turning the squares on their sides, and baking them in muffin cups. When the dough expands during baking, the squares open up in the individual cups like a fan, and because the cut sides are facing up, you can see all the layers of the lamination. I started making them when I was the head baker at Per Se. Thomas Keller was coming to town and had called ahead to ask that I have these ready on his arrival. I followed the recipe from the baker who preceded me to a T. Thomas loved them, and they became part of my repertoire. The year I left Per Se, I made my own version of fantails for my family's Thanksgiving dinner and they've since become part of my regular Thanksgiving spread. The layers of the fantails may come apart when you remove them from the pan, but don't worry about it, those crunchy bits are the first thing your guests (and you!) will reach for in the bread basket.

You want to make your butter packet in advance, or while the dough is in the refrigerator. Place the packet in the refrigerator to chill until you're ready to laminate the dough, then remove it from the refrigerator to soften it slightly when called to do so in the recipe.

Note This recipe calls for cracked butcher's pepper, which is a larger grind than what you get out of a pepper mill. If you were to analyze what comes out of a mill, it is a mixture of powder and larger chunks. Butcher's pepper consists solely of the chunks. It is sold at specialty food stores and butcher shops. To make your own, coarsely grind peppercorns in a spice grinder. Pass the ground pepper through a fine-mesh strainer. Reserve the strained pepper for seasoning meats or to use in cooking. Use the chunks of pepper left in the strainer for these fantails.

Note You will need one standard 12-cup muffin tin to make these.

For the dough		
All-purpose flour	4 cups plus more for dusting	480 grams
Granulated sugar	¼ cup	50 grams
Instant yeast	1 tablespoon	9 grams
Fine sea salt	2 teaspoons	12 grams
Cracked butcher's pepper	1 tablespoon plus 2 teaspoons	15 grams
Whole milk	1 cup	240 grams
Large egg	1	50 grams
Large egg yolk	1	17 grams
Unsalted butter, cubed and softened	10 tablespoons (1 stick plus 2 tablespoons)	140 grams
Nonstick cooking spray		
Butter Packet (page 122), chilled	12 tablespoons (1½ sticks)	170 grams
For the honey butter		
Unsalted butter, melted	8 tablespoons (1 stick)	113 grams
Mild-flavored honey (such as wildflower or clover)	3 tablespoons	60 grams
Fine sea salt	½ teaspoon	3 grams
Flaky sea salt	for sprinkling	

Make the dough

- Put the flour, sugar, yeast, salt, and pepper in a medium bowl and stir to combine.
- Place the milk, egg, and egg yolk in the bowl of a stand mixer. Place the dry ingredients and butter on top. Fit the mixer with the dough hook and mix on low speed for 2 minutes. Increase the speed to medium and mix for 5 minutes. Remove the bowl from the stand and wipe the dough hook clean with a wet hand. Place a clean kitchen towel or plastic wrap over the bowl and set the dough aside at room temperature to ferment for 1 hour.
- Line a baking sheet with parchment paper and spray the parchment with nonstick cooking spray.
- Use a plastic bowl scraper to scrape the dough out of the bowl and onto the prepared baking sheet. Using wet hands, pat and form the dough gently into an 8-inch square. Refrigerate the dough for at least 1 hour and up to 8 hours. (If you are refrigerating the dough for longer than 1 hour, remove it from the refrigerator after 1 hour, wrap it in plastic wrap, and return it to the refrigerator.)

Laminate the Dough

Lock in the butter

- Remove the butter packet from the refrigerator and set it on the counter to soften until it is bendy but still cool; this could take anywhere from 5 to 20 minutes, depending on how cold it is and on the texture of the dough. You want the butter to be slightly softer and more malleable than the dough but not so soft that it will ooze out of the dough.
- Lightly dust a large flat work surface with flour. Remove the dough from the refrigerator, unwrap the dough, and place it on the floured surface. Lightly dust the top of the dough and the rolling pin with flour and roll out the dough to a rectangle that is roughly 14 inches from side to side and 11 inches from top to bottom, dusting the work surface, rolling pin, and top of the dough lightly with flour as you roll the dough, so it doesn't stick.
- Open the parchment packet to expose the butter and flip the packet over to place the butter on the dough, centering the 10-inch length of the butter packet on the 11-inch length of dough. Run your hand over the parchment paper so that the heat of your hand helps to peel off the paper. Peel off and discard the parchment paper. Fold the left and right sides of the dough over the butter so they meet in the middle and pinch the two edges of dough together with your fingers. Gently press the top and bottom edges of the dough together to seal the packet closed and lock in the butter.

Make two letter folds

- Lightly dust a large flat work surface with flour. Lightly dust the top of the dough and the rolling pin with flour and roll the dough to 18 inches from top to bottom, dusting the work surface, rolling pin, and top of the dough lightly with flour as you roll the dough, so it doesn't stick. Using a pastry wheel or a bench knife, trim the top and bottom edges of the dough just enough to expose the layer of butter in the center of the dough. Reserve the trimmings to make Baked Trimmings (page 129) or discard them. Fold the top edge down two-thirds and fold the bottom edge to meet the top edge, so the dough is folded into thirds, like a letter.

· Rotate the dough 90 degrees so the closed edges are facing left and right and one of the open edges (with the visible layers) is facing you. Lightly dust the work surface, rolling pin, and dough with flour and roll out the dough to roughly 18 inches from top to bottom, dusting with flour as needed. Trim the top and bottom edges to expose the butter layers and add the trimmings to your baked trimmings or discard them. Fold the top edge down and the bottom edge up to make a second letter fold.

· Wrap the laminated block of dough in plastic wrap and place it in the freezer to chill for 1 hour. Move the dough from the freezer to the refrigerator for at least 8 hours and up to 12 hours to retard the dough.

Cut the fantails

· Remove the laminated block of dough from the refrigerator and set it on the counter to rest for 20 to 30 minutes, until you can feel that the butter layers inside the dough are just becoming malleable (but not soft) when you bend the block slightly.

· Spray a 12-cup muffin tin with nonstick cooking spray.

· Lightly dust a large flat work surface with flour. Unwrap the dough and place it on the floured surface with the long edge parallel to you. Lightly dust the top of the dough and the rolling pin with flour. If the dough is smaller than a 7½-inch square, roll the dough out to those dimensions.

· Cut the dough into 1½-inch squares with a pastry wheel or a large chef's knife.

· Turn the fantail cubes on their sides and place 2 pieces in each muffin cup. Cover the muffin tin with a damp, lightweight kitchen towel and set it aside in a warm place for about 1 hour to proof the fantails until they just start to puff up.

Make the honey butter

· While the fantails are proofing, place the butter, honey, and fine sea salt in a medium bowl. Whisk vigorously to combine.

Bake the fantails

· Arrange the oven racks so one is in the center position. Preheat the oven to 350°F.

· Place the muffin tin on the center rack of the oven and bake the fantails for 25 to 30 minutes, until the tops are deep golden brown, rotating the muffin tin from front to back halfway through the baking time so the pastries brown evenly.

▪ Remove the muffin tin from the oven. Immediately brush the fantails with the honey butter and sprinkle each fantail with a generous pinch of flaky sea salt. Set the muffin tins on a cooling rack and let the fantails cool in the pan for 5 to 10 minutes. Remove the fantails and serve them warm or at room temperature.

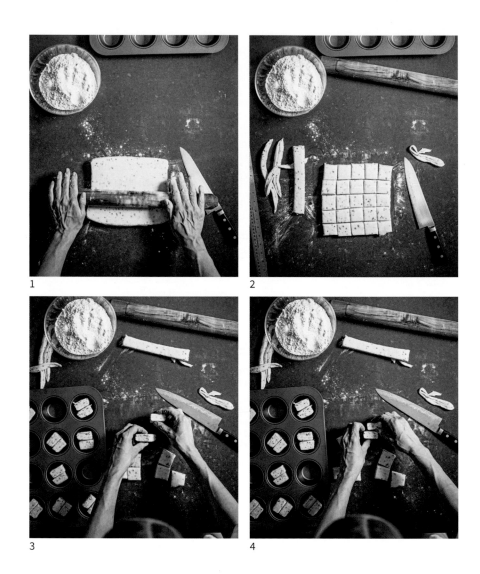

1

2

3

4

Variation
Chive Fantails

At Sadelle's, I made two types of fantails: Black Pepper Fantails with Salted Honey Butter (page 205) and these. The fresh, grassy, onion flavor of the chives is really delicious with the rich, buttery dough. You need a very sharp knife to cut the chives as finely as you must for this and also to keep from bruising them. To make these, follow the recipe for black pepper fantails, adding the chives to the dough in place of the black pepper, and brushing the baked fantails with the butter instead of the honey butter.

Fresh chives	3 bunches	65 grams
Unsalted butter, melted	8 tablespoons (1 stick)	113 grams
Flaky sea salt	for sprinkling	

▪ Line up a dozen or so chives at a time so they are all facing the same direction, and slice them as finely as possible. Put them in a bowl and slice the remaining chives, a dozen at a time.

▪ Add the chives to the fantail dough in place of the butcher's pepper and proceed with the recipe. After the fantails are out of the oven, brush them with the melted butter and a healthy sprinkle of flaky salt.

A Short and Sweet Chapter on Fried Dough

Frying dough is one of my favorite things to do. I started deep-frying at Babbo, where we always had one deep-fried item on the dessert menu. I had imagined that frying at home would be a big mess, but it turned out to be easy, and also really enjoyable, and soon I was frying everything from chicken to cannoli at home on a fairly regular basis.

Perfect deep-fried pastries are crisp on the outside, light and pillowy on the inside, and they are not greasy. The key to making sure your pastries are not greasy lies in the temperature of the oil. When baking a batter or dough, the water inside it turns to steam and evaporates. Deep-frying, however, is a direct application of heat to the surface. There is no air gap between the dough and the hot oil, so the water immediately turns to steam. If the oil is not hot enough, instead of steam escaping, the oil will penetrate more.

This chapter consists of recipes for only three deep-fried pastries (plus their accompaniments). I wanted to give just a few recipes for thoughtfully designed fried pastries that I love, are original, and are uniquely mine.

Master Class
A Home Baker's Guide to Deep-Frying

The key to a pleasant deep-frying experience is to set yourself up correctly. Here's what to do before you get started:

The fry oil

Choose the right oil. I call for you to use either canola or corn oil in these recipes (I look for organic versions). The important thing about the oil is that it be neutral flavored. The oil is a medium for cooking the pastries, but you don't want the pastries to take on the flavor of the oil.

The fry pot

Choose the correct pot, as described in the individual recipe, in which you are going to fry your pastries. The key to choosing a pot is for there to be enough surface area so the pastries can float in the oil in a single layer, but that it is not so big that you need an insane amount of oil to deep-fry. I use a large (12-quart) stainless-steel stockpot. Also, you must dry the pot really well. If there are any droplets of water in the pot, the water will pop when you begin to heat the oil, causing the oil to splatter out of the pot.

Set up your station

Get your frying station ready, including your batter, the pot you're frying in, your frying oil, and the sugar that the pastries will be tossed in when they're done. This is the time to also set up your baking sheet, tools for turning the pastries in the oil and removing them from the oil, and a cooling rack to drain the pastries on. (I've given detailed instructions for this in the individual recipes.) Line a baking sheet with paper towels and set a cooling rack on top of the paper towels. This is where you will put the pastries to drain after they come out of the oil. Have a pair of tongs and/or a spider handy.

Add oil

Add the oil. Save the container the oil came in; you will use it to hold the dirty oil after frying, which makes it easy to discard.

Temperature

Fasten a deep-fry/candy thermometer to the side of the pot. When I attended the French Culinary Institute, one of the tools I was required to own was a candy thermometer. I still have and use the same one. I use the thermometer as a "stir stick," first making a counterclockwise stir with it, then stirring in the other direction, and finally running it down the center of the pot one way and then the other. Because all of the heat is coming from the bottom, it is important to move the oil around so that it heats evenly.

Heat the oil over medium-high heat until it reaches 350°F. Heating the oil over medium-high rather than high heat means it doesn't heat too quickly, so you don't inadvertently heat the oil too much. Keep your oil at a steady temperature. A professional fryer maintains the temperature of the oil, but when frying at home, you have to do that manually, by adjusting the temperature of the stove—moving the temperature between medium and medium-high. Keep your eye on the thermometer and adjust the heat as needed to maintain a temperature as close to 350°F as possible as you fry.

Adding the pastries

Carefully add the pastries to the oil. I use my hand to carefully slide pastries into the oil, so the oil doesn't splatter. If the dough is sticking to my fingers, I wet them. Add only as many pastries as fit comfortably in a single layer. If you add more than that, the pastries will stick together, and also, the cold batter will cause the oil temperature to sink, resulting in heavy, greasy pastries.

Dispose of used oil

When you are done frying, turn off the heat and let the oil cool to room temperature. Use a funnel to pour the oil into the bottle you poured it out of. Close the bottle and put the bottle in the trash. You do not want to pour the oil down the sink.

Churros and Hot Chocolate

Makes 2 to 3 dozen (3-inch) churros

Churros are made from pâte à choux, a batter that is leavened by beaten eggs. It's the same batter used to make éclairs, profiteroles, and French doughnuts, or crullers. Rather than pipe the batter directly into hot oil, which is customary, I pipe the churros onto a baking sheet and then carefully slide them into the oil one at a time. This method prevents much of the risk of the hot oil splattering. If you have leftover churros, freeze them. When you're ready to eat them, place them on a baking sheet and put them in a 325°F oven for about 20 minutes, until they're warmed through.

Make the hot chocolate before making the churro batter, so you just need to warm it up when you're ready to serve. I put the hot chocolate on the stove to warm just before I begin to fry the churros.

Eggs have a wonderful capacity to expand your baked goods. They were the original leaveners, used before bakers started relying on baking soda and baking powder.

Note You will need large pastry bags and a star pastry tip with a 7/16-inch-wide opening (my preference is an open-star pastry tip, such as Ateco #825) to make these.

For the cinnamon sugar		
Vanilla Sugar (page 219; or granulated sugar)	1 cup	200 grams
Ground cinnamon	1 tablespoon	6 grams
Fine sea salt	⅛ teaspoon	1 gram
For the churros		
Water	2 cups	470 grams
Unsalted butter, cubed	8 tablespoons (1 stick)	113 grams
Cinnamon sticks	2	
Nonstick cooking spray		
All-purpose flour	2 cups	240 grams
Fine sea salt	1¼ teaspoons	8 grams
Large eggs	3	150 grams
Canola or corn oil	10 cups (or as needed)	2,200 grams

Hot Chocolate (recipe follows)

Make the cinnamon sugar

· Whisk the sugar, cinnamon, and salt together in a medium bowl and set aside.

Make the churro batter · Place the water, butter, and cinnamon sticks in a medium saucepan and heat over medium-high heat until the butter is melted and the liquid begins to simmer. Turn off the heat and carefully cover the saucepan with plastic wrap. Set aside to infuse the liquid for 30 minutes. Remove the plastic wrap and discard the cinnamon sticks.

The plastic wrap traps the moisture in the pan,
which helps to infuse the liquid with the cinnamon.

Get prepared · While the liquid is infusing, set up a stand mixer and have the paddle attachment handy. Fit a pastry bag with a 7/16-inch star tip and set aside.
· Spray the perimeters of two baking sheets with nonstick cooking spray and line both with parchment paper. Press around the perimeters of the baking sheet with your hands so the paper adheres to the pan. Spray the top of the parchment paper generously with nonstick cooking spray.
· Combine the flour and salt in a small bowl and set aside.
· Return the saucepan with the cinnamon-infused water to the stove. Return the liquid to a boil over high heat. Add the flour and salt and cook for 2 minutes, stirring constantly with a wooden spoon until a very thin film of dough forms on the bottom of the saucepan. Remove the pan from the heat.
· Transfer the batter to the bowl of the stand mixer. Fit the mixer with the paddle attachment and mix the dough on medium speed for about 5 minutes to cool the dough toward room temperature; you can gauge the temperature by cupping your hands on the outside of the bottom of the bowl. Add the eggs one at a time, beating on medium speed until the egg is completely blended in and stopping to scrape down the sides of the bowl before adding the next egg. Once you've added all the eggs, beat until the dough is smooth and homogenous, about 5 minutes.

Pipe the churros · Scoop the dough into the pastry bag.
· Place one of the prepared baking sheets with the long side parallel to the counter's edge. Starting in the upper left corner (if you're right-handed; do the opposite if you're left-handed), apply gentle, even pressure to the pastry bag to pipe toward you to make a 3-inch churro on the baking sheet. Scrape the tip on the baking sheet to "cut" the batter, and continue piping churros across the baking sheet, leaving about 1 inch between each. Pipe a second row of churros below the first row. Place the baking sheet in the refrigerator to chill. Pipe the remaining batter on the second prepared baking sheet and place it in the refrigerator to chill while you heat the oil, and for as long as 8 hours.

Fry the churros

- Fill a large (12-quart) pot 2 inches deep with oil. Fasten a deep-fry or candy thermometer to the side of the pot and heat the oil over medium-high heat until the thermometer registers 350°F.
- Line a baking sheet with paper towels and place a cooling rack on top of the baking sheet. Place the setup near the stove. Have a pair of metal tongs handy and place the bowl of cinnamon sugar nearby.
- Remove one baking sheet of piped churros from the refrigerator. One at a time, pick up the churros with a metal spatula and gently slide 6 or 8 of them into the oil, being careful to add only as many as will fit comfortably in the pot in a single layer. (Return the baking sheet to the refrigerator so the churros hold their shape while the first batch of churros is frying.) Fry the churros for 5 to 7 minutes, using the tongs to turn them so they fry on both sides. Use the tongs to remove the churros one at a time from the oil and place them on the cooling rack to drain.
- Remove the second baking sheet from the refrigerator. Check the temperature of the oil and wait, if necessary, for the oil to return to 350°F. Carefully slide 6 or 8 more churros into the oil and fry them as you did the first batch.

Finish and serve the churros and hot chocolate

- While the next batch is frying, dip the just-fried churros one at a time into the bowl with the cinnamon sugar to coat them all over.
- Place the finished churros on a serving platter and continue coating the next batch of churros in the cinnamon sugar as they come out of the oil. Continue frying and sugaring the remaining churros.
- When you have finished preparing the churros, heat the hot chocolate in a medium saucepan over medium-low heat or in a microwave.
- To serve, pour the hot chocolate into a small pitcher or small coffee or espresso cups or heat-proof glasses, and serve with the warm churros.

Hot Chocolate

Makes about 2 cups

I have been obsessed with creating the most perfect, creamy, thick, and rich hot chocolate ever since first having Spanish hot chocolate, which is so thick and rich that it is served in a shot glass with a spoon, like pudding. This version is slightly thinner, because I wanted it to be drinkable. Enjoy it with churros or on its own.

Granulated sugar	½ cup	100 grams
Cornstarch	1 tablespoon	9 grams
Cocoa powder (preferably Valrhona)	1 tablespoon	7 grams
Fine sea salt	⅛ teaspoon	1 gram
Bittersweet chocolate	4 ounces (or ⅔ cup chocolate chips)	113 grams
Whole milk	1 cup	240 grams
Heavy cream	1 cup	238 grams
Dark rum (optional)	1 teaspoon	5 grams

• To make the hot chocolate, whisk the sugar, cornstarch, cocoa powder, and salt together in a small bowl and set aside.

• Roughly chop the chocolate (unless you are using chocolate chips).

• Pour 1 to 2 inches of water in the bottom of a small saucepan and choose a bowl that fits over the saucepan to make a double boiler. Make sure the water is not touching the bottom of the bowl; if it is, pour some out. Bring the water to a boil over high heat and reduce the heat to medium-low to maintain a gentle simmer.

• Add the chocolate to the bowl of the double boiler and melt the chocolate, using a heat-proof rubber spatula to stir and scrape down the sides of the bowl so the chocolate melts evenly and doesn't burn. Remove the bowl from the double boiler and wipe the bottom of the bowl to make sure no water drips. Set aside for 15 to 20 minutes to cool the chocolate to room temperature.

• Set a fine-mesh strainer over a heat-proof container.

• Combine the milk and cream in a medium saucepan and bring to a boil over medium-high heat. Once the mixture reaches a boil, reduce the heat to medium-low and add the melted chocolate, whisking until the chocolate is completely mixed in. Add the dry ingredients and whisk to combine. Cook the hot chocolate over medium-low heat, whisking constantly, until the hot chocolate begins to thicken, 2 to 5 minutes. Turn off the heat and whisk in the rum, if you are using it. Pour the hot chocolate through the strainer to strain out any lumps. If you are serving it right away, strain it directly into a serving vessel, such as a small pitcher.

Vanilla Sugar

Makes 1 cup

I make this using leftover vanilla pods. Anytime I use a vanilla pod, I rinse it off, let it dry, and collect it in a container. Once I have collected enough, I grind them up with sugar to make this delicious vanilla sugar. This approach is something you see often in the restaurant industry, where you do everything you can to save money. How many vanilla beans you put in your sugar depends on how many you have; the whole point of this recipe is to recycle, so it would defeat the purpose to go out and buy vanilla beans. To dry them out, I put the pods on a plate and set them in a warm place in the kitchen for about 24 hours, until they feel dry to the touch. Use vanilla sugar in an application where vanilla is welcome, and where the sugar is a special component. I like to use it to sprinkle in Classic Roll-Out Sugar Cookies (page 391) to create vanilla sugar cookies. It would also be a great choice when you're using sugar in place of flour to roll out dough, such as for Kouign Amann (page 171).

Granulated sugar	1 cup	200 grams
Dried vanilla beans	2 to 12	

Place the sugar and vanilla beans in the bowl of a food processor fitted with a metal blade and grind for about 2 minutes, until the bean is as finely ground as the sugar, with some larger pieces remaining. Pass the sugar through a fine-mesh strainer to sift out the large pieces; discard the contents of the strainer. Transfer the sugar to a covered container and store at room temperature until you're ready to use it. It will keep almost indefinitely.

Sufganiyot with Blood Orange Jam

Makes 2 to 3 dozen doughnuts

Sadelle's, which I opened in 2015, was conceived as a modern interpretation of a Jewish bakery. When Hanukkah rolled around, I wanted to offer sufganiyot, the jelly-filled doughnuts that are traditionally made during that holiday. I started with what is essentially a brioche dough, but then I swapped melted butter for cold—an idea I adopted from the blog *Ideas in Food.* The idea behind the swap is that yeast likes heat, so when the warm, melted butter reacts with the yeast, it gives a boost to the fermentation process; this causes the dough to rise more aggressively, which in turn results in a light, airy doughnut.

I wanted to use something seasonal for the filling, so I made a blood orange jam, which is delicious and also really pretty. You can also use a jam of your choice.

Note You will need a large disposable pastry bag and a ¼-inch round icing tip (such as an Ateco #802 tip) to make this.

Unsalted butter	22 tablespoons (2¾ sticks)	311 grams
Whole milk	¾ cup	180 grams
All-purpose flour	4 cups plus 2 tablespoons plus more for dusting	498 grams
Granulated sugar	¼ cup plus 1 tablespoon	63 grams
Instant yeast	1 tablespoon plus 2 teaspoons	15 grams
Fine sea salt	2 teaspoons	12 grams
Large eggs	4	200 grams
Nonstick cooking spray		
Canola or corn oil	10 cups (or as needed)	2,200 grams
For filling and finishing the sufganiyot		
Blood Orange Jam (recipe follows)	1 cup	340 grams
Confectioners' sugar	¼ cup	30 grams

Warm the liquids
- Melt the butter in a small saucepan over medium-low heat. Turn off the heat.
- In another small saucepan, warm the milk over medium-low heat until it is warm to the touch.

Make and ferment the dough
- Combine the flour, granulated sugar, yeast, and salt in a medium bowl.
- Place the warm milk and eggs in the bowl of a stand mixer and add the dry ingredients. Fit the mixer with the dough hook and mix on low speed for 2 minutes. Increase the speed to medium and mix for 3 minutes to develop the gluten. Turn off the mixer, add about one-fifth of the warm butter, and mix on low speed for a few seconds until the butter is no longer sloshing around

in the bowl. Increase the speed to medium-high and mix until the butter is completely integrated, about 3 minutes. Turn off the mixer, add more butter, and mix it in as before. Repeat, stopping the mixer and adding the butter in increments, and beating it in before adding more. When you have added and beaten in all of the butter, turn off the mixer.

• Take the bowl off the stand, remove the dough hook, and wipe it clean with a wet hand. Cover the bowl with plastic wrap and set it in a warm place to ferment the dough for 2 hours, turning it once halfway through that time. To turn the dough, uncover the bowl and use a wet hand to fold the top edge down two-thirds and fold the bottom edge to meet the top edge, so the dough is folded like a letter. Fold the sides inward in the same way to form a sort of ball, then re-cover the bowl. At the end of 2 hours, turn the dough again. Re-cover the bowl with plastic wrap and place it in the refrigerator overnight to retard the dough.

Retarding dough slows down the fermentation and adds to the flavor, and also makes the dough easier to roll out and shape.

Roll out the dough and cut the doughnuts

• Dust two baking sheets and your countertop generously with flour. Set the baking sheets aside.

• Remove the bowl from the refrigerator, remove the plastic wrap, and use a plastic bowl scraper to scrape the dough out onto the floured surface. Dust the top of the dough with flour and pat the dough down slightly with your hands to make it easier to roll out. Dust a rolling pin with flour and roll the dough out to a ⅜-inch-thick 13- x 14-inch rectangle, dusting the top of the dough, rolling pin, and work surface periodically to keep the dough from sticking to the rolling pin or countertop.

• Using a straightedge and pastry wheel, cut the dough into 2¼-inch squares. Lift each square with an offset spatula and place the squares on the prepared baking sheets, dividing them evenly. Cut a piece of plastic wrap to fit over one baking sheet. Spray one side of the plastic with nonstick cooking spray and gently place it, sprayed side down, over the baking sheet. Repeat, covering the second baking sheet with a sprayed sheet of plastic wrap. Put the baking sheets in a warm place to proof the dough for 2 to 3 hours, until the dough squares have swelled to one and a half times their original size.

Prepare to fry the doughnuts

• Fill a large (12-quart) pot 2 inches deep with the oil. Fasten a deep-fry or candy thermometer to the side of the pot and heat the oil over medium-high heat until the thermometer registers 350°F.

• Line a baking sheet with paper towels and place a cooling rack on top of the baking sheet. Place the setup near the stove. Have a pair of metal tongs and a slotted spoon or spider handy.

Fry the doughnuts · Remove the plastic wrap from one of the baking sheets. Wet your fingers— this will help you handle the dough without squishing it—and gently pick up and drop 4 or 5 squares of dough into the oil, holding your hand fairly close to the oil when you drop the dough in so it doesn't splash up out of the pot, and fry for about 10 seconds, until the doughnuts have begun to expand. Turn the doughnuts with the tongs and fry them for a total of 2 minutes, flipping them from time to time so they brown evenly on both sides.

Turning the doughnuts often helps to keep them evenly shaped.

· Use the tongs to remove the doughnuts from the oil and place them on the cooling rack to drain. Check the temperature of the oil and wait, if necessary, for the oil to return to 350°F. Add another 4 or 5 dough squares to the oil and fry them as you did the first batch. Add them to the cooling rack to drain. Continue frying the remaining doughnuts and adding them to the cooling rack. Let the doughnuts cool to room temperature.

Fill the doughnuts · Fit a large disposable pastry bag with an Ateco #802 tip and spoon 1 cup (340 grams) of the jam into the bag. Set it aside.
· Line two baking sheets with parchment paper.
· Using the tip of a small sharp knife, make 2 slits about 1 inch deep to form an X in the side of each doughnut. Insert the tip of the pastry bag into the X and gently squeeze the jam into the center of the doughnut. You want about 1½ teaspoons (about 15 grams) of jam per doughnut so that the jam is in harmony with the dough and doesn't overpower it. (If you want to be precise, put the unfilled doughnut on a scale and tare [zero out] the scale. Then pipe the jam into the doughnut and place it on the scale again to check if you have piped in 15 grams; if not, add more.) If the jam pops up out of a doughnut, lay the doughnut on your work surface with the X facing up and gently shake it to help the jam fall down inside. Place the filled doughnut on one of the prepared baking sheets and fill the remaining doughnuts with the remaining jam.
· Put the confectioners' sugar in a fine-mesh strainer and dust the sugar over the doughnuts.

Blood Orange Jam

**Makes about 4 cups
(1,300 grams)**

This jam is a bit sweeter than traditional orange marmalade, so you get the lovely flavor and vibrant orange-red color of the blood oranges, without the bitter intensity that turns off some people, including myself. I use apple stock to set the jam; apples, specifically the skins and seeds, contain naturally occurring pectin, the substance used to set jam.

Pectin is found in varying degrees in all fruit. Acidic fruit, such as pears, quince, tart apples, and citrus fruit, are generally high in pectin. Commercial pectin is pectin in powdered form that has been extracted from fruit. Sugar is hydroscopic, which means it attracts water molecules. As the fruit breaks down in the process of making jam, the water molecules in the fruit head to the sugar molecules, leaving the pectin molecules in the fruit by themselves. The pectin molecules then form their own network, which suspends the fruit juices and creates a thick, jammy consistency. Natural apple pectin is easy to make by simply boiling apple skins and cores, where the majority of the pectin in apples is found. Natural pectin doesn't create a gummy consistency that some commercial varieties do.

Granny Smith apples	1½ pounds (about 4 large)	680 grams
Blood oranges	6 pounds (14 to 16)	2,700 grams
Granulated sugar	3¼ cups	650 grams

Make the apple stock

· Wash the apples, remove their stems, and quarter them; do not peel or core them. Place the apples in a large (6- to 8-quart) saucepan, cover them with 6 cups (1.5 liters) cold water, and bring the water to a boil over high heat. Reduce the heat to medium-low to maintain a steady simmer and simmer the apples for 1 hour. Turn off the heat and pass the stock through a fine-mesh strainer; discard the contents of the strainer. (Do not press down on the apples as this will make a cloudy stock and a cloudy jam.)

Get prepared

· Place two small plates in the freezer. (You will use these later to test the jam for doneness.)

Make the jam

· Peel 2 of the oranges with a vegetable peeler. Cut the peel into ⅛-inch-wide strips, place the strips in a small saucepan, and fill the saucepan halfway with cold water. Bring the water to a boil over high heat and boil for 1 minute. Turn off the heat and strain the orange peels. Return the orange peels to the saucepan and fill the saucepan with cold water. Bring the water to a boil over high heat and repeat, boiling the peels for 1 minute and straining them again.

· Place a cooling rack on a baking sheet. Transfer the bread slices to the rack, laying them in a single layer. Let the bread drain while you heat up the oil in the next step or cover the baking sheet and place it in the refrigerator overnight.

Fry the French toast   · Fill a large (12-quart) pot 2 inches deep with oil. Fasten a deep-fry or candy thermometer to the side of the pot and heat the oil over medium-high heat until the thermometer registers 375°F.

· Line a baking sheet with paper towels and place a cooling rack on top of the baking sheet. Place the setup near the stove. Have a pair of metal tongs handy.

· Carefully slide 2 slices of French toast into the hot oil and fry them for about 3 minutes per side, until they are deep golden brown on each side, using tongs to turn them. Remove the French toast slices from the oil and lay them on the cooling rack to drain. Check the temperature of the oil and wait, if necessary, for the oil to return to 375°F. Repeat, frying 2 more slices of bread as you did the first 2, and lay them on the cooling rack alongside the other slices to drain. Fry the remaining bread in the same way, making sure the oil is at the correct temperature before adding the bread to the oil.

· Cut each slice in half on a diagonal. Serve with the maple syrup or confectioners' sugar with strawberry jam on the side.

Strawberry Jam

In the summer I look for tiny Tristar strawberries at farmers' markets to make this. But in the winter, a plastic container of grocery store strawberries still makes a delicious jam.

Makes about 1¼ cups

Strawberries	1 pound	454 grams
Granulated sugar	1 cup	200 grams
Fresh lemon juice	1 teaspoon	5 grams

Get prepared

· Place two small plates in the freezer. (You will use these later to test the jam for doneness.)

Make the jam

· Use a paring knife to remove and discard the stems from the strawberries and cut the strawberries into quarters. Place the quartered berries in a medium (2½-quart) saucepan. Add the sugar and lemon juice and cook over medium heat, stirring constantly with a wooden spoon, until the sugar dissolves and the strawberries begin to release their juice. Increase the heat to medium-high and cook, stirring occasionally, for 20 to 25 minutes, smashing the fruit against the sides of the pan with the back of the spoon as it cooks. Turn off the heat.

· To test to see if the jam has set up sufficiently, remove one of the plates from the freezer. Place a spoonful of jam on the plate and return the plate to the freezer for 2 minutes, then gently slide your finger across the plate and through the jam; if the skin on top of the jam wrinkles, it's done. If not, put the jam back on the heat and cook it for a few more minutes, then test again in the same way using the second plate you put in the freezer.

· Remove the saucepan from the heat, pour the jam into a heat-proof storage container, and set aside to cool to room temperature with the lid slightly ajar. Cover and refrigerate the jam until you are ready to use it, or for up to several months.

Pies and Tarts

Pie making and I go way back. I started making pies as a child with my mother; cherry lattice pie was one of the first things we made together. During college, I remember proudly offering a blueberry pie that I had baked as a "thank-you" to a group of friends who helped me move apartments. And, of course, I have made many different pies for Thanksgiving. Today, pies are one of my favorite things to make, and one of the things I bake most often at home. I like sharing pie, bringing it to a dinner party or picnic. And, I also love eating pie, especially for breakfast.

Making pie is not difficult, but it does require planning because you want to make your dough in advance, so it has time to relax and chill. And it requires some skills in terms of rolling out the crust and lining the pie plate. In this chapter, you will find all the information you need for you to succeed. I have worked a lot on my piecrust over the years and I am proud of where those efforts have taken me, so I am happy to share what I've learned in this chapter, as well as my greatest pie hits from decades of passionate pie baking.

Master Recipe
for Pâte Brisée

**Makes 2 pounds (1 kilogram)
of dough; or enough for
1 double-crust pie or
half of a slab pie**

A pie is only as good as its crust. I'm very particular about piecrust, and I too seldom come across a good one, one that is tender, flaky, redolent of butter, baked to a rich, golden brown, and that doesn't shrink up when baked.

When I first started making pies at home, I became frustrated by how much my piecrusts would shrink in the oven. The crusts tasted great, and they had a good, flaky texture. But because of that shrinkage, they looked too homemade. After some tinkering, I found that by removing some of the water from the crust recipe I was using, I got less shrinkage, and a prettier pie. More water makes the dough more pliable, and the dough then shrinks back when baked; by reducing the water, you reduce the dough's stretch, and also its shrinkage. This is especially important when making a lattice-topped crust, because you want the lattice to look attractive and to keep its shape. Many pâte brisée recipes call for you to add more water if you think it's necessary when mixing the dough, but I don't give a range. I am confident that the amount of water I call for is the amount you will need, and it is the amount of water that I can guarantee will give you a tender, flaky crust that won't shrink when baked. Even if the dough looks to the novice baker like it needs more water to come together, the flour will continue to absorb the water, and you'll find that as you begin to roll the dough out, there will, in fact, be enough water.

Classic pâte brisée has a very small amount of sugar in it, and mine has a little bit more; I like the touch of sweetness it adds, and the sugar also makes the crust brown beautifully. I make this crust with a combination of all-purpose and whole-wheat flours. The whole wheat adds to the tenderness of the crust and also imparts a hint of nuttiness to the flavor.

If you are making a slab pie, such as Raspberry Rhubarb Lattice-Topped Slab Pie (page 241), Concord Grape Slab Pie (page 265), or Grapefruit Shaker Slab Pie (page 285), you will need to make two batches of this dough. Don't double the recipe as it will not fit easily in your mixing bowl; also, you would likely have to overwork the dough to mix in the butter, and great piecrust depends on your working the dough as little as possible.

Unsalted butter, cold	24 tablespoons (3 sticks)	339 grams
All-purpose flour	2½ cups	300 grams
Whole-wheat pastry flour	1¼ cups	150 grams
Granulated sugar	3 tablespoons	38 grams
Fine sea salt	1½ teaspoons	9 grams
Water, cold	½ cup	118 grams

- Cut the butter into ½-inch-thick pieces. Lay the pieces in a single layer on a plate and put the plate in the freezer for 10 minutes.
- Combine the all-purpose flour, whole-wheat pastry flour, sugar, and salt in the bowl of a stand mixer. Fit the mixer with the paddle attachment and mix on low speed to combine the ingredients. Remove the butter from the freezer, add it to the mixer bowl, and combine on low speed for about 1 to 2 minutes, until the mixture resembles coarse crumbs with some large chunks of butter remaining. Turn off the mixer and use your hands to check the size of the butter; if there are any pieces larger than a nickel, pinch them between your fingertips to flatten them. Add the water and combine on low speed until the dough comes together but is still slightly shaggy; do not mix it until the dough is smooth and homogenous, like cookie dough.

The more you mix pie dough, the tougher the crust will be because you develop more gluten. And, when you overmix the dough, the chunks of butter break up; those chunks are what create the nice layers in a crust.

- Put the dough on your work surface. If you are making the Chestnut Honey Walnut Tart (page 281) or a slab pie, leave the dough in one piece. If you are making a traditional round pie, cut the dough in half with a bench knife.
- Lay two long sheets of plastic wrap in a crisscross formation on your work surface. Place one piece of dough in the center, where the two sheets cross. Use your hands to pat the dough into a round disk for a pie or tart, and into a rectangular block for a slab pie. Loosely wrap the dough in the plastic, leaving a few inches of slack all around. Run a rolling pin over each package of wrapped dough to roll it out in the plastic to a ½-inch-thick round or block. (For more detail, see Wrapping Dough, page xl.) Place the dough in the refrigerator to chill for at least 2 hours and up to 2 days; or freeze it for up to 1 month.

1

2

3

4

5

6

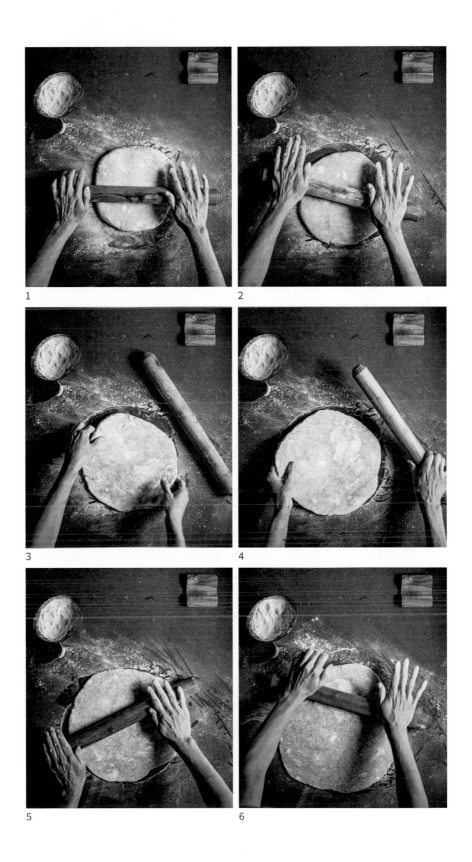

Master Class
How to Make Perfect Pie

There is a lot of subtlety that goes into making a good piecrust, the types of intuitive moves or small tips that you learn in a professional kitchen, or by baking with your mother or grandmother. In this master class, I have attempted to address all of those points, so you can apply them in these recipes to make delicious and professional-looking pies.

Plan ahead

In a professional bakery, pie dough is prepared up to several days in advance. I suggest you set yourself up the same way at home. Making the dough in advance gives the gluten time to relax, which prevents shrinkage in the crust when baked. It also ensures that the dough is properly chilled. Working with chilled dough, and relaxed gluten, makes the dough easier to roll out. Also, it is just very convenient to have the dough chilled and ready to roll when you go to make your pie. You can make pie dough up to one month in advance.

Great pie dough

A pie is only as good as its crust. I use a few different recipes for piecrust, but my basic pie dough recipe is Pâte Brisée (page 232). *Brisée* means "broken" in French, and in this dough, the butter is "broken" into the dough, creating a layered, flaky crust. Pâte sucrée, by contrast, means "sugar dough." It contains sugar and egg and is prepared like a cookie dough, with the butter and sugar creamed together. I make a Lemon Rosemary Curd Tart with Rye Crust that uses a pâte sucrée (page 288).

Butter versus lard versus shortening

The essential ingredients in pie dough are flour, water, a pinch of salt, maybe a very small amount of sugar, and some fat. Many traditional American pie dough recipes call for lard, which is rendered pork fat. Lard became taboo because of health trends, although it's currently making a comeback. I love it, but quality lard is not always easy to find, so I use good old-fashioned butter to make my pie and tart crusts.

Big chunks of very cold butter

Most pie recipes call for you to cut the butter into ¼-inch cubes. Instead, I start with sticks of butter and cut them into largish, ½-inch chunks. After cutting the butter, I place the chunks on a plate and put them in the freezer for 10 minutes, so the butter is as cold as can be without being frozen. I like to start with these larger pieces because when they are mixed in with the flour, some larger chunks remain. When the dough is rolled out, those chunks form striations of butter in the dough, and when baked, the water in the butter evaporates, resulting in microscopic flaky layers—and a light, tender, flaky crust.

Cold water   Many pie dough recipes call for you to add ice water to the dough. I find that cold water from my refrigerator works fine. Since I make sure that the butter is very cold, I don't think it is necessary to add ice-cold water. That said, if you want to use super-chilled water, it certainly won't hurt. The reason the water is added after mixing the flour with the butter is important to understand. The butter coats the proteins in the flour. It is when the water is added to the mix that the gluten starts to form. Gluten toughens dough, which is not a good thing when you're making a piecrust. A tough piecrust refers to one that is heavy and solid, not light and flaky. By mixing the flour first with cold butter, the butter coats the flour. When you add the water, the butter impedes its interaction with the flour.

Don't overmix the dough   The temptation when making pie dough is to mix it until it completely comes together, like cookie dough, but you don't want to do that. Mix it only until the dough begins to come together on the paddle, but not all the way. When you transfer the dough to the counter, it should still be a bit crumbly and shaggy, with small, observable chunks of butter. You will squish the crumbly bits together with your hands, which is gentler than using the mixer and does not develop the gluten as much.

Shape the dough   After bringing the dough together, I shape it into a round disk or brick, depending on the shape I will be rolling it out to. Then I wrap it in plastic wrap and run a rolling pin over the dough to flatten it out before putting it in the refrigerator to rest. (For more detail, see Wrapping Dough, page xl.)

If at any time the dough becomes so soft and sticky that it is difficult to shape, place it in the refrigerator to chill for a few minutes.

Let the dough rest   It's important to let pie dough rest before rolling it out. By giving the dough a good rest, the flour is able to fully absorb the water. It is only after resting that the dough will completely come together. Resting the dough also allows the glutens to relax, which makes it easier to roll out. Rested dough also shrinks less in the pie plate, making for a prettier, more professional-looking pie.

Roll out the dough   For detailed instruction, see Rolling Dough 101, page 250.

Butter the pie plate

I always butter the pie plate before lining it with dough. The butter helps the dough to adhere to the pan. I smear on enough butter that it is a visible layer on the pie plate. I usually use cold butter for this, but slightly softened also works.

Lift the dough onto the pie plate or pan

To line a pie plate, the first thing you have to do is lift the dough off the surface you rolled it on and place it on the pie plate (or tart pan). There are two ways to do this. You can fold the dough in half and carry it over. Or you can roll the dough onto your rolling pin and carry it over on the pin. I fold the dough if I am lining a round pie plate and roll the dough onto a rolling pin if I am using a jelly-roll pan, which requires a larger piece of dough. You can use whatever method you find easiest. In either case, carry the dough until it is hovering over the pie plate, tart pan, or jelly roll pan, centering it as much as you can. Then gently drop it onto the pie plate or pan and unfold or unroll it. Adjust the dough so that it is centered on the pan.

Line the pie plate or pan

Gently lift the dough with one hand and use your other hand to press it into the pan, working your way around the perimeter. Do this with a delicate touch, and resist pulling the dough, which will cause it to spring back when baked and create thin spots in the crust.

Next, gently run your finger along the rim of the pie plate, tart pan, or jelly-roll pan to press the dough onto it, just enough to ensure it adheres. This allows you to see how much dough is overhanging. Make sure it is even all the way around and sitting nicely on top of the rim.

Trim the dough

Use kitchen shears to trim the overhanging dough so there is an even 1 inch hanging over the perimeter of the pie plate, tart pan, or jelly-roll pan. (Discard the trimmings or smush them together into a disk and refrigerate or freeze the dough to make a pie another day.) If you are making a two-crust or lattice-topped pie, trim the top sheet of dough or lattice so it is flush with the outside edge of the pie plate or jelly-roll pan.

Crimp the crust

In pie making, "crimping" refers to forming the decorative, wavy, crimped edge around the perimeter of a pie. To crimp a pie, first, tightly roll the overhanging dough toward the center of the pie to create a thick lip that rests on the ridge of the plate; the dough shouldn't hang over the rim. The process will be the same whether you are making a one- or two-crust pie. For a two-crust pie, you will be rolling the bottom crust over the top crust, thereby sealing the pie closed.

As you work your way around the pie and roll the dough over itself to form this edge, use your fingers to shape the edge of the roll so that it is rounded and even.

Once you have rolled the entire edge of the pie, place the index finger and thumb of one hand on the edge of the pie and push the index finger of your other hand between those fingers toward the center of the pie to form a V or U shape. Continue around the perimeter of the pie until you have crimped the entire crust.

Chill the pie

There is a lot of chilling when you're making pie. First, you chill the butter. Then you chill the finished dough before rolling it out. You chill the pie plate or pan after you've lined it with pie dough. And then, after forming and filling the pie, you chill it again just before baking. Chilling the pie after it's been formed helps it hold its shape better during baking. If you've ever wondered why pies in professional bakeries look so much prettier than homemade ones often do, it's because they are chilled or even frozen before baking.

Freeze the pie

In my kitchens, we often freeze a fruit pie, and then take the pie from the freezer and put it directly into the oven. To bake a frozen pie, put it directly in the oven from the freezer and add 10 to 20 minutes to the total baking time, using the visual indicators for doneness in the recipe.

Bake the pie

With all pies, it's really important that they bake for enough time. Depending on how cold the pie is when you put it into the oven, and depending on your oven, the baking time might vary, so it's important to look for visual cues for doneness. The crust needs to be a rich shade of golden brown. For a fruit pie, the filling must be bubbling through the lattice in the center of the pie or the hole in the top. If the filling is not bubbling in the center (not *just* around the sides of the pie), that means the fruit hasn't cooked down enough. If you were to take the pie out at this point, you would end up with a pie with too much liquid that weeps when you cut a slice. Custard pies need to be baked until they are set. A set pie will move slightly when you jiggle the pan, but it won't slosh around like liquid. You want to avoid baking custard-baked pies for so long that they crack on top, but sometimes this is inevitable. Always put a baking sheet under pies before baking. This is particularly important with fruit pies, as this way, the bubbling fruit won't bubble over the edge of the pan onto your oven floor.

Blind baking

Also called pre-baking, blind baking refers to baking the crust before adding the filling. For custard-baked pies, such as Johnny Cash's Mother's Pineapple Rum Chess Pie (page 275) and Sweet Potato Pie (page 269), the crust is blind baked before adding the filling, which prevents it from being underbaked and becoming soggy. You will also blind bake the crust for pies or tarts whose fillings are not baked at all, such as Lemon Rosemary Curd Tart with Rye Crust (page 288), or when the filling takes less time to cook than the crust takes to brown. To blind bake a crust, you line the shaped, unbaked crust with parchment paper and then weigh it down with pie weights (ceramic beads sold for this purpose) to keep the crust from puffing up when baked. Dried beans can also be used as pie weights;

just make sure to label them as "pie weights" when you're done with them, as they will not be good for cooking once they've been baked.

Pro Tips for a Lattice Crust

Who doesn't love the look of a well-done lattice-topped pie? But it's hard to get it right, and either the bottom crust and the filling come out underdone or the lattice top gets too brown and shrinks in the process. The fact is, if you do things properly, you can bake your pie correctly *and* end up with a perfect, pretty lattice crust. Here are a few tips.

▪ Start with chilled dough. Remove the dough from the refrigerator and soften it just enough that you are able to roll it out. You will chill the dough again before cutting it and as needed at any time during the process of making your lattice. Putting the dough back in the refrigerator to chill and stiffen slightly is the remedy for warm, soft, sticky dough. I call for you to roll the dough out onto a sheet of parchment paper so you can easily lift it onto a baking sheet in one piece, and then place the baking sheet in the refrigerator.

▪ Have all your tools on hand—rolling pin, pastry wheel, straightedge, flour for dusting—before you start, that way you won't be running around your kitchen looking for these things while your dough softens up on the counter.

▪ Dust the parchment work surface generously with flour. The last thing you want is to cut the strips for your lattice and find you can't lift them off the parchment, or that they become misshapen in the process.

▪ Before cutting the lattice strips, lift the dough to make sure it is not sticking. If it is, with the help of a bench knife, gently lift the dough and dust underneath with flour.

▪ Work quickly. (All of these tips, you might notice, are getting at the same thing: work with cold dough!)

Raspberry Rhubarb Lattice-Topped Slab Pie

Makes 1 slab pie; serves 12 to 15

Slab pies are made in a jelly-roll pan instead of a pie plate, so they're about twice the size of a conventional pie. I like making them in the summer, with seasonal fruit, like this raspberry rhubarb version. Because they have more crust and less fruit than a standard round pie, slab pies are easy to pick up and eat with your hands, so they're great to take to a picnic or serve at a backyard barbecue. They're also great for breakfast. Strawberry rhubarb is the classic combination, but I use raspberries here instead. Raspberries are less sweet, which allows the tart flavor of the rhubarb to come through. This pie is thickened with arrowroot, a starch derived from plants. I prefer it as an alternative to cornstarch.

Note You will need a jelly-roll pan to make this.

For the crust

Master Recipe for Pâte Brisée (page 232)	2 recipes (each formed into a separate block)	
Unsalted butter, softened	for greasing	
All-purpose flour	for dusting	

For the filling

Rhubarb	1½ pounds	681 grams
Raspberries	1 pound	454 grams
Granulated sugar	2 cups	400 grams
Orange	1 (for zesting)	
Vanilla beans	2	
Arrowroot powder	¼ cup plus 2 tablespoons	44 grams
Fine sea salt	1 teaspoon	6 grams

For baking the pie

Large egg	1	50 grams
Fine sea salt	big pinch	
Demerara (turbinado) sugar	2 tablespoons	26 grams

Make the Crust

Get prepared

- Remove both blocks of dough from the refrigerator and set them on the counter to rest for 10 to 15 minutes, until they are pliable but not soft.
- Grease the bottom and sides of a jelly-roll pan with butter and set aside.
- Line the underside of a baking sheet with parchment paper. Make room in your refrigerator to place the jelly-roll pan and the baking sheet later.

Roll out the dough and line the pan

- Lightly dust a large flat work surface with flour. Unwrap one block of dough and place it on the floured surface. Lightly dust the dough and the rolling pin with flour and roll the dough into a ⅛-inch-thick rectangle (at least

15 x 20 inches), rotating the dough and dusting the work surface, dough, and rolling pin with flour as needed to prevent the dough from sticking to the work surface as you roll. (For more detailed instruction, see Rolling Dough 101, page 250.)

- Gently roll the dough around your rolling pin or fold the dough in half. Place the dough on the jelly-roll pan. Unroll or unfold the dough and adjust it as needed so it is centered over the pan. Use your hands to guide the dough into the bottom creases and up the sides of the pan. (For more detailed instruction, see Master Class: How to Make Perfect Pie, page 236.) Using kitchen shears, trim the dough so it hangs over the edge of the pan by 1 inch all around. Gather the trimmings and pat them into a thin square block. Wrap the block in plastic wrap and place it in the refrigerator to chill until you're ready to use it. Put the pie shell in the refrigerator while you cut the lattice strips and make the filling, and up to overnight. (If you are refrigerating the shell overnight, cover it with plastic wrap before refrigerating.)

Roll out the dough for the lattice

- Dust the work surface again lightly with flour. Unwrap the second block of dough and place it on the floured surface. Dust the top of the dough and the rolling pin with flour and roll the dough out to a ⅛-inch-thick rectangle (it will be roughly 15 x 20 inches), rotating the dough and dusting the work surface, dough, and rolling pin lightly with flour as needed to prevent the dough from sticking to the work surface as you roll. Move the dough to the underside of the parchment-lined baking sheet, folding the edges over the sheet if they are hanging over. Place the baking sheet in the refrigerator to chill the dough for 30 minutes, until it is firm, and up to overnight. (If you are refrigerating the dough overnight, cover it with plastic wrap before refrigerating.)

- Lightly dust your work surface with additional flour. Remove the square block of dough trimmings from the refrigerator, unwrap it, and place it on the floured surface. Dust the top of the dough and the rolling pin with flour and roll the dough out to a ¼-inch-thick square (it will be about 12 inches square), rotating the dough and dusting the work surface, dough, and rolling pin lightly with flour as needed to prevent the dough from sticking to the work surface as you roll. Lay a piece of parchment paper on the work surface and slide the square onto the paper. Remove the baking sheet with the dough on the underside from the refrigerator. Lay the sheet of parchment paper with the dough you just rolled on top of the first sheet of dough and return the dough to the refrigerator to chill for 30 minutes, until it is firm, and up to overnight. (If you are refrigerating the dough overnight, cover it with plastic wrap before refrigerating.)

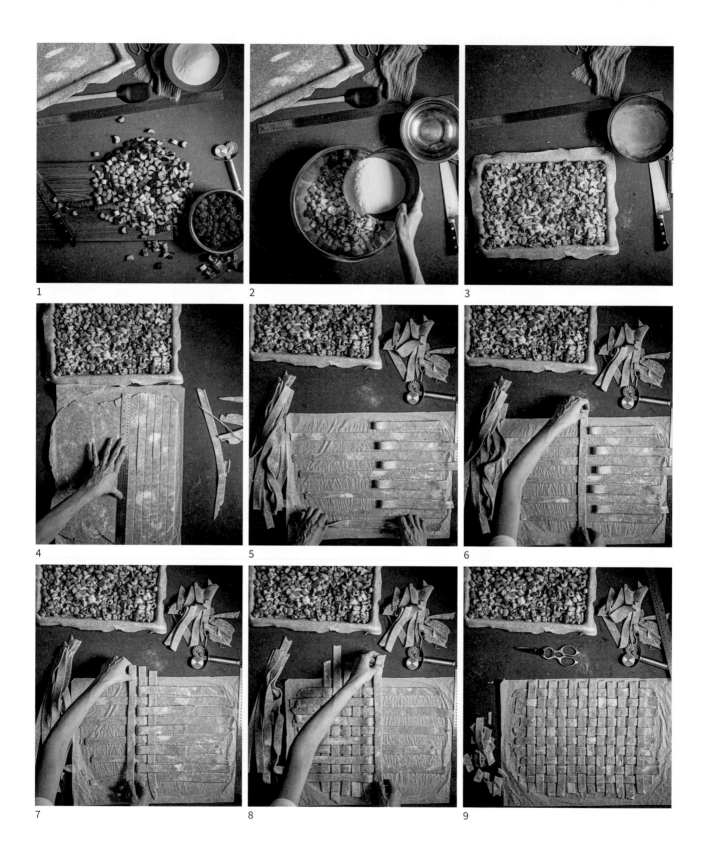

Cut the lattice strips ▪ Remove the baking sheet with the dough for the lattice from the refrigerator and slide the top sheet onto your work surface. Return the baking sheet to the refrigerator. Using a straightedge and pastry wheel, or a long knife, trim the left and right edges of the dough to form clean, straight lines. Discard the scraps or gather them for another use. Cut the dough into 12 (1-inch-thick) strips. Slide the parchment paper with the strips to the side. Remove the baking sheet with the lattice dough from the refrigerator and slide the remaining sheet of parchment and dough onto your work surface with the short side parallel to you. Slide the parchment with the cut strips onto the sheet and return it to the refrigerator.

Refrigerating the lattice strips firms them up. This allows you to handle them more easily, resulting in a neater, prettier pie.

▪ Using a straightedge and pastry wheel, or a long knife, trim the left and right edges of the dough to form clean, straight lines. Cut the dough into 1-inch-wide strips. Remove the baking sheet with the lattice strips from the refrigerator. Slide the parchment with the long lattice strips on top of the lattice strips that you cut first and return them to the refrigerator while you make your filling.

Prepare the filling ▪ Wipe the rhubarb with a damp paper towel or rinse it under running water and dry it. Cut off and discard the ends of the stalks and slice the rhubarb into ½-inch-thick pieces. Put the rhubarb in a large bowl and put the raspberries on top.
▪ Place the granulated sugar in a medium bowl and use a fine Microplane to grate the orange zest—only the outermost, bright-colored layer—over the sugar. Split the vanilla beans down the middle with a small sharp knife and use the knife to scrape the seeds out of the beans; smear the seeds onto the sugar and zest. (Use the beans to make Vanilla Sugar, page 219, or discard them.) Work the sugar between your fingertips to disperse the zest and vanilla throughout. Add the arrowroot and salt and whisk to combine. Add to the bowl with the rhubarb and raspberries and gently fold with a rubber spatula to coat the fruit with the sugar mixture.
▪ Remove the pie shell from the refrigerator and scoop the raspberry rhubarb filling into it, using a rubber spatula to get all the gooey sugary ingredients out of the bowl. Use the spatula to even out the filling.

Form the lattice ▪ Set the pie shell on the work surface with a long edge of the pan parallel to you. Remove the lattice strips from the refrigerator and lay 7 of the long strips horizontally across the pie, leaving about ½ inch between each strip. Weave in the vertical strips to form a woven lattice top, leaving about ½ inch between each strip.

- Trim the edges of the lattice top so the dough is flush with the inside rim of the pan. Gather the trimmings and leftover strips into a ball and pat them into a disk. Wrap the dough in plastic and run a rolling pin over it to flatten it to ½ inch thick. Place the dough in the refrigerator or freezer to use another time. There should be enough leftover dough to make a one-crust pie.
- Turn over the parchment on the parchment-lined baking sheet so the clean side is facing up; turn over the pan so it is right side up and line it with the parchment paper.

Crimp the crust

- Gently roll the overhang of dough up to the rim of the pan, rolling up any lattice overhang into the crust. Crimp the crust of the pie to seal it closed. (For detailed instruction, see "Crimp the crust" in Master Class: How to Make Perfect Pie, page 238.) Place the pie in the refrigerator to chill for 30 minutes to 1 hour. (You can also freeze the pie at this point for up to 2 weeks. To bake a frozen pie, put it directly in the oven from the freezer. Add 10 to 20 minutes to the total baking time, using the visual indicators for doneness in the recipe.)

Refrigerating a lattice-topped pie before baking prevents the lattice from shrinking. Because you went to all the effort to form the lattice, which is solely for decorative purposes, you don't want it to lose its shape in the oven.

Bake the pie

- Arrange the oven racks so one is in the center position. Preheat the oven to 375°F.
- Remove the pie from the refrigerator. Whisk the egg with the salt to make an egg wash. Brush the wash generously over the pie dough; discard the remaining egg wash. Sprinkle the demerara sugar over the crust. Place the pie on the parchment-lined baking sheet to catch the juices that will bubble over. Place the pie on the center rack of the oven to bake for 50 minutes to 1 hour, until the crust is golden brown and the filling is bubbly, rotating the baking sheet from front to back halfway through the baking time so the crust browns evenly. Remove the pie from the oven and place it on a cooling rack to cool for at least 1 hour before serving. Use a serrated knife to cut the pie and use an offset spatula to lift the slices out of the pan. Serve warm or at room temperature.

Variation
Blueberry Blackberry Slab Pie

Makes 1 slab pie; serves 12 to 15

Let me tell you a little story about how this pie came to be, and how it became my favorite of summer desserts. We have friends in Connecticut, and we were headed there for the weekend for a barbecue. I had never made a slab pie before, and I got it into my mind that I wanted to bring one. I went to Locust Grove, a favorite stand for spectacular fruit at the Union Square Greenmarket in Manhattan. My intention was to make a blackberry slab pie, but the cost of the tiny little baskets of berries was such that I didn't have enough cash to buy as many as I needed. I ended up buying half blackberries and half blueberries, which are much less expensive, and making a black- and blueberry pie. It just turned out phenomenally. I make it with a combination of brown sugar and demerara sugar, and not too much of either, so you can really taste the flavor and tartness of the berries.

Note You will need a jelly-roll pan to make this.

For the filling		
Light brown sugar	¾ cup (lightly packed)	150 grams
Demerara (turbinado) sugar	½ cup	100 grams
Arrowroot powder	¼ cup plus 2 tablespoons	44 grams
Fine sea salt	½ teaspoon	3 grams
Blueberries	2 pints (4 cups)	570 grams
Blackberries	2 pints (4 cups)	570 grams
Fresh lemon juice	2 tablespoons	30 grams

▪ To make the filling, whisk the brown sugar, demerara sugar, arrowroot, and salt together in a large bowl. Add the blueberries, blackberries, and lemon juice and toss gently to coat the berries with the sugar mixture. Use the filling in place of the filling in the Raspberry Rhubarb Lattice-Topped Slab Pie (page 241).

Rolling Dough 101

I know how frustrating it can be to try to roll dough at home when you don't know how, or when you are not that efficient at it. I have many memories of rolling dough when I was a kid. I worked slowly, so the dough would get warm and stick to the counter and the rolling pin. I wasn't much better when I started rolling dough as a novice home baker. Having gone through those experiences and come out a very fast and efficient baker, my goal is to teach you what I taught myself so that you won't have to suffer as I did.

Temperature

The first thing to think about when rolling dough is its temperature. You want the dough to be just pliable enough to roll. You can't roll out rock-hard dough, straight from the refrigerator. That's why I call for you to let dough rest at room temperature before rolling it out. But if you let it rest too long, and it becomes too soft, that's when it starts to stick. Take the dough out of the refrigerator, put it on your counter, and let it sit until it feels pliable but still firm, 10 to 15 minutes, before rolling it out.

Be organized

Once the dough is ready to roll, *you* need to be ready to roll. So, get organized. After taking the dough out of the refrigerator, have your work space cleared. For me that means my kitchen counter with a Roul'Pat (see page xxviii) on it. Whatever it is for you, make space, and have your rolling pin ready, as well as anything else you might need, such as a bench knife, cookie cutter, straightedge, pastry wheel, knife, and flour (or in some cases sugar) for dusting your work surface. Whatever is going to happen with the dough *after* it is rolled, make sure that is ready, too, whether it is a baking sheet lined with parchment paper, or a pie plate or pan that you'll be lining with dough. You don't want to be lining a baking sheet with parchment paper, or washing and drying a pie plate while your rolled-out dough is warming up on the counter.

Move quickly

Once you start rolling, you need to feel the urgency to get the dough rolled out and be onto the next step as quickly as possible. Even the firmest block of dough is going to start to feel very soft very quickly because it warms up from the friction of the rolling pin and the heat of your hands. So, just focus and roll. The whole process shouldn't take more than a minute or two.

The finer points of rolling	Rolling dough shouldn't be a series of random motions. It's best done in a methodical way in order to obtain a sheet that is of an even thickness, is a regular shape that you can work with (such as a circle or rectangle), and that doesn't stick to the counter.
Dust with flour	Dusting the work surface, rolling pin, and top of the dough with flour is essential in preventing the dough from sticking to the work surface or the rolling pin. That said, as essential as flour is, you want to use as little as necessary. A lot of novice bakers dust like crazy. You don't want the dough swimming in a pool of flour. Having all that excess flour is messy, and it also ends up in the dough, changing the flavor and texture of the finished pastry. (A silicone Roul'Pat mat [see page xxviii] will enable you to roll with a minimal amount of flour.) If the dough is truly sticking to the extent that you can't work with it, put it in the refrigerator to chill for 10 to 15 minutes, until it firms up enough that you can resume rolling it out.
Roll from the center outward	Regardless of whether you are rolling a round of dough into a circle or a block of dough into a rectangle, you want to start with the rolling pin in the center of the dough and work outward, away from you. I roll starting from the center and up toward 12 o'clock, working my way around to 3 o'clock, then I have to rotate the dough.
Rotate the dough	As you roll outward, you will rotate the round or block of dough by 90 degrees every few rolls so that you are still rolling from 12 o'clock to 3 o'clock. To rotate the dough, you lift it up off the counter and dust underneath it with flour, which prevents it from sticking to the counter.
Apply even pressure	When rolling out the dough, apply gentle, even pressure. If you lean on the rolling pin, you will end up with an uneven sheet of dough. On the other hand, you can't expect the dough to do all the work for you; I've found with novice home bakers that they tend to apply too *little* pressure as opposed to too much.

Sour Cherry Double-Crust Pie

Makes 1 (9-inch) pie; serves 6 to 8

The sour cherry season is a short span in early summer. I buy sour cherries to make this pie as soon as I see them at the Union Square Greenmarket. If you can't find fresh sour cherries, use frozen. Order them from an online source, or pit and freeze them when they are in season, which is what I often do. You don't need to thaw frozen cherries (or any frozen fruit) before baking them in a pie. Just throw them into a large bowl and go from there.

Note You will need a cherry pitter to make this (unless you start with frozen, pitted sour cherries). You will also need a 9-inch glass pie plate.

For the crust

Master Recipe for Pâte Brisée (page 232)	1 recipe	
Unsalted butter	for greasing	
All-purpose flour	for dusting	

For the filling

Sour cherries	2 quarts	1,200 grams
Light brown sugar	1¼ cups (lightly packed)	250 grams
Arrowroot powder	3 tablespoons	24 grams
Fine sea salt	½ teaspoon	3 grams
Fresh lemon juice	1 tablespoon	15 grams
Almond extract	1 teaspoon	5 grams

For baking the pie

Large egg	1	50 grams
Fine sea salt	big pinch	
Demerara (turbinado) sugar	2 tablespoons	26 grams

Make the crust

Get prepared

- Remove both rounds of dough from the refrigerator and set them on the work surface to rest for 10 to 15 minutes, until they are pliable but not soft.
- Grease the bottom and sides of a 9-inch pie plate with butter.
- Line a baking sheet with parchment paper.

Roll out the dough and line the pie plate

- Lightly dust a large flat work surface with flour. Unwrap one round of dough and place it on the floured surface. Lightly dust the dough and the rolling pin with flour and roll the dough into a ⅛-inch-thick round (15 inches in diameter), rotating the dough and dusting the work surface, dough, and rolling pin with flour as needed to prevent the dough from sticking to your work surface as you roll. (For more detailed instruction, see Rolling Dough 101, page 250.)

- Gently fold the dough in half, pick it up, and place it on the pie plate with the fold running down the center of the plate. Unfold the dough and adjust it so the circle of dough is centered over the plate. Use your hands to guide the dough into the bottom crease and up the sides of the plate. Using kitchen shears, trim the dough so it hangs over the edge of the pie plate by 1 inch all around. Put the pie shell in the refrigerator up to overnight while you roll out the second round of dough and make the filling. (If you are refrigerating the pie shell overnight, cover it with plastic wrap before refrigerating.)
- Dust the work surface again lightly with flour. Unwrap the second round of dough and repeat, rolling it out to a ⅛-inch-thick round. Gently fold the dough in half to pick it up and place it on the parchment-lined baking sheet. Place the baking sheet in the refrigerator for at least 30 minutes or up to overnight for the dough to chill while you make the filling. (If you are refrigerating the baking sheet overnight, cover it with plastic wrap before refrigerating.)

Make the filling and fill the pie shell

- Remove and discard the cherry stems. Have one small and one large bowl on your work surface. Use a cherry pitter to pit the cherries, letting the pits drop into the smaller bowl and dropping the pitted cherries into the larger bowl. Discard the pits.
- Put the brown sugar, arrowroot, and salt in a medium bowl and whisk to combine. Add this mixture to the bowl with the cherries. Add the lemon juice and almond extract and stir with a rubber spatula to combine.
- Remove the pie shell from the refrigerator and scoop the cherry filling into the shell, using a rubber spatula to get all the goop out of the bowl. Use the spatula to even out the filling.

Cover the pie and crimp the crust

- Remove the dough round from the refrigerator and place it on top of the pie, centering it on the pie and pressing down on the dough very gently. (Reserve the parchment-lined baking sheet to bake the pie.) Using kitchen shears, trim the top so it is flush with the outside ridge of the pie plate. Discard the trimmings.
- Gently roll the edge of the bottom dough up over the edge of the top dough to create a double-thick edge of dough that rests on the lip of the pie plate. Crimp the edge of the pie to seal it closed. (For detailed instructions, see "Crimp the crust" in Master Class: How to Make Perfect Pie, page 238.) Place the pie in the refrigerator to chill for 30 minutes to 1 hour. (You can also freeze the pie at this point for up to 2 weeks. To bake a frozen pie, put it directly in the oven from the freezer and add 10 to 20 minutes to the total baking time, using the visual indicators for doneness in the recipe.)

Bake the pie

- Arrange the oven racks so one is in the center position. Preheat the oven to 375°F.
- Remove the pie from the refrigerator. Use a small cookie cutter or the large side of a pastry tip to cut a 1-inch hole in the center of the pie and remove a little piece of dough; this hole allows the steam to escape as the pie bakes.
- Whisk the egg with the salt to create an egg wash. Brush the wash generously over the pie dough; discard the remaining egg wash. Sprinkle the demerara sugar over the crust. Place the pie on the parchment-lined baking sheet to catch the juices that will bubble over.
- Place the baking sheet on the center rack of the oven and bake the pie for 60 to 70 minutes, until the juices are bubbling and the crust is golden brown, rotating the pie from front to back halfway through the baking time so the crust browns evenly. Remove the pie from the oven and place it on a cooling rack to cool for at least 1 hour before serving. Use a serrated knife to cut the pie. Serve warm or at room temperature.

Lattice-Topped Peach Pie

**Makes 1 (9-inch) pie;
serves 6 to 8**

Peach pie is a classic; its perfection lies in its simplicity. To make the perfect peach pie, you need to start with great peaches, and use correct technique. It requires more work than other fruit pies, because you have to remove the skin from the peaches, unlike, say, a blueberry pie where you just throw the berries straight in. That extra effort is one of the things that elevates peach pie for me.

Note You will need a 9-inch glass pie plate to make this.

For the crust		
Master Recipe for Pâte Brisée (page 232)	2 recipes	
Unsalted butter, softened	for greasing	
All-purpose flour	for dusting	
For the peaches		
Ripe peaches	3 pounds (8 medium to large)	1,362 grams
Light brown sugar	½ cup (lightly packed)	100 grams
Arrowroot powder	3 tablespoons	24 grams
Freshly grated nutmeg	¼ teaspoon	<1 gram
Fine sea salt	½ teaspoon	3 grams
Fresh lemon juice	1 tablespoon	15 grams
For baking the pie		
Large egg	1	50 grams
Fine sea salt	big pinch	~1 gram
Demerara (turbinado) sugar	2 tablespoons	26 grams

Make the Crust

Get prepared

- Remove both rounds of dough from the refrigerator and set them on the work surface to rest for 10 to 15 minutes, until they are pliable but not soft.
- Grease the bottom and sides of a 9-inch pie plate with butter.
- Line the underside of a baking sheet with parchment paper. Make room in your refrigerator to place the baking sheet later.

Roll out the dough and line the pie plate

- Lightly dust a large flat work surface with flour. Unwrap one round of dough and place it on the floured surface. Lightly dust the dough and the rolling pin with flour and roll the dough out to a ⅛-inch-thick round (15 inches in diameter), rotating the dough and dusting the work surface, dough, and rolling pin with flour as needed to prevent the dough from sticking to the work surface as you roll. (For more detailed instruction, see Rolling Dough 101, page 250.)
- Gently fold the dough in half, pick it up, and place it on the pie plate with the fold running down the center of the plate. Unfold the dough and adjust

it so the circle of dough is centered over the plate. Use your hands to guide the dough into the bottom crease and up the sides of the plate. Using kitchen shears, trim the dough so it hangs over the edge of the pie plate by 1 inch all around. Put the pie shell in the refrigerator while you make the lattice and filling, and up to overnight. (If you are refrigerating the pie shell overnight, cover it with plastic wrap before refrigerating.)

· Dust the work surface again lightly with flour. Unwrap the second ball of dough and place it on the floured surface. Dust the top of the dough and the rolling pin with flour and roll the dough out to a ⅛-inch-thick square (15 inches in diameter), rotating the dough and dusting the work surface, dough, and rolling pin lightly with flour as needed to prevent the dough from sticking to the work surface as you roll. Using a straightedge and pastry wheel, or a long knife, trim the left and right edges to form clean, straight lines. Discard the trimmings. Cut the remaining dough square into 6 (2-inch-wide) strips. Carefully lift the strips off the work surface and lay them on the underside of the parchment-lined baking sheet. Place the baking sheet in the refrigerator to chill the strips for 30 minutes, until they are firm, and up to overnight. (If you are refrigerating the strips overnight, cover them with plastic wrap before refrigerating.)

Make the filling and fill the pie shell

· Fill a medium saucepan with water and bring it to a boil over high heat. Place a cup of ice cubes in a medium bowl and fill the bowl with cold water to make an ice bath. Have a spider (or fine-mesh strainer) handy. Line a large plate or a baking sheet with paper towels.

· Use a paring knife to score Xs in the skin on the bottom of each peach.

· Lower 2 of the peaches into the boiling water and cook for 1 minute. Use the spider to lift the peaches out of the water and gently place them in the ice bath. Add 2 more of the remaining peaches to the boiling water and boil for 1 minute. While the second 2 peaches are boiling, transfer the first 2 peaches from the ice bath to the paper towels to drain. Repeat with 2 peaches at a time, boiling the remaining peaches and cooling them in the ice bath in the same way. When you have removed the last peaches from the ice bath, use your fingers to pull off and discard the skins. (If the skins are not peeling easily, return the peaches to the boiling water for 1 minute, cool in the ice bath, and try again.)

· Cut each peach in half and remove and discard the pits. Place the peach halves facedown on a cutting board and slice them into 1-inch-thick pieces. Place the peach slices in a large bowl.

· Put the brown sugar, arrowroot, nutmeg, and salt in a medium bowl and whisk to combine. Add this mixture to the bowl with the peaches. Add the lemon juice and stir with a rubber spatula to combine.

• Remove the pie shell from the refrigerator and scoop the peach filling into the shell, using a rubber spatula to get all of the sugary ingredients out of the bowl. Use the spatula to even out the filling.

Create the lattice top and crimp the crust

• Remove the lattice strips from the refrigerator. Arrange 3 of the strips vertically over the pie. Place one of the remaining strips in the center of the pie at a 45-degree angle to those that are already on the pie, weaving it so it goes over the first strip, under the middle strip, and over the last strip. Weave the last 2 strips on either side of the first strip, following the opposite pattern, weaving them under the first strip, over the middle strip, and under the last strip. Flip the parchment and use it to line the baking sheet with the clean

5

6

7

8

9

10

side facing up. Set the baking sheet aside; you will place the pie on it before you put it in the oven.

- Using scissors, trim the strips so they are flush with the outside ridge of the pie plate. (Gather the trimmings and pat them into a round. Wrap in plastic wrap and place in the refrigerator to chill and use at another time.) Gently roll the edge of the bottom dough up over the strips to create a double-thick edge of dough that rests on the lip of the pie plate. Crimp the edge of the pie to seal it closed. (For detailed instruction, see "Crimp the crust" in Master Class: How to Make Perfect Pie, page 238.) Place the pie in the refrigerator to chill for 30 minutes to 1 hour. (You can also freeze the pie at this point for up to 2 weeks. To bake a frozen pie, put it directly in the oven from the freezer and add 10 to 20 minutes to the total baking time, using the visual indicators for doneness in the recipe.)

Bake the pie

- Arrange the oven racks so one is in the center position. Preheat the oven to 375°F.
- Remove the pie from the refrigerator. Whisk the egg with the salt to create an egg wash. Brush the wash generously over the pie dough; discard the remaining egg wash. Sprinkle the demerara sugar over the crust and place the pie on the parchment-lined baking sheet to catch the juices that will bubble over.
- Place the baking sheet on the center rack of the oven and bake the pie for 70 to 80 minutes, until the juices are bubbling and the crust is golden brown, rotating the pie from front to back halfway through the baking time so the crust browns evenly. Remove the pie from the oven and place it on a cooling rack to cool for at least 1 hour before serving. Use a serrated knife to cut the pie. Serve warm or at room temperature.

Apple
Crumb Pie

**Makes 1 (9-inch) pie;
serves 6 to 8**

A version of this recipe for crumb-topped sour cream apple pie was one of many that I tested for Gina DePalma's *Dolce Italiano* cookbook more than a decade ago. It was love at first bake. I have made changes to the original recipe over the years, but I still think of Gina whenever I make it. I love the appley flavor the Golden Delicious apples impart so much that I think it's my favorite apple pie I've ever made.

Note You will need a 9-inch glass pie plate to make this.

For the topping		
All-purpose flour	1¼ cups	150 grams
Light brown sugar	½ cup (lightly packed)	100 grams
Ground ginger	½ teaspoon	1 gram
Freshly grated nutmeg	¼ teaspoon	<1 gram
Fine sea salt	½ teaspoon	3 grams
Unsalted butter, cold and cubed	6 tablespoons	84 grams
Sour cream	3 tablespoons	45 grams
Pure vanilla extract	1 teaspoon	5 grams
For the crust		
Master Recipe for Pâte Brisée (page 232)	½ recipe	
Unsalted butter	for greasing	
All-purpose flour	for dusting	
For the apple filling		
Golden Delicious apples	1¾ pounds (4 large)	860 grams
Granulated sugar	¾ cup	150 grams
Vanilla bean	1	
All-purpose flour	2 tablespoons	18 grams
Fine sea salt	¼ teaspoon	2 grams
Sour cream	⅓ cup	73 grams
Large egg yolks	3	51 grams

Prepare the topping

· Line a baking sheet with parchment paper.

· Put the flour, brown sugar, ginger, nutmeg, and salt in the bowl of a food processor fitted with a metal blade and pulse to combine. Add the butter and process until the butter has broken up into the dry ingredients and the mixture is a coarse cornmeal texture. Add the sour cream and vanilla and mix until everything comes together into a homogenous dough. Drop the topping in tablespoon-size clumps onto the prepared baking sheet. Place the baking sheet in the freezer for several hours, until the topping is frozen solid.

· Remove the baking sheet from the freezer and put the topping in the bowl of a food processor fitted with a metal blade. Process until the chunks have broken up into tiny pea-size pieces. Refrigerate the pieces in a small container until ready to use, and for up to 3 days.

Make the Crust

Prepare the crust
· Remove the dough from the refrigerator and set it on the work surface to rest for 10 to 15 minutes, until it is pliable but not soft.
· Grease the bottom and sides of a 9-inch pie plate with butter.

Roll out the dough and line the pie plate
· Lightly dust a large flat work surface with flour. Unwrap the round of dough and place it on the floured surface. Lightly dust the dough and rolling pin with flour and roll the dough into a 15-inch-diameter circle, rotating the dough and dusting the work surface, dough, and rolling pin with flour as needed to prevent the dough from sticking to the work surface as you roll. (For more detailed instruction, see Rolling Dough 101, page 250.)
· Gently fold the dough in half, pick it up, and place it on the pie plate with the fold running down the center of the plate. Unfold the dough and adjust it so the circle of dough is centered over the plate. Use your hands to guide the dough into the bottom crease and up the sides of the plate. Using kitchen shears, trim the dough so it hangs over the edge of the pie plate by 1 inch all around. Tightly roll the overhanging dough toward the center of the pie plate to create a lip that rests on the ridge of the plate. Crimp the crust. (For more detail, see "Crimp the crust" in Master Class: How to Make Perfect Pie, page 238.) Put the pie shell in the refrigerator while you make the filling, and up to overnight. (If you are refrigerating the pie shell overnight, wrap it with plastic wrap before refrigerating.)

Make the filling
· Peel the apples and discard the peels. Working one at a time, stand the apples upright on a cutting board and cut around the cores to quarter the apples. Discard the cores. Lay the apple quarters flat on your cutting board and slice them ⅛ to ¼ inch thick. Place the slices in a large bowl and set aside.
· Put the sugar in a medium bowl. Split the vanilla bean down the middle with a small sharp knife and use the knife to scrape the seeds out of the bean. Add the seeds and bean to the bowl with the sugar and use your fingertips to distribute the seeds throughout the sugar. Add the flour and salt and whisk to combine. Add the sour cream and egg yolks and whisk to combine. Pour this custard mixture over the apples, using a rubber spatula to get all of the custard out of the bowl. Gently stir the custard and apples together with the spatula or your hands, making sure to distribute the custard among the apples.

Assemble and bake the pie

- Arrange the oven racks so one is in the center position. Preheat the oven to 375°F.
- Line a baking sheet with parchment paper.
- Remove the pie shell from the refrigerator and scoop the apple filling into the shell, using a rubber spatula to get all of the sugary stuff out of the bowl. Use the spatula to even out the filling.
- Cover the pie with the crumb topping, gently patting the crumbs into place so they don't roll off the pie. Place the pie on the parchment-lined baking sheet to catch the juices that will bubble over.
- Place the baking sheet on the center rack of the oven and bake the pie for 1 hour and 10 minutes to 1 hour and 20 minutes, until the crumb is golden brown and the custard is bubbling through the crumbs, rotating the pie from front to back halfway through the baking time so the crust browns evenly. Remove the pie from the oven and place it on a cooling rack to cool for at least 1 hour before serving. Use a serrated knife to cut the pie. Serve at room temperature.

Concord Grape Slab Pie

Makes 1 slab pie; serves 12 to 15

I first made this pie as a celebration of grape season. Every fall, Union Square Greenmarket in New York has the most wonderful array of Concord grapes. Concord grapes are different from any other varieties. They have a sweet-tart jamminess that is the true flavor of grape juice and grape jam. I also like to use Mars grapes, which are similar to Concord grapes but without the seeds, or Muscat grapes, both of which are also delicate, seasonal grapes. I don't recommend you use the conventional green or red grapes you find at grocery stores. They're so sweet and their skins are so tough; they won't make a good pie filling.

The beauty of fruit pie is that there is something for every season. I cut circles from the dough to decorate the top of the pie, which for me are a reflection of the grapes. Concord grapes have to be seeded, but when you taste them in this pie, I think you'll agree they're worth the effort. You can seed and freeze them up to 1 month in advance.

Note You will need a jelly-roll pan and a 1-inch round cookie cutter to make this.

For the crust

Master Recipe for Pâte Brisée (page 232)	2 recipes (each formed into a single block)	
Unsalted butter, softened	for greasing	
All-purpose flour	for dusting	

For the filling

Concord grapes	3½ pounds	1,589 grams
Light brown sugar	¾ cup (lightly packed)	150 grams
Demerara (turbinado) sugar	½ cup	100 grams
Cornstarch	¼ cup	33 grams
Juice from ½ lemon		
Fine sea salt	2 pinches	

For baking the pie

Large egg	1	50 grams
Fine sea salt	big pinch	
Demerara (turbinado) sugar	2 tablespoons	26 grams

Make the Crust

Get prepared

- Remove both blocks of dough from the refrigerator and set them on the work surface to rest for 10 to 15 minutes, until they are pliable but not soft.
- Grease the bottom and sides of a jelly-roll pan with butter.
- Line the underside of a baking sheet with parchment paper. Make room in your refrigerator to place both pans.

Roll out the dough and line the pan

- Lightly dust a large flat work surface with flour. Unwrap one block of dough and place it on the floured surface. Lightly dust the dough and the rolling pin with flour and roll the dough to a ⅛-inch-thick rectangle (at least

15 x 20 inches), rotating the dough and dusting the work surface, dough, and rolling pin with flour as needed to prevent the dough from sticking to the work surface as you roll. (For more detailed instruction, see Rolling Dough 101, page 250.)

- Gently roll the dough around your rolling pin and place it on the jelly-roll pan. Unroll the dough with the fold running down the center of the pan and adjust it as needed so the sheet of dough is centered over the pan. Use your hands to guide the dough into the bottom creases and up the sides of the pan. (For more detailed instruction, see Master Class: How to Make Perfect Pie, page 236.) Using kitchen shears, trim the dough so it hangs over the edge of the pan by 1 inch all around. Gather the trimmings, pat them into a disk, and wrap them in plastic wrap. Refrigerate or freeze the trimmings to use another time. Put the pie shell in the refrigerator while you prepare the top crust, and up to overnight. (If you are refrigerating the pie shell overnight, cover it with plastic wrap before refrigerating.)

- Dust the work surface again lightly with flour. Unwrap the second block of dough and place it on the floured surface. Dust the top of the dough and the rolling pin with flour and roll the dough out to a ⅛-inch-thick rectangle (15 x 20 inches), rotating the dough and dusting the work surface, dough, and rolling pin lightly with flour as needed to prevent the dough from sticking to the work surface as you roll. Gently roll the dough around your rolling pin to move to the underside of the parchment-lined baking sheet, folding the edges over the sheet if they are hanging over. Place the baking sheet in the refrigerator to chill the dough until it is firm, and up to overnight. (If you are refrigerating the dough overnight, cover the baking sheet with plastic wrap before refrigerating.)

- Remove the baking sheet with the dough from the refrigerator. Gently unfold the sides and use various sizes of circular cutters (cookie cutters, biscuit cutters, or the back sides of icing tips will all do the trick) to cut circular patterns in the dough. Gather the trimmings and add them to the trimmings disk from the bottom crust. Return the dough circles to the refrigerator for at least another 20 minutes, until firm, and up to overnight. (If you are refrigerating the dough overnight, cover the baking sheet with plastic wrap before refrigerating.)

Prepare the filling

- Line a baking sheet with parchment paper.
- Remove the grape stems and lay the grapes out in a single layer on the prepared baking sheet. Put the pan in the freezer until the grapes are frozen solid, about 1 hour. (The grapes can be frozen in advance; transfer the frozen grapes to quart-size storage containers or sealable plastic bags, close the containers or bags, and return them to the freezer for up to 1 month.)

- Remove about half of the grapes from the freezer. Use a small serrated knife to cut each grape in half through the stem end. Use the tip of the knife to remove the seeds and discard. Put the grapes in a large mixing bowl or large measuring cup. Once you have finished with those grapes, remove the remaining grapes from the freezer and cut them in half and deseed them. If you have more than 8 cups (1,300 grams) of grapes, reserve the rest to snack on. Transfer the grapes to a large bowl.

Make the filling

- Put the brown sugar, demerara sugar, cornstarch, lemon juice, and salt in a small bowl and whisk to combine. Pour the mixture over the grapes in the bowl and gently toss with your hands or a rubber spatula to coat the grapes with the other ingredients.
- Remove the pie shell from the refrigerator and scoop the filling into the shell, using a rubber spatula to get all of the sugary stuff out of the bowl and to even out the filling.

Cover and crimp the crust

- Remove the dough circles from the refrigerator and place them decoratively on top of the pie. Place the parchment paper with the clean side facing up on the baking sheet and set it aside; you'll place the pie on the lined baking sheet before putting it in the oven.
- Roll the overhang of bottom dough up to the rim of the pan. Crimp the crust of the pie to seal it closed. (For detailed instruction, see "Crimp the crust" in Master Class: How to Make Perfect Pie, page 238.) Place the pie in the refrigerator to chill for 30 minutes to 1 hour. (You can also freeze the pie at this point for up to 2 weeks. To bake a frozen pie, put it directly in the oven from the freezer. Add 10 to 20 minutes to the total baking time, using the visual indicators for doneness in the recipe.)

Bake the pie

- Arrange the oven racks so one is in the center position. Preheat the oven to 375°F.
- Remove the pie from the refrigerator. Whisk the egg with the salt to make an egg wash. Brush the wash generously over the pie dough; discard the remaining egg wash. Sprinkle the demerara sugar over the crust. Place the pie on the parchment-lined baking sheet to catch the juices that will bubble over. Place the baking sheet on the center rack of the oven to bake the pie for 1 hour to 1 hour and 10 minutes, until the juices are bubbling and the crust is golden brown, rotating the pie from front to back halfway through the baking time so the crust browns evenly. Remove the pie from the oven and place it on a cooling rack to cool for at least 1 hour before serving. Use a serrated knife to cut the pie and use an offset spatula to lift the slices out of the pan. Serve warm or at room temperature.

Sweet Potato Pie

**Makes 1 (9-inch) pie;
serves 6 to 8**

I started making sweet potato pie as an alternative to pumpkin pie. I love pumpkin pie, but I had been baking it and eating it for so many Thanksgiving seasons, I wanted a change. This is made with Garnet yams, which are rich and moist and lightened with beaten egg whites that are folded in. I also add orange juice, which brightens up the flavor. The result is a perfectly balanced filling that is rich and delicious, creamy and light, and not overly sweet.

This pie is best when made the day before you plan to serve it. I let mine sit out on the work surface, but if you are concerned because it contains eggs, you can also refrigerate it.

Note You will need a 9-inch glass pie plate to make this. You will also need pie weights (or dried beans) to blind bake the crust.

For the crust

Master Recipe for Pâte Brisée (page 232)	½ recipe	
Unsalted butter	for greasing	
All-purpose flour	for dusting	

For the filling

Garnet sweet potatoes	2 pounds, about 6 medium	908 grams
Unsalted butter, cubed and softened	8 tablespoons (1 stick)	113 grams
Light brown sugar	1 cup (lightly packed)	200 grams
Finely grated orange zest	1 orange	
Fine sea salt	1½ teaspoons	9 grams
Ground cinnamon	1 teaspoon	2 grams
Ground ginger	¼ teaspoon	<1 gram
Freshly grated nutmeg	¼ teaspoon	<1 gram
Fresh orange juice	½ cup	124 grams
Evaporated milk	½ cup	120 grams
Large eggs, separated	3	150 grams

Make the Crust

- Remove the dough from the refrigerator and set it on the work surface to rest for 10 to 15 minutes, until it is pliable but not soft.
- Grease the bottom and sides of a 9-inch pie plate with butter.

Roll out the crust and line the pie plate

- Lightly dust a large flat work surface with flour. Unwrap the round of dough and place it on the floured surface. Lightly dust the dough and the rolling pin with flour and roll the dough out to a ⅛-inch circle (at least 15 inches in diameter), rotating the dough and dusting the work surface, dough, and rolling pin with flour as needed to prevent the dough from sticking to the work surface as you roll. (For more detailed instruction, see Rolling Dough 101, page 250.)

• Gently fold the dough in half, pick it up, and place it on the pie plate with the fold running down the center of the plate. Unfold the dough and adjust it so the circle of dough is centered over the plate. Use your hands to guide the dough into the bottom crease and up the sides of the plate. Using kitchen shears, trim the dough so it hangs over the edge of the pie plate by 1 inch all around. Tightly roll the overhanging dough toward the center of the pie plate to create a lip that rests on the ridge of the plate. Crimp the crust. (For more detail, see "Crimp the crust" in Master Class: How to Make Perfect Pie, page 238.) Put the pie shell in the refrigerator while you make the filling and up to overnight. (If you are refrigerating the pie shell overnight, cover it with plastic wrap before refrigerating.)

Blind bake the crust

• Arrange the oven racks so one is in the center position. Preheat the oven to 375°F.

• Remove the pie shell from the refrigerator. Cut a piece of parchment paper that is larger than the pie and lay it on top of the crust. Using your fingers, press on the paper to line the crust, working it into the crease and making sure it fits snugly against the sides all the way to the crimped edge. Fill the pie with pie weights or dried beans.

• Put the pie shell on the center rack of the oven to bake for 40 to 50 minutes, until the edges are light golden brown and dry looking, and the shell is beginning to brown, rotating the pie shell from front to back halfway through the baking time so it browns evenly. Remove the piecrust from the oven and place it on a cooling rack to cool to room temperature with the pie weights or beans in place. Gently lift the edges of the parchment paper to remove the paper and weights. Put the weights or beans in a container to use the next time you need pie weights. (If you used dried beans, be sure to label them as pie weights before returning them to your pantry, so you don't try to cook them.)

Make the filling

• Peel the sweet potatoes and cut them into 1-inch pieces. Put the sweet potatoes in a pot fitted with a steamer insert, fill the pot with enough water so it comes just below the insert, and bring the water to a boil over high heat. Cover and steam the sweet potatoes until they are very tender when pierced with the tip of a knife. Turn off the heat, uncover the pot, and set the sweet potatoes aside to cool for about 5 minutes, until they are cool enough to handle.

• Reduce the oven temperature to 325°F.

Mix the filling
· Transfer the sweet potatoes to the bowl of a food processor fitted with a metal blade and process until smooth. Add the butter, brown sugar, orange zest, salt, cinnamon, ginger, and nutmeg, and process until the additions are mixed in and the butter has melted. Transfer the pie filling to a large bowl, using a rubber spatula to get all of the filling out of the food processor bowl. Add the orange juice and then the evaporated milk, stirring with a whisk to combine. Set the filling aside to cool to room temperature, 30 to 40 minutes. Then whisk in the egg yolks.

· Place the egg whites in the bowl of a stand mixer. Fit the mixer with the whisk attachment and whisk the whites on medium-high speed until they hold a peak, 4 to 5 minutes. Add the whites to the bowl with the sweet potato mixture and use the spatula to gently fold them into the filling. Pour enough filling into the prepared piecrust to come to the bottom of the crimped edge; pour any remaining filling into small ramekins or a small baking dish to bake and snack on. Use a small offset spatula to smooth out the filling.

Bake the pie
· Line a baking sheet with parchment paper.

· Place the pie on the baking sheet and put it on the center rack of the oven to bake for approximately 40 minutes, rotating the baking sheet from front to back halfway through the baking time, until the filling has puffed up and the custard is set; it will jiggle, but firmly, when you wiggle the pie. Remove the pie from the oven and set it on a cooling rack to cool to room temperature before serving.

Johnny Cash's Mother's Pineapple Rum Chess Pie

Makes 1 (9-inch) pie; serves 6 to 8

If you've never heard of Johnny Cash's mother's pineapple pie: it's a thing. A quick Internet search will turn up endless recipes for the pie, all more or less the same, with the main variable being canned or fresh pineapple. Most recipes use canned. I use fresh. The most important factor in this is making sure the pineapple is ripe; if it's not ripe, it won't be sweet enough, and you also won't get as silky a texture. So just be patient; let the pineapple sit on your counter until it's ripe. To tell, first smell it; a fragrant pineapple is a ripe pineapple. Also, pluck one of the greens from the crown; if it comes out easily, the pineapple is ripe.

Note You will need a 9-inch glass pie plate to make this. You will also need pie weights (or dried beans) to blind bake the crust.

For the crust

Master Recipe for Pâte Brisée (page 232)	½ recipe	
Unsalted butter	for greasing	
All-purpose flour	for dusting	

For the filling

Ripe pineapple	1	
Large eggs	3	150 grams
Granulated sugar	1 cup	200 grams
Coarse cornmeal	2 tablespoons	22 grams
Fine sea salt	½ teaspoon	3 grams
Unsalted butter, melted and cooled slightly	8 tablespoons (1 stick)	113 grams
Dark rum	3 tablespoons	45 grams

Make the Crust

- Remove the dough from the refrigerator and set it on the work surface to rest for 10 to 15 minutes, until it is pliable but not soft.
- Grease the bottom and sides of a 9-inch pie plate with butter.

Roll out the dough and line the pie plate

- Lightly dust a large flat work surface with flour. Unwrap the round of dough and place it on the floured surface. Lightly dust the dough and the rolling pin with flour and roll the dough out to a ⅛-inch-thick circle (at least 15 inches in diameter), rotating the dough and dusting the work surface, dough, and rolling pin with flour as needed to prevent the dough from sticking to the work surface as you roll. (For more detailed instruction, see Rolling Dough 101, page 250.)
- Gently fold the dough in half, pick it up, and place it on the pie plate with the fold running down the center of the plate. Unfold the dough and adjust

it so the circle of dough is centered over the plate. Use your hands to guide the dough into the bottom crease and up the sides of the plate. Using kitchen shears, trim the dough so it hangs over the edge of the pie plate by 1 inch all around. Tightly roll the overhanging dough toward the center of the pie plate to create a lip that rests on the ridge of the plate. Crimp the crust. (For more detail, see "Crimp the crust" in Master Class: How to Make Perfect Pie, page 238.) Put the pie shell in the refrigerator while you make the filling, and up to overnight. (If you are refrigerating the pie shell overnight, cover it with plastic wrap before refrigerating.)

Blind bake the crust

- Arrange the oven racks so one is in the center position. Preheat the oven to 375°F.

- Remove the pie shell from the refrigerator. Cut a piece of parchment paper that is larger than the pie and lay it on top of the crust. Using your fingers, press on the paper to line the crust, working it into the crease and making sure it fits snugly against the sides all the way to the crimped edge. Fill the pie with pie weights or dried beans.

- Put the pie shell on the center rack of the oven to bake for 40 to 50 minutes, until the edges are light golden brown and dry looking, and the shell is beginning to brown, rotating the pie shell from front to back halfway through the baking time so it browns evenly. Remove the piecrust from the oven and place it on a cooling rack to cool to room temperature with the pie weights or beans in place. Gently lift the edges of the parchment paper to remove the paper and weights. Put the weights or beans in a container to use the next time you need pie weights. (If you used dried beans, be sure to label them as pie weights before returning them to your pantry, so you don't try to cook them.)

Make the filling

- Use a large serrated knife to cut the top and the bottom off of the fresh pineapple. Stand the pineapple on the cutting board and use the knife to cut the peel from the sides, working from top to bottom and rotating the pineapple as you cut until you've removed the entire peel. Discard the top, bottom, and peel. Quarter the pineapple through the core. One at a time, lay each quarter on its side, cut out and discard the cores, and cut into ¼-inch-thick slices. Place the slices in a food processor fitted with a metal blade and pulse for about 30 seconds, until the pineapple is about the texture of applesauce. Place a fine-mesh strainer over a bowl and put the pulp in the strainer so the bowl catches the juice.

- Put the eggs, sugar, cornmeal, and salt together in a medium bowl and whisk to combine. Add the pineapple pulp and stir with a rubber spatula. Add the butter, rum, and 2 tablespoons of the juice that you strained out of the pineapple. Whisk to combine.

Bake the pie ▪ Line a baking sheet with parchment paper and place the pie shell on it. Open the oven and pull out the center rack. Place the baking sheet with the pie shell on the oven rack and pour the batter into the prepared pie shell. (The filling is so thin that I add it to the pie shell when the pie shell is on the rack to avoid spilling it.) Gently slide the oven rack back in and close the oven door.

▪ Bake the pie in the oven for about 1 hour, rotating it from front to back halfway through the baking time so the crust browns evenly, until the custard is set; it will jiggle, but firmly, when you wiggle the pie. Remove the pie from the oven and set it on a cooling rack to cool to room temperature.

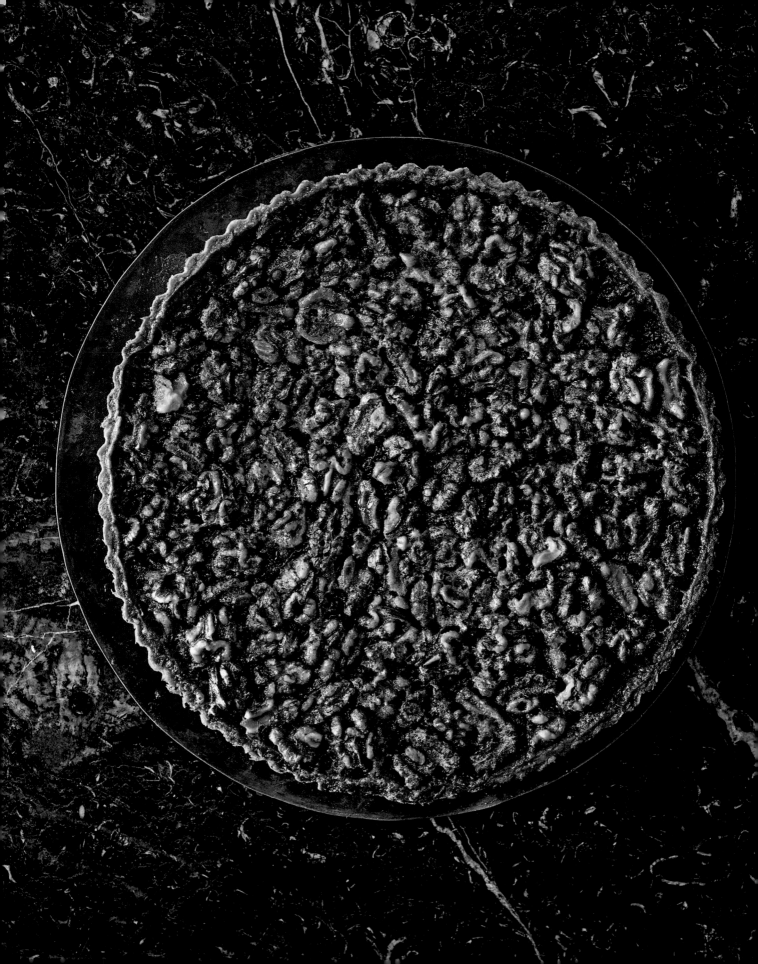

Chestnut Honey Walnut Tart

**Makes 1 (10½-inch) tart;
serves 8 to 10**

While I was working on this book, I rented a house in the South of France for my family for a week over Thanksgiving. We were joined by my sister and brother-in-law. The house had a great cooking kitchen, and we decided to make a somewhat traditional Thanksgiving feast based on what we found at the market in the small town of Vaison-la-Romaine. I saw beautiful fresh walnuts that were just coming into season and bought a big bag of them. I had already bought a jar of chestnut honey, so I made a pecan pie à la Française, substituting walnuts for the pecans and chestnut honey for the corn syrup used in a classic pecan pie, and baking it in a French tart pan. The walnuts were completely fresh and crunchy, and the chestnut honey was nutty and strong in flavor. It was really delicious. You can get chestnut honey at specialty food and cheese markets or use buckwheat honey or another honey instead.

Note You will need a 10½-inch fluted or straight-sided tart pan with a removable bottom to make this. You will also need pie weights (or dried beans) to blind bake the crust.

For the tart shell

Master Recipe for Pâte Brisée (page 232)	1 recipe (formed into a single block)	
Unsalted butter	for greasing	
All-purpose flour	for dusting	

For the filling

Walnut halves	2 cups	210 grams
Large egg	1	50 grams
Large egg yolk	1	17 grams
Unsalted butter	16 tablespoons (2 sticks)	226 grams
Chestnut honey	⅔ cup	210 grams
Granulated sugar	½ cup	100 grams
Fine sea salt	1 teaspoon	6 grams
Heavy cream	½ cup	119 grams

Make the Tart Shell

Get prepared

- Remove the block of dough from the refrigerator and set it on the work surface to rest for 10 to 15 minutes, until it is pliable but not soft.
- Grease the bottom and sides of a 10½-inch tart pan with butter.

Roll out the dough and fit it into the tart pan

- Lightly dust a large flat work surface with flour. Unwrap the dough and place it on the floured surface. Lightly dust the dough and the rolling pin with flour. Working from the center outward, roll the dough to a ⅛-inch-thick circle (at least 16 inches in diameter), rotating the dough and dusting the work surface, dough, and rolling pin with flour as needed to prevent the dough from sticking to the work surface as you roll. (For more detailed instruction, see Rolling Dough 101, page 250.)

· Roll the dough onto the rolling pin and lift it up over the tart pan, centering it. Unroll the dough so it falls directly onto the pan and gently work the dough into the creases of the pan. Working your way around the perimeter of the pan, press your fingertips around the inside of the pan to make sure the fluted ridges (if you're working with a fluted tart pan) are filled with dough. Trim the overhanging dough with kitchen shears, leaving 1 inch of dough sticking up beyond the edge of the pan. Put the tart shell in the refrigerator to chill for at least 30 minutes and up to overnight. (If you are refrigerating the tart shell overnight, cover it with plastic wrap before refrigerating.)

Blind bake the crust

· Arrange the oven racks so one is in the center position. Preheat the oven to 375°F.

· Remove the tart shell from the refrigerator and run a paring knife along the edge of the pan to trim the overhanging dough. Gather the trimmings, pat them into a thin disk, and wrap them in plastic. Refrigerate or freeze the trimmings to use another time; or discard them. You should have enough scraps from this tart to make one single-crust pie.

· Cut a piece of parchment paper that is larger than the tart and lay it on top of the shell. Using your fingers, press on the paper to line the shell, working it into the crease and making sure it is fits snugly against the sides all the way to the edges of the tart pan. Fill the tart shell with pie weights or dried beans.

· Place the tart shell on a baking sheet and place it on the center rack of the oven to bake for about 30 minutes, until the edges are light golden brown and dry looking, and the bottom of the shell is beginning to brown, rotating the tart shell from front to back halfway through the baking time so it browns evenly. Remove the baking sheet from the oven and place it on a cooling rack to cool to room temperature with the pie weights or beans in place. Gently lift the edges of the parchment paper to remove the paper and weights. (If you used dried beans, be sure to label them as pie weights before returning them to your pantry, so you don't try to cook them.)

· Decrease the oven temperature to 300°F.

Prepare the filling

· Spread the walnuts on a baking sheet and toast until they are golden brown and fragrant, about 20 minutes, shaking the pan at least once while the nuts are toasting. Remove the baking sheet from the oven and set aside to allow the walnuts to cool slightly.

· Increase the oven temperature to 325°F.

· Whisk the egg and egg yolk together in a small bowl and set aside.

- Spread the walnuts out over the bottom of the prepared tart shell.
- Combine the butter, honey, sugar, and salt in a small saucepan and cook over medium heat, stirring occasionally, until the butter melts and the mixture starts to bubble. Remove the pan from the heat and whisk in the cream. Add the whisked eggs and whisk to combine. Pour the filling evenly over the walnuts.

Bake the pie

- Carefully transport the baking sheet with the tart shell to the center rack of the oven and bake for 35 to 40 minutes, until the tart is set, rotating the tart from front to back halfway through the baking time; the tart will be firm, but the middle will jiggle slightly when shaken. Remove the baking sheet from the oven and place it on a cooling rack. Let the tart cool completely before slicing.

Grapefruit Shaker Slab Pie

Makes 1 slab pie; serves 12 to 15

When my friend Devra asked me to make a birthday dessert for a friend of hers, my first thought, of course, was to make a birthday cake. But when Devra told me that her friend *loves* grapefruit, I got inspired to make a grapefruit shaker pie. A classic shaker pie is custard-based with whole slices of citrus, usually lemon, in it. Using grapefruit and baking it in the form of a slab pie is a delicious twist.

There are endless varieties of grapefruit, and if you have access to nice grapefruit such as Ruby Red or Oro Blanco, that's great. But this recipe works well with even the most ordinary grocery store grapefruit. The grapefruit is sliced and then macerated in sugar overnight, to soften it.

Note You will need a jelly-roll pan to make this.

For the filling
Grapefruit	2½ pounds (3 to 4 small)	1,100 grams
Granulated sugar	3¼ cups	650 grams

For the crust
Master Recipe for Pâte Brisée (page 232)	2 recipes (each formed into a single block)	
Unsalted butter	for greasing	
All-purpose flour	for dusting	

For completing the filling
Large eggs	4	200 grams
Fine sea salt	1 teaspoon	6 grams
All-purpose flour	6 tablespoons	54 grams
Unsalted butter, melted and cooled slightly	8 tablespoons (1 stick)	113 grams

For baking the pie
Large egg	1	50 grams
Fine sea salt	big pinch	about 1 gram
Granulated sugar	2 tablespoons	26 grams

Prepare the grapefruit for the filling

· The evening before you plan to bake the pie, wash and dry the grapefruit and place them in the freezer for 15 to 20 minutes to firm them up; this makes slicing them easier. Remove one grapefruit from the freezer and lay it on its side on a cutting board. Use a long sharp knife to chop off one end at the point where there is not much pith, mostly fruit; discard the end. Slice the grapefruit as thinly as possible into rounds and discard the other end. Place the grapefruit slices in a large shallow bowl. Slice the remaining grapefruit in the same way, discarding the ends and adding the slices to the bowl. Add the sugar and toss to coat the grapefruit slices with the sugar. Cover the bowl with plastic wrap and set it aside overnight to allow the grapefruit to soften.

Make the crust

Get prepared

- Remove both blocks of dough from the refrigerator and set them on the work surface to rest for 10 to 15 minutes, until they are pliable but not soft.
- Grease the bottom and sides of a jelly-roll pan with butter and set aside. Line the underside of a baking sheet with parchment paper. Make room in your refrigerator to place the jelly-roll pan and the baking sheet later.

Roll out the dough and line the pan

- Lightly dust a large flat work surface with flour. Unwrap one block of dough and place it on the floured surface. Lightly dust the dough and the rolling pin with flour and roll the dough into a 15- x 20-inch rectangle (for a 12- x 17-inch pan; if your pan is not exactly those dimensions, roll the dough out to 3 inches wider and 3 inches longer than the pan you are using), rotating the dough and dusting the work surface, dough, and rolling pin with flour as needed to prevent the dough from sticking to the work surface as you roll. (For more detailed instruction, see Rolling Dough 101, page 250.)
- Gently roll the dough around your rolling pin or fold the dough in half. Place the dough on the jelly-roll pan. Unroll or unfold the dough and adjust it as needed so it is centered over the pan. Use your hands to guide the dough into the bottom creases and up the sides of the pan. (For more detailed instruction, see Master Class: How to Make Perfect Pie, page 236.) Using kitchen shears, trim the dough so it hangs over the edge of the pan by 1 inch all around. (Gather the trimmings and pat them into a square block. Wrap in plastic wrap and place in the refrigerator to chill and use another time.) Put the pie shell in the refrigerator while you make the top crust and filling, and up to overnight. (If you are refrigerating the pie shell overnight, cover it with plastic wrap before refrigerating.)
- Dust the work surface again lightly with flour. Unwrap the second block of dough and place it on the floured surface. Dust the top of the dough and rolling pin with flour and roll the dough out to a ⅛-inch-thick rectangle (at least 15 x 20 inches), rotating the dough and dusting the work surface, dough, and rolling pin lightly with flour as needed to prevent the dough from sticking to the work surface as you roll. Move the dough to the underside of the parchment-lined baking sheet, folding the edges over the sheet if they are hanging over. Place the baking sheet in the refrigerator to chill the dough for 30 minutes, until it is firm, and up to overnight. (If you are refrigerating the dough overnight, cover it with plastic wrap before refrigerating.)

Finish preparing the filling

- Remove the plastic wrap from the bowl with the grapefruit slices.
- Combine the eggs and salt in a medium bowl, whisk thoroughly to break up the yolks and whites, and add to the bowl with the grapefruit. Add the flour and butter and stir with a rubber spatula or your hands to combine.
- Remove the pie shell from the refrigerator. Using your hands, lift the

grapefruit slices from the bowl and arrange them neatly over the surface of the pie, layering the larger slices on the bottom and the smaller ones on top. Pour the remaining liquid left in the bowl over the grapefruit slices, filling the pan to ¼ inch below the rim. Remove the top crust from the refrigerator and carefully lay it on the pie, centering it over the pie. Using kitchen scissors, trim the top sheet of dough so it is flush with the outside rim of the pan. Add the trimmings to the block of scraps. Turn over the parchment on the parchment-lined baking sheet so the clean side is facing up; turn the pan so that it is right side up, and line it with the parchment paper.

Crimp the edge
· Gently roll the edge of the bottom dough up over the edge of the top dough to create a double-thick edge that rests on the lip of the pan. Crimp the edge of the pie to seal it closed. (For detailed instructions, see "Crimp the crust" in Master Class: How to Make Perfect Pie, page 238.) Place the pie in the refrigerator to chill for 30 minutes to 1 hour. (You can also freeze the pie at this point for up to 2 weeks. To bake a frozen pie, put it directly in the oven from the freezer. Add 10 to 20 minutes to the total baking time, using the visual indicators for doneness in the recipe.)

Bake the pie
· Arrange the oven racks so one is in the center position. Preheat the oven to 375°F.
· Remove the pie from the refrigerator and place the jelly-roll pan on the baking sheet to catch the juices that will bubble out of the pie. Using a paring knife, make diagonal cuts in the top sheet of dough at a 45-degree angle to the edge of the pie, across the surface of the pie, leaving about 1½ inches between each cut. Do the same in the opposite direction at the opposite 45-degree angle to create a diamond pattern. Whisk the egg and salt together in a small bowl to make the egg wash. Brush the egg wash generously over the surface of the pie; discard the remaining egg wash. Sprinkle the crust with the sugar.
· Place the baking sheet with the pie on it on the center rack of the oven and bake for 50 minutes to 1 hour, until the crust is golden brown and the filling is bubbly, rotating the baking sheet from front to back halfway through the baking time so the crust browns evenly. Remove the pie from the oven and place it on a cooling rack to cool slightly before serving. Serve warm or at room temperature.

I lightly butter a pie or tart pan with cold butter before lining it with dough. The stickiness of the cold butter helps the dough adhere. It also prevents the crust from sticking to the pan when baked, which makes it easier to remove a slice in one neat piece.

Lemon Rosemary Curd Tart with Rye Crust

Makes 1 (9-inch) tart; serves 6 to 8

My first restaurant job was at a place called the WineSellar & Brasserie in San Diego; it was a tiny, highly regarded fine-dining restaurant located in an industrial park. I was in the midst of a career transition—from chemical engineer to cook. I was still working as an engineer and had heard about this place, so I called them up and volunteered to work for free. They were like, "Okay. Yeah!" At that time, I hadn't really decided if I was going to pursue a career in savory or sweet cooking. When I arrived for my first day of work, the chef told me he needed someone to work the pastry kitchen. So that's what he trained me to do, and I started making the desserts for the restaurant. One of the first things he taught me to make was lemon curd. We would fold the curd with whipped cream and use it to fill little tart shells. I took the memory of that curd and developed this tart. The curd has fresh rosemary in it, which adds an herbal layer of flavor. The crust for this tart is a rye pâte sucrée, which has a deep, nutty flavor and provides a nice balance for the rich curd. Pâte sucrée, which means "sugared dough" in French, differs from pâte brisée in that it has more sugar and acts more like cookie dough. The curd is poured into the tart before it sets up, and then the tart is chilled overnight, so when you slice it, you cut really clean lines in the curd.

Note You will need a 9-inch fluted or straight-sided tart pan with a removable bottom to make this.

For the crust

Rye Pâte Sucrée (recipe follows)	½ recipe	
Unsalted butter	for greasing	
All-purpose flour	for dusting	

For the filling

Fresh rosemary	2 large sprigs	
Granulated sugar	¾ cup	150 grams
Fresh lemon juice (preferably from Meyer lemons)	½ cup	124 grams
Large egg yolks	6 to 7	100 grams
Fine sea salt	⅛ teaspoon	1 gram
Unsalted butter, cubed and softened	12 tablespoons (1½ sticks)	169 grams

Make the Crust

Get prepared
- Remove the dough from the refrigerator and set it on the work surface to rest for 15 to 20 minutes, until it is pliable but not soft.
- Grease the bottom and sides of a 9-inch tart pan with butter.

Roll out the crust and line the pan

· Lightly dust a large flat work surface with flour. Unwrap the dough and place it on the floured surface. Lightly dust the dough and the rolling pin with flour. Working from the center outward, roll the dough to a ⅛-inch-thick circle (at least 15 inches in diameter), rotating the dough and dusting the work surface, dough, and rolling pin with flour as needed to prevent the dough from sticking to the work surface as you roll. (For more detailed instruction, see Rolling Dough 101, page 250.)

· Roll the dough onto the rolling pin and lift it up over the tart pan, centering it. Unroll the dough so it falls directly onto the pan and gently work the dough into the creases of the pan. Working your way around the perimeter of the pan, press your fingertips along the inside of the pan to make sure the fluted ridges (if you're working with a fluted tart pan) are filled with dough. Trim the overhanging dough with kitchen shears, leaving 1 inch of dough sticking up beyond the edge of the pan. (Note: This dough may break or tear when you're working with it. Smooth tears together with your fingertips, and you can even tear a piece of dough from the trimmings and use it to patch up any holes.) Put the tart shell in the refrigerator to chill for at least 30 minutes and up to overnight. (If you are refrigerating the tart shell overnight, cover it with plastic wrap before refrigerating.)

Blind bake the crust

· Arrange the oven racks so one is in the center position. Preheat the oven to 375°F.

· Remove the tart shell from the refrigerator and run a paring knife along the edge of the pan to trim the overhanging dough. Discard the trimmings.

· Cut a piece of parchment paper that is larger than the tart and lay it on top of the crust. Using your fingers, press on the paper to line the crust, working it into the crease of the pan and making sure it fits snugly against the sides all the way to the edge of the crust. Fill the tart with pie weights or dried beans.

· Place the tart shell on a baking sheet and place it on the center rack of the oven to bake for 20 minutes. Remove the baking sheet from the oven. Gently lift the edges of the parchment paper to remove the paper and weights. (If you used dried beans, be sure to label them as pie weights before returning them to your pantry, so you don't try to cook them.) Return the tart to the oven, rotating it from front to back so the edges of the crust brown evenly, and bake for 10 minutes, until the edges are light golden brown and dry looking, and the bottom of the shell is beginning to brown. Place the tart shell on a cooling rack to cool to room temperature.

Prepare the filling

· Pour 1 to 2 inches of water into the bottom of a small saucepan and choose a bowl that fits over the saucepan to make a double boiler. Make sure the water is not touching the bottom of the bowl; if it is, pour some water out. Bring the water to a boil over high heat, then reduce the heat to medium-low to maintain a gentle simmer.

▪ Remove the bowl you chose for the double boiler. Remove the rosemary leaves from the stems, discard the stems, and roughly chop the leaves. Place the rosemary in the bowl. Add the sugar, lemon juice, egg yolks, and salt and whisk to combine. Set the bowl on the double boiler and cook, whisking constantly, until the mixture starts to thicken and the temperature registers 180°F using a digital bread thermometer, 3 to 5 minutes. (When the curd is done, it will coat the back of a spoon and leave a line when you run your finger through it.) Remove the bowl from the double boiler and wipe the bottom of the bowl to make sure no water drips. Whisk constantly until the curd has cooled to 140°F. Pass the curd through a fine-mesh strainer into the bowl of a food processor fitted with a metal blade or the jar of a large blender. With the food processor or blender running, add the butter 2 or 3 tablespoons at a time.

▪ Pour the curd into a medium bowl and place the bowl in the refrigerator or over a bowl or pan filled with about 2 inches of ice water. Cool until the curd is about room temperature, stirring occasionally to help it cool and to prevent a skin from forming, about 20 minutes. While it is warm but still runny, pour the curd into the prepared tart shell. Place the tart in the refrigerator overnight or for at least 2 hours to set the curd.

Rye Pâte Sucrée

**Makes enough for
1 (9-inch) tart**

Pâte sucrée is tart dough fortified with sugar and egg. It has a fine, crumbly quality like a sugar cookie. This crust contains more rye flour than all-purpose flour; it has a very nutty flavor, which balances nicely with the lemon rosemary curd. Rye flour also contains less gluten than wheat flour, which means the crust doesn't shrink as much in the oven as a standard crust does, which makes for a visually elegant tart. You can use this dough to make any of the single-crust round pies in this chapter. You could also use it to make a double-crust or slab pie; you would just need to double or quadruple the recipe.

Large egg yolks	2	34 grams
Heavy cream	1 tablespoon	15 grams
Rye flour	1 cup	120 grams
All-purpose flour	½ cup	60 grams
Granulated sugar	¼ cup	50 grams
Fine sea salt	½ teaspoon	3 grams
Unsalted butter, cold and cubed	8 tablespoons (1 stick)	113 grams

· Place the egg yolks and cream in a small bowl and whisk to combine.

· Place the rye flour, all-purpose flour, sugar, and salt in the bowl of a stand mixer. Fit the mixer with the paddle attachment and mix on low speed to combine the ingredients. Add the butter and mix for about 3 minutes, until the mixture resembles coarse sand. Add the egg mixture, mixing until the dough comes together into a homogenous dough.

· Lay a sheet of plastic wrap on your work surface. Turn the dough out onto the piece of plastic wrap. Use your hands to form the dough on the plastic into a roughly round shape and fold the edges of the plastic over the dough to loosely wrap. Using a rolling pin, roll the dough in the plastic to form a ½-inch-thick round. (For more detail, see Wrapping Dough, page xl.) Place the dough in the refrigerator to chill for at least 2 hours and up to 2 days; or freeze the dough for up to 1 month.

English
Sausage Rolls

**Makes 30
(2-inch) rolls**

Sausage rolls, which consist of tender pastry wrapped around pork sausage and cut into finger-food-size rolls, are a classic British party food. They are perfect, rich and delicious two-bite hors d'oeuvres to serve with apéritifs, or as a snack with beer.

Note You will need one large disposable pastry bag.

All-purpose flour	2 cups plus more for dusting	240 grams
Whole-wheat pastry flour	2 cups	210 grams
Fine sea salt	2 teaspoons plus a pinch	12 grams
Unsalted butter, cold and cubed	18 tablespoons (2 sticks plus 2 tablespoons)	226 grams
Cold water	1 cup	235 grams
Large egg yolks	2	34 grams
Sweet Italian sausage	3 pounds	1,362 grams
For baking the rolls		
Large egg yolk	1	17 grams
Fine sea salt	large pinch	

Make the dough

· Place the all-purpose flour, whole-wheat pastry flour, and 2 teaspoons of the salt in the bowl of a food processor fitted with a metal blade and process for about 30 seconds to combine the ingredients. With the processor running, add the butter through the feed tube and process for about 15 seconds, until the butter is well cut into the flour with tiny pea-size pieces of butter remaining. Transfer the mixture to a large bowl.

· Whisk the water and one of the egg yolks together in a small bowl. Using your hands, form a well in the center of the dry ingredients and pour the water and egg into the well. Use a plastic bowl scraper or a rubber spatula to bring the dry ingredients from the edges of the bowl into the center, rotating the bowl as you continue to bring the dry ingredients inward until there are no visible dry spots.

· Lay two long sheets of plastic wrap in a crisscross formation on your work surface. Use a plastic bowl scraper to scrape the dough out of the bowl onto the plastic, in the center, where the two sheets cross. Use your hands to pat the dough into a rectangular block. Loosely wrap the dough in the plastic, leaving a few inches of slack all around. Run a rolling pin over each package of wrapped dough to roll it out in the plastic, to a ½- to 1-inch-thick block. (For more detail, see Wrapping Dough, page xl.) Place the dough in the refrigerator for at least 1 hour, until it is firm, and up to overnight.

Prepare the sausage

- Remove the sausage meat from the casings and discard the casings. Put half of the sausage meat into a disposable pastry bag and push down gently on the sausage to pack it in, so there are no air gaps in the bag. Cut a 2-inch opening in the tip of the bag. Put the remaining sausage in a covered container and put the container and the pastry bag of sausage in the refrigerator until you are ready to fill the sausage rolls.

Roll out the dough

- Lightly dust a large flat work surface with all-purpose flour and roll the dough out until it measures 13 inches from top to bottom and 22 inches from side to side (it will be about ⅛ inch thick). Use a straightedge and pastry wheel or knife to trim the long edges (the top and bottom of the rectangle) so they are straight. Discard the trimmings. With the straightedge and pastry wheel, cut 3 (4- to 4½-inch-wide) strips parallel to you.

Fill and shape the pastry

- Working with one strip at a time, pipe a 1¼-inch-thick strip of sausage down the length of the pastry. Working quickly, pull the top edge of the dough up and over the line of sausage and push down to hold the dough in place while you bring the bottom edge of the dough up over the sausage to meet it. Pinch the two sides together to seal the log closed. Roll the log so the seam is centered on the bottom and use your hands to pat the log into an even shape. Use the remaining dough strips and sausage to assemble 2 more logs.

Bake the rolls

- Arrange the oven racks so one is in the top third of the oven and the other in the bottom third. Preheat the oven to 400°F.
- Line two baking sheets with parchment paper.
- Working with one log at a time, place each log on a cutting board and cut it into 2-inch rolls with a serrated knife. Place the cut rolls on one of the prepared baking sheets and repeat, cutting the remaining logs into rolls and adding them to the baking sheets.
- Whisk the remaining egg yolk with a pinch of salt to make an egg wash Brush the wash generously on the rolls; discard the remaining egg wash.
- Place the baking sheets in the oven and bake the rolls for 30 to 35 minutes, until the tops are golden brown and the sausage is cooked through, rotating the baking sheets from front to back and from one rack to the other halfway through the baking time. (The best way to test for doneness is to take one roll out of the oven and cut into it; if the sausage is pink, cook the rolls for another 3 to 5 minutes and test again.) Remove the rolls from the oven and place them on cooling racks to cool slightly before serving. Serve warm or at room temperature.

Swiss Chard Tart with Parmesan Pâte Brisée

Makes 1 (9-inch) tart; serves 10

I really have a place in my heart for the South of France and the foods of that region, and that's where this tart originates. This is my version of a tourtes de blettes, a Swiss chard tart from Nice. I make this in a springform pan, so it's a very deep-dish pie. The French version can be sweet, with apples and raisins added to the filling, or savory, and my version is decidedly savory, with a Parmesan pâte brisée and additional Parmesan and garlic in the filling. The crust is blind baked before adding the filling to make sure it turns out crispy and golden brown, and the filling, which is custard-based, is baked at a lower temperature. The tart is best when it is still ever-so-slightly warm from the oven.

Note You will need a 9-inch springform pan to make this. You will also need 2 pounds of pie weights (or dried beans) to blind bake the crust.

For the Parmesan pâte brisée

Unsalted butter, cold and cubed into 1-inch pieces	12 tablespoons (1½ sticks) plus 1 tablespoon, softened	169 grams plus 14 grams
All-purpose flour	2 cups plus more for dusting	240 grams
Parmesan, grated on the fine holes of a box grater	½ cup	50 grams
Granulated sugar	2 teaspoons	9 grams
Fine sea salt	¾ teaspoon	4.5 grams
Cold water	¼ cup	59 grams

For the filling

Swiss chard (red, white, or rainbow)	2½ pounds (about 5 bunches)	
Extra-virgin olive oil	2 tablespoons	
Garlic cloves, thinly sliced	3	
Large eggs	4	200 grams
Whole milk	½ cup	120 grams
Parmesan, grated on the fine holes of a box grater	2 cups	200 grams
Fine sea salt	1½ teaspoons	9 grams
Ground black pepper	¼ teaspoon	<1 gram

Make the dough

· Cut the cold cubed butter into ½-inch-thick pieces. Lay the pieces in a single layer on a plate and put the plate in the freezer for 10 minutes.

· Place the flour, Parmesan, sugar, and salt in the bowl of a stand mixer. Fit the mixer with the paddle attachment and mix on low speed to combine the ingredients. Remove the butter from the freezer, add it to the mixer bowl, and combine on low speed for about 1 minute, until the mixture resembles coarse crumbs with some large chunks of butter remaining. Turn off the mixer and use your hands to check the size of the butter; if there are any pieces larger than a nickel, pinch them between your fingertips to flatten them. Add the water and combine on low speed until the dough comes together but is still slightly shaggy; do not mix it until the dough is smooth and homogenous, like cookie dough.

· Lay two long sheets of plastic wrap in a crisscross formation on your work surface. Place one piece of dough in the center, where the two sheets cross. Use your hands to pat the dough into a round disk. Loosely wrap the dough in the plastic, leaving a few inches of slack all around. Run a rolling pin over the dough to roll it out in the plastic, to a ½-inch-thick round. (For more detail, see Wrapping Dough, page xl.) Place the dough in the refrigerator to chill for at least 2 hours and up to 2 days; or freeze the dough for up to 1 month.

Prepare to roll out the dough

· Remove the dough from the refrigerator and set it on your counter to rest at room temperature for 10 to 15 minutes, until it is pliable but not soft.

· Grease a 9-inch springform pan with the remaining butter.

Roll out the dough and line the pan

· Lightly dust a large flat work surface with flour. Unwrap the round of dough and place it on the floured surface. Lightly dust the dough and the rolling pin with flour and roll the dough out to a ⅛-inch-thick round (at least 15 inches in diameter), rotating the dough and dusting the work surface, dough, and rolling pin with flour as needed to prevent the dough from sticking to the work surface as you roll. (For more detailed instruction, see Rolling Dough 101, page 250.)

· Roll the dough onto the rolling pin and lift it up over the springform pan, centering it. Unroll the dough so it falls directly onto the pan and gently work the dough into the creases of the pan. If the dough forms folds on the inside of the pan, gently smooth them out with your fingers. Place the pan in the refrigerator to chill the dough for at least 30 minutes, and up to overnight. (If you are refrigerating the tart shell overnight, cover it with plastic wrap before refrigerating.)

Blind bake the tart shell

· Arrange the oven racks so one is in the center position. Preheat the oven to 375°F.

· Remove the tart shell from the refrigerator. Run a paring knife along the rim of the pan to trim the edge so it is even with the top of the pan; discard the trimmings.

· Cut a piece of parchment paper larger than the tart and lay it on top of the crust. Using your fingers, press the paper to line the crust, working it into the crease and making sure it is close and snug to the top edge. Fill the shell with pie weights or dried beans.

· Put the tart shell on the center rack of the oven to blind bake for 35 to 40 minutes, until it is golden brown with some light golden spots. Remove the crust from the oven and place it on a cooling rack to cool to room temperature with the weights or beans in place. Gently lift the edges of the parchment paper to remove the paper and weights. Put the weights or beans in a container to use the next time you need pie weights. (If you used dried beans, be sure to label them as pie weights before returning them to your pantry, so you don't try to cook them.)

▪ Reduce the oven temperature to 325°F.

Make the filling

▪ Remove the leaves from the stalks of the chard with a small paring knife. Save the stems, and sauté them for dinner. Wash the leaves and dry them in a colander. Stack 5 or 6 leaves together, roll them up lengthwise to form a log shape, and thinly slice the log to julienne the leaves. Put the julienned chard in a large bowl and repeat, julienning the remaining leaves and adding them to the bowl.

▪ Heat the olive oil in a large stockpot over medium-high heat for about 2 minutes. Add the garlic and sauté for about 1 minute, stirring constantly, until the garlic is fragrant and light golden brown. Add the chard and reduce the temperature to medium-low. Cook, turning the chard frequently with tongs so it cooks evenly, until it has completely wilted, about 3 minutes. Turn off the heat and return the chard to the large bowl.

▪ Put the eggs, milk, Parmesan, salt, and pepper in a medium bowl and whisk to thoroughly combine the ingredients. Pour this custard mixture into the bowl with the chard and toss to coat. Pour the filling into the prepared crust.

Bake the tart

▪ Place the tart on the center rack of the oven and bake for 40 to 45 minutes, until the custard has puffed up slightly and is set in the middle; the custard will jiggle slightly but firmly when shaken. Remove the tart from the oven and place it on a cooling rack to cool slightly.

▪ To remove the tart from the pan, unclasp the outer ring and gently lift it off of the tart. Slide the tart off the bottom of the pan onto a cutting board. Use a large sharp knife to cut it into 10 equal slices. Serve warm.

Layer Cakes and Frostings

Having a young son, I attend a lot of kids' birthday parties, and I make a lot of birthday cakes. For me, birthday cake means layer cake, because layer cakes make for such a grand presentation, and that little bit of extra effort that it takes to frost a cake makes it feel like something for a special occasion—if not a birthday, then the holidays, an anniversary of some sort, or any other celebration. That said, the artistry I bring to layer cakes is in baking the perfect cake, and pairing it with the ideal frosting, but not in elaborately decorating. When it comes to frosting the cake, I keep it very simple. If I do want something a bit more elegant, I rely on fresh flowers, which is the easiest way to make a cake look beautiful when you don't know how or don't have the patience to make icing roses. I use fresh flowers as garnish only; they should not be eaten. And avoid using any flowers that might be toxic. Here are five traditional layer cakes (plus a layered crepe cake), all classics, because layer cakes are classic. I hope you enjoy making these as much as I do.

Pumpkin Layer Cake with Salted Caramel Buttercream and Brown Sugar Frosting

Makes 1 (8-inch) cake

This cake has a finer crumb than pumpkin quick bread because the butter and sugar are creamed together, whereas for a typical pumpkin quick bread, the ingredients would simply be stirred together and then poured into a loaf pan. Creaming butter with sugar aerates the batter and contributes to a finer crumb. And buttermilk weakens the gluten in the flour, which makes the crumb softer. Both result in a lighter, more delicate cake. I use canned pumpkin puree to make this. When you roast your own pumpkin, there are many variables—the variety of the squash, how it was roasted, how flavorful or how watery each individual pumpkin is—all of which affect whatever you're baking. Canned pumpkin puree, by contrast, is a reliable, consistent product. And it doesn't have anything in it other than pumpkin. This cake does not get a "crumb coating" like the other cakes in this chapter (see Master Class: Building and Frosting a Layer Cake, page 306). The recipe makes just enough Brown Sugar Frosting (page 303) to frost the cake without a crumb coating. It's such a rich cake, you wouldn't want more.

Note You will need three (8- x 2-inch) cake pans to make this.

Unsalted butter, melted	2 tablespoons for greasing	28 grams
All-purpose flour	3 cups plus more for dusting	360 grams
Pumpkin puree	1 (15-ounce) can	425 grams
Buttermilk, well shaken	1½ cups	375 grams
Ground cinnamon	1½ teaspoons	3 grams
Ground cloves	1½ teaspoons	3 grams
Freshly grated nutmeg	1½ teaspoons	1.5 grams
Fine sea salt	1 teaspoon	6 grams
Baking soda	1 tablespoon	15 grams
Large eggs	6	300 grams
Pure vanilla extract	1½ teaspoons	7 grams
Unsalted butter, cubed and softened	24 tablespoons (3 sticks)	339 grams
Granulated sugar	1½ cups	300 grams
Light brown sugar	1½ cups (lightly packed)	300 grams
Salted Caramel Buttercream (recipe follows)		
Brown Sugar Frosting (recipe follows)		

Get prepared

- Arrange the oven racks so one is in the top third of the oven and the other is in the bottom third. Preheat the oven to 325°F.
- Lightly coat the sides and bottoms of three (8- x 2-inch) cake pans with melted butter. Line the bottoms of the pans with parchment paper and lightly brush the paper with melted butter. Dust the pans with flour, invert, and lightly tap on the bottoms to tap out any excess flour. Set aside.

Make the batter

- Combine the pumpkin puree and buttermilk in a medium bowl. Whisk them together and set aside.

Master Class
Building and Frosting a Layer Cake

When it comes to decorating cakes, I keep things simple. The only flowers you'll see on a cake of mine are fresh ones. That said, I am a perfectionist, and I want my cakes to look pretty. I also have a proper understanding of how a layer cake should be assembled, and I use this to make sure my cakes are level, evenly frosted with no crumbs in the frosting, and have an attractive texture on the outside.

One of the nice things about making layer cakes is that you can bake the cake layers in advance. Wrap them in plastic wrap and freeze for up to one month. The night before you want to frost them, transfer them to the refrigerator to thaw. When you're ready to frost and serve the layer cake, just take the layers out of the refrigerator to come to room temperature while you make the frosting. Assembling the cake in steps, for me, means not feeling rushed, which makes the process more enjoyable.

Cut the cake layers in half

Some cakes are assembled using whole cake layers, and for other cakes, each layer is cut in half. The latter yields a cake with thinner layers, which also means there are more of them, which means more frosting. If the recipe calls for you to cut the layers in half, place the cake layer on your cutting board like a wheel of cheese and use a long serrated bread knife to score around the side to mark the halfway point of the cake. Carefully saw along the score, keeping your knife centered as you go.

Frost between the layers

Lay one cake layer, cut side up, on a cardboard cake round, a cake stand, or platter. Reserve the bottom half of one of the divided layers for the top. Place the specified amount of frosting in the center of the cake layer. Technically, the frosting is supposed to be half the depth of the cake layer itself, so if the cake is 1 inch thick between the layers, there should be ½ inch of frosting. I aim to reflect that proportion in my recipes, but I'm a little relaxed about it. Use an offset spatula to spread the frosting evenly to the edges of the cake.

An offset spatula is offset by about ½ inch from the handle, which gives you an angle, so your hand is not in the way of what you're doing and allows you to have more control. An offset spatula is essential when you're frosting a cake.

Stack the cake layers   After applying frosting on the first cake layer, put a second cake layer on top. Preferably the cut side should go facedown. After placing a layer on the cake, press gently to secure it to the previous layer; the frosting is the glue that will help keep it in place. Frost the second layer as you did the first.

Continue building the cake   Continue stacking the cake layers, pressing gently as you add them to create a stable cake, and frosting each layer before adding the next layer.

Top the cake   Place the reserved layer with the bottom flat side up on the top of the cake.

Apply a "crumb coat" of frosting   A crumb coat or crumb layer refers to a thin layer of frosting that you apply to a cake before frosting it. The purpose of this layer is to pick up any stray crumbs, so they don't end up in your final, decorative layer of frosting. To apply a crumb coat, put a couple of tablespoons of frosting on the top of the cake and use an offset spatula to spread it in a thin layer over the cake. Then do the same along the sides of the cake, using the frosting to fill in the gaps between the layers to create smooth, even sides. After applying a thin, crumb coat layer of frosting over the surface of the cake, chill the cake so the frosting firms up, providing a clean and stable base for the final frosting.

Frost the cake   Applying the final layer of frosting is the easiest part of frosting a cake, and probably also the most fun and most rewarding. We're not making a wedding cake or icing rosettes, so we're not using any special tips or doing any special tricks, just applying a clean, even layer of frosting on the top. To do this, place the specified amount of frosting on the top of the cake, then use the offset spatula to smooth it to the edges, using your wrists to move the spatula in a figure-eight motion to create pretty swirls. Do the same with the sides, applying about 2 tablespoons of frosting at a time; any more than that and it will fall off the cake before you have time to spread it out.

Decorate the cake   Usually, frosting the cake is where I stop, but if I decide I want to go a step further and decorate it, it's going to be very simple. For my son, Wyatt, I might put colored sprinkles on top. Occasionally I will use a piping bag to pipe a border around the top and bottom. If I want an elegant cake, I decorate the top with fresh flowers.

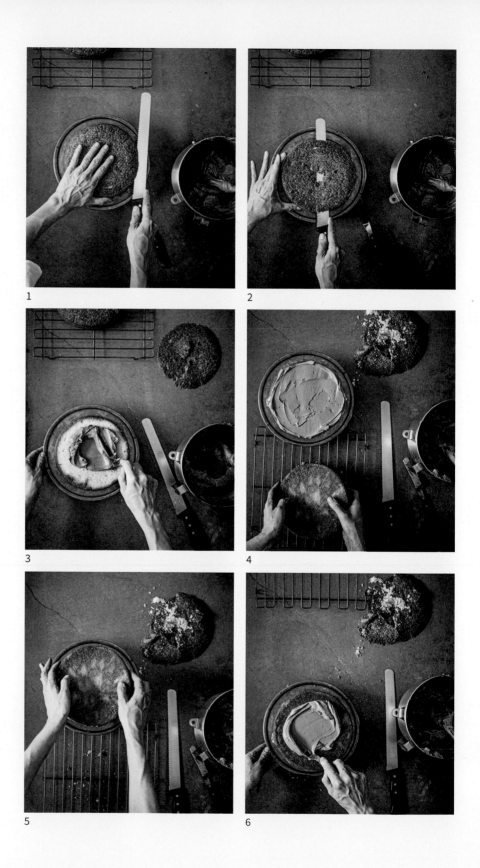

7   8

9   10

A Tutorial on Frosting and Buttercream

Frosting is essentially sugar and fat whipped together to create a smooth, voluptuous consistency. Buttercream is a category of frosting and is often referred to as "buttercream frosting." There are three traditional types of buttercream: Swiss, Italian, and French. These buttercreams begin with a meringue into which butter is beaten. When you make meringue, the proteins in the egg whites denature, or unwind, to form a stable network of bonds that trap air. The trapped air is what makes meringue light and airy, and buttercream made with a meringue base is also light. American frosting (sometimes referred to as American buttercream), by contrast, is made by simply beating sugar into butter; no eggs or cooking are involved. Confectioners' sugar is the sugar most commonly used to make American frosting, as the cornstarch in it acts as a stabilizer.

My Chocolate Buttercream (page 327) and White Buttercream (page 337) are based on Swiss buttercream. I prefer that to the French and Italian versions because it is the most consistent and foolproof, and the resulting frosting is rich and light at the same time. The meringue base allows you to add more butter than you could if the only other ingredient were sugar, resulting in a frosting that is very buttery and refined without being too sweet. A warning: a lot of kids don't like buttercream; they find it too buttery and they want the traditional frosting of sugar and butter beaten together.

My Salted Caramel Buttercream (page 302), Brown Sugar Frosting (page 303), and Classic Cream Cheese Frosting (page 334) all fall into the category of American buttercream. Because these frostings do not begin with meringue, their texture tends to be more dense. My Chocolate Fudge Frosting (page 317) does contain eggs, but it also does not start by making a meringue. It is a dense, rich, fudgy frosting.

Frosting is at the perfect temperature and consistency just after it's made, so it's ideal to make frosting just before you're ready to use it. If you make the frosting ahead of time and refrigerate it, the butter in it will harden and the frosting will be impossible to spread. If you do want to make it in advance, refrigerate the frosting until you're ready to use it and for up to 3 days. Remove it from the refrigerator and set it aside to come to room temperature; don't leave it for so long that it becomes very soft and greasy. Transfer the frosting to the bowl of a stand mixer, fit the mixer with the paddle attachment, and beat on high speed until it is light and fluffy. While you are beating it, the frosting will go through a phase where it looks like it has broken or separated. Have faith and keep beating until it comes back together into a light, fluffy consistency.

The key to making any successful frosting is that you start with cool, malleable butter. If you are adding the butter to a meringue that is still warm, it acts to cool the meringue. You can also aerate cool butter, whereas, when warm, it will melt and not hold its shape. The resulting frosting will be greasy and runny instead of fluffy and luxurious. If your frosting becomes too greasy or too soft while you are mixing, turn off the mixer. Fill a bowl larger than the mixer bowl with ice and water. Place the bowl of ice water under the mixer bowl and continue to mix the frosting, allowing the ice water to cool the buttercream in the process.

Wyatt's Chocolate Birthday Cake with Chocolate Fudge Frosting

Makes 1 (8-inch) cake

For my son's sixth birthday, he asked for chocolate cake. I envisioned a moist, deep chocolaty layer cake with a fudge frosting. I was playing off what my childhood ideal of a chocolate cake would have been. After four or five tries, I succeeded in making a cake that was rich and moist and chocolaty and not too sweet, and that my son liked enough that he wanted it named after him. It's unusual to see a chocolate cake recipe that uses unsweetened chocolate, as this does, as well as cocoa powder. Unsweetened chocolate has fat in it, and lends a fudgy quality to this double chocolate cake.

I think there's something appealing about a cake that relies on something other than butter for its fat—in fact, some of the moistest cakes we have, old-fashioned cakes such as carrot cake and apple cake, are traditionally made with oil. Still, there's nothing like butter for flavor, so for this cake I use a combination of butter and oil to get a super-moist texture and the buttery flavor.

Note You will need two (8- x 2-inch) cake pans to make this.

Unsalted butter, melted	2 tablespoons for greasing	28 grams
Cake flour (preferably unbleached)	1¾ cups plus more for dusting	210 grams
Unsweetened chocolate	3 ounces (or ½ cup unsweetened chocolate chips)	85 grams
Cocoa powder (preferably Valrhona)	½ cup	43 grams
Baking powder	1 teaspoon	5 grams
Baking soda	1 teaspoon	5 grams
Fine sea salt	¾ teaspoon	4.5 grams
Whole milk	2 cups	480 grams
Canola or vegetable oil	¼ cup	55 grams
Pure vanilla extract	1½ teaspoons	8 grams
Granulated sugar	1¾ cups	350 grams
Unsalted butter, cubed	8 tablespoons (1 stick)	113 grams
Large eggs	2	100 grams
White vinegar	1 tablespoon	15 grams
Chocolate Fudge Frosting (recipe follows)		

Get prepared

• Arrange the oven racks so one is in the center position. Preheat the oven to 350°F.

• Lightly coat the sides and bottoms of two (8- x 2-inch) cake pans with melted butter. Line the bottoms of the pans with parchment paper and lightly brush the paper with melted butter. Dust the pans with cake flour, invert, and lightly tap on the bottoms to tap out any excess flour. Set aside.

Make the batter
- Pour 1 to 2 inches of water into the bottom of a small saucepan and choose a bowl that fits over the saucepan to make a double boiler. Make sure the water is not touching the bottom of the bowl; if it is, pour some water out. Bring the water to a boil over high heat, then reduce the heat to medium-low to maintain a gentle simmer.
- Roughly chop the chocolate (unless you are using chocolate chips). Add the chocolate to the bowl of the double boiler and melt it, using a heat-proof rubber spatula to stir and scrape down the sides of the bowl so the chocolate melts evenly and doesn't burn. Remove the bowl from the heat, and wipe the bottom of the bowl to make sure no water drips. Set aside to cool the chocolate to room temperature, 15 to 20 minutes.
- Whisk the cake flour, cocoa powder, baking powder, baking soda, and salt together in a separate medium bowl. If there are any lumps of cocoa powder in the mixture, pass the dry ingredients though a fine-mesh strainer; push the lumps through with your fingers to break them up. Set aside.
- Combine the milk, oil, and vanilla in a small bowl and set aside.
- Combine the sugar and cubed butter in the bowl of a stand mixer. Fit the mixer with the paddle attachment and beat on medium speed for 2 to 3 minutes, stopping to scrape down the sides of the bowl with a rubber spatula once or twice during that time. Add the eggs one at a time, beating well after adding the first egg and stopping to scrape down the sides of the bowl before adding the second egg. Add the second egg and beat until the mixture is light and fluffy. Turn off the mixer and add the melted chocolate and the vinegar. Beat on medium speed until the additions are blended in, stopping to scrape down the sides of the bowl with a rubber spatula once or twice during that time. With the mixer on low speed, add the dry ingredients in three additions and the milk in two, alternating between the wet and dry ingredients and ending with the dry ingredients. (The batter will be very runny; it's supposed to be this way, so don't be alarmed.) Remove the bowl from the mixer stand and fold the batter with a rubber spatula so it comes completely together, making sure to scrape the very bottom of the bowl.

Bake the cakes
- Pour the batter into the two prepared cake pans, dividing it evenly.
- Place the cakes on the center rack of the oven to bake for 40 to 45 minutes, until the centers spring back when touched and a small knife or toothpick inserted into the center of each cake comes out clean. Remove the cakes from the oven and set them aside to cool in their pans for 10 minutes. Quickly invert the cakes onto a cooling rack and remove and discard the parchment paper. Let the cakes cool to room temperature before frosting them.

Assemble and frost the cake
- Place one of the cakes, flat side up, on a cake plate or flat round platter. Place ½ cup of the frosting onto the center of the cake and use an offset spatula to spread the frosting to the edges. Place the second cake on top of the first, also flat side up, pressing gently on the cake to secure it. Use the remaining frosting to cover the top and the sides of the cake, moving the offset spatula in a figure-eight motion to create swirls.
- Place the cake in the refrigerator for at least 30 minutes before serving to allow the frosting to set. If you are planning ahead, you can also refrigerate the cake overnight and then remove it from the refrigerator for about 30 minutes to come to room temperature before serving.

Chocolate Fudge Frosting

**Makes about
3 cups**

This frosting contains raw egg, so refrigerate the frosted cake until you're ready to serve it. Warning: Consuming raw eggs may increase your risk of food-borne illness.

Unsweetened chocolate	6 ounces (or 1 cup unsweetened chocolate chips)	170 grams
Unsalted butter, cold and cubed	8 tablespoons (1 stick)	113 grams
Confectioners' sugar	2¼ cups	270 grams
Large eggs	2	100 grams
Hot water (100°–110°F)	3 tablespoons	45 grams
Fine sea salt	pinch	1 gram

· Pour 1 to 2 inches of water into the bottom of a small saucepan and choose a bowl that fits over the saucepan to make a double boiler. Make sure the water is not touching the bottom of the bowl; if it is, pour some water out. Bring the water to a boil over high heat, then reduce the heat to medium-low to maintain a gentle simmer.

· Roughly chop the chocolate (unless you are using chocolate chips). Add the chocolate and cubed butter to the bowl of the double boiler and melt them, using a heat-proof rubber spatula to stir and scrape down the sides of the bowl so the chocolate and butter melt evenly and the chocolate doesn't burn. Remove the bowl from the heat and wipe the bottom of the bowl to make sure no water drips. Set aside the chocolate to cool to room temperature, 15 to 20 minutes.

· Combine the confectioners' sugar, eggs, water, and salt in the bowl of a stand mixer. Fit the mixer with the paddle attachment and beat on medium speed just to combine the ingredients. Add the melted chocolate and the butter and beat on medium speed until the mixture sets up to the consistency of thick, fudgy frosting, about 5 minutes. If it does not set up, this means the chocolate was too warm when you added it to the mixing bowl; to fix this, place the bowl of frosting in a bowl of ice water and stir frequently until the frosting is thick and fudgy. Use the frosting to frost the cake as soon as the cake has cooled to room temperature.

Orange Crepe Cake with Hojicha Cream

**Makes 1
(9-inch) cake**

At Sadelle's, the bakery team used to make crepes for cheese blintzes. They would stack up the crepes really high, and every time I saw all those stacked crepes, I would think: I want to make a crepe cake! Now I get my chance.

Crepe cake (sometimes called a *mille crêpes*) is made by layering crepes with pastry cream. On the one hand, it's very simple to make; it's like an arts and crafts project. But it does take time and patience; you have to cook about twenty-five crepes, one at a time, so you just need to settle in and enjoy the process. Here I use a hojicha-infused pastry cream between the layers. Hojicha is Japanese roasted green tea; the roasting gives the tea a subtle, unusual, caramelized flavor that adds a nice dimension to the cake.

This recipe calls for the crepe batter to be made a day in advance, which is typical with crepes. Resting the batter allows the flour to absorb more of the liquid; the starches in the flour swell as they bond to the water molecules, which gives the batter a thicker, more viscous consistency. This makes the batter easier to cook without tearing the crepes in the process. Make the pastry cream the day before. That way, the next day you only need to make the crepes and assemble the cake before serving it.

Note You will need a 10-inch crepe pan or nonstick skillet.

For the crepes		
Whole milk	3 cups	720 grams
All-purpose flour	2½ cups	300 grams
Large eggs	6	300 grams
Granulated sugar	3 tablespoons	39 grams
Unsalted butter, melted	2 tablespoons	28 grams
Fine sea salt	1½ teaspoons	9 grams
Vanilla beans	2	
Grand Marnier	½ cup	118 grams
For the pastry cream		
Whole milk	4½ cups	1,080 grams
Loose-leaf hojicha tea	6 tablespoons	18 grams
Vanilla bean	1	
Granulated sugar	1 cup	200 grams
Cornstarch	½ cup	65 grams
Fine sea salt	¼ teaspoon	2 grams
Large egg yolks	12	204 grams
Unsalted butter, cubed and softened	8 tablespoons (1 stick)	113 grams
Heavy cream	1½ cups	357 grams
For cooking the crepes and assembling the cake		
Unsalted butter, melted	2 tablespoons	28 grams
Granulated sugar	¼ cup	50 grams
Water	2 tablespoons	28 grams

Make the crepe batter   Place ¼ cup (60 grams) of the milk, the flour, eggs, sugar, butter, and salt in the bowl of a food processor fitted with a metal blade. Split the vanilla beans down the middle with a small sharp knife and use the knife to scrape the seeds out of the beans into the bowl. (Use the beans to make Vanilla Sugar, page 219, or discard them.) Blend until the batter is smooth. Transfer the batter to a large bowl and whisk in the remaining milk and the Grand Marnier. Strain the batter through a fine-mesh strainer into a 2-quart container or two (1-quart) containers. Cover and refrigerate overnight or for at least several hours.

Make the pastry cream   • Put the milk in a large saucepan and warm it over medium heat until it is bubbling around the edges. Turn off the heat. Add the tea, whisk to combine, and carefully cover the saucepan with plastic wrap. Set aside for the tea to infuse in the milk for 30 minutes. Remove the plastic wrap and pass the milk through a fine-mesh strainer, pressing on the tea leaves to extract as much flavor from them as possible. Discard the leaves.

• Wipe the saucepan clean of any tea leaves and return the steeped milk to the saucepan. Split the vanilla bean down the middle with a small sharp knife and use the knife to scrape the seeds out of the bean. Add the seeds and bean to the saucepan with the milk.

• Pour half of the sugar into a medium bowl and add the remaining sugar to the saucepan with the milk. (The halves of sugar can be eyeballed; they don't need to be exact. The sugar added to the milk helps to keep it from scorching on the bottom of the pan.) Warm the milk and sugar over medium-high heat, stirring occasionally to prevent the milk from scorching, until it begins to bubble around the edges.

• Meanwhile, place a dampened kitchen towel under the bowl with the sugar; this will prevent the bowl from sliding around when you begin whisking. Add the cornstarch and salt to the bowl and whisk to combine. Add the egg yolks and whisk for about 30 seconds to lighten them slightly. Drizzle in 1 cup of the hot milk, whisking constantly. Add the remaining milk 1 cup at a time, whisking constantly. Return the mixture to the saucepan and bring it to a boil over high heat, stirring constantly with the whisk. (You need to be able to see that it's boiling, and if you're whisking too furiously, it froths and you can't see it.) When it starts to boil, reduce the heat to medium-low and cook for 2 minutes to swell the cornstarch, whisking furiously to work out any lumps that have formed in the cream. (The reason we're cooking the custard at this point is not to thicken it—it will be thick before the 2 minutes are up—but to cook the starch in the cornstarch so you don't taste it, and also to destroy the alpha amylase enzyme in the eggs, which can cause the custard to break down after it's cooked.)

- Remove the saucepan from the heat, add the butter, and whisk once more, until the butter has melted and combined with the cream. Remove the vanilla bean.
- Set a fine-mesh strainer over a bowl or storage container. Pass the pastry cream through the strainer to remove any lumps, pressing on the cream with a rubber spatula to push it through the strainer. Place a sheet of plastic wrap on top of the pastry cream and press it so it sits directly on the surface to prevent a skin from forming. Cover the container with a lid and refrigerate for at least 1 hour and up to 3 days.

When pastry cream cools, steam rises up out of the cream and it causes the outermost layer of the cream to dry out and form a skin. The skin acts as a barrier, preventing additional steam from escaping during the cooling process. To prevent a skin from forming, I cover the surface with plastic wrap. If you want to go a step further, puncture the plastic with a sharp knife; this allows the steam to escape while still preventing a skin from forming.

Cook the crepes
- Preheat a 10-inch crepe pan or nonstick skillet over medium heat.
- Remove the crepe batter from the refrigerator and stir to recombine the ingredients. Use a pastry brush to lightly coat the pan with melted butter. Lift the pan from the heat and ladle ¼ cup of batter into the center. Swirl and gently shake the pan so the batter covers the surface evenly. Return the pan to the heat and cook for about 1 minute, until the surface looks dry and the crepe can be easily separated from the pan at the edge using an offset spatula. Use the offset spatula to lift the edges of the crepe, then slide it underneath the crepe to loosen it from the pan. With the spatula under one side of the crepe, lift the crepe up and then flip it over. (I use my fingers for this. I have "hot hands," which basically means that my fingers do not feel the hot temperatures! But because most home cooks will not be like me, please use a spatula.) Cook the crepe on the second side for 30 seconds, until golden brown. Using the offset spatula, lift the crepe onto a plate. Repeat, cooking the remaining crepe batter in the same way, using the melted butter sporadically to coat the pan and stacking the crepes on top of one another.

Finish the cream filling
- Pour the cream into the bowl of a stand mixer. Fit the mixer with the whisk attachment and whisk on medium speed until soft peaks form, about 1 minute. Increase the speed to high and whisk until stiff peaks form, about 1 minute more.
- Transfer the pastry cream to a large bowl. Add about one-quarter of the whipped cream and whisk vigorously to combine the whipped cream with the pastry cream; don't worry about deflating the whipped cream, it's a necessary

Continued

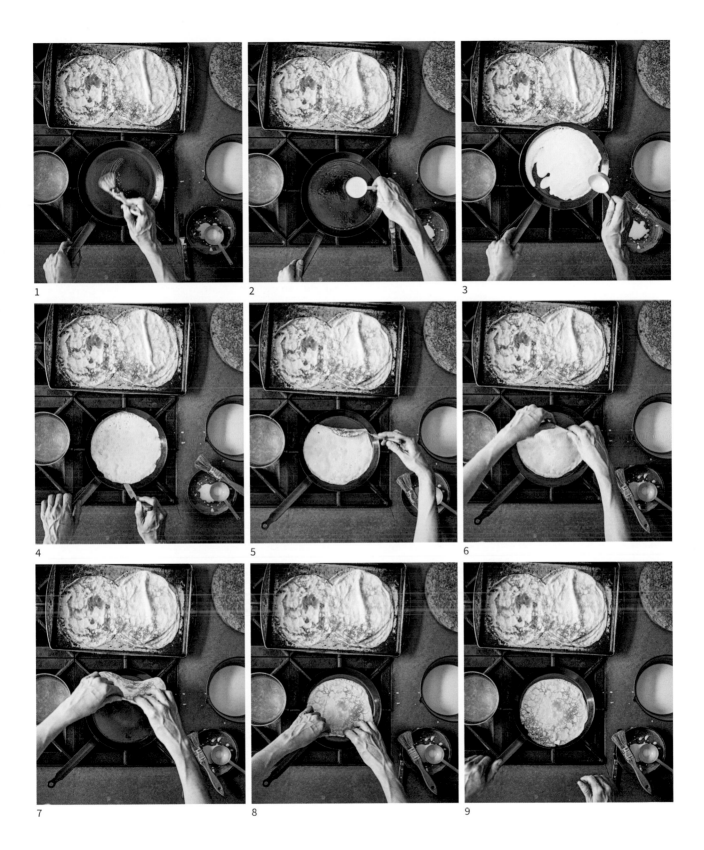

1 2 3

4 5 6

7 8 9

Layer Cakes and Frostings ▪ 323

sacrifice. Once the first addition of whipped cream has been thoroughly whisked in, add half of the remaining whipped cream and gently fold it into the pastry cream with a whisk, trying not to deflate the whipped cream. Add the remaining whipped cream and fold it in.

Assemble the cake

• Place one crepe on a cake platter or flat serving plate. Place ⅓ cup (60 grams) of the pastry cream in the center of the crepe and use an offset spatula to spread it to the edges in an even layer, with the layer of cream slightly thinner in the center of the crepe; this will help the crepes to stack evenly as you build the cake. Place another crepe on top of the first one, place another ⅓ cup of the pastry cream on top, and spread it out in the same way. Continue layering the crepes and pastry cream, reserving the prettiest crepe for the top.

• Place the sugar in a medium saucepan and cover it with the water. Shake the pan to distribute the water so there are no dry patches of sugar and bring the mixture to a full boil over high heat. Boil the water and sugar together until the sugar caramelizes to a medium amber, 5 to 8 minutes, shaking the pan every now and then so the sugar browns evenly and doesn't burn. Turn off the heat and gently brush the caramel over the crepe cake.

• To serve, use a large knife to cut the crepe cake into slices.

Perfect Yellow Cake with Chocolate Buttercream

Makes 1 (8-inch) cake

Is there a more quintessential birthday cake than yellow cake with chocolate buttercream frosting? Because I have a young son, I often make birthday cakes for him and his friends, and you can't go too crazy with little kids. This is the cake I find myself making for them most often. The chocolate buttercream has a touch of salt in it, which is really good in the same way that a touch of salt makes brownies so good.

Note You will need two (8- x 2-inch) cake pans to make this.

Unsalted butter, melted and cooled slightly	1 tablespoon for greasing	14 grams
Cake flour	3⅓ cups plus more for dusting	400 grams
Baking powder	2 teaspoons	10 grams
Baking soda	½ teaspoon	3 grams
Fine sea salt	1 teaspoon	6 grams
Canola or vegetable oil	½ cup	110 grams
Buttermilk, well shaken	1 cup	250 grams
Pure vanilla extract	2 teaspoons	10 grams
Large eggs	3	150 grams
Large egg yolks	3	51 grams
Granulated sugar	2 cups	400 grams
Unsalted butter, cubed and softened	12 tablespoons (1 stick plus 4 tablespoons)	170 grams

Get prepared

- Arrange the oven racks so one is in the center position. Preheat the oven to 350°F.
- Lightly coat the sides and bottoms of two (8- x 2-inch) cake pans with melted butter. Line the bottoms of the pans with parchment paper and lightly brush the paper with melted butter. Dust the pans with cake flour, invert, and lightly tap on the bottoms to tap out any excess flour. Set aside.

Make the batter

- Whisk together the cake flour, baking powder, baking soda, and salt in a medium bowl and set aside.
- In another small bowl, combine the oil, buttermilk, and vanilla and set aside.
- Crack the eggs into a small bowl and add the yolks to them.
- Combine the sugar and butter in the bowl of a stand mixer. Fit the mixer with the paddle attachment and beat on medium speed for 3 minutes. (The mixture will not become light and fluffy because there is less butter to the ratio of sugar; we add oil later to compensate for the missing butter.) Turn off the mixer and scrape down the sides of the bowl with a rubber spatula. Add

the eggs 2 at a time, beating the eggs into the batter on medium speed until they are completely incorporated before adding more, and scraping down the sides of the bowl between additions. Once you have added all the eggs, beat the batter on medium-high speed for 1 minute to aerate the batter, which will make for a lighter cake. Scrape down the sides of the bowl with the spatula and add the dry ingredients in three additions, alternating with the buttermilk, and ending with the dry ingredients, making sure to scrape the very bottom of the bowl.

Bake the cakes

- Divide the batter between the two cake pans and use an offset spatula to smooth out the tops.
- Place the cakes on the center rack of the oven to bake for 40 to 45 minutes, until the tops are nicely browned, have puffed up, and spring back slightly when touched in the center; a small knife or toothpick inserted into the center of each cake will come out clean. Remove the cakes from the oven and set them aside to cool in their pans for 10 minutes. Quickly invert the cakes onto a cooling rack and remove and discard the parchment paper. Let the cakes cool to room temperature before frosting them. Once the cakes have cooled, carefully flip them right side up.

Assemble and frost the cake

- Use a large serrated knife to slice the rounded humps off the tops of both cakes. Place one of the cakes on a cake plate or flat round platter, right side up. Place 1 cup of the buttercream onto the center of the cake and use an offset spatula to spread the buttercream evenly to the edges. Place the second cake on top of the first, with the bottom side up, pressing gently on the cake to secure it. Scoop 1 cup of the remaining buttercream onto the center of the cake and spread it over the top and sides to create a thin crumb coating. Place the cake in the refrigerator to chill for 20 to 30 minutes to let the crumb coating set up. (While the crumb coating is chilling, leave the buttercream at room temperature; it will be impossible to spread if it is chilled.) Remove the cake from the refrigerator. Use the remaining buttercream to cover the top and sides of the cake, using the offset spatula to create a smooth, even coat.

Chocolate Buttercream

Makes about 4 cups

Start melting the chocolate to make this buttercream as soon as the cake comes out of the oven. That way the chocolate and cake cool down together, and the buttercream will be ready when the cake has cooled.

Bittersweet chocolate	8 ounces (or 1½ cups chocolate chips)	226 grams
Semisweet chocolate	8 ounces (or 1½ cups chocolate chips)	226 grams
Large egg whites	3	99 grams
Granulated sugar	¾ cup	150 grams
Unsalted butter, cubed and softened	24 tablespoons (3 sticks)	339 grams
Fine sea salt	½ teaspoon	3 grams

· Pour 1 to 2 inches of water into the bottom of a small saucepan and choose a bowl that fits over the saucepan to make a double boiler. Place the bowl on the saucepan and make sure the water is not touching the bottom of the bowl; if it is, pour some water out. Remove the bowl and bring the water to a boil over high heat, then reduce the heat to medium-low to maintain a gentle simmer.

· Roughly chop the bittersweet and semisweet chocolates (unless you are using chocolate chips). Put the chocolate in the bowl of the double boiler and melt, using a heat-proof rubber spatula to stir and scrape down the sides of the bowl so the chocolate melts evenly and doesn't burn. Remove the bowl from the heat and set aside to cool to room temperature, 15 to 20 minutes.

· While the chocolate is cooling, combine the egg whites and sugar in the bowl of a stand mixer and whisk by hand to combine.

· Add more water to the pan you used as a double boiler so it's as deep as it was when you started, and bring the water to a simmer over medium heat. Place the bowl with the egg whites over the pot of simmering water and cook, whisking constantly, until the mixture is warm to the touch and the sugar has dissolved, 2 to 3 minutes. (To check that the sugar has dissolved, dip your thumb and index fingers into the mixture and rub them together to see if you feel grains of sugar.) Remove the bowl from the simmering water and wipe the bottom to make sure no water drips. Return the bowl to the mixer stand. Fit the mixer with the whisk attachment and whisk the egg whites and sugar on high speed for 5 minutes, until the whites hold stiff peaks and have cooled to room temperature (to check the temperature, place your hand on the outside of the mixing bowl; if it feels warm, keep whisking).

• Turn off the mixer and replace the whisk attachment with the paddle attachment. With the mixer on high speed, add the butter 2 to 4 tablespoons at a time, waiting for it to blend in before adding the next tablespoons. When all the butter has been added, turn off the mixer and add the melted chocolate and the salt. Beat on medium speed until the chocolate is incorporated. Turn off the mixer and use the rubber spatula to scrape down the sides and bottom of the bowl and gently fold in any dark streaks of chocolate. Use the buttercream as soon as the cake has cooled to room temperature.

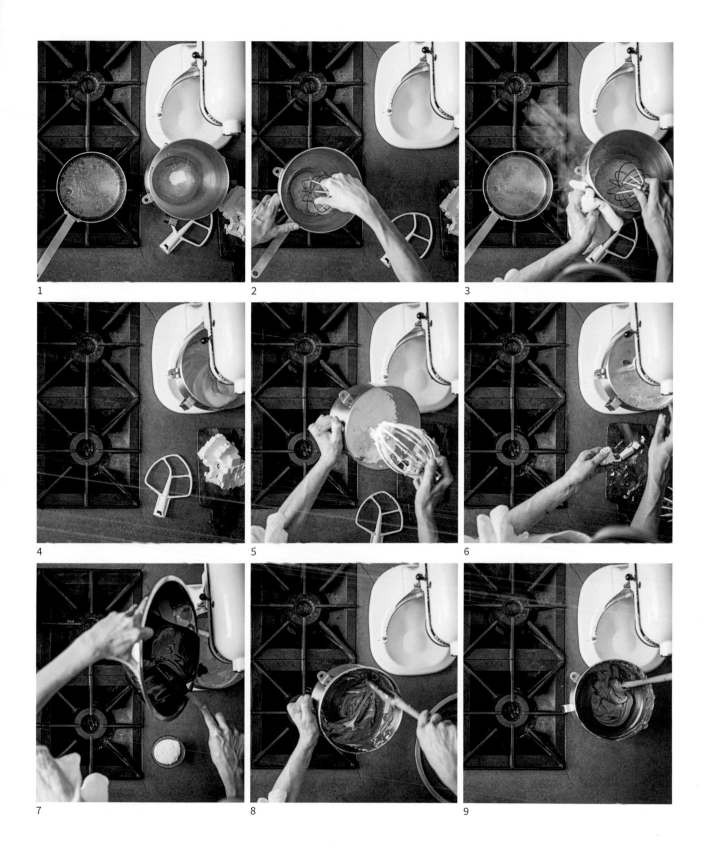

My Favorite Carrot Cake with Classic Cream Cheese Frosting

Makes 1 (8-inch) cake

I love carrot cake, and this recipe, which is based on the one I learned at the French Culinary Institute, is my favorite. Carrot cake is so good that I don't fuss too much with it, but this version does have one twist: it contains coarsely ground pecans, which impart a nice flavor and texture. It also contains crushed pineapple, which makes for a moist and flavorful cake. I like carrot cake all year round, but I especially like it in the springtime, just before vegetables and fruits begin reappearing at the market.

Note You will need two (8- x 2-inch) cake pans to make this.

Ingredient	Amount	Weight
Unsalted butter, melted and cooled slightly	2 tablespoons for greasing	
All-purpose flour	1½ cups plus more for dusting	180 grams
Pecans	1 cup	115 grams
Golden raisins	¾ cup	113 grams
Baking powder	1 teaspoon	5 grams
Baking soda	1 teaspoon	5 grams
Fine sea salt	1 teaspoon	6 grams
Ground cinnamon	1 teaspoon	2 grams
Ground allspice	¼ teaspoon	<1 gram
Freshly grated nutmeg	¼ teaspoon	<1 gram
Canned crushed pineapple, drained	½ cup	110 grams
Fresh lemon juice	2 tablespoons	30 grams
Carrots	3 medium	200 grams
Granulated sugar	1¼ cups	250 grams
Large eggs	3	150 grams
Pure vanilla extract	1 teaspoon	5 grams
Canola or vegetable oil	¾ cup	165 grams
Classic Cream Cheese Frosting (recipe follows)		

Get prepared

· Arrange the oven racks so one is in the center position. Preheat the oven to 300°F.

· Lightly coat the sides and bottoms of two (8- x 2-inch) cake pans with melted butter. Line the bottoms of the pans with parchment paper and lightly brush the paper with melted butter. Dust the pans with flour, invert, and lightly tap on the bottoms to tap out any excess flour. Set aside.

· Spread the pecans on a baking sheet and toast them in the oven for 18 to 20 minutes, shaking the pan once during that time for even toasting, until the nuts are golden brown and fragrant. Remove the baking sheet from the oven and set aside to cool the nuts to room temperature.

· Meanwhile, increase the oven temperature to 350°F.

- Place the raisins in a small bowl and cover with hot water. Set aside to soak for 5 minutes. Drain the raisins in a fine-mesh strainer and let them sit in the strainer so they continue to drain until you're ready to use them.

Make the batter
- Whisk the flour, baking powder, baking soda, salt, cinnamon, allspice, and nutmeg together in a medium bowl.
- Place the pineapple in the bowl of a food processor fitted with a metal blade. Add the lemon juice and puree. Transfer the puree to a medium bowl.
- Peel the carrots and grate them on the fine holes of a box grater. Measure out 1½ cups (185 grams); discard the remaining carrots or reserve them for another use, such as to toss in a salad or scrambled eggs. Add the carrots to the bowl with the pineapple puree and stir to combine.
- Wipe the food processor bowl clean and process the pecans until they are finely ground. Add to the bowl with the dry ingredients and whisk to combine. Set aside.
- Combine the sugar and eggs in a large bowl and whisk for about 1 minute to lighten the mixture. Add the vanilla extract and the oil and whisk to combine. Add the carrot-pineapple mixture and the raisins and fold them in with a rubber spatula. Add the dry ingredients and stir with a rubber spatula to combine, making sure to scrape the very bottom of the bowl.

Bake the cakes
- Divide the batter evenly between the two prepared pans and use an offset spatula to smooth out the tops of the cakes.
- Place the cakes on the center rack of the oven and bake for 40 to 45 minutes, until the tops are nicely browned and a small knife or toothpick inserted into the center of each cake comes out clean. Remove the cakes from the oven and set them aside to cool for about 10 minutes. Quickly invert the cakes onto a cooling rack and remove the parchment paper. Let the cakes cool to room temperature before frosting them. Once the cakes have cooled, carefully flip them back right side up.

Assemble and frost the cake
- Use a long serrated knife to slice the rounded humps off the tops of both cakes. (Snack on the humps while you frost the cake.) Place one of the cakes, right side up, on a cake plate or flat round platter. Place 1 cup of the frosting on the center of the cake and use an offset spatula to spread it evenly to the edges. Place the second cake, bottom side up, on top of the first and place 1 cup frosting in the center of the cake. Use the offset spatula to spread the frosting in a thin layer over the top and sides of the cake to form a crumb coating. Place the cake in the refrigerator for 20 to 30 minutes to let the coating set up. (Leave the frosting at room temperature while the cake is chilling.) Remove the cake from the refrigerator. Use the remaining frosting to cover the top and sides of the cake, moving the offset spatula in a figure-eight motion to create swirls.

Classic Cream Cheese Frosting

Makes about 4 cups

The recipe makes a healthy amount of cream cheese frosting, which is essential to a good carrot cake.

Cream cheese, cubed and softened	16 ounces	454 grams
Unsalted butter, cubed and softened	16 tablespoons (2 sticks)	226 grams
Confectioners' sugar	2 cups	240 grams
Pure vanilla extract	1 teaspoon	5 grams

▪ Place the cream cheese and butter in the bowl of a stand mixer. Fit the mixer with the paddle attachment and beat on medium speed until they are combined and fluffy. Turn off the mixer and scrape down the sides of the bowl with a rubber spatula. Add the confectioners' sugar and vanilla. Start the mixer on low speed so that the confectioners' sugar doesn't fly out of the bowl. Beat on low for about 30 seconds and then raise the speed to medium-high and beat for about 1 minute until the frosting is smooth.

White Layer Cake

Makes 1 (8-inch) cake

I grew up eating white Betty Crocker cakes, made by my mother, with white "buttercream" that she made from Crisco and confectioners' sugar. I loved it. That white on white cake is a special memory for me, and I still find myself craving that cake. In my early twenties, my mom even mailed me one that she'd baked from a Duncan Hines mix. This white cake is my attempt to mimic the experience of the cake my mom made for me, but made from scratch, and with quality ingredients—like real butter in the buttercream! When I make it for kids, I throw in sprinkles and turn it into a confetti cake. I prefer classic jimmies, such as Betty Crocker "Carousel Mix," to organic or natural sprinkles.

To use this recipe to make cupcakes, line 18 muffin cups with cupcake liners and fill each one three-quarters full. Bake the cupcakes for 20 to 22 minutes, and frost and decorate them as you desire.

Note You will need two (8- x 2-inch) cake pans to make this.

Unsalted butter, melted and cooled slightly	2 tablespoons for greasing	28 grams
Cake flour	2½ cups plus more for dusting	300 grams
Baking powder	3 teaspoons	15 grams
Fine sea salt	1 teaspoon	6 grams
Large egg whites	4	140 grams
Pure vanilla extract	2 teaspoons	10 grams
Unsalted butter, cubed and softened	12 tablespoons (1½ sticks)	169 grams
Granulated sugar	1½ cups	300 grams
Whole milk	1 cup	240 grams
Sprinkles	¾ cup	130 grams
White Buttercream (recipe follows)		

Get prepared
- Arrange the oven racks so one is in the center position. Preheat the oven to 350°F.
- Lightly coat the sides and bottoms of two (8- x 2-inch) cake pans with melted butter. Line the bottoms of the pans with parchment paper and lightly brush the paper with melted butter. Dust the pans with cake flour, invert, and lightly tap on the bottoms to tap out any excess flour and set aside.

Make the batter
- Whisk the cake flour, baking powder, and salt together in a medium bowl and set aside.
- Whisk the egg whites and vanilla together in a medium bowl.
- Combine the cubed butter and sugar in the bowl of a stand mixer. Fit the mixer with the paddle attachment and beat on medium speed for 2 to

3 minutes, stopping to scrape down the sides of the bowl with a rubber spatula once or twice, until the mixture is light and fluffy. Turn off the mixer, add half of the egg whites and vanilla mixture, and beat until the eggs are incorporated, stopping to scrape down the sides of the bowl with the spatula. Add the remaining egg whites and vanilla mixture and beat until incorporated. With the mixer on low speed, add the dry ingredients in three additions and the milk in two, alternating between them and starting and finishing with the dry ingredients. Remove the mixer from the stand and fold the batter with a rubber spatula so it comes completely together, making sure to scrape the very bottom of the bowl. If you plan to use sprinkles, fold them into the batter now.
▪ Divide the batter between the two prepared cake pans and use an offset spatula to smooth the tops.

Bake the cakes

▪ Place the cakes on the center rack of the oven to bake for about 30 minutes, until the cakes pull away from the sides of the pans and a small knife or toothpick inserted into the center of each cake comes out clean. Remove the cakes from the oven and set them aside to cool in their pans for 10 minutes. Quickly invert the cakes onto a large cooling rack and remove and discard the parchment paper. Let the cakes cool to room temperature before frosting them. Once the cakes have cooled, carefully flip them right side up.

Assemble and frost the cake

▪ Use a large serrated knife to slice the rounded humps off the tops of both cakes. (Snack on the humps while you frost the cake.) Then slice each cake in half like a hamburger bun. Reserve the nicest of the two bottom halves to top the cake.
▪ Place the remaining bottom half, cut side up, on a cake plate or flat round platter. Place 1 cup of the buttercream on the center of the cake and use an offset spatula to spread it evenly to the edges of the cake. Place a second cake layer on top of the first, pressing gently to secure it. Place 1 cup of the remaining buttercream on the center of the cake and use the offset spatula to spread it evenly to the edges. Repeat with the third cake layer, pressing it gently to secure it and spreading about 1 cup of buttercream on it. Place the fourth cake layer, flat side up, on the cake and press gently to secure it. Place 1 cup of the remaining buttercream on top and spread it over the top and sides of the cake to create a thin crumb coating. Place the cake in the refrigerator to chill for 20 to 30 minutes to let the crumb coating set up. (While the crumb coating is chilling, leave the buttercream at room temperature; it will be impossible to spread if it's chilled.) Remove the cake from the refrigerator. Use the remaining buttercream to cover the top and sides of the cake, using the offset spatula to create a smooth, even coat.

White Buttercream

Makes about 4½ cups

Granulated sugar	1 cup	200 grams
Large egg whites	4	140 grams
Unsalted butter, cubed and slightly softened	28 tablespoons (3½ sticks)	396 grams
Fresh lemon juice	2 tablespoons	30 grams
Pure vanilla extract	1 teaspoon	5 grams

▪ Choose a saucepan on which you can place the bowl of a stand mixer. Pour enough water into the saucepan to fill it 1 to 2 inches deep. Place the bowl on the saucepan and make sure the water is not touching the bottom of the bowl; if it is, pour some water out. Remove the bowl and bring the water to a boil over high heat, then reduce the heat to medium-low to maintain a gentle simmer.

▪ While the water is coming to a boil, whisk the sugar and egg whites together in the bowl. Return the bowl to the pan of simmering water and cook, whisking constantly, until the mixture is warm to the touch and the sugar has dissolved. (To check that the sugar has dissolved, dip your thumb and index fingers into the mixture and rub them together to see if you feel grains of sugar.) Remove the bowl from the simmering water and wipe the bottom to make sure no water drips. Place the bowl on the stand mixer. Fit the mixer with the whisk attachment and whisk on high speed for 5 minutes until the whites hold stiff peaks and have cooled to room temperature. (To check the temperature, place your hand on the outside of the bottom of the mixing bowl; if it feels warm rather than room temperature, keep whisking.)

▪ Turn off the mixer and replace the whisk attachment with the paddle attachment. With the mixer running on high speed, add the butter 2 tablespoons at a time, beating in the butter before adding the next tablespoons. When all of the butter has been added, beat the buttercream for 1 to 2 minutes, until it is light and fluffy. Add the lemon juice and vanilla and beat on medium speed to combine. If the buttercream separates from the addition of the lemon juice, beat it on high speed until it comes together again. Use the buttercream as soon as the cake has cooled to room temperature.

Quick Breads and Casual Cakes

Quick breads is an old-fashioned term that distinguishes these cake-like breads from yeasted ones. Quick breads are quick because they don't contain yeast, which means they don't require time to rise. They are leavened, instead, by baking powder and/or baking soda. These breads are often called casual cakes or keeping cakes, because they keep for a few days without getting stale; some even get better with time. Quick breads are often baked in a loaf pan, but muffins and scones also fall into this category. The recipes in this chapter are relatively easy projects that can be made in one go—no waiting, resting, chilling, or decorating necessary. This is a good place to start if you are a novice baker, or if you want to bake something quick and easy. They make great snacks, gifts, and casual desserts. These are my favorite kinds of cake: simple, unadorned, and not too sweet.

Ricotta Chocolate Chip Pound Cake

**Makes 1
(9-inch) loaf**

When I was developing the menu for Sadelle's, I wanted to take nostalgic New York City favorites, such as babka and rugelach, and make them as good as they could be. Chocolate chip cake was not originally on my list of New York classics, until I visited Wall's Bake Shop, an old-timey bakery on Long Island. I really liked the simplicity of their cake, so I started to develop my own version. *Food & Wine* magazine called it "a feat of physics," because the chocolate chips don't sink in the cake—they are dispersed throughout—which is something I worked very hard to achieve. Chocolate chips, even the mini ones, want to sink to the bottom of the batter. To prevent this, I chop the chocolate very finely before folding the chips into the batter. The smaller, lighter chips float rather than sinking to the bottom of the pan. The cake is great with coffee for breakfast or as an afternoon snack, but it also doubles as a dessert.

This cake is very easy to put together, but it's a bit tricky to bake. It's baked in a loaf pan, which is much higher than a cake pan, so the challenge is to make sure it's cooked all the way through. Where the toothpick test is sufficient for most cakes—and you can certainly use that for this cake--to make sure it is baked properly, I check the internal temperature with a digital thermometer, a bread baker's trick that I apply to this cake.

Please note that as much as I like to use the best possible ingredients in everything I bake, I have made this both with artisanal ricotta from a cheese shop and with inexpensive ricotta from a grocery store, and to be honest, I don't think I can tell the difference.

Note You will need a 9- x 4-inch Pullman loaf pan (or a 9- x 4-inch standard loaf pan) to make this.

Nonstick cooking spray		
Semisweet chocolate chips	1¼ cups	220 grams
All-purpose flour	1⅔ cups	200 grams
Baking powder	1 tablespoon	15 grams
Fine sea salt	1 teaspoon	6 grams
Whole milk ricotta	1⅔ cups	367 grams
Unsalted butter, cubed and softened	12 tablespoons (1½ sticks)	170 grams
Granulated sugar	1½ cups	300 grams
Large eggs	3	150 grams
Pure vanilla extract	1 tablespoon	15 grams

Get prepared

- Arrange the oven racks so one is in the center position. Preheat the oven to 350°F.
- Cut a piece of parchment paper that measures 8 x 12 inches. Spray the bottom and the sides of a 9- x 4-inch loaf pan with nonstick cooking spray.

Line the pan with the parchment so it covers the bottom and goes up the longer sides of the pan.

▪ Chop the chocolate chips until they are about one-third their original size. Pass them through a fine-mesh strainer to strain out the chocolate dust; discard the dust (or reserve it to make Hot Chocolate, page 218) and set the chocolate chips aside.

Make the batter

▪ Whisk the flour, baking powder, and salt together in a medium bowl and set aside.

▪ Put the ricotta in a food processor fitted with the S-shape blade and process until creamy and smooth, about 1 minute. Set aside.

▪ Combine the butter and sugar in the bowl of a stand mixer. Fit the mixer with the paddle attachment and beat on medium speed for 2 to 3 minutes, stopping to scrape down the sides of the bowl with a rubber spatula once or twice, until the mixture is light and fluffy. Add the eggs one at a time, stopping to scrape down the sides of the bowl between additions. Add the vanilla, mix it in, and scrape down the sides of the bowl. Add the ricotta and mix on medium-low until it is blended in; note that the mixture will look "broken," not homogenous. Turn off the mixer, scrape down the bowl, and add the dry ingredients. Mix on low speed until only traces of flour remain visible. Turn off the mixer and take the mixer bowl off the stand. Add the chocolate chips and fold them in with a rubber spatula until they are evenly dispersed, and no flour is visible, making sure to scrape the very bottom of the bowl.

In baking, you often add eggs one at a time, mixing each one in before adding the next. The reason for this is to emulsify the eggs into the batter, suspending the fats with the other ingredients and making for a stable, emulsified batter. A batter that is not stable will lose air holes and the resulting cake will not be as light or delicate and will be more likely to sink.

Bake the cake

▪ Scoop the batter into the prepared pan and use a small offset spatula to smooth and level out the top.

▪ Place the cake on the center rack of the oven and bake for 1 hour to 1 hour and 10 minutes, until a digital thermometer registers 200°F when inserted into the center. Remove the cake from the oven and place the pan on a cooling rack to cool for 15 minutes. Remove the cake from the pan by lifting up on the ends of the parchment paper and return to the rack. Discard the parchment paper and let the cake cool completely.

Orange, Coconut, and Poppy Seed Cake

**Makes 1
(9-inch) cake**

If I could have one bite of cake before I die, this, which is my spin on a "whole orange cake," would be that cake. It differs from other citrus cakes in that it doesn't call for the zest and juice, but for the *whole orange*. You boil the oranges to soften and cook the rinds, and then you put them in a blender and puree them, which makes the cake very moist, and also offers a unique flavor component and richness. It is the quintessential *me* cake; it has so many layers of flavor that all work together really well. Plus, it's gluten free. It is also Passover-friendly in that it is nonleavened and contains no wheat flour.

Note You will need a 9-inch springform pan to make this.

Navel oranges	2 medium	
Nonstick cooking spray		
Almond flour (made from skinless almonds)	3 cups	300 grams
Shredded unsweetened coconut	2¾ cups	261 grams
Poppy seeds	¼ cup	35 grams
Baking powder	1 teaspoon	5 grams
Fine sea salt	1 teaspoon	6 grams
Large eggs	6	300 grams
Granulated sugar	2¾ cups	550 grams
Sliced almonds	½ cup	50 grams
For finishing the cake		
Apricot jam	⅓ cup	95 grams
Water	1 tablespoon	15 grams

Boil the oranges

▪ Place the oranges in a medium saucepan and add enough water to cover them completely. Place a small heavy plate or saucepan on top of the oranges to weigh them down and keep them submerged. Bring the water to a boil over high heat. Reduce the heat to maintain a steady simmer and cook the oranges for 2 hours, replenishing the water with more boiling water to keep the oranges submerged. Turn off the heat, remove the plate, and use a slotted spoon to remove the oranges from the water and place them aside to cool to room temperature; discard the cooking water. (To cool the oranges more quickly, cut them into quarters when they come out of the cooking water.) When the oranges have cooled completely, put them in the bowl of a food processor fitted with a metal blade and puree. Measure 1½ cups (365 grams) of the orange puree and stir the rest into a bowl of plain yogurt or a smoothie—along with a spoonful of honey, as the orange rind makes the puree slightly bitter. (You can make the puree up to 2 days in advance; transfer to an airtight container and refrigerate until you're ready to use it.)

Get prepared

· Arrange the oven racks so one is in the center position. Preheat the oven to 350°F.

· Spray the bottom and sides of a 9-inch springform pan with nonstick cooking spray. Cut a piece of parchment paper to fit on the bottom of the pan and place it in the pan. Spray the parchment with nonstick spray and set the pan aside.

Make the batter

· Combine the almond flour, coconut, poppy seeds, baking powder, and salt in a large bowl and whisk them together.

· Combine the eggs and the sugar in the bowl of a stand mixer. Fit the mixer with the paddle attachment and beat on medium speed for 2 to 3 minutes, stopping to scrape down the sides of the bowl with a rubber spatula once or twice, until the mixture is light and fluffy. Add the orange puree and beat on medium speed until it is mixed in. Add the dry ingredients and beat on low speed until no dry ingredients are visible, stopping to scrape down the sides of the bowl as needed. Remove the bowl from the mixer and use a rubber spatula to finish mixing the batter, making sure to scrape the very bottom of the bowl.

Bake and glaze the cake

· Scoop the cake batter into the prepared pan and use a small offset spatula to even out the top. Sprinkle the almonds over the cake.

· Place the cake on the center rack of the oven and bake for 50 minutes. Lower the oven temperature to 325°F and bake for an additional 15 to 30 minutes, until the cake is golden brown and the center springs back when touched. Remove the cake from the oven and set it on a cooling rack to cool for about 10 minutes in the pan. Run a small sharp knife around the edges of the pan to loosen the cake from the pan. Unclasp and remove the ring from the side of the pan and let the cake cool completely.

· Meanwhile, place the jam and water in a small saucepan and heat over medium heat, whisking frequently, until the jam has melted. Pass the mixture through a fine-mesh strainer to remove the solids; discard the solids. Brush the glaze on the top of the warm or cooled cake.

Spelt Bull's-Eye Scones with Raspberry Jam

Makes 9 scones

There are basically two different types of scones in the world: one, which is referred to as a "cream scone," is made with cream but no egg; these are the scones you typically think of as English scones. Then there are scones with egg in them, which have a biscuit-like quality. I prefer scones made with egg because the egg, which is dense in fat, adds moisture and richness. This recipe contains eggs, and the resulting scones are flaky and buttery and not dry, with the added bonus of a big spoonful of jam in the center. They are, in my view, the perfect scone.

I often make my own jam, but when I don't have any on hand, I walk across the street to the deli in my Brooklyn neighborhood and buy a jar of Bonne Maman jam, which is incredibly good quality, especially considering you can get it at just about any regular grocery store.

Buttermilk, well shaken	½ cup	125 grams
Large eggs	2	100 grams
All-purpose flour	2 cups	240 grams
Spelt flour	2 cups	210 grams
Granulated sugar	¼ cup plus 1 tablespoon	63 grams
Baking powder	1 teaspoon	5 grams
Fine sea salt	2 teaspoons	12 grams
Unsalted butter, cold and cubed	20 tablespoons (2½ sticks)	283 grams
Raspberry Jam (recipe follows; or store-bought)	¾ cup	218 grams

Make the batter

· Whisk the buttermilk and eggs together in a small bowl to break up the egg yolks.
· Put the all-purpose flour, spelt flour, sugar, baking powder, and salt in the bowl of a stand mixer. Fit the mixer with the paddle attachment and mix on low speed to combine, about 30 seconds. Add the butter and continue to mix on low speed until the butter and flour have combined to look like moist crumbs. (Don't mix so much that you form a solid ball of dough.) Turn off the mixer and add the buttermilk and eggs. Mix on low speed until the dough just comes together and no trace of dry crumbs remain. Cover the mixer bowl with plastic wrap and refrigerate the dough until it is firm, about 2 hours, and up to overnight. (This time allows the flours to absorb some of the liquid and the gluten to relax, which helps to create a tender scone.)

Form and bake the scones

· Arrange the oven racks so one is in the top third of the oven and the other is in the bottom third. Preheat the oven to 375°F.
· Line two baking sheets with parchment paper.

- Remove the dough from the refrigerator and pull about a ½-cup (110-gram) portion. Roll the dough into a ball and pat it into a 2½- to 3-inch-wide disk. Continue with the rest of the dough, dividing the disks among the two baking sheets, spacing them evenly. Once you've formed all the scones, use your thumbs to press a tablespoon-size crater into the center of each scone. Spoon 1 tablespoon of jam into each crater you created.
- Place one baking sheet on each oven rack and bake for 25 to 30 minutes, until the scones are light brown, rotating them from front to back and top to bottom halfway through the baking time. Remove the scones from the oven and let them cool for about 5 minutes on the baking sheet. Use a spatula to transfer the scones to a cooling rack to cool to room temperature.

Raspberry Jam

**Makes about
1½ cups**

Turning 1 pound of raspberries into raspberry jam couldn't be easier—and the results are so delicious and worth the effort. Because this is a small quantity of jam, it cooks (and can burn) very quickly, so it's important to keep an eye on it and stir it frequently.

Raspberries	1 pound (about 3 half-pints)	454 grams
Granulated sugar	1 cup	200 grams

Get prepared

- Place two small plates in the freezer. (You will use these later to check the jam for doneness.)

Make the jam

- Combine the raspberries and sugar in a small (2-quart) saucepan and cook over medium-high heat, stirring constantly, until the sugar dissolves and the raspberries break down and release their juice. When the liquid released from the raspberries comes to a boil, reduce the heat to medium-low to maintain a gentle simmer and cook, stirring constantly, for 8 to 12 minutes, until the jam has thickened, reducing the heat if the jam is sputtering out or sticking to the bottom of the pan.
- To test to see if the jam has set up sufficiently, remove one of the plates from the freezer. Place a spoonful of jam on the plate and return the plate to the freezer for 2 minutes, then gently slide your finger through the jam; if the skin on top of the jam wrinkles, it's done. If not, put the jam back on the heat and cook it for a few more minutes, then test again in the same way using the second plate you put in the freezer.
- Remove the saucepan from the heat, pour the jam into a heat-proof storage container, and set aside to cool to room temperature with the lid slightly ajar. Cover and refrigerate the jam until you are ready to use it, or for up to several months.

Steamed Persimmon Pudding

**Makes 1
(2-quart) cake**

The first time I made steamed persimmon pudding, I was living in Southern California, where every autumn there was a bounty of persimmons at the farmers' market. The market tables would be stacked high with Fuyu and Hachiya persimmons, and on a particular Saturday morning, I came home with a big bag of Hachiyas.

This recipe is based on Marion Cunningham's steamed persimmon pudding, which I clipped from an old *Williams-Sonoma* magazine, and which was the basis for my first persimmon pudding.

The Hachiyas, which are more domed in shape compared to squat Fuyus, must be very ripe, soft, and pulpy when you use them for this recipe to succeed. If they are firm and not ripe, their tannin content is too high and they will taste astringent. I like to place the persimmons in the vegetable drawer of my refrigerator to let them slowly ripen until they are soft enough to puree.

Steamed pudding—sometimes called steamed cake—is a rich and moist cross between cake and pudding. It is made in a sealed aluminum mold, which is put into a pot of simmering water with the lid closed, so the cake steams rather than bakes, which makes for a rich, dense, and moist result.

When I first started making steamed cake, I didn't have a steamed cake mold, so I improvised by using a Bundt cake pan and sealing the top closed with aluminum foil. Later, I found a pretty steamed cake mold at Fante's, a wonderful kitchenware shop in Pennsylvania, where I am from. I suggest you buy a mold rather than improvising. I hope it will mark the beginning of a long future for you and steamed cake. This cake is so rich, it really should be served on its own, but if you want to dress it up a bit, serve it with unsweetened whipped cream. I often take it to holiday parties; not only is it really pretty, it is also easy to transport. If you are taking the cake somewhere, unmold while it is still warm, to prevent the cake from sticking to the pan, let it cool down, and then carefully put the cake back into the mold. Put the lid back on the mold to carry it where you're going.

Note You will need a 2-quart (approximately 2-liter) pudding mold and its lid, or a 2-quart Bundt pan and aluminum foil to make this.

Walnuts	1 cup	105 grams
Nonstick cooking spray		
Hachiya persimmons, ripe	3	
Baking soda	2 teaspoons	10 grams
All-purpose flour	1 cup	120 grams
Ground cinnamon	1 teaspoon	2 grams
Fine sea salt	¾ teaspoon	4.5 grams
Unsalted butter, cubed and softened	8 tablespoons (1 stick)	113 grams
Granulated sugar	1½ cups	300 grams
Large eggs	2	100 grams
Dark rum	2 tablespoons	30 grams
Fresh lemon juice	1 tablespoon	15 grams
Pure vanilla extract	1½ teaspoons	8 grams
Golden raisins	1 cup	150 grams

Get prepared

- Arrange the oven racks so one is in the center position. Preheat the oven to 300°F.
- Spread the walnuts on a baking sheet and toast until they are golden brown and fragrant, about 20 minutes, shaking the pan at least once while the nuts are toasting. Remove the pan from the oven and set aside for the walnuts to cool slightly. When they are cool, coarsely chop the walnuts.
- Spray the inside of a 2-quart pudding mold and its lid, or a 2-quart Bundt pan, with nonstick cooking spray.
- Place the pudding mold in a 4-quart stockpot and add enough water to come almost all the way up the sides of the mold but not cover it. Remove the mold. Fold a kitchen towel in quarters and place it in the bottom of the pot. Bring the water to a boil over high heat.

Make the batter

- Cut off the tops of the persimmons and peel with a small serrated knife. Cut the persimmons in half, removing any white stem. Transfer the persimmons to a food processor fitted with a metal blade and puree until smooth. Measure out 1 cup (220 grams) of the puree and reserve the rest to snack on. Transfer the puree to a small bowl. Add the baking soda and whisk to combine. (The baking soda will cause the puree to coagulate into a solid mass, so don't be alarmed.) Set the puree aside.
- Whisk the flour, cinnamon, and salt together in a medium bowl and set aside.
- Combine the butter and sugar in the bowl of a stand mixer. Fit the mixer with the paddle attachment and beat on medium speed for 2 to 3 minutes, stopping to scrape down the sides of the bowl with a rubber spatula once or twice, until the mixture is light and fluffy. Add the eggs one at a time and mix on medium speed after each addition, stopping to scrape down the

sides of the bowl before adding the next egg. Add the rum, lemon juice, and vanilla and mix until combined. Reduce the mixer speed to low, add the dry ingredients, and mix until only some patches of dry ingredients remain. Add the persimmon mixture and mix on low speed until the puree has broken up and is mixed throughout the batter, about 30 seconds; the puree will never become fully homogenized in the batter. Remove the bowl from the stand. Add the walnuts and raisins and mix them in with a rubber spatula, making sure to scrape the very bottom of the bowl.

Steam the pudding
· Spoon the batter into the prepared mold or pan and use the back of the spoon to smooth and level the top. Secure the lid onto the mold (or cover it tightly with aluminum foil) and carefully lower it into the pot of boiling water. Adjust the temperature of the burner to maintain a steady simmer. Put the lid on the stockpot and steam the pudding for 2 hours, adding boiling water to the pot as needed so the water comes at least three-fourths of the way up the side of the pudding mold. After 2 hours, uncover the pot, remove the mold from the pot using kitchen towels to hold it, and remove the lid from the mold, taking care not to burn yourself with the steam that will rise. Check the cake for doneness by inserting a long toothpick or skewer into the center. If the tester comes out clean, the cake is done. If it does not come out clean, replace the lid, return the mold to the pot, and steam the cake for an additional 10 minutes before checking again.

· Remove the mold from the water to a wire cooling rack and let it rest for 15 to 20 minutes before unmolding the cake. Remove the lid from the mold. Put a serving plate on top of the pudding and invert the pudding onto the plate. Serve the pudding at room temperature or chilled.

Polenta Cake with Dried Apricot Compote

**Makes 1
(9-inch) cake**

When my friend the food writer Charlotte Druckman was writing a story about New York City bodegas (small grocers) for the website Food52, she asked me for a recipe she could include that was made with ingredients you could find at a bodega. This is that recipe, and when I make it, I do buy all the ingredients at my local bodega in Brooklyn. It is a simple cake to make: mix up the batter, scoop it into a cake pan, and bake. It's not too sweet, so it's a cake you might leave on the table for your family to snack on one sliver at a time. I used to serve this with kumquat compote, but kumquats have such a short season that I started using dried apricots instead, because you can find them anytime, anywhere—even at the bodega.

Note You will need a 9-inch cake pan or springform pan to make this.

Nonstick cooking spray		
All-purpose flour	1¼ cups	150 grams
Polenta (coarse cornmeal)	¾ cup	115 grams
Baking powder	2 teaspoons	10 grams
Fine sea salt	1 teaspoon	6 grams
Unsalted butter, cubed and softened	8 tablespoons (1 stick)	113 grams
Granulated sugar	¾ cup	150 grams
Lemon, zested	1	
Large eggs	3	150 grams
Pure vanilla extract	1 teaspoon	5 grams
Whole milk	½ cup	120 grams
Dried Apricot Compote (recipe follows)		

Get prepared

- Arrange the oven racks so one is in the center position. Preheat the oven to 350°F.
- Spray a 9-inch cake pan or springform pan with nonstick cooking spray and set aside.

Make the batter

- Put the flour, polenta, baking powder, and salt in a medium bowl and stir to combine. Set aside.
- Place the butter, sugar, and lemon zest in the bowl of a stand mixer. Fit the mixer with the paddle attachment and beat on medium speed for 2 to 3 minutes, stopping to scrape down the sides of the bowl with a rubber spatula once or twice, until the mixture is light and fluffy. Add the eggs one at a time, mixing until each egg is incorporated and stopping to scrape down the sides of the bowl before adding another egg. Add the vanilla and mix to combine. With

the mixer running on low speed, add the dry ingredients in three additions and the milk in two, alternating between the dry and wet ingredients and ending with the dry ingredients. Turn off the mixer and remove the bowl from the stand. Finish mixing the cake with a rubber spatula, making sure to scrape the very bottom of the bowl.

Bake the cake

- Scoop the batter into the prepared pan and use a small offset spatula to smooth and level the top. Place the cake on the center rack of the oven and bake for 30 minutes, until it springs back when touched in the center, and a small knife or toothpick inserted into the center comes out clean. Remove the cake from the oven and set aside to cool for about 10 minutes. Invert the cake onto a cooling rack to cool completely. Gently turn the cake right side up to slice.
- Slice the cake and serve with apricot compote on the side.

Dried Apricot Compote

**Makes about
2½ cups**

During the winter, practically the only seasonal fruit you can find is citrus (and even that is coming from California), so you have to think creatively. One of the things I reach for at this time of year is dried fruit, and in particular dried apricots, which I cook with orange juice and a little honey to make a sweet compote. I like their sweet-tart quality, fresh or dried. I prefer brownish, sulfite-free apricots, because I think they are more natural and also have a tangier flavor, but I often use the bright orange ones because that is what they sell at my bodega. Leftover compote is delicious stirred into plain yogurt.

Dried apricots	1¼ cups	23 grams
Hot water (100°–110°F)	2 cups	470 grams
Fresh orange juice	⅔ cup	165 grams
Mild-flavored honey (such as wildflower or clover)	3 tablespoons	60 grams
Fine sea salt	pinch	

· Slice the apricots ⅛ to 3⁄16 inch thick and place in a small bowl. Cover with the water and set aside to soak for 10 minutes.

· Transfer the apricots and their soaking liquid to a small saucepan. Add the orange juice, honey, and salt and bring to a boil over high heat. Reduce the heat to medium-low to maintain a steady simmer and cook until the liquid is thick and syrupy, about 45 minutes. Turn off the heat and set aside to cool to room temperature. Serve, or refrigerate the compote in a covered container for up to 2 weeks.

Zucchini Olive Oil Cake with Citrus Glaze

This cake is vegan—it utilizes flaxseeds in place of eggs. It also uses shredded zucchini, which contains moisture and gets absorbed by the cake, so it gets even more moist over time. It's what is sometimes referred to as a keeping cake, which is a way of describing a cake that will still be delicious after three or four days. It is not too sweet, so it makes a great breakfast option.

Note You will need a 9-inch springform pan to make this.

Makes 1 (9-inch) cake

For the cake

Ingredient	Amount	Weight
Nonstick cooking spray		
All-purpose flour	1½ cups plus more for dusting	180 grams
Flaxseed meal	3 tablespoons	22 grams
Warm water	3 tablespoons	45 grams
Zucchini	1 pound (2 small to medium)	500 grams
Whole-wheat pastry flour	½ cup	53 grams
Fine sea salt	¾ teaspoon	4 grams
Baking powder	1 teaspoon	5 grams
Baking soda	½ teaspoon	2.5 grams
Freshly grated nutmeg	½ teaspoon	<1 gram
Orange	1	
Granulated sugar	1 cup plus 2 tablespoons	226 grams
Extra-virgin olive oil	¾ cup	165 grams

For the glaze

Ingredient	Amount	Weight
Juice from 1 lemon	2 tablespoons	30 grams
Juice from ½ orange	2½ tablespoons	37 grams
Confectioners' sugar	1¾ cups plus 2 tablespoons	230 grams

Get prepared

· Arrange the oven racks so one is in the center position. Preheat the oven to 350°F.

· Spray the bottom and sides of a 9-inch springform pan with nonstick cooking spray. Dust the pan with all-purpose flour, invert, and lightly tap the bottom to remove any excess flour. Set aside.

· Stir the flaxseed meal and water together in a small bowl and set aside to soak for at least 10 minutes, or until you're ready to add it to the batter.

· Place a box grater on a clean kitchen towel. Trim the bottoms from the zucchini and, holding the zucchini by the stem, grate the zucchini on the large holes of the grater, discarding both ends. Close the towel with the zucchini inside and wring it out over the sink to remove as much water as possible. Set aside.

Make the batter
- Put the all-purpose flour, whole-wheat pastry flour, salt, baking powder, baking soda, and nutmeg together in a large bowl and whisk to combine.
- Use a fine Microplane to grate the orange zest over a bowl, grating only the outermost, bright-colored layer.
- Combine the sugar and orange zest in the bowl of a stand mixer. Fit the mixer with the paddle attachment and mix on low speed for 20 seconds to distribute the zest. Add the olive oil and mix on medium speed for about 30 seconds. Add the soaked flaxseed meal and continue to mix on medium speed for about 1 minute to lighten and emulsify the batter. Turn off the mixer and add the zucchini. Mix on low speed to distribute the zucchini, about 30 seconds. Turn off the mixer, add the dry ingredients, and mix on low speed until the wet and dry ingredients are combined. Turn off the mixer and remove the bowl from the stand. Finish mixing the cake with a rubber spatula, making sure to scrape the very bottom of the bowl.

Bake the cake
- Scoop the batter into the prepared pan and use a small offset spatula to smooth the top of the batter.
- Place the cake on the center rack of the oven and bake for 55 to 65 minutes, until the cake is brown on top, has pulled away from the sides of the pan, and springs back when gently pressed in the middle. Remove the cake from the oven and set it on a cooling rack to cool for about 10 minutes in the pan. (The cake will collapse in the center as it cools, so don't worry when you see this.) Run a small sharp knife around the edges of the pan to loosen the cake from the pan. Unclasp and remove the ring from the side of the pan and let the cake cool completely.

Glaze the cake
- While the cake is cooling, to make the glaze, whisk together the lemon juice, orange juice, and confectioners' sugar until no lumps remain. Spoon or brush the glaze over the cake while it is still warm; it is a thin glaze, and it soaks into the cake and is just barely visible in the end. Slide the cake off the bottom of the springform pan onto a cake stand or serving plate.

Cinnamon Swirl Sour Cream Bundt Cake

Makes 1 (10-inch) Bundt cake

In Nancy Silverton's book *Pastries from the La Brea Bakery,* she has a recipe for a crème fraîche coffee cake that I have been making for years. Over time, I have tweaked it until it may not be recognizable to Nancy, but to me, it still feels like hers. Where some coffee cakes are so dry and boring all you want to do is eat the crumbly part off the top, the amount of sour cream in this cake creates a moist and tangy cake that balances perfectly with a cup of morning coffee.

Note You will need a 10-inch Bundt pan to make this.

Nonstick cooking spray		
All-purpose flour	3 cups plus more for dusting	360 grams
Dark brown sugar	½ cup (lightly packed)	100 grams
Ground cinnamon	2 teaspoons	4 grams
Baking powder	2 teaspoons	10 grams
Fine sea salt	1 teaspoon	6 grams
Unsalted butter, cubed and softened	16 tablespoons (2 sticks)	226 grams
Granulated sugar	1½ cups	300 grams
Lemon	1	
Large eggs	2	100 grams
Sour cream	2 cups	454 grams
Pure vanilla extract	1 teaspoon	5 grams
Confectioners' sugar	¼ cup	30 grams

Get prepared

- Arrange the oven racks so one is in the center and make sure there is enough room above to accommodate a Bundt pan. Preheat the oven to 350°F.
- Spray the inside of a 10-inch Bundt pan with nonstick cooking spray. Dust the pan with flour, invert, and lightly tap the bottom to remove any excess flour. Set aside.
- Put the brown sugar and cinnamon in a small bowl and whisk to combine. Set aside.

Make the batter

- Put the flour, baking powder, and salt together in a medium bowl, whisk to combine, and set aside.
- Combine the butter and granulated sugar in the bowl of a stand mixer. Use a fine Microplane to grate the lemon zest over the bowl, grating only the outermost, bright-colored layer. Fit the mixer with the paddle attachment and beat on medium speed for 2 to 3 minutes, stopping to scrape down the sides of the bowl with a rubber spatula once or twice, until the mixture is light and fluffy. Add the eggs one at a time, beating on medium speed until they are thoroughly combined and stopping to scrape down the sides of the

bowl before adding the next egg. Add the sour cream and vanilla and beat on medium speed until the sour cream is mixed in. Scrape down the sides of the bowl and add the dry ingredients. Mix on low speed until no flour is visible. Be careful, because flour can fly out of the bowl when you start mixing. Turn off the mixer and remove the bowl from the stand. Finish mixing the cake with a rubber spatula, making sure to scrape the very bottom of the bowl.

Bake the cake

- Drop half of the batter in spoonfuls around the bottom of the prepared Bundt pan. Use the back of the spoon to even out the batter. Sprinkle about two-thirds of the cinnamon–brown sugar mixture over the batter. Spoon the remaining batter on top of the cinnamon–brown sugar layer and use the back of the spoon to smooth it out. Sprinkle the remaining cinnamon–brown sugar over the top layer of batter.
- Place the cake on the center rack of the oven to bake for 1 hour to 1 hour and 10 minutes, until a toothpick inserted into the center comes out clean and the cake springs back when you press gently with your finger. Remove the cake from the oven and set it aside to cool in the pan for 10 minutes. Invert the cake onto a cooling rack to cool completely.
- Transfer the cake to a serving plate. Put the confectioners' sugar in a fine-mesh strainer and dust it lightly over the cake.

Flourless Chocolate Olive Oil Cake

Makes 1 (9-inch) cake

I love any cake made with olive oil—oil-based cakes tend to be really moist, and the olive oil in this chocolate cake imparts another layer of flavor. This cake contains polenta, which gives it a nice crunch. It's so rich and dense that my son, Wyatt, calls it a brownie cake.

Note You will need a 9-inch springform pan to make this.

Nonstick cooking spray		
Bittersweet chocolate	8 ounces (or 1⅓ cups chocolate chips)	226 grams
Extra-virgin olive oil	½ cup	110 grams
Granulated sugar	1 cup	200 grams
Large eggs, separated	5	250 grams
Polenta (coarse cornmeal)	3 tablespoons	36 grams
Fine sea salt	1 teaspoon	6 grams

Get prepared

- Arrange the oven racks so one is in the center position. Preheat the oven to 350°F.
- Spray the bottom and sides of a 9-inch springform pan with nonstick cooking spray. Line the bottom with a parchment-paper round and then spray the bottom with additional nonstick spray. Set aside.

Prepare a double boiler and melt the chocolate

- Unless you are using chocolate chips, chop the chocolate into ⅓-inch pieces.
- Pour 1 to 2 inches of water into the bottom of a small saucepan and choose a bowl that fits over the saucepan to make a double boiler. Make sure the water is not touching the bottom of the bowl; if it is, pour some water out. Bring the water to a boil over high heat, then reduce the heat to medium-low to maintain a gentle simmer.
- Put the chocolate in the bowl of the double boiler and melt it, using a heat-proof rubber spatula to stir and scrape down the sides of the bowl so the chocolate melts evenly and doesn't burn. Remove the bowl from the double boiler and wipe the bottom of the bowl so no water drips. Add the olive oil and whisk to combine. Add ¾ cup (150 grams) of the sugar, the egg yolks, polenta, and salt and whisk to combine. Set aside.

Whip the egg whites and mix the batter

- Place the egg whites in the bowl of a stand mixer. Fit the mixer with the whisk attachment and whip on medium-high speed until the egg whites have started to froth, about 2 minutes. With the mixer running, add the remaining ¼ cup (50 grams) sugar in a slow, steady stream. Increase the speed to high and continue to whip until soft peaks have formed, about 2 minutes. Add one-third of the egg whites to the chocolate batter and gently fold them in with a rubber spatula. (I do this by moving the bowl counterclockwise with my left hand as I work my spatula around the edge and up through the center with my right hand.) Add the remaining egg whites and gently fold them in.

I like to beat my egg whites just this side of stiff peaks. This helps them to better expand in the oven as the cake bakes, resulting in a lighter cake. Heat causes expansion in the oven; by not beating the egg whites to their maximum potential, you allow them the room to expand.

Bake the cake
- Pour the batter into the prepared cake pan and use a small offset spatula to smooth and level the top.
- Place the cake on the center rack of the oven and bake for 30 to 35 minutes, until it has puffed up with some small cracks on the surface and feels slightly firm and not jiggly to the touch. Remove the cake from the oven and set it on a cooling rack to cool for about 10 minutes in the pan. (The cake will collapse in the center as it cools; that is part of its rustic beauty.) Run a small sharp knife around the edges of the pan to loosen the cake from the pan. Unclasp and remove the ring from the side of the springform pan and let the cake cool completely. Slide the cake off the bottom of the pan onto a cake stand or serving plate.

Date Walnut Cake with Dulce de Leche

Makes 1 (8-inch) cake

This date cake is a variation of one I made while working at Babbo for Gina DePalma. The walnuts are toasted and ground into a fine walnut flour and the dates are skinned and puréed. The resulting cake pairs perfectly with a dulce de leche, which is easy to make from scratch, or a vanilla custard, like we did at Babbo.

Note You will need an 8-inch square baking pan to make this.

Nonstick cooking spray		
Walnuts	1 cup	105 grams
Dates (with pits, preferably Medjool)	2 cups	335 grams
All-purpose flour	1½ cups	180 grams
Baking powder	1 teaspoon	5 grams
Baking soda	½ teaspoon	3 grams
Fine sea salt	¾ teaspoon	4.5 grams
Buttermilk, well shaken	1 cup	250 grams
Large eggs	2	100 grams
Dark brown sugar	½ cup (lightly packed)	100 grams
Unsalted butter, melted and cooled slightly	8 tablespoons (1 stick)	113 grams
Pure vanilla extract	1 teaspoon	5 grams
Dulce de Leche (recipe follows)		

Get prepared

- Arrange the oven racks so one is in the center position. Preheat the oven to 300°F.
- Spray the bottom and sides of an 8-inch square baking pan with nonstick cooking spray. Cut an 8-inch-wide piece of parchment paper and lay it in the pan so it lines the bottom and sides. Trim the paper so it overhangs the edges of the pan by ½ inch. Spray the parchment with nonstick cooking spray.
- Spread the walnuts on a baking sheet and toast them in the oven for 18 to 20 minutes, shaking the pan once during that time for even toasting, until the nuts are golden brown and fragrant. Remove the baking sheet from the oven and set aside to cool the nuts to room temperature.
- Increase the oven temperature to 350°F.
- Place the dates in a small heat-proof bowl and add enough boiling water to cover. Set aside to soak for 10 to 15 minutes, until the skins begin to pull away from the flesh. Strain the dates through a fine-mesh strainer and use your fingers to remove and discard the skins and pits. Set the dates aside.

Make the batter
- Whisk the flour, baking powder, baking soda, and salt together in a medium bowl and set aside.
- Put the walnuts in a food processor fitted with a metal blade and pulse until they are smaller than a lentil; any smaller and they will begin to turn into a paste, like a nut butter. Transfer the ground walnuts to the bowl with the dry ingredients and set aside. (There is no need to wipe down the bowl of the food processor.)
- Place the dates in the bowl of the food processor. Add ½ cup of the buttermilk and process to form a smooth paste, about 1 minute. Scrape the paste into a medium bowl, add the remaining ½ cup buttermilk, and whisk to combine. Set aside.
- Combine the eggs and brown sugar in the bowl of a stand mixer. Fit the mixer with the paddle attachment and beat on medium-high speed until the mixture has lightened in color, about 2 minutes, stopping to scrape down the sides of the bowl with a rubber spatula once during that time. With the mixer running, drizzle in the melted butter and vanilla and mix to combine. Add the date puree and mix on low speed until blended. Turn off the mixer and scrape down the sides of the bowl with a rubber spatula. Add the dry ingredients and mix on low speed until smooth. Turn off the mixer and remove the bowl from the stand. Finish mixing the cake with a rubber spatula, making sure to scrape the very bottom of the bowl.

Bake the cake
- Scrape the batter into the prepared baking pan and use a small offset spatula to even out the top.
- Place the cake on the center rack of the oven and bake for 45 to 50 minutes, until a toothpick inserted into the center comes out clean. Remove the cake from the oven and let it cool for about 5 minutes in the pan. Pull the parchment paper ends to lift the cake out. Remove and discard the parchment paper and place the cake on a serving plate. While the cake is still warm, use a chopstick to poke holes in the cake, leaving about 1 inch between each hole. Drizzle half of the dulce de leche over the cake so it fills the holes and drips down the sides.
- Cut the cake into 9 squares and serve with the remaining dulce de leche on the side.

Dulce de Leche

**Makes about
2 cups**

Dulce de leche is Argentine caramel, made by cooking milk and sugar together slowly for a long time until the mixture turns into a thick, rich, delicious caramel. If you've never made it, you should try it; it's not at all difficult to do. You will have some left over after serving it with the date walnut cake; drizzle it over ice cream.

Whole milk	4 cups	960 grams
Granulated sugar	1¼ cups	250 grams
Baking soda	½ teaspoon	3 grams
Vanilla bean	1	
Fine sea salt	½ teaspoon	3 grams

Place the milk, sugar, and baking soda in a large saucepan. Split the vanilla bean down the middle with a small sharp knife and use the knife to scrape the seeds out of the bean. Add the seeds and bean to the saucepan. Stir to dissolve the sugar and warm the milk over medium-high heat until the mixture begins to bubble around the edges. Reduce the heat to medium-low to maintain a steady simmer and simmer for 60 minutes, stirring every 10 to 15 minutes, until the mixture is a tan color, and then increase the stirring to every 5 minutes, until the dulce de leche is a beautiful deep amber. Turn off the heat. Remove the vanilla bean. (Use the bean to make Vanilla Sugar, page 219, or discard it.) Pass the caramel through a fine-mesh strainer into a large bowl. Whisk in the salt. Serve warm. (If you are making the dulce de leche in advance or if you have some left over, allow it to cool to room temperature, transfer it to a covered container, and refrigerate until you're ready to serve it, or for up to 2 weeks. Before serving, reheat the dulce de leche in a medium saucepan over medium-low heat, stirring often.)

Banana Bread

**Makes 1
(9-inch) loaf**

I add a *lot* of banana to this batter, so you can really taste it. And I don't add walnuts, because I want it to be all about the banana. It's a keeping cake, which means it keeps for three or four days without going stale, and, in fact, it gets more moist and more delicious during this time.

Note You will need a 9- x 4-inch loaf pan to make this.

Nonstick cooking spray		
All-purpose flour	1¼ cups	150 grams
Granulated sugar	¼ cup plus 2 tablespoons	76 grams
Baking powder	½ teaspoon	3 grams
Baking soda	½ teaspoon	3 grams
Fine sea salt	½ teaspoon	3 grams
Ground cinnamon	½ teaspoon	1 gram
Peeled bananas	3 to 4 medium	250 grams
Large egg	1	50 grams
Buttermilk, well shaken	⅓ cup	83 grams
Unsalted butter, melted and cooled slightly	6 tablespoons	85 grams
Pure vanilla extract	1 teaspoon	5 grams

Get prepared

- Arrange the oven racks so one is in the center position. Preheat the oven to 350°F.
- Spray a 9- x 4-inch loaf pan with nonstick cooking spray.

Make the batter

- Whisk the flour, sugar, baking powder, baking soda, salt, and cinnamon together in a medium bowl and set aside.
- In a separate medium bowl, mash the bananas with a fork until they are pureed with some small chunks remaining (about 1 cup). Add the egg, buttermilk, melted butter, and vanilla and whisk them in with the bananas. Add the dry ingredients and use a rubber spatula to fold them in until no flour is visible, making sure to scrape the very bottom of the bowl.

Bake the bread

- Scoop the batter into the prepared loaf pan and use a small offset spatula to smooth and level out the top.
- Place the banana bread on the center rack of the oven and bake for 50 to 55 minutes, until a toothpick inserted into the center comes out clean, rotating the pan from front to back halfway through the baking time. Remove the banana bread from the oven and let it cool in the pan for 10 minutes. Invert the banana bread onto a cooling rack and flip it again so it is right side up. Let it cool on the rack.

Pumpkin Muffins

Makes 1 dozen muffins

When I was child growing up in central Pennsylvania, I used to go with my parents and grandmother to a restaurant called the Country Cupboard. It was very homey; when you sat down, they brought a bread basket to the table, filled with warm white dinner rolls and pumpkin muffins. I loved the muffins so much, my parents would purchase some to take home, which they would keep in the freezer to heat up for special occasions. It's funny that we treated them like something so special, because really, they're very basic. In trying to replicate those muffins, I relied on a recipe I found in a collection from our local church.

Note You will need one 12-cup standard-size muffin tin to make these.

Nonstick cooking spray		
Whole-wheat pastry flour	2 cups	210 grams
Baking soda	1 teaspoon	5 grams
Ground cinnamon	1 teaspoon	2 grams
Fine sea salt	¾ teaspoon	4 grams
Ground cloves	½ teaspoon	1 gram
Freshly grated nutmeg	¼ teaspoon	1 gram
Light brown sugar	1¼ cups (lightly packed)	250 grams
Canned pumpkin puree	⅔ cup	150 grams
Large eggs	2	100 grams
Canola oil	½ cup	110 grams
Fresh orange juice	⅓ cup	82 grams
Black raisins	½ cup	75 grams

Get prepared

- Arrange the oven racks so one is in the center position. Preheat the oven to 350°F.
- Spray a 12-cup muffin tin with nonstick cooking spray and set aside.

Make the batter

- Put the whole-wheat pastry flour, baking soda, cinnamon, salt, cloves, and nutmeg in a medium bowl and whisk to combine. Set aside.
- Put the brown sugar, pumpkin puree, eggs, oil, orange juice, and raisins in a separate large bowl and stir to combine. Add the dry ingredients and fold them together with a rubber spatula, making sure to scrape the very bottom of the bowl.

Fill the cups and bake the muffins

- Scoop the batter into the prepared muffin tin, filling each cup about three-quarters of the way.
- Place the muffins on the center rack of the oven to bake for 25 to 30 minutes, until a toothpick inserted into the center of one comes out clean, rotating the

tin from front to back halfway through the baking time. Remove the muffin tin from the oven and let the muffins cool in the pan for about 10 minutes. Run a small paring knife around the outside of each muffin to loosen it. Tilt the muffin tin over and coax the muffins out onto a cooling rack. Turn the muffins right side up and let them cool completely.

Orange, Oat, and Flax Muffins

Makes 1 dozen muffins

I like to eat healthfully, and as a baker, I like experimenting with ways to make healthy baked goods that don't taste like health food. These gluten-free, dairy-free muffins—made with oat flour, loaded with fruit, and sweetened with brown sugar—are my version of a modern "morning glory" muffin. They're made with all whole ingredients, including flaxseed meal, which is ground flaxseeds; in recent years, it has been added to baked goods to make them "healthy" the way that bran was added to baked goods when I was growing up. I started making these for a bakery I was consulting for in Pennsylvania. It was the thing I grabbed to have with my morning coffee.

Note You will need two (6-cup) jumbo muffin tins to make these.

Nonstick cooking spray		
Golden raisins	1 cup	150 grams
Dried cherries	1 cup	150 grams
Dried blueberries	½ cup	85 grams
Granny Smith apple	1	130 grams
Dark brown sugar	¾ cup (lightly packed)	150 grams
Large eggs	3	150 grams
Mild-flavored honey (such as wildflower or clover)	1½ tablespoons	30 grams
Fresh orange juice	1¼ cups	309 grams
Extra-virgin olive oil	½ cup	110 grams
Flaxseed meal	2⅓ cups	230 grams
Oat flour	1¾ cups	161 grams
Baking soda	2 teaspoons	10 grams
Ground cinnamon	1 teaspoon	2 grams
Fine sea salt	1 teaspoon	6 grams
Demerara (turbinado) sugar	1½ tablespoons	22 grams

Get prepared

- Arrange the oven racks so one is in the center position. Preheat the oven to 375°F.
- Spray two (6-cup) jumbo muffin tins with nonstick cooking spray and set aside.
- Place the raisins, cherries, and blueberries in a medium bowl, cover with hot tap water, and set aside to soak for 5 minutes. Drain in a fine-mesh strainer; set the strainer on top of a bowl to drain off any excess water while you prepare the muffin batter.
- Peel the apple and grate it on the large holes of a box grater; set aside. (I place the grated apple on top of the dried fruit until I'm ready for them.)

Make the batter
- Whisk the brown sugar, eggs, and honey together in a large bowl. Add the orange juice and olive oil and whisk to combine.
- Put the flaxseed meal, oat flour, baking soda, cinnamon, and salt in a medium bowl and whisk to combine. Add the dry ingredients to the bowl with the brown sugar mixture and whisk until smooth. Add the dried fruit and apple and stir with the whisk to combine, making sure there are no clumps of grated apple in the batter. Set aside for 5 minutes to allow the flaxseed meal to absorb the liquid in the batter.

Fill the cups and bake the muffins
- Scoop the batter into the prepared muffin tins, filling each cup about three-quarters of the way. Sprinkle the muffins with the demerara sugar.
- Place the muffins on the center rack of the oven for 25 to 30 minutes, until a toothpick inserted into the center of one comes out clean, rotating the pans from front to back halfway through the baking time. Remove the tins from the oven and let the muffins cool in the pans for about 10 minutes. Run a small paring knife around the outside of each muffin to loosen it. Tilt one muffin tin over and coax the muffins out onto a cooling rack. Repeat with the second tin of muffins. Turn the muffins right side up and let them cool completely.

Cookies and Bars

Cookies are a strong part of my repertoire, and also my family traditions. When I was growing up, my mother went all out with cookies at Christmastime. She would bake several different kinds, and at the same time I would push my own cookies through my Easy-Bake oven. I carry on the tradition (minus the Easy-Bake) with my son. We usually bake at least five types of holiday cookies, including Classic Roll-Out Sugar Cookies decorated with Royal Icing (page 391), Pistachio Biscotti (page 397), and Hazelnut Linzer Cookies with Pineapple Jam (page 406), among others. I also have a strong affinity both for making and eating what I call snacking cookies—those familiar favorites that you make to serve and enjoy as an everyday afternoon snack, such as Chocolate Chunk Cookies (page 380), Fudgy Brownies (page 419), and Oatmeal Raisin Cookies (page 382). The cookies in this chapter are those that I make time and again, that are crowd-pleasers and satisfy my quest for the perfect (and often simplest) thing.

Tahini White Chocolate Chunk Cookies

Makes 16 to 20 cookies

Not long ago, it seemed like all of a sudden, many of the bakers I know started baking with tahini, or sesame seed butter. Their curiosity intrigued me, and I began poking around and experimenting with different brands of tahini and ways to use tahini in baked goods. These cookies are one product of that experimenting. They are basically peanut butter cookies made with tahini (in place of peanut butter), which imparts a toasty, nutty flavor to the cookies. Even though I love the taste memory of peanut butter cookies, I like these even more.

I make these cookies with brown rice flour. Because rice flour is not ground as fine as wheat flour, it takes longer to absorb liquid, which gives the cookies a grainier, crispier texture. And, because rice flour is gluten free, the cookies are gluten free.

Note Regular grocery store tahini will work fine in this recipe, but if you want to make the very best version of these cookies, seek out tahini made with Ethiopian sesame seeds; my favorite is Soom. When buying sesame seeds, look for those that haven't been hulled. You can find them online or buy toasted sesame seeds in a shaker can in the Japanese section of grocery stores; these are not hulled, and they have great flavor.

White chocolate	6 ounces (or 1 cup white chocolate chips)	170 grams
Brown rice flour	1¾ cups	224 grams
Baking powder	½ teaspoon	3 grams
Baking soda	½ teaspoon	3 grams
Unsalted butter, cubed and softened (see page 379)	9 tablespoons (1 stick plus 1 tablespoon)	126 grams
Dark brown sugar	½ cup (lightly packed)	100 grams
Fine sea salt	1 teaspoon	6 grams
Tahini (sesame seed butter)	½ cup	128 grams
Pure vanilla extract	1 tablespoon	15 grams
Large egg	1	50 grams
Sesame seeds (not hulled)	¼ cup	35 grams
Granulated sugar	2 tablespoon	26 grams

Get prepared

- Arrange the oven racks so one is in the top third and the other is in the bottom third. Preheat the oven to 350°F.
- Line two baking sheets with parchment paper.
- Unless you are using chips, chop the chocolate into ¼- to ½-inch chunks and set aside.

Make the dough

- Whisk the brown rice flour, baking powder, and baking soda together in a large bowl.
- Combine the butter, brown sugar, and salt in the bowl of a stand mixer. Fit the mixer with the paddle attachment and beat on medium speed for 2 to

3 minutes, stopping to scrape down the sides of the bowl with a rubber spatula once or twice, until the mixture is light and fluffy. Turn off the mixer, scrape down the sides of the bowl, add the tahini, and mix it in. Add the vanilla and egg and beat on medium speed until the mixture is light and fluffy, 1 to 2 minutes. Turn off the mixer, add the dry ingredients, and mix on low speed until no flour is visible. Add the white chocolate and mix on low speed until the chocolate is evenly dispersed.

Form and bake the cookies

- Put the sesame seeds and granulated sugar in separate small bowls. Scoop a 2-tablespoon (50-gram) portion of dough and roll it between the palms of your hands into a ball. Roll the ball in the sesame seeds, pushing down slightly so the seeds adhere, then roll the ball in the sugar to coat it on all sides. Place the ball on one of the prepared baking sheets. Continue forming and rolling the dough in the same way, placing the balls on the prepared baking sheets as they are ready and leaving about 2 inches between each one. When you have rolled all of the balls, flatten each ball with the palm of your hand to about 3 inches in diameter and ¾ inch thick.
- Put one baking sheet on each rack of the oven and bake the cookies for 12 to 14 minutes, until they are light golden brown, rotating them from front to back and from one rack to the other halfway through the baking time. Remove the cookies from the oven and set them aside to cool slightly. Transfer the cookies to a cooling rack to cool completely.
- Store the cookies in an airtight container at room temperature for up to 1 week or freeze for up to 3 months.

Softening Butter

Many people think they have to plan ahead to make cookies because they need to soften the butter for a long time, but that's not the case. The ideal temperature for butter when you start to make cookies is 65°F to 70°F, which takes 10 to 15 minutes after removing it from the refrigerator. At that temperature, the butter is solid, so when you pound it with your mixer in the process of creaming the butter with the sugar—the foundation of most cookie recipes—the coarse shards of sugar break through the butter to make it fluffy. As butter gets warm, it becomes liquid, so instead of the sugar breaking through a solid substance and holding air, which makes the mixture light and fluffy, the mixture becomes flat and greasy. If you've softened your butter so much that it is greasy, put it in the refrigerator to firm it up. It's better to err on the side of butter that is too cold than too warm, as the process of creaming will soften butter that is too cold.

Chocolate Chunk Cookies

**Makes about
3 dozen cookies**

I know: there are a lot of chocolate chip cookies in the world. What makes these different—and I think better—is the addition of confectioners' sugar. Classic chocolate chip cookie dough is made with both granulated and brown sugar. These cookies are made with those sugars plus confectioners' sugar, which contains cornstarch. The starch absorbs moisture and results in cookies that are tender and chewy all the way through. I use a combination of dark semisweet chocolate and milk chocolate in these cookies. I know that dark chocolate is thought to be more "sophisticated," and while I do like dark chocolate, I have to confess that I like milk chocolate even more. I also think the milk chocolate gives the cookies a homey, nostalgic flavor.

Bittersweet chocolate	8 ounces (or 1¼ cups chocolate chips)	226 grams
Milk chocolate	8 ounces (or 1¼ cups chocolate chips)	226 grams
All-purpose flour	3 cups	360 grams
Baking powder	1½ teaspoons	8 grams
Baking soda	1 teaspoon	5 grams
Fine sea salt	1 teaspoon	6 grams
Large eggs	2	100 grams
Large egg yolks	4	68 grams
Pure vanilla extract	2 teaspoons	10 grams
Unsalted butter, cubed and softened (see page 379)	14 tablespoons (1 stick plus 6 tablespoons)	196 grams
Dark brown sugar	1¼ cups (lightly packed)	250 grams
Granulated sugar	¾ cup	150 grams
Confectioners' sugar	½ cup	60 grams

Make the dough

· Unless you are using chocolate chips, chop the bittersweet and milk chocolate into ¼- to ½-inch chunks. Put the chunks in a bowl and set aside.
· Place the flour, baking powder, baking soda, and salt in a medium bowl and whisk to combine.
· Combine the eggs, egg yolks, and vanilla in a small bowl and whisk to combine.
· Combine the butter, brown sugar, granulated sugar, and confectioners' sugar in the bowl of a stand mixer. Fit the mixer with the paddle attachment and beat on medium speed for 2 to 3 minutes, stopping to scrape down the sides of the bowl with a rubber spatula once or twice, until the mixture is light and fluffy. Add the egg mixture in three additions, beating until it is completely integrated with the batter and stopping to scrape down the sides of the bowl

between each addition. Turn off the mixer, add the dry ingredients, and mix on low speed until no flour is visible. Add the chocolate and mix on low just to combine. Chill the dough overnight or for at least 2 hours.

Prepare to bake the cookies

- Arrange the oven racks so one is in the top third of the oven and the other is in the bottom third. Preheat the oven to 375°F.
- Line two baking sheets with parchment paper.

Form and bake the cookies

- Scoop the dough in 2-tablespoon (50-gram) portions and roll them between the palms of your hands into balls. Place the balls on the prepared baking sheets, leaving about 2 inches between each ball, and fitting 8 to 10 balls on each baking sheet. Flatten each ball with the palm of your hand to about 3 inches in diameter and ¾ inch thick. Return the remaining dough to the refrigerator.
- Place one baking sheet on each oven rack and bake for 16 to 18 minutes, until the centers of the cookies no longer look wet and the edges are deep golden brown, rotating the baking sheets from front to back and from one rack to the other halfway through the baking time. Remove the baking sheets from the oven and let the cookies cool for 2 minutes on the baking sheets. Use a spatula to remove the cookies to a cooling rack to finish cooling.
- Remove the remaining dough from the refrigerator, roll the remaining balls, flatten them, and bake them as you did the first batch.
- Store the cookies in an airtight container at room temperature for up to 1 week or freeze for up to 3 months.

Oatmeal Raisin Cookies

Makes 18 to 20 cookies

After eating these cookies at Sadelle's, the *New York Times* restaurant reviewer Pete Wells wrote that they were "one of the best oatmeal cookies in existence." The secret is letting the dough rest for four days. Yes, you read that right! One day will do if that's all you have, but four is ideal. While the dough rests, the oats absorb the moisture, which gives the cookie its perfect texture: slightly crispy around the edges with a chewy center.

Note The weight of 2 cups of oats varies by brand. So even though I prefer weighing to measuring when baking, for this recipe, I suggest you measure the oats.

Black raisins	1 cup	150 grams
All-purpose flour	1⅓ cups	160 grams
Ground cinnamon	2 teaspoons	4 grams
Baking soda	1½ teaspoons	9 grams
Fine sea salt	1 teaspoon	6 grams
Unsalted butter, cubed and softened (see page 379)	12 tablespoons (1 stick plus 4 tablespoons)	170 grams
Light brown sugar	¾ cup (lightly packed)	150 grams
Granulated sugar	¼ cup plus 2 tablespoons	76 grams
Large egg	1	50 grams
Large egg yolk	1	17 grams
Pure vanilla extract	2 teaspoons	10 grams
Old-fashioned rolled oats	2 cups	

Make the dough

- Place the raisins in a small bowl, cover with hot tap water, and set aside to soak for 30 minutes. Drain the raisins in a fine-mesh strainer and let them sit in the strainer to drain any remaining water while you mix the cookie dough.
- Put the flour, cinnamon, baking soda, and salt in a medium bowl and whisk to combine.
- Combine the butter, brown sugar, and granulated sugar in the bowl of a stand mixer. Fit the mixer with the paddle attachment and beat on medium speed for 2 to 3 minutes, stopping to scrape down the sides of the bowl with a rubber spatula once or twice, until the mixture is light and fluffy. Turn off the mixer, scrape down the sides of the bowl, and add the egg, egg yolk, and vanilla. Mix on medium speed until combined. Turn off the mixer, scrape down the sides of the bowl, add the dry ingredients, and mix on low until almost no flour is visible. Add the oats and mix on low speed to combine. Add the raisins and mix on low to distribute. Turn off the mixer and remove the bowl from the stand. Cover the bowl and chill for 4 days.

Prepare to bake the cookies
- Arrange the oven racks so one is in the top third of the oven and the other in the bottom third. Preheat the oven to 350°F.
- Line two baking sheets with parchment paper.

Form and bake the cookies
- Remove the dough from the refrigerator and uncover. Scoop a 2-tablespoon (50-gram) portion of dough and roll it between the palms of your hands into a ball. Place the ball on one of the prepared baking sheets. Continue scooping and rolling the dough, leaving 2 inches between each ball and fitting 9 to 10 balls on each baking sheet. Return any remaining dough to the refrigerator.
- Place one baking sheet on each oven rack and bake for 16 to 18 minutes, until the centers of the cookies no longer look wet and the edges are deep golden brown, rotating the baking sheets from front to back and from one rack to the other halfway through the baking time. Remove the baking sheets from the oven and let the cookies cool for 2 minutes on the baking sheets. Use a spatula to remove the cookies to a cooling rack to finish cooling.
- Remove the remaining dough from the refrigerator, roll the remaining balls, and bake them as you did the first batch.
- Store the cookies in an airtight container at room temperature for up to 1 week or freeze for up to 3 months.

Chewy Gingersnaps

For me, the perfect gingersnap cookie is crispy on the outside and chewy on the inside, with a good ginger kick. This is it! I think of these as a holiday cookie, although there's no reason you can't enjoy them year-round.

**Makes about
2 dozen cookies**

All-purpose flour	2¼ cups	270 grams
Baking soda	2 teaspoons	10 grams
Fine sea salt	½ teaspoon	3 grams
Ground ginger	1½ teaspoons	3 grams
Ground cinnamon	1 teaspoon	2 grams
Ground cloves	1 teaspoon	2 grams
Ground cardamom	⅛ teaspoon	< 1 gram
Granulated sugar	1¼ cups	250 grams
Canola oil	½ cup plus 1 tablespoon	125 grams
Large egg	1	50 grams
Molasses	¼ cup	79 grams
Fresh ginger, peeled and grated on the medium holes of a box grater	1 tablespoon	15 grams

Make the dough

- Whisk the flour, baking soda, salt, ground ginger, cinnamon, cloves, and cardamom together in a medium bowl and set aside.
- Combine 1 cup (200 grams) of the sugar, the oil, and egg in the bowl of a stand mixer. Fit the mixer with the paddle attachment and mix on medium speed for 2 minutes, until the mixture begins to lighten in color. Turn off the mixer and scrape down the sides of the bowl. Add the molasses and grated fresh ginger and beat on medium speed to combine. Turn off the mixer, add the dry ingredients, and beat on low speed until no flour is visible. Turn off the mixer and remove the bowl from the stand. Cover the bowl with plastic wrap, and refrigerate until the dough has chilled and firmed up, at least 2 hours and up to 2 days.

Prepare to bake the cookies

- Arrange the oven racks so one is in the top third of the oven and the other is in the bottom third. Preheat the oven to 350°F.
- Line two baking sheets with parchment paper.

Form and bake the cookies

· Remove the dough from the refrigerator and uncover. Place the remaining ¼ cup (50 grams) sugar in a small bowl. Scoop a 1-tablespoon (25-gram) piece of dough and roll it between the palms of your hands into a ball. Roll the ball in the bowl with the sugar to coat it all over. Place the ball on one of the prepared baking sheets. Continue with the remaining dough, leaving 2 inches between each ball on the baking sheets.

· Place one baking sheet on each oven rack and bake for 11 to 13 minutes, until the cookies have risen and fallen, rotating them from front to back and from one rack to the other halfway through the baking time. Remove from the oven and let the cookies cool on the baking sheets for about 10 minutes. Use a spatula to remove the cookies to a cooling rack to cool completely.

· Store the cookies in an airtight container at room temperature for up to 1 week or freeze for up to 3 months.

Chocolate Sugar Cookies

Makes 16 to 18 (2-inch) cookies

These are everything I want in a chocolate sugar cookie: they're really chocolaty, not too sweet, ever-so-slightly salty, and a bit chewy. And, they have that beautiful crackle on top that, for me, is the sign of a perfect rise-and-fall cookie. A rise-and-fall cookie refers to one that rises in the oven and then falls when you take it out. The rise-and-fall process is a result of the baking soda reacting with the cocoa powder and brown sugar before the cookie is set. When the cookies are removed from the oven, they fall, giving them that crackle top. How quickly the cookie rises before it sets up is the key to achieving that finish. For these cookies, to ensure they rise quickly, I don't refrigerate the dough before baking, which causes the cookies to rise more quickly than if the dough were cold. I use Valrhona cocoa powder to make these, which in my opinion is the best there is, but if you can't find Valrhona, the cookies will be delicious with whatever cocoa powder you use. And I make them with dark brown sugar in place of the more typical granulated sugar, which gives a depth of flavor to an otherwise straightforward cookie.

All-purpose flour	2 cups	240 grams
Cocoa powder (preferably Valrhona)	½ cup	43 grams
Baking soda	1 teaspoon	5 grams
Fine sea salt	½ teaspoon	3 grams
Unsalted butter, cubed and softened (see page 379)	16 tablespoons (2 sticks)	226 grams
Dark brown sugar	1½ cups (lightly packed)	300 grams
Large egg	1	50 grams
Pure vanilla extract	1 teaspoon	5 grams
Granulated sugar	½ cup for rolling	100 grams

Get prepared

- Arrange the oven racks so one is in the center position. Preheat the oven to 350°F.
- Line two baking sheets with parchment paper.

Make the dough

- Put the flour, cocoa powder, baking soda, and salt in a medium bowl and whisk to combine the ingredients. Set aside.
- Put the butter and brown sugar in the bowl of a stand mixer. Fit the mixer with the paddle attachment and beat on medium speed for 2 to 3 minutes, stopping to scrape down the sides of the bowl with a rubber spatula once or twice, until the mixture is light and fluffy. Turn off the mixer, add the egg and vanilla, and beat until the egg is thoroughly incorporated, 1 to 2 minutes, stopping to scrape down the sides of the bowl once during that time. Add

the dry ingredients and mix on low speed until no flour is visible, stopping to scrape down the sides of the bowl once during the process.

Form and bake the cookies

· Pour the granulated sugar into a small bowl. Scoop a 2-tablespoon (50-gram) portion of dough and roll it between the palms of your hands into a ball. Roll the ball in the bowl with the sugar to coat it all over. Place the ball on one of the prepared baking sheets. Continue scooping and rolling the dough, leaving about 2 inches between each ball.

· When you have filled one baking sheet, place it on the center rack of the oven and bake for 12 to 14 minutes, until the cookies have puffed up and have cracked as they've fallen back down, rotating the baking sheet from front to back midway through the baking time. Remove the baking sheet from the oven and let the cookies cool to room temperature for about 2 minutes. Use a metal spatula to transfer them to a cooling rack to cool completely.

· While the cookies are baking, roll 6 more balls and place them on the second baking sheet. While the first batch is cooling, put the second batch of cookies in the oven and bake them as you did the first batch. Repeat with the third batch of cookies.

· Store the cookies in an airtight container at room temperature for up to 1 week or freeze for up to 3 months.

Classic Roll-Out Sugar Cookies

**Makes about 5 dozen
(2-inch) cookies**

Every year, my son and I make these cookies together. I make the dough and cut out the cookies, and then he decorates them with colored sugar. This recipe makes a big batch, because I like to give the baked cookies away. If the yield is more than you need, bake off all of the cookies and freeze them to enjoy another time. You can snack on them straight from the freezer or bring them to room temperature.

Please note: The yield and baking time for this recipe are for cookies made with a 2-inch round cookie cutter; if you use a different size or shape of cutter, the yield and baking time may change. To know if your cookies are done, rely on the indicators given in the recipe, rather than the time.

If this dough is too cold, it will crack when you roll it out. If it is too warm, it will stick to the rolling pin and work surface. You want to soften it until it is just pliable. If you soften it too much, return it to the refrigerator to firm it up a bit before you start or continue rolling.

Note You will need a 2-inch round cookie cutter to make this. If you are icing the cookies, you will need at least one large disposable pastry bag and one ⅛-inch round icing tip.

All-purpose flour	4½ cups plus more for dusting	540 grams
Baking powder	1 teaspoon	5 grams
Fine sea salt	1 teaspoon	6 grams
Unsalted butter, cubed and softened (see page 379)	20 tablespoons (2 sticks plus 4 tablespoons)	283 grams
Granulated sugar	2 cups	400 grams
Large eggs	2	100 grams
Pure vanilla extract	2 teaspoons	10 grams
Optional for decorating		
Colored or plain sanding sugar	about 2 tablespoons for sprinkling	
Royal Icing (recipe follows)	2 recipes	
Sprinkles, for decorating (optional)		

Make the dough

· Whisk the flour, baking powder, and salt together in a medium bowl and set aside.

· Combine the butter and sugar in the bowl of a stand mixer. Fit the mixer with the paddle attachment, and beat on medium speed for 2 to 3 minutes, stopping to scrape down the sides of the bowl with a rubber spatula once or twice, until the mixture is light and fluffy. Add the eggs one at a time, mixing on medium speed until each egg is blended in and stopping to scrape down the sides of the bowl before adding the next egg. Add the vanilla and mix to combine. Add the dry ingredients and mix on low speed until no flour is visible, stopping to scrape down the sides of the bowl as needed.

▪ Lay two long sheets of plastic wrap in a crisscross formation on your work surface. Scoop the dough out of the bowl onto the center of the cross of plastic wrap and use your hands to pat the dough into a rectangular block. Loosely wrap the dough in the plastic, leaving a few inches of slack all around. Run a rolling pin over the dough to roll it out in the plastic, to a ½- to 1-inch-thick rectangle. Turn the dough out onto your work surface and wrap it loosely in plastic wrap. (For more detail, see Wrapping Dough, page xl.) Place the dough in the refrigerator for at least 2 hours and up to 3 days to firm up.

Prepare to bake the cookies

▪ Arrange the oven racks so one is in the top third of the oven and the other is in the bottom third. Preheat the oven to 350°F.

▪ Line two baking sheets with parchment paper.

Roll out and cut the dough

▪ Remove the block of dough from the refrigerator. Unwrap the dough, and use a bench knife or serrated knife to cut it in half. Set one half on your work surface to soften until it is barely pliable but not soft, about 10 minutes. Rewrap the other half of the dough and return it to the refrigerator.

▪ Lightly dust a large flat work surface with flour and place the block of dough on the floured surface. Lightly dust the top of the dough and the rolling pin with flour. Starting from the center of the dough and working outward with the rolling pin, roll out the dough to an even rectangle ⅜ inch thick, dusting the work surface, dough, and rolling pin as needed to keep the dough from sticking. (For more detailed instruction, see Rolling Dough 101, page 250.)

▪ Using a 2-inch cookie or biscuit cutter, cut circles from the dough, making the cuts close together to get as many cookies as possible from the dough. Use a small offset or metal spatula to lift the cookies off the work surface and onto the prepared baking sheets, leaving about 1 inch between them. Gather the scraps of dough, wrap them in plastic, and place them in the refrigerator to chill.

If you are decorating the cookies with sugar

▪ Sprinkle a light layer of sugar on the cookies. If you are decorating the cookies with royal icing, do not sprinkle sugar on them.

Bake the cookies

▪ Place one baking sheet on each oven rack and bake the cookies for 12 to 14 minutes, until the edges are lightly browned, rotating the baking sheets from front to back and from one rack to the other halfway through the baking time. Remove the baking sheets from the oven and set aside to cool for about 2 minutes. Use a metal spatula to lift the cookies from the baking sheet and transfer them to a cooling rack to cool completely.

• Remove the second block of dough from the refrigerator and roll it out and cut the cookies in the same way. Add the scraps to the first ball of scraps. Gather the dough scraps and chill them. Roll the scraps once and cut and bake them as you did the previous batches. Discard any scraps remaining after cutting those.

• Store the cookies in an airtight container at room temperature for up to 1 week or freeze for up to 3 months.

If you are icing the cookies

• After the cookies have baked and cooled, line two (or more) baking sheets with parchment paper. Arrange 12 cookies on each pan. If you don't have enough baking sheets to hold all of the cookies, lay the parchment on a flat work surface and place the cookies on the paper. Fit a large disposable pastry bag with a ⅛-inch round icing tip, such as Ateco #6. Have a small offset spatula nearby to clean up the cookies.

Pipe the outlines of the cookies

• Spoon half of the icing into the pastry bag. Working with one cookie at a time, hold the piping bag about ¼ inch above the cookie and gently squeeze the pastry bag to slowly pipe the icing around the perimeter of the cookie, leaving a ⅛-inch border free of icing. If you make a mistake, use the offset spatula to remove the icing from the cookie and start again. Once you have outlined all of the cookies, if you still have icing in the bag, empty the icing out into the bowl with the icing of that color. Remove and rinse out the tip and return it to the pastry bag.

"Flood" the cookies

• Gradually add enough water (a teaspoon or two) to the remaining icing in the mixing bowl, stirring as you add it, until the icing starts to run like honey. Fill the pastry bag with the flooding icing, using the end of the bag to "plug" the tip so the icing doesn't leak out of the bag while you're filling it.

Flood is a term used for filling in the outline when decorating cookies or cakes.

• Squeeze a big dollop of icing into the middle of one cookie and drag the pastry tip through the icing to spread it toward the piped edges. Continue squeezing icing out onto the cookie and using the tip to spread it until the icing floods the entire surface of the cookie.

• If you are using sprinkles, sprinkle them on the cookie while the icing is wet.

• Line a baking sheet or work surface with parchment paper and put the cookie on the parchment. Continue flooding the remaining cookies with the remaining icing and adding them to the parchment-lined baking sheet. When one baking sheet is full, line another with parchment paper and place the iced cookies on that.

At home, I have a small work space, so I squeeze as many cookies onto each baking sheet as possible without stacking them and messing up the icing. You could also move the cookies to a dining table. Find what works best for you given your space.

▪ Let the icing dry and harden overnight before storing the cookies. Place the cookies in an airtight container, separated by sheets of parchment paper. Cover and store at room temperature for up to 2 weeks.

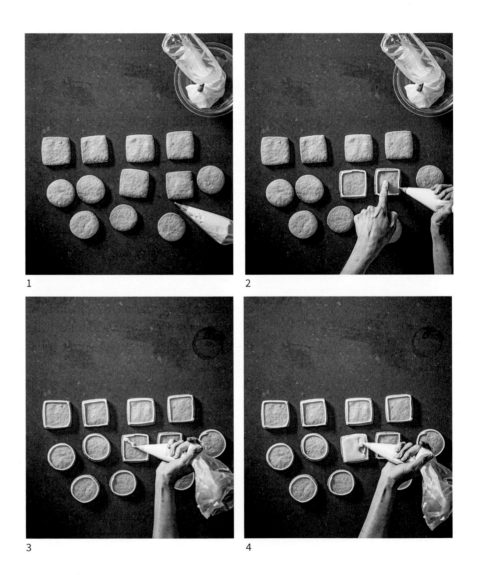

1

2

3

4

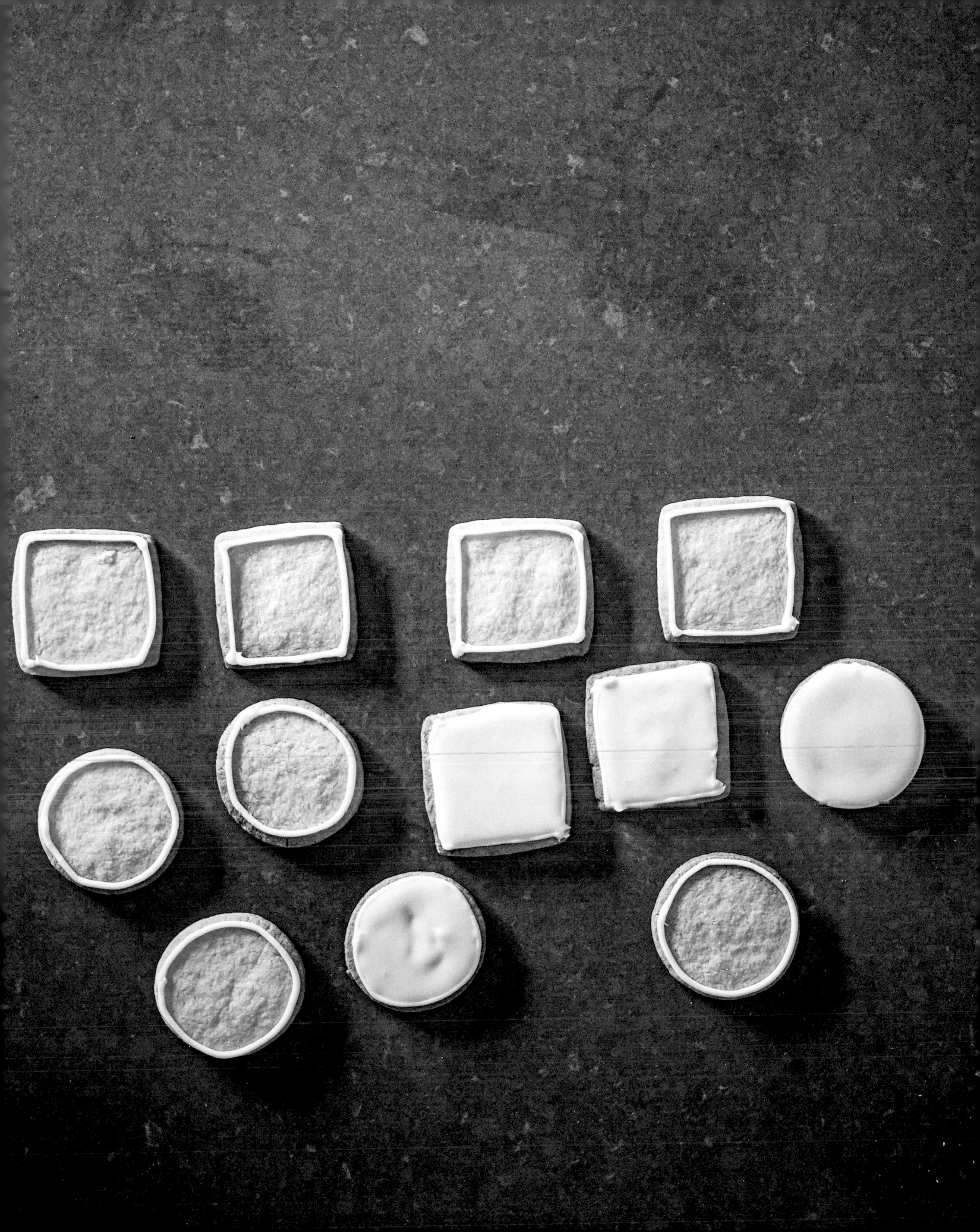

Royal Icing

**Makes enough for
2 dozen (2-inch)
cookies**

Royal icing is a decorative icing made with egg whites, confectioners' sugar, and water. It is smooth when it sets up, so you get really pretty, professional-looking cookies. But royal icing can be tricky to work with; the main consideration is the consistency. You make a stiff icing to pipe the outline of the cookies, and then thin the icing to flood or fill in the outline to cover the surface of the cookies. The perfect flooding consistency is thicker than maple syrup but thinner than honey; it needs to be thin enough that it will pool and move around nicely to flood the cookies, but not so much that it runs all over the place, out of control. You may have to make a few batches of icing before you get it just right.

The other "trick" to beautiful iced cookies is that you use the correct pastry tip. If the tip is too small, you'll hurt your wrist trying to squeeze the icing out of it. If it's too big, the icing will spill out of it too fast, resulting in messy-looking cookies. I recommend a tip that has a round ⅛-inch opening.

In terms of colored icing, I keep it simple. I make one batch of icing at a time and color each one individually. I generally make only two colors; rarely more than three. You will need two batches of icing to color the entire batch of classic sugar cookies, so this works out perfectly.

This recipe uses uncooked egg whites, and there is always a slight risk for them to contain food-borne pathogens. To avoid any potential risk, use pasteurized egg whites, which are available at most grocery stores.

Confectioners' sugar	1 (16-ounce) box	454 grams
Large egg whites	2	65 grams
Water	1 teaspoon plus more as needed	5 grams
Food coloring (optional)		

Combine the confectioners' sugar, egg whites, and 1 teaspoon of the water in the bowl of a stand mixer. Fit the mixer with the paddle attachment and mix on medium speed for 30 seconds to 1 minute, until the icing is smooth. Remove the paddle and scrape the icing off with a butter knife or small offset spatula. If you want to color the icing, add one or two drops of food coloring and stir with a rubber spatula until no streaks of color remain. Continue to add additional drops to your liking.

Pistachio Biscotti

Makes 4 to 5 dozen biscotti

My favorite biscotti hands down are dry, crunchy biscotti. What makes biscotti as hard and crunchy as they are has to do with the proportion of wet to dry ingredients. These biscotti are unusual in that the dough contains cookie crumbs. Because the cookie crumbs contain butter, they impart more flavor (and also more texture) than if you just added flour in their place. I call for you to slice these really thin, which makes the cookies delicate and crispy. I make the crumbs from Classic Roll-Out Sugar Cookies (page 391), but you could also use store-bought all-butter sugar cookies.

For the dough		
Large eggs	2	100 grams
Water	½ cup	118 grams
Sugar cookie crumbs (page 391; or store-bought)	⅔ cup (from about 5 cookies)	90 grams
All-purpose flour	4 cups plus 2 tablespoons	498 grams
Pistachios (preferably Sicilian)	2⅔ cups	347 grams
Granulated sugar	1¾ cups	350 grams
Baking powder	1½ teaspoons	8 grams
Baking soda	1 teaspoon	5 grams
Fine sea salt	2 teaspoons	12 grams
For baking the biscotti		
Granulated sugar	1½ tablespoons for sprinkling	20 grams

Get prepared
- Arrange the oven racks so one is in the center position. Preheat the oven to 350°F.
- Line a baking sheet with parchment paper.

Make the dough
- Separate the yolk and white of one of the eggs into individual small bowls. Set the bowl with the egg white aside.
- Add the whole egg and water to the bowl with the egg yolk and whisk to break up the yolks.
- Put the cookie crumbs in the bowl of a stand mixer. Fit the mixer with the paddle attachment and add the flour, pistachios, sugar, baking powder, baking soda, and salt and mix on low speed to combine. With the mixer running, add the egg and water mixture and mix for about 2 minutes, until the dough has formed clumps the size of large marbles.

Shape the logs
- Lay a sheet of parchment paper on your work surface.
- Scoop half of the dough (about 720 grams) out of the mixer bowl onto the parchment-lined baking sheet. Roll the dough into a log 3 inches wide,

12 inches long, and 1 inch thick. Repeat, forming a second log on the same baking sheet. Rearrange the logs if necessary, making sure there are 3 inches between them.

Bake and slice the biscotti

- Whisk the egg white in the small bowl. Brush the tops of the biscotti logs with the egg white and sprinkle with the sugar.
- Place the baking sheet on the center rack to bake the logs for 35 minutes, rotating the baking sheets from front to back halfway through the baking time. Remove the logs from the oven and let cool to room temperature.

Warm biscotti loaves will crumble when you slice them. As the loaves cool, the water escapes in the form of steam, and at the same time, the structure of the logs continues to set. The cooled, set loaves won't crumble when sliced.

- Reduce the oven temperature to 250°F. Arrange the oven racks so one is in the top third of the oven and the other is in the bottom third.
- Slide one log onto a cutting board and use a serrated knife to slice the loaf at a 90-degree angle into ⅜-inch- to ½-inch-thick slices. Lay the slices, cut sides up, in a single layer on a baking sheet and repeat with the second loaf, laying those slices on a second baking sheet. (There is no need to leave space between the cookies as they are not going to spread like many cookies do; the point of the second baking is simply to dry them out.)

The key to cleanly sliced biscotti is to rest the knife where you want the slice and then to press down quickly.

Bake the sliced biscotti

- Return the biscotti to the oven and bake for 20 minutes. Remove the baking sheets from the oven and use tongs or your fingers to turn each biscotti. Return the baking sheets to the oven, rotating them from front to back and from one rack to the other. Bake the biscotti for an additional 15 to 20 minutes, until they are dry and crunchy. To test for doneness, remove one biscotti from the oven and place it on your work surface for about 5 minutes to cool down, then break it open to see if it is dry all the way through. If the biscotti are not crunchy enough, bake for an additional 5 minutes. Remove the biscotti from the oven and set aside to cool to room temperature.
- Store the biscotti in an airtight container at room temperature for up to 1 week or freeze for up to 3 months.

Raspberry Jam Bars

Makes 28 bars

I was in Copenhagen a few years ago teaching a baking class at Meyers Bageri, a bakery there owned by Claus Meyer, one of the founders of Noma. There they made these traditional jam bars, called Hindbærsnitter, that I couldn't stop eating. Before I left, I asked them for the recipe, and they were kind enough to share it with me. These are not like the "open-face" jam bars I was familiar with. The jam is sandwiched between two thin sheets of dough, almost like a Pop-Tart, with a crust made from almond flour. So, you can even fool yourself into thinking they're a "breakfast cookie." Put whatever jam you want inside. I like raspberry for both the flavor and the bright red color. Often when I am working with a sticky dough, which this is, I roll it out between two sheets of parchment paper. For these, I go the extra step of creating a paper packet for the dough, which ensures that it is rolled out to a specific dimension and even thickness. If you don't mind jam bars with uneven edges, skip the step of creating the paper packets and simply roll the dough out to a ten-inch square.

Large egg	1	50 grams
All-purpose flour	3 cups	360 grams
Granulated sugar	1 cup	200 grams
Almond flour	⅔ cup	67 grams
Fine sea salt	1 teaspoon	6 grams
Vanilla bean	1	
Unsalted butter, cubed	20 tablespoons (2 sticks plus 4 tablespoons)	283 grams
Large egg white	1	
Raspberry Jam (page 350; or store-bought)	1½ cups	435 grams
Granulated sugar	about 2 tablespoons for sprinkling	26 grams

Get prepared

- Cut a piece of parchment paper from a roll to 24 inches long. Fold the edges inward to create the 10 x 10-inch paper packet. Repeat, creating a second 10-inch-square parchment-paper packet.
- Whisk the egg in a small bowl to break up the yolk.

Make the dough

- Combine the all-purpose flour, sugar, almond flour, and salt in the bowl of a stand mixer. Split the vanilla bean down the middle with a small sharp knife and use the knife to scrape the seeds out of the bean. Add the seeds to the mixer bowl. (Use the bean to make Vanilla Sugar, page 219, or discard it.) Fit the mixer with the paddle attachment and mix on low speed for about 30 seconds, just to combine the ingredients. Add the butter and mix on low speed until the mixture is the texture of coarse cornmeal, with no chunks of butter remaining, but not so long that the dough begins to clump together. Turn off the mixer, add the egg, and mix on low speed until a dough forms around the paddle, 2 to 3 minutes, stopping to scrape down the paddle once or twice.

- Turn the dough out of the bowl onto your work surface and use a bench knife or serrated knife to cut it in half; each half will be approximately 475 grams (about 17 ounces). Place one half of the dough in the center of one of the paper packets and use your fingertips to pat the dough into a square. Fold the edges of the packet inward to cover the dough. Flip the packet so the seams of paper are facing down and run a rolling pin over it to press the dough to the edges of the packet, forming a 10-inch square of dough of even thickness. Repeat, wrapping the remaining dough in parchment and rolling it to create an identical packet. Place both dough packets on a flat surface in your refrigerator and refrigerate for 1 to 2 hours, until thoroughly chilled, and up to overnight.

Prepare to bake the jam bars
- Arrange the oven racks so one is in the center position. Preheat the oven to 350°F.
- Line a baking sheet with parchment paper.

Form the jam bars
- Whisk the egg white in a small bowl to break it up. Remove one dough packet from the refrigerator, unwrap it, and place it on the prepared baking sheet. Brush the egg white in a ½-inch-wide border around the edges of the dough. Spoon the jam onto the dough and use a small offset spatula to spread it evenly over the surface, leaving the ½-inch border brushed with egg white free of jam. Unwrap the second packet of dough and gently place the dough on top of the packet. Use your fingertips to gently press along the edges of the dough to seal the top and bottom together. If any jam has squeezed out the sides of the sealed dough, use a damp paper towel to wipe off the jam so it doesn't burn in the oven.
- Press the edges of the top and bottom sheets of dough together with the back side of a fork to further seal them. Again, if any jam squeezes out, use a damp paper towel to wipe it off. Pierce the dough all over with the tines of the fork, making sure to get all the way through both the top and bottom layers of dough. Brush the dough with the remaining egg white and sprinkle with the sugar.

Bake the jam bars
- Place the baking sheet on the center rack of the oven to bake the jam bars for 35 to 40 minutes, rotating them front to back halfway through the baking time so they bake evenly, until the top is light golden brown and the edges are deep golden brown; some spots may darken even further from the jam that has

leaked out. Remove the baking sheet from the oven and place it on a cooling rack until the bars have cooled completely.

▪ Set the baking sheet on a cutting board. Holding onto the parchment paper, gently slide the jam bars onto the work surface. Using a large knife, cut into 28 bars. Store the bars in an airtight container at room temperature for up to 1 week or freeze for up to 3 months.

To cut bars, blondies, brownies, slab pies, or any other rectangular baked goods into even pieces, first make a cut down the center, then make an even number of cuts on either side of the center. Rotate the pan 90 degrees and do the same thing, making a cut down the center that is perpendicular to the first cuts, and then making an even number of cuts on either side of the center line.

Chocolate Shortbread

Makes 18 to 20 (2-inch) cookies

These shortbread cookies are very chocolaty and not too sweet; they make a great afternoon snacking cookie. I also use the cookies to make ice cream sandwiches and grind them into crumbs to use in Chocolate Babka (page 100).

All-purpose flour	1⅓ cups plus more for dusting	160 grams
Cocoa powder (preferably Valrhona)	⅔ cup	57 grams
Baking soda	⅛ teaspoon	1 gram
Fine sea salt	½ teaspoon	3 grams
Unsalted butter, cubed and softened (see page 379)	11 tablespoons (1 stick plus 3 tablespoons)	155 grams
Granulated sugar	½ cup	100 grams

Make the dough

· Put the flour, cocoa powder, baking soda, and salt in a medium bowl and whisk to combine the ingredients. Set aside.

· Place the butter and sugar in the bowl of a stand mixer. Fit the mixer with the paddle attachment and beat on medium speed for 2 to 3 minutes, stopping to scrape down the sides of the bowl with a rubber spatula once or twice, until the mixture is light and fluffy. Turn off the mixer, scrape down the sides of the bowl with a rubber spatula, and add the dry ingredients. Mix on low speed until the dough comes together and wraps around the paddle.

· Lay two long sheets of plastic wrap in a crisscross formation on your work surface. Scoop the dough out of the bowl onto the center of the cross of plastic wrap and use your hands to pat the dough into a rectangular block. Loosely wrap the dough in the plastic, leaving a few inches of slack all around. Run a rolling pin over the dough to roll it out in the plastic, to a ½-inch-thick rectangle. (For more detail, see Wrapping Dough, page xl.) The dough does not need to be refrigerated before rolling it out (it is already a stiff dough), but if you are planning ahead, you can refrigerate the dough for up to 3 days.

Prepare to bake the shortbread

· Arrange the oven racks so one is in the top third of the oven and the other is in the bottom third. Preheat the oven to 325°F.

· Line two baking sheets with parchment paper.

Roll out and cut the shortbread

· Lightly dust a large flat work surface with flour. Remove the dough from the refrigerator, remove and discard the plastic wrap, and place the dough on the floured surface.

- Lightly dust the top of the dough and the rolling pin with flour. Starting from the center of the dough and working outward with the rolling pin, roll out the dough to an even rectangle ⅜ inch thick, dusting the work surface, dough, and rolling pin as needed to keep the dough from sticking. (For more detailed instruction, see Rolling Dough 101, page 250.)
- If you are making the cookies to serve and eat on their own, use a straight-edge and a pastry wheel or long knife to trim the top and bottom edges of the dough to create straight lines; reserve the scraps. Cut the dough into 2-inch squares. Use an offset spatula to lift the dough squares up and transfer them to the parchment-lined baking sheets, leaving about 2 inches between each cookie. Prick each square several times with the tines of a fork. If you are making the cookies to turn into crumbs, use a pastry wheel or long knife to cut the dough into roughly 2-inch pieces and prick them with the tines of a fork.

Bake the shortbread
- Place one baking sheet on each oven rack and bake the shortbread for about 17 minutes, until the tops are dry to the touch and the cookies have begun to fall after rising, rotating the baking sheets from front to back and from one rack to the other halfway through the baking time. Remove the cookies from the oven and set them aside for about 2 minutes to cool on the baking sheets. Use an offset spatula or a metal spatula to transfer the shortbread to a cooling rack to cool completely.
- While the cookies are baking, gather the scraps and roll them into a ball. Pat the dough into a thin block, wrap it in plastic, and place it in the refrigerator to chill. Roll out, cut, and bake the scraps as you did the first batch.
- Store the shortbread in an airtight container at room temperature for up to 1 week or freeze for up to 3 months.

Hazelnut Linzer Cookies with Pineapple Jam

Makes 20 to 22 sandwich cookies

Not long ago, I went to a small, beautiful tea shop called Té Company in the West Village in Manhattan and tried their delicious little sandwich cookies filled with pineapple jam. I had never tasted pineapple jam like this before. It was infused with rosemary; I thought it was very special, particularly paired with hazelnut cookies. This is my version of those cookies. It is similar to a linzer cookie, but the cookie itself is crisper and not as tender as a traditional linzer cookie. These filled sandwich cookies are really good the day after they're assembled, but after two days, the filling turns the cookies soggy and they begin to go downhill. Use Raspberry Jam (page 350), Blood Orange Jam (page 224), Lemon Rosemary Curd (page 288), or your favorite store-bought jam, if one of those is more convenient or more to your liking than the pineapple jam in this recipe.

Note You will need a 2-inch round cookie or biscuit cutter and a smaller cutter to make these.

Hazelnuts	1 heaping cup	140 grams
All-purpose flour	2⅓ cups	280 grams
Baking powder	1 teaspoon	5 grams
Fine sea salt	1 teaspoon	6 grams
Granulated sugar	1¾ cups	350 grams
Unsalted butter, cubed and softened (see page 379)	16 tablespoons (2 sticks)	226 grams
Large egg	1	50 grams
Pure vanilla extract	1 teaspoon	5 grams
Pineapple Jam (recipe follows)	1 cup	

Get prepared

· Arrange the oven racks so one is in the center position. Preheat the oven to 300°F.

· Spread the hazelnuts on a baking sheet and toast them in the oven for 20 to 25 minutes, shaking the pan once during that time for even toasting, until the nuts are golden brown and fragrant. Remove the baking sheet from the oven and set aside to cool the nuts to room temperature.

· Put the nuts in the center of a clean kitchen towel, gather the towel to close it, and rub the nuts in the towel between your hands to remove as much of the skins as possible. Open the towel, discard the skins, and transfer the hazelnuts to the bowl of a food processor fitted with a metal blade.

· While the nuts are cooling, whisk the flour, baking powder, and salt together in a medium bowl.

Make the dough

• Add ½ cup (100 grams) of the sugar to the bowl of the food processor and pulse until the nuts are very finely ground, 30 seconds to 1 minute. (It is important to pulse rather than run the machine continuously, so you don't end up with hazelnut butter.)

• Transfer the hazelnut-sugar crumbs to the bowl of a stand mixer. Add the butter and the remaining 1¼ cups (250 grams) sugar. Fit the mixer with the paddle attachment and beat for about 20 seconds on the lowest speed to prevent the sugar-nut mixture from flying out of the mixer. Increase the speed to medium and beat for 2 to 3 minutes, until light and fluffy. Turn off the mixer and scrape down the sides of the bowl with a rubber spatula. Add the egg and vanilla and mix on medium speed until the egg is completely incorporated. Stop, scrape down the sides of the bowl, and add the dry ingredients. Mix on low speed until no flour is visible, stopping to scrape down the sides of the bowl once during this time.

• Lay two long sheets of plastic wrap in a crisscross formation on your work surface. Use a plastic bowl scraper to scoop the dough out of the bowl onto the center of the cross of plastic wrap and use your hands to pat the dough into a rectangular block. Loosely wrap the dough in the plastic, leaving a few inches of slack all around. Run a rolling pin over the dough to roll it out in the plastic to a ½- to 1-inch-thick rectangle. (For more detail, see Wrapping Dough, page xl.) Place the dough in the refrigerator to chill for 1 hour, and up to 2 days.

Prepare to bake the cookies

• Arrange the oven racks so one is in the top third of the oven and the other is in the bottom third. Preheat the oven to 325°F.

• Line two baking sheets with parchment paper.

Roll out and cut the cookies

• Remove the dough from the refrigerator, unwrap the dough, and use a bowl scraper or knife to cut the dough in half. Rewrap and return one half of the dough to the refrigerator.

• Lightly dust a large flat work surface with flour. Place the dough on the floured surface, lightly dust the top of the dough and a rolling pin with flour, and starting from the center and working outward, roll the dough out to a ⅛-inch-thick rectangle. (For more detailed instruction, see Rolling Dough 101, page 250.)

• Using a 2-inch cookie or biscuit cutter, cut circles from the dough, making the cuts close together to get as many cookies as possible from the dough. Use a small offset or metal spatula to lift the cookies off the work surface and onto the prepared baking sheets, leaving about 2 inches between each cookie. Gather the scraps of dough into a ball and set aside.

• Remove the second half of the dough from the refrigerator and roll and cut the dough in the same way that you did for the first batch. After cutting all of the circles, use a small circular cutter to cut smaller circles, like doughnut holes, in the center of each of the 2-inch rounds. Use a small offset or metal spatula to lift the circles with the holes in them off the work surface and onto the prepared baking sheets, leaving about 2 inches between each cookie.

▪ Gather the scraps, add them to the first bunch of scraps, and pat them into a thin disk. Wrap the dough in plastic and place it in the refrigerator for at least 2 hours and up to 3 days to firm up.

Bake the cookies

▪ Place one baking sheet on each oven rack and bake the cookies until they are golden brown around the edges, 15 to 18 minutes for the "doughnut" cookies, and 18 to 20 minutes for the whole rounds, rotating them from front to back and from one rack to the other halfway through the baking time. Remove the baking sheets from the oven and let the cookies cool on the baking sheets for 5 to 10 minutes. Use a small offset or metal spatula to transfer the cookies to a cooling rack to cool to room temperature.

▪ Roll out, cut, and bake the scraps, cutting an equal number of tops and bottoms.

Assemble the cookies

▪ Set up an assembly line with full round cookies, the jam, and then the cookies with the holes cut out all laid out in a line.

▪ Spoon 1 heaping teaspoon of jam on the bottom (flat) side of one full cookie round and use a small offset spatula to spread the jam over the surface, leaving a small border around the edge with no jam. Place a "doughnut" cookie on top with the flat side of the cookie facing the jam, and gently press on the top to smush the jam down in an even layer. Repeat, using the rest of the cookies and jam to assemble the rest of the cookie sandwiches.

▪ Store the cookies in an airtight container at room temperature for up to 1 week or freeze for up to 3 months.

Pineapple Jam

**Makes about
2½ cups**

Limes	3	
Ripe pineapple	1 medium to large	
Granulated sugar	1½ cups	300 grams
Water	1 cup	235 grams
Fresh rosemary	2 sprigs	
Fine sea salt	½ teaspoon	3 grams

- Place two small plates in the freezer. (You'll use these later to test the jam for doneness.)
- Use a fine Microplane to grate the zest of one lime into a bowl, grating only the outermost, bright-colored layer.
- Cut off the top and bottom of the pineapple, remove the skin, and discard. Cut the pineapple into quarters and cut out and discard the cores. Turn each quarter onto its side and slice it into ⅛- to ¼-inch-thick wedges. Place the pineapple in the bowl of a food processor fitted with a metal blade and process to a rough pulp with no large chunks remaining. Transfer the pulp to a medium saucepan. Add the sugar, water, lime zest, and the juice from the remaining 2 limes. Bring the mixture to a boil over medium-high heat and cook, stirring frequently, for 20 to 30 minutes, until the jam is thick enough that you can draw a clean line in it with a wooden spoon across the bottom of the pan. Reduce the heat to low, add the rosemary sprigs and the salt, and cook for 10 to 15 minutes more, stirring frequently so the jam doesn't burn on the bottom, until the jam is very thick.
- To test to see if the jam has set up sufficiently, remove one of the plates from the freezer. Place a spoonful of jam on the plate and return the plate to the freezer for 2 minutes, then gently slide your finger through the jam; if the skin on top of the jam wrinkles, it's done. If not, put the jam back on the heat and cook it for a few more minutes, then test again in the same way using the second plate you put in the freezer.
- Remove the saucepan from the heat, pour the jam into a heat-proof storage container, and set aside to cool to room temperature with the lid slightly ajar. Cover and refrigerate the jam until you are ready to use it, or for up to several months.

Spiced Graham Crackers with Chocolate Marshmallows

Makes 3 to 4 dozen graham crackers

Even though most of us have been eating graham crackers all our lives, many people are surprised to learn that there is even such a thing as homemade graham crackers. I put cinnamon and cayenne pepper in mine, so they're a little bit spicy, but obviously you can skip the cayenne if you want. I make these most often when I am making s'mores with Chocolate Marshmallows (page 415), which I do for my family when we go camping, or in the winter, to toast the marshmallows in the fireplace.

I call for you to roll out this dough between two sheets of parchment paper. It is a sticky dough that gets even stickier as it warms up in the process of being rolled out.

All-purpose flour	2 cups plus more for dusting	240 grams
Whole-wheat pastry flour	¾ cup	79 grams
Dark brown sugar	1 cup (lightly packed)	200 grams
Ground cinnamon	1 tablespoon	6 grams
Baking soda	1 teaspoon	5 grams
Fine sea salt	1 teaspoon	6 grams
Cayenne pepper	¼ teaspoon	2 grams
Unsalted butter, cold and cubed	8 tablespoons (1 stick)	113 grams
Mild-flavored honey (such as wildflower or clover)	⅓ cup	105 grams
Whole milk	¼ cup	60 grams
Pure vanilla extract	2 teaspoons	10 grams
Granulated sugar	about 2 tablespoons for sprinkling	26 grams

Make the dough

· Combine the all-purpose flour, whole-wheat pastry flour, brown sugar, cinnamon, baking soda, salt, and cayenne in the bowl of a stand mixer. Fit the mixer with the paddle attachment and mix on low speed to combine. Turn off the mixer. Add the butter and mix on low speed until the mixture is the consistency of coarse cornmeal and no chunks of butter remain, about 2 minutes, stopping once to scrape down the sides of the bowl with a rubber spatula. Turn off the mixer.

· Whisk the honey, milk, and vanilla in a small bowl and add to the mixer bowl. Mix on low speed until the dough comes together and no flour is visible, 1 to 2 minutes, stopping once during that time to scrape down the sides of the bowl with a rubber spatula. Turn off the mixer.

· Lay two long sheets of plastic wrap in a crisscross formation on your work surface. Use a plastic bowl scraper to scoop the dough out of the bowl onto the center of the cross of plastic wrap and use your hands to pat the dough into a rectangular block. Loosely wrap the dough in the plastic, leaving a few inches of slack all around. Run a rolling pin over the dough to roll it out in the plastic to a ½- to 1-inch-thick rectangle. Refrigerate the dough for at least 2 hours, until it is firm, and for up to 2 days.

Roll out and cut the dough
- Remove the dough from the refrigerator, unwrap the dough, and use a bench knife or serrated knife to cut it in half. Rewrap half of the dough and return it to the refrigerator.
- Lay a sheet of parchment paper on a large flat work surface and dust it lightly with all-purpose flour. Place the dough on the parchment and dust the top lightly with flour. Place another sheet of parchment on top of the dough. Working as quickly as possible to prevent the dough from warming up and becoming sticky, roll out the dough between the sheets of parchment paper to ⅛ inch thick. (A few times during the rolling process, quickly lift the top sheet of parchment paper, dust the dough with flour, and lay the paper back down. Flip the dough over and do the same on the other side. If the dough becomes too sticky to roll, place it, sandwiched between the two sheets of parchment paper, in the refrigerator to chill until it firms up slightly before continuing to roll it out.) Place the dough, sandwiched in the parchment paper, in the refrigerator. Remove the second half of dough from the refrigerator and roll it out and refrigerate it as you did the first batch. Lay the second sheet of dough on top of the first sheet in the refrigerator. Chill the dough for at least 30 minutes, until it is firm.
- Remove one sheet of dough from the refrigerator. Peel off the top sheet of parchment paper and then lay it back on the dough. Flip the dough over and remove the remaining sheet of parchment paper; use it to line a baking sheet with the clean side facing up.

The reason you remove the parchment paper only to set it back on the dough is so that the dough is not stuck to the paper; this makes it easier to lift off of the paper after it is rolled out.

- Using a straightedge and pastry wheel or long knife, trim the top and bottom edges of the dough to create straight lines; reserve the scraps and set them aside. Cut the dough into 2½-inch squares, adding the outermost strips with uneven edges to the trimmings. Use an offset spatula to lift the dough squares up and transfer them to the parchment-lined baking sheet, fitting as many squares as you can on the paper in a single layer. Place the baking sheet with the squares in the refrigerator while you cut the second sheet of dough.

Note that graham cracker dough is very sticky, so it is more important to work quickly than it is to measure impeccably.

- Remove the baking sheet with the cut dough from the refrigerator and use the offset spatula to lift the squares off the work surface and onto the parchment paper that you laid on the first layer of cookies. Return the baking sheet to the refrigerator to chill the graham squares for at least 30 minutes and as long as overnight.
- Gather the scraps of dough into a ball and pat the ball into a thin block with your hands. Place the dough in the refrigerator to chill for 15 to 20 minutes, until it firms up. Remove the dough from the refrigerator and roll and cut it as you did the others. Discard any remaining scraps.

Prepare to bake the graham crackers

- Arrange the oven racks so one is in the top third of the oven and the other is in the bottom third. Preheat the oven to 325°F.
- Line two baking sheets with parchment paper.

Bake the graham crackers

- Remove the baking sheet with the graham cracker squares from the refrigerator. Transfer 8 cookies to each of the prepared baking sheets, spacing them evenly. Prick the squares with the tines of a fork and sprinkle them with a thin layer of granulated sugar. Return the remaining dough squares to the refrigerator.
- Place one baking sheet on each oven rack and bake the graham crackers for 16 to 18 minutes, until they are crispy and light golden brown around the edges, rotating the baking sheets from front to back and from one rack to the other halfway through the baking time. Remove the graham crackers from the oven and set them aside to cool for 5 to 10 minutes on the baking sheet. Use a spatula to move the graham crackers onto a cooling rack to cool completely. The graham crackers should be crunchy throughout once they have cooled. If they are not, return them to the oven and bake for an additional 2 to 3 minutes.
- Bake the remaining cookies in the same way.
- Store the graham crackers in an airtight container at room temperature for up to 1 week or freeze for up to 3 months.

Chocolate Marshmallows

Makes 2 to 3 dozen marshmallows

I love s'mores, but my pet peeve is when the chocolate doesn't melt all the way through from the heat of the marshmallow. My solution to this problem is to put the chocolate *in* the marshmallow, eliminating the chocolate bar altogether, which is how these marshmallows came about. The secret to getting these marshmallows so chocolaty is that I cook the cocoa powder with the sugar syrup. This is something Gina DePalma taught me when I worked at Babbo. When we made chocolate sorbetto, Gina was insistent that we simmer cocoa powder for at least fifteen minutes. If it wasn't cooked long enough, she said the sorbetto didn't taste as good, and she would get angry—and you didn't want to face Gina when she was angry in the kitchen!

Marshmallows are set up with gelatin, which is derived from collagen. Gelatin is sold in the form of powder and sheets. I call for powdered gelatin because it is more widely available to the home cook. It needs to be rehydrated before using it, so you will see that step in this recipe.

Note You will need an 8-inch square baking pan to make this and a candy thermometer.

Nonstick cooking spray		
Cold water	1 cup	235 grams
Powdered gelatin	3 packets	22 grams
Granulated sugar	2⅓ cups	467 grams
Light corn syrup	½ cup	158 grams
Cocoa powder (preferably Valrhona)	½ cup	43 grams
Mild-flavored honey (such as wildflower or clover)	2 tablespoons	40 grams
Fine sea salt	¼ teaspoon	2 grams
Pure vanilla extract	1 teaspoon	5 grams
For dusting		
Cocoa powder (preferably Valrhona)	3 tablespoons	22 grams
Confectioners' sugar	2 teaspoons	5 grams

Get prepared

• Spray an 8-inch square baking pan with nonstick cooking spray. Line the pan with aluminum foil and use your hands to smooth out the foil as much as possible. Spray the foil generously with nonstick cooking spray.

Make the marshmallow

• Pour ½ cup (118 grams) of the water into the bowl of a stand mixer. Fit the mixer with the whisk attachment and sprinkle the gelatin over the water. Set the bowl on the mixer stand and let it rest for about 5 minutes to hydrate the gelatin.

- Put the granulated sugar, corn syrup, cocoa powder, honey, salt, and the remaining ½ cup (118 grams) water in a medium saucepan and whisk to combine the ingredients. Cook over medium-high heat until a candy thermometer reads 240°F, stirring occasionally. This is the end of what is known in candy making as the "soft-ball stage." Turn off the heat.

When I'm cooking sugar, I often use the thermometer I'm using to gauge the temperature to stir, so I don't dirty another tool.

- With the mixer on high, gradually add the sugar syrup, pouring it down the inside of the bowl so it doesn't splash against the whisk, shooting the syrup all over the sides of the bowl. Whip for 15 minutes, until the marshmallow cools to room temperature; check the temperature by cupping your hands around the bottom of the bowl. Turn off the mixer, add the vanilla, and mix on medium speed to distribute the vanilla.
- Scoop the marshmallow into the prepared pan with a rubber spatula or a large metal spoon. Spray a large offset spatula with nonstick cooking spray (or grease it with neutral-flavored oil) and use it to spread the marshmallow to the corners of the pan and even out the top.

Dust and cut the marshmallows

- Place the cocoa powder and confectioners' sugar in a small bowl and stir to combine. Transfer the mixture to a fine-mesh strainer and lightly dust the mixture over the top of the marshmallow to cover it with a light drift of the powder; reserve the remaining powder. Set the pan of marshmallow aside to rest, uncovered, for 8 to 10 hours to let the marshmallows set. (If you let the marshmallows rest any longer than about 10 hours, they will begin to get a dry crust.)
- Invert the pan to transfer the marshmallow to a cutting board. Remove and discard the aluminum foil and dust the bottom and sides with the remaining cocoa powder mixture. Use a long sharp knife to cut the marshmallow into 1½-inch cubes. Dust the sides of each marshmallow with the remaining coating powder.
- Store the marshmallows in an airtight container at room temperature for up to 1 week.

Fudgy Brownies

Makes 16 brownies

If there are two brownie camps—one made up of those who prefer cakey brownies and one of those who prefer fudgy—I definitely belong in the fudgy camp. I bake these at 400°F, which makes the outside edges cook faster than they would at the usual 350°F, resulting in brownies that are moist and fudgy on the inside with a delicate, thin crust on the outside. In my opinion, brownies just don't get any better; I've been making this recipe, which I originally adapted from one in Alice Medrich's book *Cookies and Brownies* for more than twenty years.

Note You will need an 8-inch square baking pan to make these.

Nonstick cooking spray		
Unsweetened chocolate	4 ounces (or ⅔ cup unsweetened chocolate chips)	113 grams
Unsalted butter, cubed	8 tablespoons (1 stick)	113 grams
Granulated sugar	1¼ cups	250 grams
Pure vanilla extract	1 teaspoon	5 grams
Fine sea salt	¼ teaspoon	3 grams
Large eggs	2	100 grams
All-purpose flour	½ cup	60 grams

Get prepared

- Arrange the oven racks so one is in the center position. Preheat the oven to 400°F.
- Spray the bottom and sides of an 8-inch square baking pan with nonstick cooking spray. Cut a piece of parchment paper 8 inches wide and 15 to 16 inches long. Lay the paper in the pan so it travels up and over two of the sides. Spray the paper with nonstick cooking spray.

Make the batter

- Pour 1 to 2 inches of water into the bottom of a small saucepan and choose a bowl that fits over the saucepan to make a double boiler. Make sure the water is not touching the bottom of the bowl; if it is, pour some water out. Bring the water to a boil over high heat, then reduce the heat to medium-low to maintain a gentle simmer.

When I am using a double boiler, while the water is coming to a simmer, I weigh the ingredients directly into the bowl that will rest on top of the simmering water.

- Unless you are using chocolate chips, roughly chop the chocolate. Put the butter and chocolate into the bowl of the double boiler and melt them, using

a heat-proof rubber spatula to stir and scrape down the sides of the bowl so the chocolate doesn't burn.

- Remove the bowl from the double boiler and wipe the bottom of the bowl so no water drips. Add the sugar and vanilla and whisk them in. Add the eggs one at a time and whisk until the batter is shiny and smooth, 1 to 2 minutes. Add the flour and stir with a rubber spatula until no flour is visible.

Bake the brownies

- Using a rubber spatula, transfer the batter to the prepared pan. Use the spatula to smooth out the top of the batter.
- Place the brownies on the center rack of the oven and bake for 20 minutes, rotating the pan from front to back halfway through the baking. Remove the brownies from the oven and cool on a cooling rack. The tops will appear dry, but the insides will remain fudgy if you poke the center with a toothpick or cake tester. Holding the sides of the parchment paper, lift the brownies out of the pan and place them on a cutting board. Using a large knife, cut the brownies into 16 equal pieces.
- Store the brownies in an airtight container at room temperature for up to 1 week or freeze for up to 3 months.

Milk Chocolate and Raspberry Blondies

Makes 2 dozen blondies

I'm not always fan of blondies. I often find them to be too sweet, but these are different. First, they are made with salted butter. Then they are dotted with raspberry jam, which is a bit tart, and sprinkled with sea salt, so they have a nice balance, and in my opinion, they really break the blondie mold.

Note You will need an 8- x 12-inch baking pan to make this.

Nonstick cooking spray		
All-purpose flour	2 cups	240 grams
Baking powder	1 teaspoon	5 grams
Milk chocolate	8 ounces (1¼ cup milk chocolate chips)	226 grams
Dark brown sugar	1½ cups (lightly packed)	300 grams
Large eggs	2	100 grams
Salted butter, melted and cooled slightly	16 tablespoons (2 sticks)	226 grams
Pure vanilla extract	2 teaspoons	10 grams
Raspberry Jam (page 350; or store-bought)	½ cup	145 grams
Flaky sea salt (such as Maldon; optional)	1 teaspoon for sprinkling	

Get prepared

- Arrange the oven racks so one is in the center position. Preheat the oven to 350°F.
- Spray the bottom and sides of an 8- x 12-inch baking pan with nonstick cooking spray.
- Whisk the flour and baking powder together in a small bowl and set aside.
- Unless you are using chocolate chips, chop the chocolate into ⅜-inch pieces. Pass the chocolate through a fine-mesh strainer to sift out any dust and discard the dust.

Make the batter

- Combine the brown sugar and eggs in a medium bowl and whisk until the mixture is smooth and lightened in color. Gradually add the butter, stirring with the whisk as you add it and taking care that it doesn't slosh out of the bowl. Use the whisk to stir in the vanilla. Add the flour mixture and fold it in with a rubber spatula until almost no flour is visible. Add the chocolate and fold it in until the chocolate is evenly distributed and no flour is visible.

Bake the blondies

- Using a rubber spatula, transfer the batter to the prepared pan. Use the spatula to get the batter into the corners of the pan and to smooth out the top.

Drop in the jam in ½-teaspoon-size drops, distributing it over the surface of the batter. Draw a small paring knife back and forth through the batter, running it through the jam across the length of the pan and then back across the sides. Sprinkle the salt, if you are using it, over the top.

▪ Place the blondies on the center rack of the oven and bake for about 30 minutes, until the batter has puffed up, rotating the pan from front to back halfway through the baking time. Remove the pan from the oven and put it on a cooling rack; let the blondies cool to room temperature in the pan. Use a large knife to cut the blondies into 24 equal pieces.

The blondies may not look completely set when they come out of the oven. Not overbaking them is the secret to a moist, chewy texture.

▪ Store the blondies in an airtight container at room temperature for up to 1 week or freeze for up to 3 months.

Acknowledgments

It took four years to write this book, and the recipes and knowledge took more years than that. I always wanted to write a baking book but never felt that I was ready. One evening in the summer of 2015, Charlotte Druckman introduced my desserts and me to Nancy Silverton. And it was through this introduction that the cookbook came to be. Nancy tasted my desserts and then proceeded to immediately ask me if I wanted to write a cookbook. She generously put her agent, Janis Donnaud, in touch with me. I cannot thank Charlotte enough. Not only for her introduction to Nancy, but also for so many other things including helping me fine-tune the book's introduction. I also cannot thank Nancy enough. Not only for the introduction to Janis, but also for being a mentor to me through her work and her books. And thank you, Nancy, for letting me test quite a few of these recipes in your beautiful home kitchen. I feel quite blessed to have such a smart and talented agent in Janis. Thank you, Janis, for being a tough cookie when I needed straightforward feedback.

This book would not have been possible without Carolynn Carreño, my writer. Carolynn, I love how you captured my voice, even when I didn't think I had one. Your writing and work is amazing. And I am grateful that you practically wrote two books in just this one! You put in so much work and meticulousness to yield consistency in all of the recipes. Thank you. I also must thank my editor, Lexy Bloom. Your vision in bringing my science and engineering background more front and center makes me proud of the book. And makes the book feel like who I am. Thank you to Tom Pold and the entire team at Knopf. From the meticulousness of the copy editing to the beautiful design, the book is beyond what I could have imagined it to be. Thank you to my photographer, Johnny Miller. Your photographs make my pastries look like works of art. When I said "moody," you got it and ran with it. And thank you so much to your lovely and extremely talented team, including Rebecca Bartoshesky, who assembled beautiful and moody props, and Rebecca Jurkevich—thank you for all of your help in styling the food. I picked up so many good tips and tricks and I am grateful that we worked together.

The recipes and knowledge within this book come from years of work and learning and I want to thank all of those mentors and teachers along the way. In particular, Gina De Palma, a true mentor to me. You are still missed but your recipes live on. Dorie Greenspan, I learned so much by baking through your recipes at home. Jim Lahey, my knowledge of bread and fermentation blossomed while working at Sullivan Street Bakery under your tutelage. Toni Lynn Dickinson, I learned so much from you while at the French Culinary Institute—from creaming butter and sugar to sacrificing batter in cake-making. Thank you. I also could not have written this book without the help of the many assistants I have had, including Zoe Kanan, Joe Bowie, Ali Spahr, Harlie Orr, Tiffany Bryant, Mel Levi, and Sergey Linnikov.

And last but not least, thank you to my son, Wyatt, for tasting all of the pastries. And thank you to Ken, for everything else.

Index

(Page references in *italics* refer to illustrations.)

A NOTE ABOUT THE AUTHORS

MELISSA WELLER received a James Beard Award nomination for Outstanding Baker in 2016. A French Culinary Institute graduate, she trained at Babbo and Sullivan Street Bakery in New York City. She was chef-partner at High Street on Hudson; the head baker at Per Se, Bouchon Bakery, and Roberta's; an owner and founder of Sadelle's; and the head baker at Walnut Street Café in Philadelphia. She lives in Brooklyn.

CAROLYNN CARREÑO is a James Beard Award–winning journalist, the author of the cookbook *Bowls of Plenty,* and the coauthor of thirteen cookbooks. She lives in San Diego and Mexico City.

A NOTE ABOUT THE TYPE

The text in this book was set in Miller, a transitional-style typeface designed by Matthew Carter (b. 1937) with assistance from Tobias Frere-Jones and Cyrus Highsmith of the Font Bureau. Modeled on the roman family of fonts popularized by Scottish type foundries in the nineteenth century, Miller is named for William Miller, founder of the Miller & Richard foundry of Edinburgh.

The Miller family of fonts has a large number of variants for use as text and display, as well as Greek characters based on the renowned handwriting of British classicist Richard Porson.

Composed by North Market Street Graphics
Lancaster, Pennsylvania

Printed and bound by C&C Offset Printing Co., Ltd.
Tai Po, Hong Kong

Designed by Pei Loi Koay